LINKAGE INC.

Best Practices in Organization Development and Change

Culture • Leadership
Retention • Performance
Coaching

Case Studies
Tools
Models
Research

Louis Carter, David Giber, and Marshall Goldsmith
Editors

JOSSEY-BASS/PFEIFFER
A Wiley Company
www.pfeiffer.com

Published by

JOSSEY-BASS/PFEIFFER
A Wiley Company
989 Market Street
San Francisco, CA 94103-1741
415.433.1740; Fax 415.433.0499
800.274.4434; Fax 800.569.0443

www.pfeiffer.com

One Forbes Road
Lexington, MA 02421
781.862.3157; Fax 781.860.5138
www.linkageinc.com
www.linkageinc.com/ler

Jossey-Bass/Pfeiffer is a registered trademark of Jossey-Bass Inc., A Wiley Company.
ISBN: 0-7879-5666-X

Library of Congress Cataloging-in-Publication Data
Copyright © 2001 by Linkage, Inc.

Best Practices in organization development and change: culture, leadership, retention,
performance, coaching / editors Louis Carter, David Giber, Marshall Goldsmith;
foreword by Richard Beckhard

    p. cm.
  Includes biographical references and index.
  ISBN 0-7879-5666-X
  1. Organizational change—Case studies. I. Carter, Louis. II. Giber, David J.
III. Goldsmith, Marshall.

  HD58.8 B485 2001
  658.4´06—dc21
                                                 2001038195

Printing 10 9 8 7 6 5 4 3 2 1

TABLE OF CONTENTS

PART THREE: CONCLUSION

PART ONE

INTRODUCTION

ACKNOWLEDGMENTS

LINKAGE TEAM

LINKAGE EDUCATIONAL RESOURCES

Louis Carter, Publisher, Director of Products

Taavo Godtfredsen, Regional Vice President

Melissa McLaughlin, Manager

Marc Pramuk, Director

Derek Smith, Research Consultant

INTERIOR ELEMENTS

Lynda Jemson

CONSULTANTS

Richard Beckhard, former professor, Sloan School of Management, and author, *Agent of Change.*

Warner Burke, chair and professor, Department of OD and Leadership, Teachers College, Columbia University, and author, *Organization Development: A Process of Learning and Changing.*

Jay Conger, executive director, The Leadership Institute, University of Southern California, and author, *Learning to Lead.*

John Sullivan, professor of HR and head of the Human Resource Management Program at San Francisco State University.

Ed Lawler III, director of the Center for Effective Organizations at the Marshall School of Business and author, *Tomorrow's Organization and From the Ground Up.*

Bev Kaye, president of Career Systems International and author, *Up Is Not the Only Way and Love 'Em or Lose 'Em*

CONTRIBUTORS

Jane Brent, *Kraft Foods*

Suzanne Browning, *Boeing Corporation*

Warner Burke, *SmithKline Beecham*

Alice Cochrane, *Allstate Insurance*

Fernan Cepero, *Xerox*

Charles J. Corace, *Johnson & Johnson*

Karen Ferraro, *Case Corporation*

Ellen Johnston, *Sun Microsystems*

Jim Kane, *Linkage, Inc.*

Bill Keeley, *Westinghouse*

Karen King, *Cellular One—San Francisco*

Jodi Knox, *Deloitte Consulting Group*

Beth Lama, *Torchiana, Mastrov & Sapiro, Inc.*

Iris Lemmer, *Kraft Foods*

Carol E. Lorenz, *Nortel Networks*

Rick Maloney, *Sonoco*

Judy Milam Mason, *Dow Corning*

Claire Meany, *Cellular One— San Francisco*

Keith Montgomery, *CK Witco*

Jim Moore, *Sun Microsystems*

Lynda K. Munoz, *Advanced Micro Devices*

Scott Nelson, *Linkage, Inc.*

Ellen M. Papper, *Allstate Insurance*

Kristine Rainge, *Linkage, Inc.*

Ronald Recardo, *Catalyst Consulting Group*

Derek Smith, *Linkage, Inc.*

Elizabeth "Liz" Thach, *MediaOne Group*

Lynn Ware, *Integral Training Systems, Inc.*

Sandra Wells, *ServiceMASTER*

ABOUT THIS BOOK

The principal goal of this book is to provide you with the key ingredients taken from best-practice companies to help you create and enhance your organization and human resource development (OD/HRD) initiative. Through a case study approach, this book provides practical, easy-to-apply tools, instruments, training, concepts, and competency models that can be used as benchmarks for the successful implementation of your specific OD/HRD initiative.

Within each case study, you will learn how to:

- Analyze the need for the specific OD/HRD initiative
- Build a business case for OD/HRD
- Identify the audience for the initiative
- Design the OD/HRD initiative
- Implement the design of the initiative
- Evaluate the effectiveness of the initiative

HOW TO USE THIS BOOK

DIRECT APPLICATION

Because this book contains actual forms, guides, training, competency models, and methodologies for implementing an Organization or Human Resource Development (OD/HRD) program, you can immediately apply many of its parts directly to your job and company initiatives. Many of the evaluation and assessment forms, models, reference guides, and training exercises can be easily implemented and customized to fit your specific organizational needs. A selection of these features is available on the accompanying CD-ROM. The selected features in this book are highlighted by a CD-ROM icon. See page 549 for CD-ROM instructions.

MASTER'S DEGREE OR EXECUTIVE WORKSHOPS AND SEMINARS

This book is ideal for a master's degree or executive workshop and/or seminar on designing, implementing, and evaluating an Organization or Human Resource Development system. The case studies can be used as actual examples of OD/HRD systems and initiatives. For more information on Linkage's onsite or public workshops on various OD/HRD topics, or its actionable research and resources in OD/HRD, contact Linkage Customer Service at (781) 862-3157, or visit Linkage on the Web at: www.linkageinc.com.

ONLINE OR VIRTUAL TEAM LEARNING

This book can be shared with members of teams or students across long distances, who are not able to attend.

GETTING THE MOST FROM THIS BOOK

1. Read over the Introduction to get a feel for the book's landscape.
2. Skim over the table of contents for each chapter, mining for information on the types of OD/HRD interventions, key features in each program, competency models, strategic objectives of programs, critical success factors, and evaluation methods.
3. Examine all of the exhibits.
4. Go back and choose specific case studies to read over carefully. Work with a team to develop a list of the components in a few case studies that fit your organization. Analyze why these components are most applicable to your organization and its culture. What interventions and key features best fit your organization's goals and objectives? How might you go about implementing such a program at your organization? Why do some programs work for your organization better than others?

FOREWORD BY RICHARD BECKHARD

In June 1999, Linkage, Inc. performed a research study on the current state of Organization and Human Resource Development. The study indicated that there is a strong demand, in particular, for the following OD/HRD initiatives (Table 2) within organizations.

This handbook approaches each of these 5 OD/HRD topic areas through practical case studies. From the perspective of the practitioner, the handbook presents a practical framework for designing, implementing, and evaluating a successful OD/HRD initiative.

MAJOR FINDINGS

Linkage examined many organizations from a variety of industries that ranged in size, with a reputation for having best practice management systems, to compile this book. They were asked to share the approaches, tools, and specific methods that made their programs successful. All of these organizations have a strong financial history, formal human resource management programs that integrate company strategy with its program's objectives, and a strong pool of talent.

Perhaps more important, we chose companies that have succeeded in "anchoring change firmly in [their] corporate culture."[1] These are the companies where change is facilitated though integrated, multimode programs that include the following features.

Table 1. OD/HRD Topics with Highest Level of Demand, in Order of Demand

OD/HRD Topic	Level of Demand (Scale: 1–5, with 5 being highest level of interest)
Organization Development & Change	4.6
Leadership Development	4.5
Recruitment & Retention	4.27
Performance Management	4.24
Coaching & Mentoring	4.03

Commitment to Organizational Objectives and Culture

In each case, there was a strong commitment to the strategic objectives or goals of the organization. There was an equally strong commitment to a vision upon which change and/or development was built. Kraft's High Performance Work Systems project was created to fulfill the organization's objective to "become the undisputed leader in the food industry by the year 2001." Sun Microsystem's leadership development program was built upon 4 beliefs about leadership that reflect the organization's mission and strategic objectives. The Coaching and Mentoring process at Dow Corning was based upon a commitment to increasing the capacity of managers to manage both stability and change. They focused on 6 dimensions that emphasize learning, collaboration, performance, leading change, operating without borders, and customer service.

Changing Perceptions

Clearly, our best organizations are getting people "unstuck" from the way they are used to thinking through strong change messages and methodologies. Westinghouse's Waste Isolation Division made an impact on its employees by reinforcing the message "safety first" through setting examples such as laying off and sometimes firing employees who did not comply with safety measures. After the merger of SmithKline Beckman and Beecham, huge banners were positioned over the main entrances of the former SmithKline Beckman building in Philadelphia, Pennsylvania, and the Beecham headquarters building in London, in bold, new company letters, "Now We Are One." Other organizations such as Boeing, MediaOne, Johnson & Johnson, Sun Microsystems, and others are skillfully "unfreezing" employees from their old way of thinking through multirater feedback tools that enable them to better understand the impact of their behaviors on others and the strategic objectives of the organization. Edgar Schein describes the unfreezing stage as the first of three stages of interpersonal change (unfreezing, changing, and refreezing) in his book, *Coercive Persuasion*.[2]

Strong Support From the Top

Support from senior management has been identified by 88% of the contributors as a critical step in overcoming resistance to change. Johnson & Johnson's leadership development program was strongly supported by the chairman of its board, Ralph Larsen. In a report to the senior management team, Larsen stated, "Leadership is the single-biggest constraint to growth at Johnson & Johnson, and it is the most critical business issue we face." In addition, Larsen participated in J&J's Standards of Leadership 360-degree feedback and action planning process. Case Corporation's performance management system is built upon the strategic framework that its CEO, Jean-Pierre Rosso, implemented when he joined the organization in 1994. The framework is posted in offices, hallways, and manufacturing plants to reinforce the organization's strategic imperatives. Xerox's empowered work groups initiative was a result of CEO Paul Allaire's vision to create "work groups that will be tied directly to the customer." Other initiatives, including Boeing, Sun Microsystems, Johnson & Johnson, and Dow Corning, were supported by senior management.

Competency or Organization Effectiveness Models

Virtually all of these programs have an explicit model using behavioral competencies or organization assessment metrics. These range from the 22 behavioral competencies within Sun Microsystem's SMI Leadership Skill Profile, to the 13 or more organization metrics within Kraft Food's Organizational Assessment Tool, Xerox's CSS Empowerment Survey, Cellular One's Employee Satisfaction Survey, Nortel Network's Change Capability Evaluation, and others. Case Corporation's competency model was specific to the behaviors required of coaches and managers who facilitate the performance management process. Dow Corning's 3-Circle Profile Competency Model is based upon more than 1,000 skills. These models frequently form the basis of 360-degree feedback, and often provide a focus to the flow of the program itself.

AN APPROACH TO ORGANIZATION AND HUMAN RESOURCES DEVELOPMENT

Each case includes 6 elements of the change process associated with OD/HRD.

1. Business Diagnosis
2. Assessment

3. Program Design

4. Implementation

5. On-the-Job Support

6. Evaluation

Table 2. Best Practice Case Studies

(By Company, Industry, Number Of Employees, and Gross Revenue)

Company	Industry	Employees	Revenues
Allstate Insurance	Insurance	55,000	$25.9 B+
Advanced Micro Devices	Manufacturing	13,000	$2.5 B
Case Corporation	Manufacturing	17,700	$6.1 B
Cellular One—SF	Telecom	970	N/A
Dow Corning Corporation	Chemicals—Petroleum	9300	$2.7 B+
Johnson & Johnson	Healthcare—Pharmaceutical	94,000	$23.7 B
Kraft Foods	Manufacturing	37,500	$17 B
MediaOne Group	Telecom—Info Services	16,000	$7.4 B
Nortel Networks	Telecom—Info Services	80,000+	13 B+
ServiceMaster	Healthcare—Pharmaceutical	44,000	$6.4 B+
SmithKline Beecham	Healthcare—Pharmaceutical	20,000+	$13.4 B
Sonoco	Manufacturing—Packaging	16,500	$2.6 B+
Sun Microsystems	Computers—Electronics	30,000	$12 B+
The Boeing Company	Manufacturing	220,000	$56.1 B
Westinghouse	Government	23,500	$2.2 B+
CK Witco	Manufacturing	175	$62 M
Xerox Corporation	Manufacturing	92,700	$20 B+

Element 1

The first element is usually a diagnostic step in which the business drivers and rationale for creating the initiative are identified. Critical to this stage is creating consensus and a sense of urgency regarding the need for the initiative. A future vision that is supported by management is key. All of the systems have some model as a focal point for their work. The best of these models capture the imagination and aspirations of the organization and its change agents. Designing the system also leads to strategic questions. As taken from the *ServiceMASTER* example:

1. What do the senior leaders want to accomplish through this change?

2. What strategic business initiatives will be supported or achieved through [the] implementation?

3. What do they believe will be different, better, or the same?

As Sandy Wells of *ServiceMASTER* further points out, once the organization's leaders have made a commitment to the change initiative, more in-depth diagnostic questions that are specific to the organization and its dynamics are posed to assist in the Design phase.

1. What is going on in this organization that will enable or hinder successful implementation of this organizational change?
2. What can we do to achieve the delivery of excellent service?
3. What do we need to do to work together in this partnership?
4. What affects readiness in this organization to address change?

A well-thought-out diagnostic phase is usually connected to an evaluation of the desired business impacts in Element 6.

Element 2

Assessment is also a commonly shared element. These assessments range from Kraft Food's Organization Assessment to Boeing's Team/Project Assessment process, where individuals receive feedback about themselves in a nonthreatening environment. Assessments are delivered both to individuals and to teams, resulting in development plans and actions. Assessment has become a norm for business—the question is, how do we use the assessment to drive change in our businesses and ourselves? Organizations such as SmithKline Beecham, Sun Microsystems, MediaOne, and others use behavioral analysis tools such as Myers-Briggs Type Indicator or 360-degree assessments. Cellular One leverages a skills assessment matrix to identify strengths and opportunities for improvement and a career path options matrix to determine the specific career goals that are "appropriate and realistic" for the employee. Individual coaching often accompanies this assessment. This coaching has been extremely successful for such firms as Dow Corning, MediaOne, Johnson & Johnson, and others.

Element 3

Element 3 is program design. These outstanding programs have several unique features that deserve recognition.

- Cellular One's retention program highlights a monthly Employee Satisfaction Survey (ESS) meeting. The senior management team and the director of Organization Development and Training convene to create and manage action plans based upon data from the ESS during this meeting. Other recruitment and retention programs, such as Allstate's, use the Internet to educate and select employees. Advanced Micro Devices offers a "work/life balance" class to minimize stress and help employees to achieve a greater balance in their work, family, and personal lives.

- Dow Corning's coaching and mentoring system, which won the ASTD award for excellence in practice, features a career resource center, brown bag lunches for discussing a range of career topics, and a development coaching training program for all managers.

- Action learning is a commonly shared feature of the leadership development systems at Johnson & Johnson, Sun Microsystems, and Boeing. These programs are selective about their participants and action learning topics. Boeing has a formal selection process for action learning that identifies the employees who should participate in the program as well as the most urgent strategic business issues to be tackled. These action learning programs must answer such questions as:

What is a realistic project that still expands thinking?
How do we set senior management's expectations for the business value that the learning will produce?
How do action teams stay together as "learning groups" over time?

- 360-degree feedback and competency models remain a hot topic at such organizations as Sun Microsystems, Dow Corning, Boeing, Johnson & Johnson, Case, Sonoco, CK Witco, *ServiceMASTER*, SmithKline Beecham, and MediaOne. Boeing's leadership education system develops the lowest-ranking competencies of its top 200 executives. Other programs, such as Sun Microsystems, review their competencies from time to time to make sure that their competency models are up-to-date. Sonoco's 360-degree feedback process is done online, and the results are tabulated by a software program, so that the employees requesting feedback can see results immediately after assessors have completed the survey.

- Several organizations held senior management meetings to embed the change project and create actionable plans for the future. *ServiceMASTER* holds an offsite partnership retreat in which senior leaders strengthen the relationship necessary for implementation of the company's Integrated Service program. SmithKline Beecham created a "merger management committee" (MMC) led by the CEO of Beecham, the company that merged with SmithKline Beckman. The purpose of the committee was to work on such issues as strategy, selection, and organizational structure.

Element 4

The fourth element is program implementation. Almost all of the initiatives have a formalized training and development program or workshop to propel the change or development process into action. Components of several noteworthy training and development workshops are described here.

- After SmithKline Beecham's merger, the executive management committee (EMC) decided that in order to successfully merge their companies' cultures, they first had to discover their differences as an executive team. Using the Myers-Briggs Type Indicator, the team discovered differences in their personality styles and was better able to engage in effective dialogue and communication in a more nonthreatening manner. Because of this team-building exercise, the EMC created the organization's core values.

- During Case Corporation's training on performance management, participants create performance agreements in which they set performance objectives and measures at the beginning of the year and revise as necessary throughout the year.

- Sun Microsystem's leadership development training incorporates instruction on two strategic business objectives of the organization: maximizing profitability and strategic business partnerships. Through a customized business simulation, participants play the role of an executive competing against other executive groups for market share, quality indexes, and product reviews

Other programs implemented "enablers of change" that help to prevent the system from becoming dysfunctional.

- In order to guard employees from the "whistle-blower" syndrome, Westinghouse established an anonymous telephone hotline for employees to identify safety issues that arose during the intervention.

- Allstate implemented a detailed action checklist and questioning process that enabled change agents to determine whether the recruitment and selection system was being properly implemented. Nineteen questions in 8 categories are on this checklist including:

1. What training is in place to ensure consistent standards of excellence for recruiters and selection consultants?

2. What policies and guidelines are in place related to selection (e.g., retesting policies, handling of internal transfers)?

3. What current processes are in place to ensure that all legal requirements are met in the development and implementation of all selection policies and procedures?

4. Are partnerships in place with each client group to ensure involvement and buy-in in the development and implementation of new processes?

Element 5

These benchmark programs reach beyond the boardrooms and classrooms and provide on-the-job reinforcement and support. Work in this phase defines the follow-up support that determines whether change and development will transfer on the job. In several of the programs, the support system outside of training is one of the most salient elements of the OD/HRD initiative. SmithKline Beecham installed a pay-for-performance system to help transfer the shared goals of the organization to employees on the job. Johnson & Johnson instituted a formalized follow-up process that directs participants to perform progress checks and assessments of their degrees of improvement. After performance management training is delivered at Sonoco, managers explain business objectives, deliver developmental plans, and provide coaching and feedback to employees on a regular basis. Both Coaching and Mentoring case studies, Dow Corning and MediaOne, are excellent examples of organizations that provide ongoing support for leadership development and, more specifically, the organization's strategic business goals and objectives.

Other organizations take a more direct approach to providing on-going support and development for change by installing review processes. Allstate and Westinghouse have ongoing review, monitoring, and analysis processes in place to ensure that the new policies and procedures are being followed.

Element 6

Evaluation is the capstone—the point at which the organization can gain insight on how to revise and strengthen a program, eliminate barriers to its reinforcement and use in the field, and connect the intervention back to the original goals to measure success. All of the organizations in this book measure the impact of their initiatives in some way. Several organizations deserve noting for outstanding practices in this stage.

- Kraft Foods connected evaluation back to its original goals. A Kraft facility that implemented the HPWS process reported improvements in line efficiency and down time, which were 2 of the original objectives of the program.
- CK Witco leverages a multiple amount of change metrics. The company reported improvements in on-time shipments, inventory accuracy records, and performance to schedule as well as a reduction in reportable incident rates, customer complaints, costs, and turnover.
- Westinghouse is an excellent example of an organization that is tirelessly dedicated to measurement and evaluation of safety standards through surveys, safety examinations, and program evaluations. Westinghouse achieved award-winning results from its change program, becoming a world leader in safety.

- Boeing's leadership development program measures the effectiveness of its program based upon placement results, exit interview and survey results, and other qualitative evaluations that measure outcomes of its action learning process.
- Dow Corning measures the impact of training to on-the-job assignments. Follow-up interviews are conducted 8 weeks after training occurs.
- Xerox's Employee Motivation and Satisfaction, Empowering Work Environment and Organizational Empowerment surveys track the effectiveness of its High Performance Work Systems intervention, post-implementation.
- Case Corporation, Sonoco, MediaOne, Nortel Networks, *ServiceMASTER*, Xerox, and others track the improvements in their new systems or training programs.

CONCLUSION

Should companies invest in organization and human resource development? Spending an average of $4,886,364 on their OD/HRD initiatives, the organizations in this book would argue, yes. Most of the initiatives in this book have made a significant impact on the culture and objectives of the organization. This impact may have eased an important organizational transition or toughened an organization to compete. The value of the shifts, in terms of improved decision making and solutions, better performance, improved retention and selection, more satisfied customers, or a safer and more satisfied employee, as these organizations have proven, need to be continuously tracked and understood.

Clearly, there are prominently shared views and approaches across these various industries and OD/HRD practices of what is needed to address the challenge of making change. The formula for organization development and change remains an important goal, which companies need to keep as an asset.

ENDNOTES

1. Kotter, John. *Leading Change*, Boston: Harvard Business School Press, 1996. pp. 14–15.

2. Schein, Edgar. *Coercive Persuasion*, New York: W. W. Norton & Company, 1961.

ORGANIZATION & HUMAN RESOURCES DEVELOPMENT CASE STUDIES

Organization Development & Change

THE BROAD BAND OF ORGANIZATION DEVELOPMENT & CHANGE: AN INTRODUCTION BY W. WARNER BURKE

It was a lot simpler in the 1960s. Organization development (OD) was new. People in the field and those who were flocking to it were energized and enthusiastic about the learning and possibilities involved in changing organizations. It was simpler then because we didn't know very much; or, put another way, we didn't know any better. We knew training, process consultation, and team-building. Sometimes these activities were solutions in search of a problem. It was amazing how many clients needed training and team-building. We thought, if we could only get people to relate with one another more openly and manage conflict better, things would change. If things did change, they were at the individual, not the organizational, level. This realization was gradual, but we did learn.

Beckhard[1] for example, helped us to understand that with team-building we begin with goals not interpersonal relationships. Schein[2] showed that process consultation was much more than getting people to be open. Argyris[3] emphasized the importance of gathering valid information and gaining client commitment. Galbraith[4] taught us organization design, and Lawler[5] helped us to see more clearly the links between behavior and rewards. And by 1978 we already had the second edition of OD's first textbook.[6] These are but a few examples.

3

We also learned that there is a systematic way to go about organizational consulting. Starting with *entry* we then establish a *contract* with our client, *gather data* and conduct a *diagnosis*, provide *feedback* to the client based on this diagnosis, plan and help to implement an *intervention* in the organization, and finally assist in *evaluating* the effectiveness of the intervention. There are phases to the consulting process, we learned. And this learning has been valuable. We indeed need a way of thinking about how the consulting process should progress. And we have learned that this process is not a series of discrete steps but phases, each overlapping and blending with the other. To think in terms of phases is useful, but we also have learned that to gather data is to intervene; intervention occurs all along this phased path.

All this learning, and we have only mentioned a bare minimum, has been rich and has served us well. But as we now know, it is not enough. The operative words today are *speed* and *complexity*.

Speed

The client will not sit still for us to go through our seven phases of consulting. There is not enough time. So we've had to learn to conduct our diagnosis "out of phase," or on the run, as it were. Moreover, by the time we get there, change is already underway with our clients. We are entering midstream, not at the beginning.[7] To have the time to consult in an orderly phased way is no longer possible; it seems luxurious today. Some nostalgia is allowed, is it not?

Having to deal with this demand for speed is not all bad. Many years ago Kurt Lewin told us that the best way to understand an organization is to try to change it. Our diagnosis, then, comes from observing and collecting data about people's *reactions* to interventions, not the interventions themselves. Think metaphorically for a moment. As a child you no doubt threw a rock into a pond once or twice. If the pond was clear you could follow the rock all the way to the bottom. For purposes of organizational diagnosis, however, it would be far more beneficial to study the ripples on the pond, not so much where the rock ended up. Our diagnosis is in the ripples.

Complexity

We have finally learned that to bring about organization change we must think and act in total system terms. An organization consists of many components, all interacting with one another, and to change one part will have consequences, eventually, for all other parts. Moreover, the system totality is something more than the sum of all its components. So, whatever we do by way of intervention, it must be multiple, not one intervention (e.g., team-building) for our problem. In total system terms, there is no such thing as "one problem" and, besides, the presenting problem is rarely the problem. It is more likely a symptom. We must get to the causes. Note the plural here.

To add to our complexity and to think beyond our phased way of consulting, it is just as important to conduct our work according to a clear understanding of how organization change works—where it begins, what should happen next, and how one intervention leads to another. For organization development and change today, here are some givens:

1. We begin with the external environment. What changes in the marketplace, in technology, and with our competitors are occurring? How should we respond? Should these responses be deep, or does the response need to be one of fine tuning?

2. We must make a compelling case for the change that has been deemed to be necessary. If there is no urgent need by organizational members for the change, motivation to do anything differently is highly unlikely. A compelling case starts with #1 above, i.e., what is going on in the external environment, followed by a tentative plan for the type of responses that will be required. "Tentative plan" means that it needs to be tested for feasibility among many organizational members, especially those managers who would be most involved.

3. Coupled with the case being made is a focus on what aspects of the organization need to be affected to respond to the need. Should the focus be as fundamental as the organization mission, its *raison d'être,* or is it the culture, which is currently antithetical to what is needed? For example, is it a more empowered workforce, or is it the company's business strategy that, if not changed, in a couple of years there will be no business? Or perhaps the change need is not so fundamental, but more in terms of turning around an ailing plant? Getting rid of waste and improving our cost structure? Or perhaps providing some badly needed training or a combination of some of these possible interventions? The point of this third phase is to determine the organizational levers that need to be activated to bring about the change required.

4. Next, of course, is to design and implement the change levers.

5. We then monitor and evaluate the process so that we can answer the question, "How will we know if we have succeeded?"

Much more is involved in organization development and change than these five phases convey. The change cases in this section that follow illustrate these phases and much more. Here is a quick summary of what the following cases in this section provide regarding organization development and change.

What You Will Learn From the Cases in this Section

Seven rich cases of organization development and change are discussed in the following pages. The cases cover a wide range of change from how OD occurs every day to deep change in an organization's culture.

Kraft Foods With this case we learn about a five-stage high performance work system (HPWS) that "streamlines processes, enhances employees' skills, and aligns human and work systems to increase efficiency and reduce costs," to use the contributors' words. The case illustrates quite clearly and dramatically the phases of organization development and change briefly described earlier. With a vision of becoming "the undisputed leader in the food industry by 2001," a business case for change in order to get there was made. A mission statement was crafted, with values highlighted, and critical success factors spelled out. Organizational assessments were incorporated and a "variance analysis tool" was used to help improve work efficiency. These are just some of the interventions that were employed. A value of this case is the fact that the contributors have freely shared with us the steps they took and the tools they used.

Nortel A telecommunications company with 80,000 employees worldwide might convey the image of a huge corporate headquarters. Not so. Only three people from corporate help with change efforts, thus, this case is a good example of how to create "self-help" processes at the local level. This case also illustrates a strong effort of "silo prevention." Their "supply chain management" initiative is the primary intervention for integrating multiple businesses and product lines. For all us practitioners, Carol Lorenz, the case contributor, provides a very useful guide and tool, their "Effective Change Management Practices Checklist."

ServiceMASTER If you want to know how an organization builds in OD (their term is OE—organizational effectiveness) on an everyday basis, this is the case to read. A 5-billion-dollar company employing 60,000 people, *ServiceMASTER* is a true success story of how to provide services in a way that ensures continuing contracts with clients and customers. Four corporate objectives define the culture and drive the business—to honor God in all we do; to help people develop; to pursue excellence; and to grow profitably. This case highlights the many ways they strive to accomplish the second objective— people development. The OE people provide a wide array of services for organizational members, with special emphasis, as you might imagine, on training.

SmithKline Beecham One of the problems with a merger is that no one believes it. One of the two parties ultimately wins, and thus the so-called merger in reality was an acquisition. A true merger is possible nevertheless. This case brings to life the possibility. Key to a successful merger is developing a new mission that can only be accomplished through the joint efforts of the former two companies with each company bringing to the efforts its unique strengths and perspectives. The SmithKline Beecham "Promise" was that new mission. Key to their success was such levers as the top team's "getting its act together," the identification of 5 core values that provided focus for the new culture, the translation of those values into leadership behaviors that provided the basis for 360-degree feedback, a communication process that relied on multiple means, a pay-for-performance system, strong leadership throughout the company (especially at the top), and organization-wide surveys to monitor and evaluate progress. The success of this merger is well-documented.

Westinghouse Dealing with nuclear waste is not exactly a "dream job." How do you learn what to do and ensure safety at the same time? One way is to concentrate on developing a safety culture. This case is about culture change, or perhaps culture development is more apropos. The case is also about a comprehensive start-up enterprise with multiple processes and methods on behalf of the U.S. Department of Energy. This case illustrates very clearly that under circumstances of threat to human survival, having an unequivocal mission coupled with strong leadership is imperative to success. Also impressive is how the evaluation of the changes was conducted as well as the results that they accomplished.

CK Witco Being a specialty chemical company, it should be obvious that how well their various plants operate is critical to business success. This case is about change at the plant level. All 175 people at the plant described in this case were involved and the change effort was comparatively short, only about 5 months. In fact, speed was a central concern. The change concerned work redesign and used an innovative "fast cycle" process to create a new business strategy. Multiple interventions were deployed including a balanced scorecard for determining performance. The change effort fortunately had good leadership, and higher performance was the outcome.

Xerox Technology changes in the external environment, namely the transition to a digital world, drove change at Xerox. They wanted to make empowerment real, not just talk. A strong belief was that empowered teams would lead to higher performance as determined by an increase in customer satisfaction. Multiple levers (interventions) were used in this change effort: clearer vision for the future, empowered work groups that were largely self-directed, training at all levels, communication plan, organizational surveys, shared databases and Web sites (organizational learning), reward and recognition programs, and documented work processes. All these factors contributed to the change, and customer satisfaction increased.

Summary

To return to the beginning, these cases demonstrate in no uncertain terms that organization development and change today is not exactly simple. It is always complex, and clients always want things to happen yesterday. The cases also show how the phases of organization change work. We start with the external environment, build a case for change, and end with evaluation—and if the organization is to remain successful, the cycle of phases will begin again.

Some final points:

- Time and again, these cases abundantly illustrate the absolute necessity of strong leadership for change to occur. We see change leaders in living color here. There is no substitute for visionary leadership in times of change. By definition, if there is leadership there is followership.

- The role of the organization change specialist, both internal and external to the organization, is critical. While not always obvious, careful reading does show the clear added-value that OD (or OE) people provide.

- In addition to demonstrating how the organization change phases work, all these cases show the deployment of multiple interventions. True organization change is too complicated for one intervention. Multiple leverage is required.

- These cases were written by practitioners, people in the trenches with the client. They were there; they know what they are talking about. We are not burdened with theory that may or may not be relevant. These practitioners describe the real world of organization development and change.

Without doubt we can learn from these cases. And learn we must. Changing organizations is too intricate to be left to novices. We have indeed learned and noted at the outset, but we still have much to learn.[8] As one who has been involved for more than 35 years, helping organizations change is both thrilling and very satisfying. Learning, however, is the most exciting part.

W. Warner Burke (wwb3@columbia.edu) is a professor and chair of the department of organization and leadership at Teacher's College, Columbia University. Dr. Burke is the author or editor of more than 100 articles and 13 books. He has been recognized for his book *Organization Development: A Process of Learning and Changing* in Addison Wesley's OD Series. In 1990, he received the Distinguished Contribution to Human Resources Development Award, and in 1993, the Organization Development Professional Practice Area Award for Excellence. He is a diplomate in industrial-organizational psychology, American Board of Professional Psychology.

Endnotes

1. Beckhard, R. "Optimizing Team-Building Efforts," *Journal of Contemporary Business*, 1(3), 23–32, 1972.

2. Schein, E. H. *Process Consultation.* Reading, MA: Addison-Wesley, 1969.

3. Argyris, C. *Intervention Theory and Method.* Reading, MA: Addison-Wesley, 1970.

4. Galbraith, J. *Designing Complex Organizations.* Reading, MA: Addison-Wesley, 1973.

5. Lawler, E. E. III. *Pay and Organization Development.* Reading, MA: Addison-Wesley, 1981.

6. French, W. L, and C. H. Bell, Jr. *Organization Development* (2nd ed.). Englewood Cliffs, NJ: Prentice-Hall, 1978.

7. Burke, W. W., M. Javitch, J. Waclawski, and A. H. Church. "The Dynamics of Midstream Consulting," *Consulting Psychology Journal: Practice and Research,* 49, 83–95, 1997.

8. Burke, W. W. "Organization Change: What We Know, What We Need to Know," *Journal of Management Inquiry,* 4, 158–171, 1995.

CHAPTER ONE

Kraft Foods

A 5-stage high performance work system that streamlines processes, enhances employees' skills, and aligns human and work systems to increase efficiency and reduce costs

INTRODUCTION

Kraft Foods, Inc., headquartered in Northfield, Illinois, is the North American food business of Philip Morris Companies, Inc. Kraft's history traces back to three of the most successful food entrepreneurs of the late 19th and 20th centuries; J. L. Kraft for cheese, Oscar Mayer for meats, and C. W. Post for cereals. Today Kraft operates through eight business divisions and is the largest U.S.-based packaged food company in the world. Kraft employs approximately 37,500 people in North America and has a retail sales force of 3,000. Kraft has 50 manufacturing facilities and 14 field distribution centers in the United States supported by a network of plant-based warehouses. In Canada, there are 12 plants and four distribution centers.

Kraft's North American financial background includes 1998 revenues of $17 billion. The company reorganized in 1995 into one operating company. High Performance Work Systems (HPWS) became the change management tool for creating a consistent management philosophy for the goal of operating as one company after the reorganization. It became a way of determining such factors as total inventory, cost of production, and measurement of productivity for all of the new plants and distribution centers throughout North America.

CREATING A BUSINESS CASE FOR HPWS AT KRAFT

Since 1995, Kraft has spent time and effort divesting of businesses, acquiring more profitable businesses, and organizing into one operating company. This new approach led to the current Kraft vision to become the undisputed leader in the food industry by the year 2001. In order to contribute toward the 2001 vision, the Operations Division in particular had to reduce manufacturing and distribution costs, increase productivity, and integrate many change initiatives to streamline processes and reduce waste. After research and a proven track record, the Operations Division chose HPWS as the best way to include all necessary elements that would contribute to the vision of undisputed leadership. Kraft opened three "greenfield" or start-up plants and chose to implement an HPWS design at these locations from the beginning. This method proved to be very successful. The focus now turned to the existing plants and how to help them become just as successful. The major issues impeding their success were costs, waste, and productivity. Many of the plants had high manufacturing and distribution costs, low asset effectiveness, less than aggressive productivity targets, and organization deficiencies, such as jobs specifically designed to correct mistakes, decision making at high levels, and nonvalue-added costs.

DESIGN OF HPWS PROCESS

HPWS is designed to align systems and people to produce dramatic business results (increasing productivity while maintaining quality and cost reduction) and achieve the Kraft vision of becoming the undisputed leader in the food industry by 2001. To achieve this end, there are three essential components of HPWS:

Redesign of People and Work Processes

Most effective method of streamlining processes that increase efficiency and reduce costs enabling Kraft companies to remain competitive.

- Eliminates nonvalue-added work
- Drives work and decision making to the lowest appropriate level in the organization
- Allows salaried employees to focus on moving from core work to process improvement and growth initiatives
- Maximizes utilization of people, physical assets, and materials

Empowerment of Employees

Employees are provided the opportunity to increase their skill level in order to own the core work. Then employees are given the authority to respond to changing business needs, resulting in their ability to create extraordinary value that supports customers and stockholders. Before HPWS, employees would have to talk to managers in order to stop the line. After the implementation of HPWS, line employees are able to stop the line when they notice a problem.

Alignment of Systems and Generating "Buy-in"

HPWS aligns work and people systems to achieve the vision. The buy-in of the HPWS process from senior management was achieved through the creation and presentation of a business case. A business case was developed by senior leaders of the operations staff that laid out the expected overall benefits of the process and the expected benefits from an increased investment in employee training.

Some of the ultimate outcomes of the HPWS process are:

- Increased productivity/output per employee
- Improved morale/decreased absenteeism
- Improved safety/workers compensation costs
- Increased number of improvement initiatives
- Decreased inventory cost
- Faster cycle times
- Waste reduction
- Increased customer satisfaction

In 1998, each plant was given a set of aggressive targets to hit over the next three years. After the financial analysis, it was determined that investing in HPWS could potentially save $15.2 million in the first year, $42 million in the second year, and $57.2 million in the third year. These savings would be achieved through the performance categories of quality, cost, delivery, safety, and employee morale. The business case was approved at the executive level required to obtain funding.

In order to achieve the benefits from implementing HPWS, the Operations Division had to make an additional, incremental investment in training of 25 hours per employee. An HPWS continuum, one to five, was developed to show senior managers how an increased investment in training can help plants can evolve from current state to a high performance state. Once programs and people skills are more fully developed, the on-going training investment will decrease.

The HPWS Continuum

*Stages 1–2: Non-HPWS/
Beginning the Journey*
Benefits from training

- Some improvements in Utilization/Maintenance
- Some consolidations in Quality and Safety positions

*Stages 2–3: Making
Progress*
Benefits from systems &
training

- Cost reductions generated by an increase in ideas implemented
- Supervisor/management begin to understand role change from current style to a coaching capacity

- Increase in employee ownership and business knowledge

- Improved consistency of technical and process skills

- Continued consolidation of Quality and Maintenance activities

Stages 3–5: Well Down the Road/Fully Practicing Benefits from redesign, alignment of systems, and training

- Fewer functional resources necessary, technical absorbs functional roles and responsibilities

- Several jobs combined into one

- Increased job flexibility and "nimbleness"

- Workers make decisions to react quickly and save money

- Process steps are followed in a logical order

- Work and decisions are performed at the appropriate level

- Reduction of conversion costs

- Reduction of waste/nonvalue-added work

- Improved first-pass at quality of output

- Sense of valuable contribution dramatically improves employee morale

- Fewer supervisors necessary—role becomes a coach

- Improved/flexible scheduling

Each plant interested in beginning the HPWS implementation process is eligible for the additional training funds from the HPWS Business Case funding process. The first step is to develop, and have approved, their own business case that ensures linkage of training plans to the achievement of strategic plans. They must track the delivery of training and increased productivity then submit quarterly data reports. When developing a business case, plants must consider the basis for HPWS in that it aligns work and people systems to achieve the business results. Some work systems include work flow and processes, technology, organization structure, and information systems. Some people systems are the selection system, performance management, rewards and recognition, people and organizational development, stakeholder collaboration, and quality of work life.

Implementation: The Four Phases of Implementing HPWS

Kraft Foods applies a four-phase approach to HPWS implementation that usually completes in 24 to 30 months. The phases and the activities in each phase are as follows. The first three phases are planning steps and phase 4 is execution.

Phase 1: Organization Assessment	• Assess the degree to which the plant's business functions and its employees are receptive to change.
Phase 2: Business Case for Change	• Develop and align strategic plans to implement selected initiatives.
	• Conduct a gap analysis for each critical success factor.
	• Assess stakeholders (those people who could make or break the HPWS implementation, local and elsewhere).
	Integration of Strategic Change Initiatives
	• Determine appropriate change initiatives to build systems and capabilities needed for closing the gaps.
Phase 3: Design	• Design optimal work and people systems.
Phase 4: Implement, Change and Monitor, & Improve	• Implement the new design.
	• Make sure all systems are aligned to support an HPWS environment.
	• Continuous improvement of the new design once implemented.
	• Continued education of all employees.

Beginning the Process

The manufacturing facility has the responsibility to decide when they will embark on the HPWS process. When the plant makes the commitment, a Champion is appointed. The HPWS Champion is most often a full-time position with responsibility for leading the initiative by facilitating meetings, conducting workshops, and leading the Design Team through redesigning the work processes. An HPWS Champion is typically an individual chosen from the plant's workforce because of their unique ability to understand the business, lead groups, and facilitate meetings. Hiring an existing plant employee to be the Champion saves time and prevents pain that occurs when this new position is trying to establish credibility among plant employees. The Champion is not left to work alone leading the initiative for their facility. Each plant is assigned an Area Organization Performance (OP) Manager from the Organization Performance & Development group, a headquarters-based function. The Area OP Manager manages the performance and development from strategy to execution for all manufacturing facilities in a given geographical area (region). These individuals hold a great deal of expertise and experience in sociotechnical redesign methods. The Area OP Manager initiates the process prior to Phase 1 by working with the plant manager and the plant management staff. The Area OP Manager leads some of the more strategic and/or complicated workshops as a way to guide the process and help set direction and while showing the Champion how to manage their role.

A comprehensive tool kit is supplied to the plant via the company intranet with separate tools for each HPWS phase. The HPWS principles were used to design some of the tool kits. The Area OP Managers met with the HPWS manager who led the effort to determine what types of tools would be the best to include for the HPWS Champions. Six OP Managers, each with 10–15 years of experience, contributed to the content of the tool kits. In mid-1997, the previous contributions were synthesized, and tool kit strategy was designed, called the *Champion Tool Kit*. Combining contributions from Organization Performance and Operations, five tool kits are now available—one for each phase and one called "Introduction to HPWS." Each Champion must complete a certification process that assures he or she understands the tools and that the tools will be consistently applied through out the Operations Division facilities. The certification process includes role clarification, certification on facilitation skills, applying knowledge and application of all tools in demonstrations, and participation in simulations designed around working through each HPWS phase. In keeping with HPWS principles, all tools undergo continuous improvement revisions. Since the OP Managers are actually in the facilities observing, and sometimes using the tools, they are in the best position to make suggestions on how the tools could be improved. Tool kits for the Introduction, Organization Assessment, Business Case for Change, and Design phases each have between 45–55 tools. Some tools are designated as core tools, or tools that must be applied during the process to ensure success. Other tools are designated as noncore tools, or optional tools, and are used according to the individual business needs of a particular facility.

DESCRIPTION OF STAGES AND KEY TOOLS

The High Performance Work Systems process consists of five phases:

1. Organizational Assessment (OA)
2. Business Case for Change (BCC)
3. Design
4. Implementation
5. Monitor and Improve (M&I)

The five phase process begins with a facility self-assessment of skills, attitudes, and systems. In the second phase, a business case for change is developed. Vision and strategic direction are established and reasons for change are communicated to the work force. Work and people systems are designed (redesigned) in phase three, using socio-tech and participative design tools. Appropriate tools for change are selected from the tool kit based on the previous assessment and presented to the workforce. In phase four, change is implemented and the way people work is redesigned. Phase five is evaluation and continuous improvement. Each facility monitors and evaluates for effectiveness, improvement, and problems. Successful initiatives are benchmarked and unsuccessful initiatives are continually improved upon. The following Table 1 illustrates the activities involved in the five phases of HPWS.

Introduction to HPWS

This is not a true phase, but a tool kit was developed to explain the specific Kraft Foods strategy behind the HPWS initiative. Slides from the initial business case presented to senior managers, an introductory narrative, and phase charts, along with multipurpose tools, are included in this kit. Multipurpose tools are applied throughout the process in any phase. Examples of multipurpose tools are creative thinking techniques, how to create effective presentations, and change management information.

Phase 1—Organization Assessment (OA)

This phase determines how ready and able the organization is for the type of change that occurs when introducing and implementing an HPWS. The OA phase takes approximately six weeks. A fundamental tool uses data collection and analysis through the administration of a survey to all facility employees. Survey questions fall into four major change areas for analysis: Leadership, Systems & Processes, Job Design, and Dealing with Change. Employees are asked to read the question and use a numerical scale to answer in two ways: first, their view of the world today and second, their perception of the ideal future state. In addition to the four major change areas, the data is analyzed according to core values that were established by the design team. Table 2 provides a sample of a question per core value category.

Table 1. Calendar of HPWS Events

Event	Week Number
1. Organization Assessment Phase (OA)	
Area Organization Performance Manager and Facility/Function Manager hold initial discussion	1
Area Organization Performance Manager and Steering Team hold initial discussions	1
OA Implementation plan formulated	1
OA Survey administered	2–3
OA Data Analysis and Recommendations presented	4
Update presentation given to the work force	5
Steering Team evaluation of the OA phase success	5
OA phase culmination report completed	6
2. Business Case for Change Phase (BCC)	
Steering Team completes Guiding Successful Change Workshop	6
Steering Team develops and implements a facility-wide communication plan	7
Steering Team develops and implements a facility-wide education plan	7
Site visits are conducted to other high-performance companies	7 and beyond
Celebrate progress	7 and beyond
Continue education of Steering Team and work force	7 and beyond
Activity logs kept current	7 and beyond
Develop Business Case Workshop (1st session)	8
• Introduction and Gaining Approval tips	
• Steps 1 and 2 (of 9)	
Strategic Document Workshop (Part 1)	8
• Mission Statement	
• Vision Statement	
• Critical Success Factors fully defined	
Develop Business Case Workshop (Session 2)	11
• Steps 3 and 4	
Strategic Document Development Workshop (Part 2)	12
• Core Values identified and defined	
• Driving value identified and defined	
	3-month mark
Develop Business Case Workshop (Session 3)	13
• Step 5	

(Continued)

Table 1. Calendar of HPWS Events (*Continued*)

Event	Week Number
Facility-wide Vision Communication and Validation	14
• Strategy validated and "signed-off" by work force and other key stakeholders	
Develop Business Case Workshop (Session 4)	16
Steps 7, 8, and 9	
Gaining approval tips	
Business Case (including high-level implementation plan) presented and approved	20
Steering Team develops an overall HPWS Implementation Plan	21
Update presentation to the work force	22
Steering Team evaluation of the BCC phase success	23
BCC phase culmination report completed	24

3. Design Phase

Event	Week Number
Steering Team clarifies roles (Kraft uses a Role Clarification Workshop)	25
	6-month mark
Facility wide communication and education plan updated	26
Steering Team completes their own long term charter	27
Steering Team completes Design Team charter template	27
Design Team Selection process (using a selection tool)	28–30
Design Team and Steering Team clarify how they will work together (Kraft uses an Initiation Workshop and Inter-team Relationship Building Workshop)	31
Steering Team and Design Team complete an Introduction to Star Point Systems workshop (facilitated by Area Org. Performance Manager)	32
Design Team receives education on the Design phase and the process of redesigning work	33–35
Design Team provides update to Steering Team	36 to final approval
Steering Team and Design Team provide update to Headquarters	37 to final approval
Steering Team and Design Team update the work force	37 to final approval
Final approval of the new design	59

Table 1. Calendar of HPWS Events (*Continued*)

Event	Week Number
	14-month mark
Steering Team evaluation of the Design phase success	60
Design phase culmination report completed	61
4. Implementation	
Steering Team updates their long-term charter	62
Steering Team develops Design implementation Team Charter Update	63
Design Team to Implementation Team selection process (some Design Team members may drop off and new team members added for implementation, which is recommended)	64–66
Facility-wide communication plan updated	64
Facility-wide education plan updated	64
Overall HPWS Implementation plan updated	64
	15-month mark
Design Implementation Team receives education on team initiation, inter-team relationships, and how to implement the new design	67–68
Design Implementation Team p provides update to Steering Team	69 to final approval
Steering Team and Design Team provide update to Headquarters	70 to final approval
Steering Team and Design Team update the work force	70 to final approval
Final approval of new design Implementation Plan	74
	17-month mark
Pilot new design Implementation Plan	3 months
5. Monitor & Improve	
Evaluate pilot	3 more months
Expansion Plan complete	2 more weeks
	23.5 months

Table 2. Phase 1 Key Tool: Organization Assessment Survey Excerpts

Each question begins with: *The working environment in my organization . . .*

- **Collaborative Efforts**
seeks a lot of input for decisions that impact the whole organization

- **Continuous Improvement**
wants employees to suggest changes to the way things are done

- **Cost Effectiveness**
thinks of cost-saving ideas when making decisions

- **Customer Conscious**
has a process for external customers to tell us their requirements

- **Empowering Practices**
wants all employees to willingly own their tasks

- **Innovative Practices**
wants employees to question the way things are done

- **Job Structure**
has jobs designed that support the way work is actually done

- **Long-Term Orientation**
helps employees plan to achieve long-term goals

- **Open Communication**
gives timely information about the organization's performance

- **People Concerns**
wants everyone to be treated fairly

- **People Development**
wants workers to crosstrain and rotate jobs

- **Productivity**
gets the most use out of all equipment and resources

- **Quality**
uses procedures that make sure quality goals are met

- **Safe Practices**
expects safety hazards to be fixed quickly without approval from a manager

- **Sense of Urgency**
allows workers closest to a problem to make decisions

- **Teamwork**
helps people participate in cross-functional teams

- **Technological Awareness**
increases the organization's technical skills by using technology and training

- **Trust**
wants everyone to share good and bad news; the messenger is not punished

Overall, results from the survey measure employee responses in several areas:

1. Whether or not they believe the current environment is consistent with HPWS behavior

2. The level of perceived need (high or low) for change

3. How significant the gaps are in the general understanding of HPWS concepts

survey data may be manipulated for analysis in many different ways and can (and should be) used throughout the entire HPWS process. The Area OP Manager, along with the Champion and plant management, prepare a culmination report from the data and deliver the results to the work force. The survey data is also used to prepare the business case.

The Organization Assessment has six steps (see Exhibit 1):

1. *Initial Management Awareness* The purpose is to develop awareness and definition around HPWS and gain support from Management. A tool is provided to facilitate discussion between Management and the Area OP Manager.

2. *Data Collection* This tool helps the Area OP Manager and the Steering Team collect and analyze data that determines the change factors for implementing HPWS. The tools used for this process are:

   • HPWS Systems Survey

   • OA Survey

   • Interviews and focus groups

   • Data Analysis and determination of next steps

3. *Data Analysis* This tool documents the Organizational Assessment Phase for the facility or function. It is a guide for preparing a culmination report after all data and survey results have been compiled.

4. *Conclusions and Recommendations* See above. The results of the data analysis help determine the conclusions and recommendations for the facility or function.

5. *Planning Next Steps* The facility or function tracks its progress through the Organizational Assessment Phase as the information becomes available. An activity log provides sound documentation of activities and knowledge gained during the OA Phase.

6. *Initial Workforce Awareness* This step creates awareness of HPWS and gains support from the entire workforce. Most often this takes place in the form of a presentation that introduces and expounds the benefits of moving to an HPWS environment.

Phase 2—Business Case for Change (BCC)

The BCC phase has a two-fold purpose:

1. The facility develops a long-range plan for implementing HPWS and prepares an education/training plan reflecting the development needs of the workforce.

2. The facility develops business reasons that help it acquire the necessary funding to meet the long-range plan and the training needs.

This phase takes approximately 18 weeks to complete. During this time, a Steering Team is chartered. This is the group that oversees the process and usually consists of facility management and representatives from the hourly work force. This group also sets the strategic direction for the HPWS process. The HPWS Champion is a member of the Steering Team, and the Area OP Manager works very closely with this group to help keep everything on track. The Steering Team drives the activities that build the business case.

There are nine steps involved in developing the BCC.

1. Define the facility's mission, vision, values, and critical success factors and how these strategic documents correlate to the Kraft Foods mission, vision, values, and critical success factors.

2. Identify and develop the rationale for the change actions required to achieve the facility's mission, vision, and critical success factors.

3. Determine the strategic direction and timing of the change effort.

4. Estimate a financial break-even point.

5. Perform a "reality check" with corporate stakeholders, those people who have a vested interest in the success of HPWS.

6. Define changes in roles and responsibilities for stakeholders due to changes that naturally occur when moving to a high-performance environment.

7. Identify barriers to achieving the critical success factors.

8. Identify and define implementation support needs.

9. Present BCC to management and corporate stakeholders.

Step 1 is the foundation for this phase where facility-wide plans for communication, education, and implementation are developed. Other strategic documents to develop include a mission statement and a vision statement. The data on core values from the assessment survey in Phase 1 is drawn upon to define values that are the fundamental principles that guide the actions of individuals. In addition, critical success factors are developed that are intermediate steps critical to achieving the vision. Critical success factors provide specific, intermediate milestones for the employees to focus on, thus making the journey more manageable.

Phase 2 Key Tool: Developing Strategic Documents

The Mission articulates the facility or function's "reason for existence." The Vision articulates "the long-term direction." The Critical Success Factors spell out the "intermediate steps critical to achieving the Vision." Lastly, the

Values are the "written and unwritten rules that govern the behavior of all employees." Developing the strategic documents is just as important as the final documents themselves. The Steering Team spends a great deal of time (up to one week) formulating, debating, and validating these key documents to "make them their own," specific to their facility's or function. It continues to strengthen their sense of being a team and helps everyone focus on the same goals. This cannot happen if they just copy another facility's or function's documents.

The strategic documents form the core of the facility or function's BCC. They define the direct and indirect business results expected. Direct business results are typically measured such as sales, share, volume, consumer complaints, ROI, and so on. Indirect business results are focused more on the people aspects, for example, job satisfaction and turnover.

Each Kraft facility reviews the results from the Organization Assessment phase to develop the framework around which the Strategic Documents are built. The Steering Team looks at each value category in the assessment for insight into what things are like now and what they could be like.

Developing a Mission Statement The mission statement articulates why the organization exists. This statement is a simple set of statements that focus on today. The key components of a mission statement are:

- primary justification for existence
- line(s) of business
- customer
- products/services provided
- how products/services are provided

Steps to create the mission statement

1. Brainstorm key components
2. Determine what "we" worry about every day (customers, quality, employees, cost)
3. Determine why we exist
4. Develop a draft statement
5. Discuss
6. Finalize

Developing a Vision Statement A vision statement has a long-term focus and describes the organization in its ideal state. It provides a clear goal for members of the organization to work toward over the long term. The key components to a vision statement are:

- market share
- profitability
- impact on competition
- impact on employees
- impact on customers

Steps to create a vision statement

1. Work on one component at a time
2. Determine the defining characteristics—does it instill passion, communicate a clear, visual image, align with the future external market? Are the goals bold and outrageous, but possible? Does it contain a specific timeframe, and is it easy to remember?
3. Develop a draft statement
4. Discuss
5. Finalize

Developing Critical Success Factors (CSF) Critical success factors are the intermediate steps that provide specific milestones critical to achieving the vision. Components of critical success factors are:

- What is critical to achieve our vision?
- What can we do to achieve our vision?
- What will drive us to excellence?

Critical success factors have quantifiable measures such as a percentage, a completion date, or hard numbers. Some examples of CSFs include:

- Maximize customer service
- Provide exceptional quality and service
- Produce at lowest imaginable cost
- Develop an effective tea-based organization
- Increase the growth of product volume
- Implement and maximize use of all technology
- Maximize quality of worklife, diversity, job satisfaction, and community involvement

Directions for Developing Critical Success Factors

1. Brainstorm no more than eight and no fewer than four factors that are driving your business to change.

2. Put the change factors through a gap analysis of where the organization is now versus where it needs to be to reach the vision or the ideal.

3. The gaps form the basis for the critical success factors.

4. Write out no more than eight critical success factors.

5. Discuss, finalize, and test.

6. Define by: target action, goal, time, measure.

Critical Success Factor Test

- Is it critical to make the vision happen?
- Does it support the mission?
- Does it contain specific, understandable goals and measures?
- Will it drive us to excellence (at least 25% better than where we are now)?
- Is it something we can do?
- Do we have control over the implementation barriers?
- Is it easily understood and remembered?
- Does at least one critical success factor leverage the employee as an asset?
- Will it last more than one year?

Defining the Values Determining the values helps toward understanding the rules, both written and unwritten, that govern behavior. Begin with determining what these rules could be. Then identify the core values for your organization. Refer to the 18 core values in the Organization Assessment phase. Gain agreement among employees, management, and the Design and Steering Teams. Communicate the core values to the organization.

Before concluding the BCC, the Steering Team makes recommendations for the reward and recognition system. Careful consideration should be given to this piece due to the volatile nature of the subject among employees. Kraft is not at a point where teams are at a mature-enough level to manage total self-management, including peer evaluation, compensation decided by team members, discipline decided by team members, and so on. An alternative compensation system is usually implemented when teams are well into the fully practicing stage on the continuum.

Phase 3—Design

The purpose of the Design phase is to build on the information from all of the strategic documents and apply that toward the new design of a work process. The new design will include sociotech concepts that align people and work systems in a process of planning how the organization will look. Significant and lasting results from a new design come from using an approach that considers all of the elements of the system and creates alignment among those elements. With this in mind, Kraft's high-performance methodology believes heavily in the team approach to job performance. A facility may choose from two design methods:

1. *Whole System Design*—A method that utilizes a critical mass of about 40–100% of facility employees as the initial design team. Whole System strives for direct and full participation of all employees during the process of redesigning their own work and people systems in two two-day workshops led by an Area OP Manager. The first workshop is focused on analyzing technical or work systems and the second workshop analyzes the social or people systems to create a high-level design that jointly optimizes all systems. The Whole System approach uses simple but powerful tools and concepts that provide an opportunity for employees and their managers to collaboratively self-manage their way through the redesign process. After completing the two workshops, the Steering Team charters a smaller core design team to finalize, move forward, and implement the work from the two workshops. The smaller design team works very closely to the people who attend the workshops. This process creates democratic structures where workers are directly involved in analyzing and redesigning their own work and relocates responsibility for design with those who will make it work. The Whole System approach is a faster implementation because a "critical mass" is involved in creating their future and they have a vested interest in seeing the new design succeed. This approach provides a unique opportunity for employees to understand and visually see how their work impacts other departments. The only real down side to this approach is the four-day commitment for a large number of employees.

2. *Design Team Method*—The most familiar method where the Steering Team selects and charters a Design Team whose members represent a diagonal slice of the organization being redesigned. The Steering Team uses interviewing techniques when selecting the 8 to 15 Design Team members. The same sociotech principles are applied in this method—aligning work and people systems to create the design. Input and data are gathered from employees and stakeholders not on the Design Team in order to provide a vehicle for involvement and input

into the new design. The Design Team method generally takes from 4–10 months to finish, depending on the complexity of the process being redesigned. The benefits of this method are the low number of employees required to be away from their jobs for months at a time and the amount of in-depth knowledge they gain about the facility. However, the Design Team and the Steering Team are the only people heavily involved in the 4–10 month period of intense design work. This situation can cause anxiety among the workforce waiting for (and sometimes speculating) about the results. It is crucial that the communication plan is administered frequently.

Work and People Systems (Table 3) also include business systems of revenue, expense, and asset utilization.

Table 3. Differences in Systems

Work Systems	People Systems
The design is created to put systems in place: • organization & flow of work • tasks and activities • use of technology, software, or equipment • physical layout	The systems are designed to do these things: • organization structure • organization design • decision making • team design • performance improvement

Phase 3 Key Tool: Design Phase Activities

Regardless of the method chosen, there are universal activities in the Design phase:

1. *Design team selected*—This begins in the BCC phase. The Steering Team identifies and interviews candidates.

2. *Update the Steering Team charter*—As the HPWS process moves into the Design phase, revisions may be made based on what has been learned during the BCC phase.

3. *Clarify the role of the Steering Team*—After the Design Team is in place, the Steering Team reviews the two charters for unclear areas or points of conflict, then finds solutions.

4. *Design team initiation*—This step helps the members understand their new role as well as how to work effectively as a team. The Steering Team clarifies expectations, deadlines, and the commitment required.

5. *Education*—This is an ongoing process for both the Design Team and the Steering Team to help strengthen their understanding and knowledge of HPWS. Education can be accomplished through outside workshops on change management, teamwork, business skills, management; by reading books; or by site visits to other companies already practicing HPWS.

6. *Analyze technical systems and social systems, create the design, and gain approval*—This is the heart of the Design phase, redesigning a process. Specifically, this process includes gathering data on the "as-is" state or what the process looks like now. For example, mapping the current process in a flow chart by interviewing the workers, identifying the variances from the process map, and brainstorming possible solutions. The next step is to determine the "to-be" state, or the way the process should look. This includes developing a preliminary design, preliminary team analysis, making sure that both work and people systems are included in the preliminary design. After preliminary analyses are complete, a final design is agreed upon, including teams and what work each team will perform. The Star Point tool is an introduction to the concept of transferring more responsibility for managing a total work process from management and/or functional groups to process operators.

7. *Commitment*—To the HPWS process, this is an ongoing activity among Design Team and Steering Team members and the workforce who will live the new design.

Phase 3 Key Tool: Variance Analysis

Another key Design Team tool is the variance analysis. Data from the analysis is applied from initial development through final design.

Purpose
- To take data from process maps and subject matter expert interviews and uncover, prioritize, and analyze variances that occur in each step

- To determine how the process could be changed or managed differently so a new work process can be developed that eliminates or reduces the number of times the variance occurs

- To begin brainstorming possible solutions to the variances that can transition to the development of a new design for the process

- A *variance* is a difference in an outcome or result other than what is expected. It can occur across the process or in very specific areas

- A variance is either an information gap, a recurring error, or a recurring issue that holds up work and negatively impacts quality, cost, delivery, safety, or morale.

Description
- Design Team members develop a shared understanding of the current system through interviews and their own knowledge. They then begin to identify changes in the system that will eliminate or reduce the occurrence of variances and allow for a correction closer to the source.

- Begin with process owner interviews and brainstorm sessions. Work with several variance analysis and variance solution worksheets to develop solutions.

The Variance Analysis Process

1. *Brainstorm and collect the variances*—Some variances will come directly from the process maps and subject matter expert (process owners) interviews. Involve the process owners as much as possible to gain buy-in for the new design along the way. Make sure they are clear. For example, "communication" is not a variance. Ask what it is about communication that is causing the problem.

2. *Categorize the variances according to organizational system (people, work, business).*

Examples of where to look for work system variances:

- core technology
- facility/department design
- equipment
- production layout
- work flow
- work area layout
- skill requirements

Examples of where to look for people system variances:

- management philosophy
- organization/department design
- organization/department structure
- levels of hierarchy
- roles and responsibilities
- decision making procedures
- skill level classifications

See Table 4 for more information.

Table 4. Variance Classification Worksheet

Variance	Technical Systems	Social Systems
Inconsistent performance of same task		✓
Process has rework or overlap in machine work	✓	

3. *Identify the Key Variances*—Rank the variances in order of their importance against the critical success factors developed in the BCC. This procedure allows the Design Team to determine the most important variances. Apply the 80/20 rule when determining the most important variances to select— 80% of the problems come from 20% of the variances.

It will be up to the Design Team as to how many key variances they choose to work with. Whatever is left over should be stored for later work that could be performed by either the Design Team or the individual employee work teams. The ranking session (see Table 5) is lead by the HPWS Champion.

Table 5. Variance Ranking Worksheet

Ranking Scale
0 = No impact
1 = Very low impact
2 = Low impact
3 = Some impact
4 = High impact
5 = Very high impact

Variance	Critical Success Factor #1	Critical Success Factor #2	Total
	Secured Customer		
	Confidence (list quantitative details here) • Delivery of products for customers (x)% or schedule		
Multiple schedule changes	4	5	**Average**

4. *Analyze the Variances*—A critical cause is the most frequent cause of or has the largest impact on the variance. Work with one variance at a time. Write the variances and the associated critical cause in the spaces provied (see Table 6). Use two worksheets—one for work system variances and one for people system variances.

Table 6. Variance and Critical Cause Worksheet

Variance	Critical Cause

Next use the worksheet and look at all of the variances and their causes to determine where the variance controlled and how it could be moved closest to the source. Use the worksheet (Table 7) for work system variances then people system variances.

Table 7. Determining Variances and Their Sources Worksheet

Key Variance	Cause	Where it's found	Where it's fixed	How to move it closest to the source

5. *Develop Possible Solutions*—The Champion, Design Team, and process owners meet to make sure everyone is clear on the information from all of the variance analysis worksheets before they begin to use the worksheet to brainstorm possible solutions (see Table 8). Look at these areas when brainstorming:

- organization (department) and work flow
- tasks and activities performed
- use of technology, software, and equipment
- physical layout

Table 8. Brainstorming Worksheet

Variance	Possible Solution	Barriers to the Solution

You are now ready to create the new design. Make sure to align work and people systems; to determine current responsibilities of each job affected and the time it takes to perform the tasks of the job; to plan out how the facility or department being redesigned would function in a team environment, the team structure, and member roles and responsibilities.

Phase 4—Implementation and Monitor and Improve

The Implementation phase takes the new design and aligns all activities and support processes. The major output of the Implementation phase contains:

1. A transition hand-off plan
2. The role and accountabilities of the Steering Team during the phase
3. Preparation of employees for the changes that will take place as a result of the new design
4. A project management type plan for "phased" implementation of the new design
5. How to measure the performance of the new design

After the new design is approved, the Design Team must determine the best way to implement it. A transition hand-off plan helps them determine how to implement the new design and is a critical element to successful implementation.

Phase 4 Key Tool: Transition Hand-Off Plan

Use this tool to develop a plan for transferring work from one team or individual to another team or individual. Use the feasibility tool as an audit to determine whether the plan is possible.

A hand-off plan is a systematic process for deciding which tasks can be transferred. It's called a hand-off plan because tasks are "handed-off" to teams or individuals who can perform them. There are usually two separate hand-off plans: one for the work performed by the management, and another for the work performed by support departments like shipping, quality, human resources, or purchasing.

A *Hand-off Feasibility* analysis should be used in conjunction with the transition plan to determine if the plan to hand off tasks can actually work, based on the current work environment.

The HPWS Champion has primary responsibility for seeing that the hand-off plan gets developed. The Design Team and subject matter experts play a key role in developing the actual plan.

The Activities Analysis Log (Table 9) determines the activity, the time it takes, and its strategic importance. (The arrows in the "other" category refer to hierarchy—above/below.)

Table 9. Activities Analysis Log Worksheet

Time	Activity	Strategically Important		Automate (A) Eliminate (E) Transfer (T)
		Self	Other	
			↑↓ —	

Write the strategically important task and to whom it should be transferred on the disposition of tasks worksheet (Table 10). These categories will be area, department, and company specific. Write an "×" in the appropriate box.

Table 10. Disposition of Tasks Worksheet

Task	Team Member	Outside of Team	Team Leader	Management

Look for whether the plan overloads one individual, or if a time consuming task is given to someone already burdened with value added, but time consuming activities. Also confirm that all tasks should be performed and not eliminated or automated. Make sure the individual or team receiving the task demonstrates understanding of how performing the task effects the business (Table 11).

Table 11. Hand-Off Feasibility Worksheet

Task	To Whom	Time on Task

Monitor and Improve is the process of applying continuous improvement once the design is implemented. In most cases, this is an audit of the current situation as compared with the new design. One example of an audit is the Work Team Self-Assessment tool that can be administered quarterly or as needed. The purpose of this tool is to provide the team a view of how each team member rates working with the other team members. By sharing the results, the team gains better team communication that leads to higher productivity because the team focuses on how it interacts.

Phase 4 Key Tool: Work Team Self-Assessment

The following excerpts are questions answered by each individual team member. Results are analyzed by either the HPWS Champion or the Team Leader. Team effectiveness is rated on a scale of 1 to 5, with 5 being the best rating. Ratings are placed next to each phrase.

Role Clarity

Team members clarity around their roles

Team members clarity around responsibilities

Team members clarity around authority (clear or ambiguous)

Priorities

Team meets on a regular basis to discuss priorities.

Team meets on a regular basis to discuss work objectives and ways to manage changes in priorities as they occur.

Planning and Goal Setting

The team sets goals and develops a detailed project plan.

Decision Making

Decisions are made as a team through group participation and input.

Feedback

Team members share their perception of the behavior of others and its effect on the team performance. The team has a proven system for team members to receive timely, clear, and accurate performance feedback.

EVALUATION

Kraft measures HPWS to include business system results as well as people and work system results. Kraft expects to improve bottom line financial performance by 30–50% over a 3 to 5 year period. Expectations are that high performing organizations improve bottom line financial performance 3–7% faster than "traditionally" designed organizations. Kraft also expects improvements after redesign to average at a 6.8% greater improvement per year. In one facility where production was decreasing and costs were increasing, they managed to increase employee training and still save money. For example, salaried positions were reduced by 8%; the policy on overtime pay was re-evaluated and changed, resulting in continuous cost savings and outside support was eliminated (for example, clerks, technical writers). In addition, through redesign they realized a $.25 per-case cost reduction. Another facility who used the Whole System approach to design is reporting significant improvements in line efficiency, down time, and ability to meet case counts. They are confident that they will be a facility of choice for new product lines. All of these results were goals and objectives stated in their business case.

Kraft also sees proof that, by implementing their best practices around the tool kits, additional positive results are achieved. By consistently applying the tools across Operations, Kraft is assured that people and work systems are aligned during the redesign process. Consistent application of the tools has resulted in HPWS Champions developing skills to become internal consultants for the company. To date, 22 plants have progressed to a point in the process where they can claim the Champion as an internal consultant, therefore relying less on outside support that quickens the process and reduces costs. Another area where Kraft has seen the tools contribute to the success of the HPWS initiative is the annual Organization Performance and Development Conference. Attendance increased to 185 participants in 1999, up from 92 participants in 1998. The attendees included hourly HPWS representatives, human resources staff, plant and corporate management, and area vice presidents. The majority of topics were focused on facility and function employees presenting best practices being applied around the HPWS process. The level of excitement and interest generated at these types of conferences instills the commitment that will sustain the momentum needed to continue the success of HPWS.

Exhibit 1. Organizational Assessment—Phase I

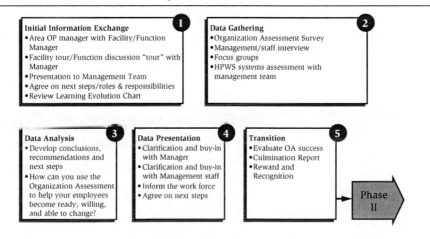

ABOUT THE CONTRIBUTORS

Iris Lemmer (ilemmer@kraft.com) has more than 18 years of experience in human resources, organization development, change management, and consulting for high-performance work systems. From 1993–1996, Lemmer helped to start up Kraft's first self-directed work team as the manager of the HPWS team. In her current role as associate director, field organization performance, operations, Lemmer is responsible for managing the design and implementation of High Performance Work Systems throughout field operations. She has also held the positions of regional organization performance manager and project manager for high performance work systems, operations at Kraft. For the first 7 years of her career, Lemmer designed and delivered training and OD interventions in the retail industry. In 1987, Lemmer joined Helene Curtis where her key focus was implementing people involvement and total quality management. Lemmer led the first sociotech redesign teams at Helene Curtis, which resulted in a 40% productivity improvement in high speed shampoo lines. In 1991, Lemmer joined Kraft Foods to help Kraft implement TQ efforts.

Jane Brent (jbrent@kraft.com) has more than 18 years of experience in customer service, sales, training, and performance management and development. Brent joined Kraft Foods in 1999 as a performance and development manager specifically focused on designing the strategy and tools for the continued growth of the HPWS process. She worked in customer service and sales for Owens-Corning Fiberglas for 7 years, exceeding sales goals, helping customers plan business strategies, and educating their employees and the general public on fiberglass products. During the next 7 years, Brent was with the commercial printer R. R. Donnelley & Sons where she focused on developing curriculum, designing and implementing development programs, and working as an internal consultant on strategy. In addition, Brent spent time participating and leading several design teams in the corporate headquarters functions. In 1996, Brent became an independent consultant, taking on contracts that included everything from introducing a new technical system to employee development strategy.

CHAPTER TWO

Nortel Networks

A change program, embedded in a larger corporate-wide initiative, designed for use in a highly distributed organization with minimal corporate staff.

INTRODUCTION

Nortel Networks (Nortel) is a leading multinational data and voice telecommunications company, employing over 80,000 people worldwide. Nortel supplies much of the world's voice and data communications equipment, including the optical networking systems that carry more than 75% of the backbone Internet traffic in North America. As a global company with several business units, Nortel Networks has been very successful with each business unit supporting different product lines and serving its own market.

However, with the evolution of the telecommunications market, customers are demanding integrated solutions that involve several Nortel Network product lines. In response to this need, in 1996 the global operations organization began the Supply Chain Management (SCM) initiative, a major change effort that integrated multiple product lines, processes, and locations to provide seamless customer service across all Nortel Networks products. This effort included major process reengineering and the implementation of an Enterprise Resource Planning System. A small corporate group out of the global operations organization led the change, but the actual implementations were managed by approximately 30 local sites around the world within the several business units.

The change demanded a high level of collaboration between the various lines of business (LOBs). A governance system of cross-LOB councils and teams was formed, with the global operations senior vice president and his team providing the leadership. The corporate global operations team was divided into 5 major areas:

- Program Management for establishing and tracking program and project milestones
- Process Development for coordinating and managing the process reengineering portion of the change effort
- Implementation Support to support the local teams in the actual implementation
- Finance for managing the budget and interfacing to the larger Corporate Finance organization
- Organizational Change Management to support the people side of the total change effort

PROGRAM OVERVIEW

General Description

The Supply Chain Management (SCM) leadership team visited several other companies that had implemented similar initiatives. One of the things they learned was that these initiatives generate tremendous changes in the organization and have significant impact on the people working there. This realization led to the appointment in late 1996 of a director of organizational change for the specific purpose of bringing a concentrated focus to bear on the "people side" of the SCM initiative. This was a full-time position, embedded in the larger SCM program and reporting directly to the senior vice president of global operations. The goal was to establish a small corporate team to partner with the local sites and build local capability to handle not only the change associated with the SCM work but also to build general resilience to change in the organization as a whole.

In addition to the director, 3 full-time people were recruited to the corporate change team. It was understood that these four positions would be dedicated to the SCM effort for at least two years, and then they would be reviewed for the need to integrate the work into other existing organizations. Major success criteria for the team included:

1. Getting alignment among the various local teams around the direction of the SCM initiative
2. Supporting the training and education necessary
3. Creating an awareness of the people and organizational changes required to support the overall initiative
4. Assisting the local sites design interventions appropriate for them
5. Doing all this with as few corporate staff as possible, with the intent of disbanding the corporate team at the appropriate time

Nortel Networks is a highly distributed organization with a very lean corporate staff. Essentially corporate staff members have significant responsibility for getting things (like process reengineering) done with little to no authority for doing so. The base of power is in the lines of business; they are the profit centers where the products are created and from whom the customers buy. Realization of this led to the formation of the SCM governance structure described briefly in the previous section. This model of having a small corporate group leading the effort and teaming with representatives from each of the local sites was adopted by the organizational change team as well. In light of the culture of Nortel Networks, it was the only approach that made sense. So in this way, the culture had a significant impact on this particular change initiative.

Prior to the formation of the corporate organizational change team, each of the lines of business had established their implementation teams. In many cases these teams had designated someone (at times several people) to address training, communications, and, to a lesser degree, organizational change processes. In nearly all cases, the local people were quite willing but lacked many of the necessary skills. The challenge for the corporate team was how to engage those people and build local capability while at the same time arriving at common mental models, messages, and ways of work around organizational change. They needed to get the approximately 30 local sites to head in a relatively common direction and not spend huge amounts of resources (time, effort, money) reinventing the same things.

To this end, there was the 4-person team at the corporate level providing coordination and guidance to the local teams. In many cases, the corporate team and local site teams actually co-created the strategies and tactics used. (See the On-the-Job Support section for additional information on the "Ambassadors of Change" virtual team.) The corporate team and the local teams together were actually a highly distributed virtual team. They needed a working definition of organizational change that would be the shared mental model for local understanding and would form the basis for the work to be done.

In their article, "An Improvisational Model of Change Management: The Case of Groupware Technologies," Wanda Orlikowski and Debra Hofman present such a definition. They discuss 3 kinds of change: 1) anticipated change, which is planned ahead of time and occurs generally as planned, 2) opportunity change, which is introduced purposefully and intentionally, and 3) emergent change, which arises spontaneously, is not planned or anticipated, but usually needs to be dealt with. In their words, " . . . managing technological change in organizations is not a pre-defined program of change charted by management ahead of time. Rather, it is an iterative series of different changes, many of which are unpredictable at the start, that evolve from practical experience with the new technologies. This requires a set of processes and mechanisms to recognize the different types of change as they occur and to respond effectively to them."1 This was the foundation upon which the Change Management Program for Nortel's Supply Chain Management initiative was built.

Strategy and Objectives

It quickly became obvious to the corporate change team that their client group was the local site implementation team. With this as its guiding beacon, the corporate organizational change team divided its work into 3 areas: Organizational Change Processes, Communications, and Education and Training, with several overarching strategies or goals articulated. Specific objectives in line with the strategies were then developed and tracked within each of the 3 areas. Program strategies and goals included:

- Build organizational and individual understanding and capabilities in change management at the local level
- Enable local sites to assess their unique situation(s), develop insights, and determine the course of action most appropriate to their site and their national and business cultures
- Mobilize existing internal resources to support the work of the local site teams; minimize the use of external resources

- Ensure collaborative working relationships with other existing corporate organizations, such as employee communications, training, and human resources; work through virtual teams and networks to set direction and accomplish deliverables

- Develop and maintain strategic external relationships to stay on the leading edge of the change management field and integrate appropriate information into the overall program

- Devise and implement mechanisms to gather client feedback on effectiveness of the change program and adapt efforts as indicated to meet the needs of the client base

5 Major Areas of Work

The work of all 3 segments of the organizational change team was divided into 5 major areas. The first area was that of actual "product type" deliverables. These included specific ongoing items such as Web sites, vision maps, training courses, newsletters, and presentation packages. Built into these were extensive feedback mechanisms (see Feedback and Evaluation section for examples, as well as Exhibit 1) to ensure that they were meeting the needs of the respective target groups.

The second major area of work was that of developing various tools and templates to help the local sites in assessing their own situations and determining the best course of action for that site. The team looked first to use or adapt already existing materials, either from inside the company or from sources external to the organization. An entire Change Capability Evaluation Guide, a Toolkit, and a Resource Manual was developed using this approach, as were training courses and guides to developing communications plans.

The third work area was a consultation and facilitation service and comprised a significant portion of the workload of the corporate team. The local teams often requested assistance in facilitating a portion of the assessment, in using the templates, in designing and/or facilitating appropriate interventions, or in capturing and sharing lessons learned. Also included here was the coordination of various networks and virtual teams in the areas of communications, training and education, and organizational change processes.

Area 4 was the process development and documentation work. A process to develop an integrated organizational change plan encompassing the communications, education and training, and change processes was designed, tested, and documented, as were various processes to adapt training materials, to design a team-based organization, and to develop a communications plan. Whenever possible, existing approaches, either internal or external, were utilized. Included as part of this area of work was the obligation not only to develop, test, and document processes but also to transfer the knowledge of actual use of the processes.

The fifth and final area was that of integration with the larger program, the Supply Chain Management initiative. Work here centered around relating the organizational change work to key milestones in the overall initiative and establishing checklists and checkpoints to ensure that progress was being made on this front as well as in the overall program. Seven critical success factors were identified along with a monitoring mechanism; this was incorporated into the progress reviews of the overall program.

ASSESSMENT

Because of the highly technical and tools-focused culture of Nortel, it was critical to get the organization to move from being "unconsciously unaware" to being "consciously unaware" of the need to address the people side of this large change effort. To this end, the Change Capability Evaluation was developed. It was designed as a self-assessment and monitoring device to assist the organization in preparing the people for the significant changes the Supply Chain Management initiative entailed. It will be presented in some detail, with the remainder of the program presented at a higher level.

Change Capability Evaluation

Overview The Change Capability Evaluation (CCE) was actually a 3-volume series that included a guide, a toolkit with the tools and specific instructions on their use, and a resource manual to give background and theoretical underpinnings and to link the CCE clearly into the monitoring process for the total initiative. The entire series was placed on the Supply Chain Management Web site and was available to be downloaded by the local sites. Sites were able to use the material as it existed, or make local adaptations, and then develop presentation materials, print the tools as needed, or obtain copies of the original articles in the Resource Manual.

The Guide The Guide had 5 major sections, a brief description of which follows.

Section 1   Introduction

In this section was an explanation of what, why, how, who, when, and outcomes of the CCE.

Section 2   Planning the Evaluation Process

This section presented an overview for planning the evaluation process, outlined steps to take in preparation for the evaluation, and presented high-level information on doing the evaluation and on gaining business unit commitment, and gave some recommendations for follow-up actions and activities.

Section 3   Conducting the Evaluation

Information in this section included the specific steps of the evaluation process and outlined team roles, responsibilities, and skills suggested for the evaluation team members.

Section 4   5 Key Areas of Focus

Contained in this section is an overview of the five areas in which the CCE focuses; these are also the organizing framework for the Toolkit itself. The 5 major areas of focus are

Leadership and the Organization

This has 4 subsections that explore how the organization has dealt with change in the past, what other change initiatives exist, what the existing organizational culture is, and what the competencies and commitment of the leadership team relative to the current change are.

Communications

Included here is information to help the organization understand its current approach to communications, learn the elements of a communications plan, and develop a communications plan for the current initiative.

Process

This section is essentially a gap analysis approach to understanding what the current work processes are, what the new ones are, where the differences are, and some ways to begin to close the gap between current and desired.

Performance Management

Output of the current work processes in the form of business metrics is the definition of performance management in this section, not individual employee job performance. The organization is helped to understand the current measures, the measures of the future, the gap, and ways to start closing the gap.

Technology

Again, gap analysis is used to help the organization understand the technology (information systems) used in the current ways of work, the new technology, and the gap. Plans to close the gaps are started.

Section 5   Managing the Change: People, Processes, and Systems

This section contains information about the people side of change in relation to the process and systems changes. It helps the organization focus on turning the results of the CCE into intervention points to be integrated into the overall timeline. A framework for designing interventions is presented as Seven Critical Success Factors. Also included are several examples of integrated change plans from some of the early adopters of the CCE.

The Toolkit The toolkit contained the actual tools for completing the assessment as well as templates for reports, examples, and supporting information. This was divided into 4 sections.

Section 1   Planning the Evaluation Process

This section contained a step-by-step description of the process for planning the evaluation. The information keyed off the higher level information in the section of the same name in the Guide. Also included were checklists for the evaluation team leader and for the facilitator(s). There were sample letters and a sample feedback form (see Exhibit 1) to be used by the local team to gauge the effectiveness of their evaluation process.

Section 2   Change Capability Dashboard

A single-page, visual representation of the results of the evaluation was needed. A dashboard was selected and in this section was an explanation of the dashboard analogy, a template that could be used by the local site to enter their data, and an example of a data-filled dashboard. In keeping with the spirit of this entire tool, local sites were free to develop their own mechanism for visually capturing results, but the dashboard was presented as the "default" mechanism.

Section 3   The Tools

This section, clearly the largest of this volume, contained the tools. They were organized using the framework presented in the guide, and were available on the Web site for downloading and immediate use. Incorporated into each tool were specific instructions for its use, outlining multiple options for gathering and compiling the data. (See Exhibit 2 for one of the tools from the toolkit.) Once again, local sites were encouraged to use the instructions as guidelines and to make local adaptations and changes as needed.

Section 4   Appendices

There were 4 appendices. One was a "how-to" on conducting facilitated sessions. A second appendix had a CCE report form and an example from one of the early adopters who used the evaluation. A third appendix had helpful hints on developing organizational change interventions. The fourth one identified where to go for more information, including Web sites, people to call, references, and so on.

INTERVENTIONS

Designing Interventions

Once a site had completed its assessment, the team wrote a report of their findings. (See Exhibit 3 for a template.) This information was typically presented to
the local implementation team as well as to the Executive Steering Committee
at the site or business unit level. Part of the report of findings was a recommendation of actions. Some teams were able to do the recommendations quite
well on their own; others requested extensive consultation services from the corporate team at this point. Still others elected to present information to the implementation team and get them and/or their local human resources teams
involved in designing interventions. The sites were free to use the information
in whatever ways were most appropriate to them, and there was no attempt to
do a composite of the information at the corporate level.

Examples of Interventions

Issues to be addressed varied considerably as did the interventions. Two
European sites brought in a motivational speaker and did a formal launch as
part of their change. Most sites held general information sessions to begin
informing the employee population about the SCM initiative and the changes
that were coming as a result. Internal speakers were often invited to these sessions, particularly members of the corporate team leading the change.

As a result of the CCE, several sites realized that they had inadequate executive
support and subsequently formed and chartered steering committees where none
had existed before. Two sites did perception gap measurements to surface the differing perceptions of "support" that existed between the implementation team
and the steering committee. The gaps were then openly discussed and addressed
in a joint meeting between the two groups, facilitated by a neutral third party.

Yet another site realized that their implementation team was focused entirely
on the business process and tool portion of the change. They decided to split their
team in half with one half continuing to focus on the process and tool implementation and the other half to focus on the people and organizational change
side. The "people" half formed the core of the local change implementation team,
and then formed an extended team including a human resources person and the
local employee communications specialist. Using portions of the CCE, they
planned out an approach to change that integrated with the overall project plan
and tracked it in their regular project review sessions. The process they used to
do the integrated plan was captured, shared with others, and reused at other sites.

Several sites recognized the need to address shifts in the organizational structure that were required to support the new ways of work. Three sites put
together organizational design teams comprising diagonal cross sections of the

organization and literally redesigned the organization to more closely align with the changes being implemented.

ON-THE-JOB SUPPORT

Support of the local site teams took many forms. One of the most significant was the "Ambassadors of Change" network. Each site had its own local people involved in the change effort at that site, but many lacked sufficient knowledge and experience to deal with the massive changes that this initiative would engender. The corporate team had a strong interest in pulling this group together to create some common vision, direction, and learning around the whole initiative, and to subsequently develop change capability at the local level— hence, the Ambassadors of Change network.

This network comprised site-based personnel involved in the people side of the SCM implementation. Most local implementation teams had appointed someone to work on the communications and training portions of the change, but few had addressed the organizational change needs. Three separate networks were formed in early 1997: one for all the communications primes, one for all the training primes, and a third for site human resource primes or others interested in organizational change and development. Each was convened, electronically at first, by a member of the corporate team, and they began work on setting strategy, creating approaches to the issues in their arena, sharing ideas, and supporting each other. It quickly became apparent that there would be great benefit in getting all three groups together in a face-to-face working session. The first of these was held in June 1997 in Richardson, Texas, and was so successful that a second one was planned for February 1998 in Paignton, England. These 3 working networks together became the Ambassadors of Change.

The Ambassadors of Change continued to meet, electronically and face-to-face when possible, to provide support, exchange ideas, provide feedback and input to the corporate team and each other, learn, have fun, and share lessons learned throughout the year. As the local sites completed their projects, most of the ambassadors went on to other jobs. However, they took with them their knowledge and learning around organizational change, thereby adding to the organization's capability in this critical area.

Other support came in the form of workshops (for implementation teams particularly) on becoming agents of change. There were workshops to redesign the organization to align with the new work processes, and a whole training portfolio around the concept of supply chain management, the processes involved, and the business context within which the initiative was couched. Whenever possible, when a workshop was done, the local sites would have someone from their site to "shadow" the presenter and learn how to do the workshop for subsequent presentation.

Another support mechanism came in the form of ongoing consultation from in-house personnel knowledgeable of and experienced in organizational change. To the extent possible, local people with the appropriate skills and knowledge were tapped to support local teams. Where this was not possible, corporate staff did travel to the sites to consult and work directly with the implementation teams, assisting in setting up and training evaluation teams, designing interventions, facilitating workshops, or helping negotiate conflict or navigate controversial situations.

FEEDBACK AND EVALUATION

Mechanisms of Feedback and Evaluation

Evaluation and feedback were built into the overall change effort; a large, single program evaluation was not done at the close of the initiative, so there are no quantifiable data, such as ROI, available. Because the implementations occurred in a series and not in parallel, it was important to capture lessons from one implementation and get those to the next site(s) on the track to improve with each successive implementation. For this reason, there were multiple lessons-learned sessions in which the participants reflected on their experiences and passed on their collective wisdom to those sites that were next up to implement. The training group did a particularly insightful lessons learned, and then teamed with an in-house expert in systems thinking to identify overarching themes and patterns of behavior that led to some of the problematic situations encountered.

A video of the Army's "After Action Reviews" was presented at one Ambassadors of Change meeting. The format of these reviews was examined and parts of the technique were subsequently incorporated into local site reviews.

The communications team did multiple "pulse checks" along the way. For example, after each newsletter went out, there was a simple survey sent to get reactions and feedback about what people liked and used and what could be done better. Subsequent newsletters shared the results and spelled out what actions were being taken (or had been taken) in response to comments. The Web site was redesigned several times based on input from users.

Simple pulse checks were also built into the Change Capability Evaluation (see Exhibit 1). Additionally there was an organizational pulse check provided as part of the CCE; this 35-question survey, called "Stages of Concern," was adapted from the field of education. Local sites administered the survey at 3 or 4 different points during their implementation to get a sense of employee concerns about the change.

The CCE was revised based on input from a user's group. Several of the early adopters worked to make recommendations and then read the several iterations of the second version before it was released in the summer of 1998. It was then that the evaluation's name was changed from "Readiness Assessment" to the current Change Capability Evaluation. The reason for this was that the feedback indicated 2 things: 1) The words Readiness Assessment implied a "do this and then you're done" approach and the users believed that the tools were also useful later in the implementation to gauge whether progress had been made in a certain area, and 2) Readiness Assessment did not translate well into Spanish or Portuguese.

Subjective Evaluations

In general, the organizational change portion of the Supply Chain Management Initiative at Nortel Networks, and the CCE in particular, was designed as a self-help, local capability-building effort. The CCE assisted the local sites in asking themselves the "right" questions. It was believed that the questions would create dialogue locally, which would lead to the realization that change interventions would be necessary. Local teams, with assistance and support from the corporate team, would then design and implement interventions that worked for them. There were many comments from local site personnel that the change program did indeed work in this way.

"This work has created a strong awareness within Nortel of the need for Change Leadership 49. . . It has applied theory to practical situations in ways that have challenged the corporation and those in it to think in different ways about how it goes about implementing its strategies."

"The focus on people development (capability building) is having results far broader than originally thought."

"The Change Capability Evaluation helped us (local site) look at our situation, gave us choices and options, and we (the local site) chose those we felt we needed."

"The Change Capability Evaluation will stand the test of time and become a recognized standard for organizations undergoing change."

Portions of the approach and program have been presented outside Nortel Networks. Sessions were given at the Change '98 and Change '99 conferences, hosted by Linkage, Inc. The general approach and the toolkit were presented at a joint regional meeting of the American Society for Training and Development (ASTD) and the Society for Human Resource Managers (SHRM). A similar presentation was given to several classes of MBA students at the University of North Carolina Keenan-Flagler School of Business. In all cases, audience comments indicated that the approach was well-grounded in theory and very practical and usable.

LESSONS LEARNED

Nortel Networks's Supply Chain Management (SCM) initiative was a major change effort involving reengineering and information technology. It took place in an operations group, distributed throughout the world, in an organization with an extremely lean corporate staff to support the effort. These are some of the lessons learned during this particular change.

Lesson #1—Utilize existing materials and resources, both internally and externally. Often existing materials can be adapted for use and there is no need to build anew. Engage or mobilize local, internal resources to support a major effort. Within the CCE toolkit is a tool for Leadership Competencies. This was developed using the internal work around performance dimensions for performance appraisals; the parts dealing with change leadership were extracted verbatim and used to form a quick self-assessment that could be done within the context of the SCM initiative.

A tool to get a quick picture of an organization's culture was needed to help the site teams understand enough about their local business culture to be able to design interventions that would be accepted within that culture. The *Harvard Business Review* had an article with a very simple tool in it. Nortel Networks bought the rights from *HBR* to reproduce and use that tool.

Local human resources personnel were mobilized to support their implementation sites. Training development was coordinated by a virtual team of 6 people from 4 different organizations within Nortel. This team was responsible for developing 40-plus courses in a 9-month time period.

Lesson #2—Do not be too much of a purist when it comes to tools. Ensure that the tools get at what is essential, but academic purity is not necessary. Obviously, any tools used need to have integrity, but it is more important that they are useful, address the issues, stimulate dialogue, and result in locally owned solutions.

Lesson #3—Build in multiple, simple, small feedback points to assess the acceptance of the change effort. These feedback points give people the opportunity for input into the process and ensure the information is collected and used, no matter how few responses there are at first. Then be sure that people know what changes were or will be made as a result of their input. In this way, credibility and integrity accrue to the change effort.

Lesson #4—Use templates and examples. It is amazing how creative people can get when they can see what is meant by a statement like, "Do a final report of the CCE and present the results to your Steering Committee." A template and an example of how another site did theirs stimulates people to begin looking at what will work for them and what they would change to make it better.

Lesson #5—No matter how difficult, integrate organizational change milestones into the overall program plan, particularly if there is a strong project management mentality present. Many times, people involved in organizational change tend to be intuitive thinkers who do not respond well to what they perceive as an "engineered" approach to organizational change. However, it is important to get milestones into the overall project management plan. Doing so makes the people involved part of an overall effort, gives a public forum for small amounts of education to occur, and tracks progress.

SUMMARY

Nortel Networks officially started the Supply Chain Management initiative in July 1996, with the organizational change portion starting late that same year. Because the implementation sites were so widely distributed (United States, Canada, England, Ireland, Latin America, Australia, and the Far East) and the corporate team was so small (3 people plus an administrative person), there was no choice but to build a self-help approach. This actually had extremely positive outcomes, because there was tremendous local ownership of the assessment results and the subsequent interventions.

The implementations were scheduled to occur through 1999 in a serial fashion. Thus it was important to be able to quickly capture the lessons and insights from one implementation and share them with the upcoming sites. This was accomplished via an internal newsletter, multiple lessons-learned sessions, and a Web site with a section dedicated to lessons learned, all 3 of which were published, coordinated, and maintained by the corporate team.

The self-help, distributed approach had other benefits as well. If there had been a large centralized staff to handle all of the work around organizational change, that staff would have learned quite a lot and increased its capabilities. However, since that was not the situation, the learning around organizational change was distributed among the implementation sites, which increased capability at the local level, not at a centralized corporate level. Learning, information sharing, and common vision and strategy was aided by the Ambassadors of Change network and by the work of numerous virtual teams.

The CCE was a central piece of the organizational change effort. It was extremely valuable in getting the local sites to ask questions that would lead them to the tactical interventions that were most useful. This had to be supported by the availability of the corporate staff for consultation, and through involving knowledgeable local resources.

The work of this change effort was centered in the Global Manufacturing organization within Nortel Networks. While there are no quantifiable results (which were not part of the success criteria), there is evidence that the approach and the CCE will be used in another discipline's organizational change. With a bit of adaptation, this is an approach that can have application in multiple arenas.

Exhibit 1. Sample Feedback Form

CHANGE CAPABILITY
EVALUATION QUESTIONNAIRE

Please complete this form so that the Change Capability Evaluation Team can review the effectiveness of its evaluation process.

Name (Optional) _____ Business Unit/Site _____

Date of Evaluation: _____

	Strongly Disagree	Disagree	Agree	Strongly Agree	Not Applicable
1. The objectives of the evaluation were clearly communicated and understood.	1	2	3	4	N/A
Comments?					
2. Best use was made of the time available.	1	2	3	4	N/A
Comments?					
3. Tools were appropriate for the evaluation.	1	2	3	4	N/A
Comments?					
4. Evaluation was structured in a way which enabled the delivery of the desired results.	1	2	3	4	N/A
Comments?					

5. What worked well? What didn't work well?

6. What were the key messages you got from the evaluation?

THANK YOU FOR YOUR FEEDBACK!

Exhibit 2. Sample Tool

History and Context
Section: Leadership and the Organization

A key predictor to an organization's ability to successfully implement major change initiatives is the way in which the organization has handled such initiatives in the past. Reviewing what worked and what did not work in previous projects will often provide insights into pitfalls to avoid and strengths to leverage. Doing an assessment of your organization's implementation history and viewing that history through the lens of recognized change management practices can help the implementation team devise ways to "work smarter" in the current or upcoming initiative. This tool will assist you in doing an Implementation History Review.

Objectives

- Identify and review past initiatives
  - How they were approached
  - Reaction in the organization
  - Ultimate outcome: how successful and contributing factors
- Identify lessons learned by comparing outcomes of past initiatives
- Evaluate current change
- Identify risk level of current initiative and record on "Change Capability Dashboard"
  - High, medium, low risk
- Prioritize actions to avoid mistakes and leverage success; incorporate in Change Capability Evaluation Report

Facilitated Session (see separate tool kit section) *or Interview*

Participants: multifunctional cross section of your organization (15–20 individuals)

Survey: Effective Management Practices Checklist

Process Options

Option A This option will require the better part of a day, or two half-day sessions to complete. Assemble a diagonal, multifunctional cross section of people (15–20) who have been with the organization for several years for a facilitated session. After making certain everyone knows each other, brainstorm a list of major change projects that the organization has been involved with over the past several years. Make certain that everyone has sufficient knowledge of each of the projects; if not, then perhaps the people who do could share their knowledge with the remainder of the group.

EXHIBIT 2. Sample Tool (*Continued*)

Have the group decide which projects were and were not relatively successful. Create two groups of projects: successful and not so successful. Extremes are important here, so encourage everyone to be *very candid*. Ensure that discussions in this session are considered confidential and that no one will be chastised for addressing issues or concerns. Then the group should select one project from each category for further analysis.

Introduce the group to the Change Management Practices Checklist (enclosed); discuss each parameter sufficiently to create a common understanding of the practices in the room. Select the first project to evaluate (either the successful one or the not so successful one). Then have everyone score that project individually on his or her worksheet. Bring the group together and ask each person to state their score on a given parameter. Record all individual scores first; there will most likely be wide variations in the scoring. Ask someone who scored the parameter high to share their perspective on why they scored the way they did; do the same with a low score. This usually engenders significant discussion and insights; record insights on a separate flip chart. The group should then decide the best way to arrive at a group score. In the interest of time, selecting the point around which most of the individual scores aggregate is probably useful. Plot the group's scores on the spreadsheet using points and a line graph. Then repeat the process with the second project. At the close of this portion of the exercise, you should have two completed worksheets and two graphs plotted, one for a successful project, and one for a not-so-successful project. Have the group study the two graphs and discuss their observations and interpretations of the data. Encourage identifications of pitfalls, what was done well, and what this means for future implementations. Record the group's learning and insights on flipcharts and keep in full view.

Have the group evaluate the current change initiative using the same criteria and the same process. Again, *complete candor* is critical. It is important not to chastise people for raising an issue or concern. Record the group's scores and again plot the line graph, noting discrepancies in the scores and discussing why these are. Compare these to the graphs from the other projects: Is the profile of the current project more like the one from the successful project or unsuccessful project? What does the profile of the current project tell the group?

(Continued)

Exhibit 2. Sample Tool (*Continued*)

The group should then rate the risk level of the current project. The group can set their own risk-level categories; however, as a general rule, if the scores of *all* parameters are above 75, the total project can be considered to be fairly low risk. If scores fall between 50 and 75, the project is medium risk; scores below 50 should be considered high risk. Overlay the team's cut-off points on the current project profile. Based on the group's scores and discussion, determine whether they believe the current project carries a low, medium, or high risk at this time and why. Have the group state clearly the reasons they believe this to be true. Devise a plan (or make recommendations) to manage high-risk items, improve the odds in medium-risk areas, and hold the line on areas that are currently low risk. Include the overall risk assessment in the Change Capability Dashboard in the History and Context space and the reasons and action items in the Change Capability Evaluation Report.

This completes the Implementation History Review Session. Be certain to thank the participants in a timely manner.

Option B In this option, the team can finish its tasks in less time than in Option A, perhaps a single half-day session. However, this option will require more time of the leader/facilitator in preparation and may be more difficult in the long run, if the group comes together and disagrees with the composite lists. In this option, the facilitator would conduct a telephone survey of the diagonal, multifunctional cross section of the organization and come to the facilitated session with the master list of projects already completed. If it is reasonably clear which projects were successful and which were not, without group discussion, it is fine to come to the facilitated session with the two lists—successful projects and not-so-successful ones. Continue with the above set of instructions at the appropriate point.

Variations on these approaches are possible and encouraged. The important points are to get out the information, to do the evaluations against the change management practices, to view the current initiative candidly, to have open discussion, and to devise appropriate plans or recommendations to manage identified risks.

Roles for either option

- Leader or facilitator
- Group members

Equipment and supplies

- Conference room large enough to hold the group comfortably
- Flip charts, markers, tape
- Pencils
- Worksheets (make copies in advance)

- Transparencies of the Effective Management Practices
- Overhead projector

It would probably be useful to make up a flip chart copy of the group's score sheets (3 needed*) and graph pages (3 needed*) in advance; an alternative would be to use transparencies although this would limit the group's ability to see multiple sets of data simultaneously.

Exhibit 2A. Effective Change Management Practices Checklist

Effective Change Management Practices Checklist

Instructions: Discuss and develop an understanding of each category, then score the extent to which you believe the specified change project met/meets the objectives. **Score each item on a scale from 0–100,** with 0 indicating that the practice was not considered and 100 indicating the project followed this practice extremely well.

PREPARATION PHASE

_____ Establish driving need

Need for change understood throughout organization?
Clear goals and objectives?
Broad base of support for the change initiative?

_____ Define the approach

Scope and approach of change effort clearly defined and understood
throughout organization?
Success criteria clearly identified and communicated?

_____ Create guiding coalition and required infrastructure

Agreement throughout the organization that change effort was/is the
"right" thing to do?
Adequate resources dedicated for life of project?

_____ Clear program management plan

Clearly articulated program plan?
Interface points with corporate direction and plans (if applicable)
well-defined with dependencies clearly understood?
Change Capability Evaluation with appropriate plans for follow-up actions?

IMPLEMENTATION PHASE

_____ Action stage

Realistic implementation plan?
Clear to everyone how implementation actions occur; how monitored; and
how course corrections are made?

---

* 1 for successful, 1 for not so successful, and 1 for current initiative

(Continued)

Exhibit 2A. Effective Change Management Practices Checklist (*Continued*)

_____ **Progress and feedback**

Mechanisms for tracking progress clearly defined and understood?

Mechanisms in place for real-time feedback (pulse checks), information sharing, emotional "escape valves," judging effectiveness?

DEVELOPMENT PHASE (Many of these activities are iterative throughout project life)

_____ **Continuity**

Plan in place to ensure continuity of change once established as the "new order" of the organization?

Plan to manage, evolve, and improve the new "state of affairs"?

_____ **Lay of the land**

Executive sponsors engaged?

Executives remain engaged throughout project?

Symptoms of "disengaging" identified and plan to manage if this occurs?

_____ **Knowledge and skill building**

Required skills for new way of work known and acquisition of same addressed?

Formal skills and behavior gap analysis done or to be done?

_____ **Change Management Capabilities**

Project management team understands and applies recognized change management practices?

_____ **Reward and recognition**

Reward and recognition of teams using good change management practices, planning and prevention of crisis behaviors (such as fire fighting)?

Reward and recognition system to reinforce behaviors appropriate to new way of work?

_____ **Learning**

Mechanisms in place for capturing and applying learning and insights to future projects?

_____ **Communications**

Clear communications plan covering all levels of organization?

Plan meets needs ranging from awareness to availability of technical detail and certification (if appropriate)?

_____ **Other (Identify and discuss)**

Exhibit 2B. Sample Group Profile

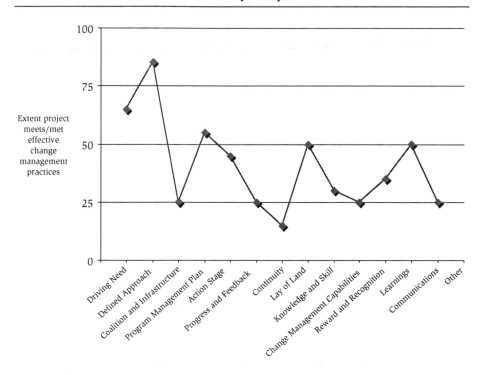

Exhibit 3. Change Capability Evaluation Final Report Form

Change Capability Evaluation Final Report

Business Unit: _____

Date: _____

Evaluation Team Members

_____

_____

_____

_____

(*Continued*)

Exhibit 3. Change Capability Evaluation Final Report Form (*Continued*)

1. INTRODUCTION

Background

The benefits and recommendations for a Change Capability Evaluation were proposed in a meeting or workshop on _____ .

The purpose of the Change Capability and Development initiative is to

- establish the areas requiring attention if the project implementation is to be successful
- evaluate the change capabilities of the business unit
- establish Change Development Activities
- identify critical areas and areas of high risk

The Change Capability Evaluation initiative was undertaken over a ___week period between (*date*) and submission of this final report on (*date*).

The Evaluation took the form of:

(List surveys, workshops, facilitated sessions, interviews.)

In addition inputs were taken from the following:

(List here any additional input, such as employee satisfaction data, customer satisfaction data, or other.)

Compelling Reasons for Change

These are the reasons for change:

(List the reasons for change; this may include business or project objectives such as enhance global operations, improve use of assets, improve processes, improve market to factory demand visibility, meet customer demands with flexibility, improve accuracy and speed, benchmark to best in class. One source of information for this could be the business case supporting the project.)

2. CONCLUSIONS

Executive Summary of Conclusions

(List in brief form the key conclusions of the evaluation team.)

Change Capability 'dashboard'

(Include here a copy of the composite results from the evaluation.)

3. RECOMMENDATIONS

Overall

(Give a brief statement of the general recommendations of the team; use the next part of this section to give specific recommendations, actions, and timelines on an area-by-area basis.)

(Continued)

Exhibit 3. **Change Capability Evaluation Final Report Form** (*Continued*)

Leadership and the Organization

History and Context (past initiatives)

Change Portfolio

Culture

Leadership Competencies and Commitment

Communications

Process

Performance Management

Technology

4. BUDGET AND RESOURCING

(Estimate what the cost of implementing the recommendations would be, what the scope of the work would be, and the resources required.)

5. APPENDICES

(Optional: Append the actual findings on an area-by-area basis and any other supporting information deemed appropriate.

Endnote

1. Orlikowski, Wanda J., and J. Debra Hofman, "An Improvisational Model of Change Management: The Case of Groupware Technologies." Sloan Management Review, vol. 38, no. 2, Winter 1997.

Bibliography

Goffee, Rob, and Gareth Jones, "What Holds the Modern Company Together?" *Harvard Business Review*, November–December, 1996.

Kim, W. Chan, and Renee Mauborgne, "Fair Process: Managing in the Knowledge Economy." *Harvard Business Review*, July–August, 1997.

Kotter, John P., *Leading Change*. Boston: Harvard Business School Press, 1996.

Mohrman, Susan Albers, Susan G. Cohen, and Allan M. Mohrman, Jr., *Designing Team-Based Organizations*. San Francisco: Jossey-Bass, 1995.

Mohrman, Susan Albers, and Allan M. Mohrman, Jr., *Designing and Leading Team-Based Organizations (A Workbook for Organizational Self-Design)*. San Francisco: Jossey-Bass, 1997.

ABOUT THE CONTRIBUTOR

Dr. Carol E. Lorenz   (lorenzc@mindspring.com) worked for Nortel Networks from 1984 through 1999. In her fifteen years with the company, Lorenz held a variety of positions in human resources, manufacturing, materials management, customer service, quality, technical training, and most recently as director of Organizational Change for Global Operations. She is the recipient of several Nortel Networks President's Awards of Excellence, the most recent one in 1997 for People Development. Lorenz received her Ph.D. from North Carolina State University in human resource development, specializing in community psychology. She has presented at numerous conferences on her work in the organizational change area and in applying systems thinking in organizational development and learning. After leaving Nortel Networks, Lorenz started her own consulting and contracting business, Carol Lorenz and Associates, offering services in organizational effectiveness.

CHAPTER THREE

ServiceMASTER

An organization development initiative that transforms healthcare service support cultures, delivers increased patient satisfaction, achieves increased cost savings and efficiencies, and develops a motivated workforce that seeks and finds meaning in daily work through service culture transformation

Creating support among all members of organizations for organizational change is a difficult task. How do change architects create the understanding and increase the readiness and enthusiasm for change, while simultaneously managing the fear process to create a "change by design"? The focus of this chapter is to describe an organizational change intervention that addresses these necessary components as a prerequisite to implementation of a significant cultural organizational change. The approach includes integration of process consultation, organizational diagnosis and feedback, systems thinking, action learning, didactic and experiential training, values integration, and work redesign. By relying on Organization Development technology utilized in the operational arena of healthcare service support departments, *ServiceMASTER* transforms support service delivery into one customer service organization, generates financial savings while increasing efficiency, and increases patient satisfaction. This is achieved by increasing the capabilities and competencies of the service partner and their teams, refocusing the work structure, and operating with a systems' view of service. The end result is a workforce that is significantly more involved—full partners in creating and sustaining change and meaning in their daily work.

ABOUT *ServiceMASTER*

ServiceMASTER, long a partner to many hospitals and healthcare systems in support service delivery, provides a variety of outsourced management services. Formed in 1947 as a carpet cleaning company, *ServiceMASTER* has developed into an international enterprise that serves healthcare organizations, educational institutions, aviation services, business and industry, and the rapidly growing consumer services market in which *ServiceMASTER* businesses TruGreen-Chemlawn, Terminix, and Merry Maids are well-known to homeowners. With 1998 revenues topping $5 billion, *ServiceMASTER* employs nearly 50,000 people, manages another 200,000 in operations in 38 countries, and serves 6.5 million customers. *ServiceMASTER* is a recipient of many awards for sound management practices. In November 1998, it was recognized by the *London Financial Times* as one of the world's most respected companies and in 1999 by *Fortune* magazine as the "most admired outsourcing organization."[1]

ServiceMASTER has gained special attention for emphasizing 4 corporate objectives that are the cornerstones of its corporate culture:

- To Honor God in All We Do
- To Help People Develop
- To Pursue Excellence
- To Grow Profitably

The strong corporate emphasis on the second value, the development of people, has come to be a trademark of the organization. In a visit to the corporate headquarters, management expert Peter Drucker, remarked to the *Service-MASTER* board of directors, "Your business is simply the training and development of people."[2] The integration of spirit, people development, and corporate excellence strongly follow Greenleaf's model of an ideal company where managers would describe their mission as being in the "business of growing people—people who are stronger, healthier, more autonomous, more self-reliant, more competent."[3] Pat Asp, corporate vice president for people, puts the mission of *ServiceMASTER* this way: "We're a service organization. When you think about that, our only asset is our people. Everything we do, all the value we create, comes through people. The way I think of it, only people can serve customers. Only people can create and innovate."[4]

With this strong heritage in training and development, it follows that any new approach to the delivery of services would include a strong emphasis in people development. This is certainly evident with the development of Integrated Service as a line of business offering by the management services division of *ServiceMASTER*. Not only is there a strong emphasis on training and development, but through the integration of organization development into every phase of business operations, the initiatives that drive transformation of the service culture result in a workforce that is changing the face of healthcare by changing themselves first.

BACKGROUND AND CONTEXT

Healthcare in America is facing myriad challenges. Some of the areas that demand the attention of hospital executives in their efforts to remain fiscally sound include:

1. Managed care and health maintenance organizations (HMOs)
2. Competition from walk-in clinics and physician-run ambulatory centers
3. Government intervention and mergers and acquisitions that create multihospital healthcare systems
4. Rising treatment expense and increasing numbers of nonpaying patients
5. Initiatives to influence proactive healthier communities

In order to more effectively deal with these and other yet-unforeseen challenges, hospital executives believe that the internal hospital culture must be responsive, adaptive, capable of learning and implementing innovative ideas, and caring enough to deliver exceptional service to patients and their families.

The damage and fear resulting from healthcare layoffs, "making do" with smaller staffs and increased work loads, and archaic command and control hierarchies must be overcome to create work environments where individual employees care enough about the whole organization to do their very best in delivering service. This is particularly true for the hospital service worker, often accorded the lowest status in an organization where education and preparation is so highly valued. Whether one is pushing carts of cleaning tools, preparing a room for the next newly admitted patient, or tending to broken fixtures, the service worker is routinely disenfranchised in employee involvement initiatives. Yet this worker has the potential to significantly impact the entire patient-hospital experience. In customer service language, they are owners of many "Moments of Truth," those individual incidents in the customer service cycle that influence customer satisfaction. Clearly, the service worker must be included in the process of improving patient satisfaction.

Structurally, most service support departments are separate functional areas, or "silos." Division of work in the traditional healthcare model does not accommodate the ebb and flow of patient admission, absenteeism, or turnover. The discrete skill sets needed within the environmental services department are not those found in the maintenance department, and individuals from one group cannot readily substitute for another. Additionally, the career paths are limited within these departments.

The demographics of the service worker show a sector of the hospital workforce that may be technically oriented (such as carpenters, engineers, and plant maintenance), may lack a high school diploma, and may not speak English as a native language. They may lack formal education beyond junior high school. Lack of self-esteem may be accompanied with few skills that facilitate higher pay and jobs that offer career advancement. Changing jobs may mean leaving the hospital to gain employment in a fast-food restaurant. Several scenarios apply here such as:

1. The worker may not aspire to learning
2. The worker may lack the self-esteem to sit in training classes with nurses and other higher-educated hospital staff
3. The facility may not have the job-related training available for skill development necessary in order to advance and attain more responsibility (and more salary)

Empowerment, self-directedness, participation, and lifelong learning are relatively unknown concepts in the service world.

SERVICE CULTURE TRANSFORMATION
THROUGH INTEGRATED SERVICE

Recent thought on the improvement of the American healthcare system calls for new ways of operating. Change is critical for survival; modern hospitals and healthcare organizations must remove parochial blinders and look to successful organizations in the private sector for lessons to increase "business acumen" and, hence, improve profitability and customer satisfaction. Among those with recommendations to the healthcare industry, Regina Herzlinger of the Harvard Business School encourages consideration of the lessons learned in the manufacturing sector for suggestions on transforming America's largest service industry.[5] The profound innovations that have revitalized much of the business arena—changes in organizational structure, in systems' perspective, in the use of technology, in development of participative cultures, and in utilization of information—have not been as widely practiced in healthcare yet hold much promise. Herzlinger maintains that many of these ideas have eluded healthcare systems. Noted futurist Ian Morrison, author of *The Second Curve,* presents the need to move from the familiar world (the "first curve," those traditional business practices and processes that represent the core of what has always been done to generate revenues and profits)[6] to transition to the "second curve" of the future. Morrison suggests that organizations must face up to the reality that the rapid rate of changes in globalization, new technologies, and consumer behavior are demanding new strategies. To those serving in support services in healthcare, translating "Second Curve" thinking into operational terms means redesigning the entire process and structure of service delivery (to incorporate the realities of creating an organization that will embrace change and learn how to adapt) and ultimately better serve customers in the process.

Integrated Service (IS) is an approach that incorporates the "profound innovations" that Herzlinger advocates and challenges the "first curve" thinking prevalent in hospital and healthcare systems. As a new approach to streamline the varied hospital support service areas, the complex variety of departments (traditionally the nonclinical infrastructure of the hospital) are combined into one customer-focused organization (Figure 1). In addition to the structural redesign of the service departments, IS is characterized by use of a proprietary software system that provides data on support operations, a centralized service center, evolution of workers into self-directed work teams, and a leadership cadre that has been selected for its ability to guide transformational change. Organization development is the "glue" that holds the model together.

Through centralization of services, economies of scale are maximized and redundancies are eliminated (for example, one central service center for a 2-hospital system with employees routed to address a customer's immediate need). Fewer service employees are usually needed since employees are trained

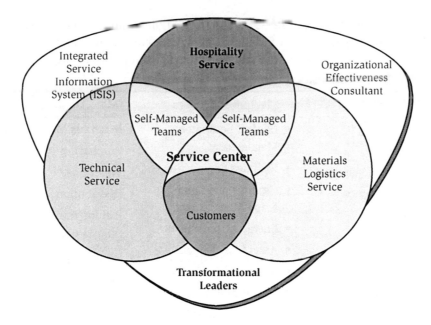

Figure 1 *ServiceMASTER* Integrated Service Structure

to cover the functions that were once the turf of a particular department: Instead of employees who are assigned to "Housekeeping" or "Transportation," they are members of a zone team that services a particular section of the facility, easily recognized by their uniforms. Employees are given the training needed to learn the technical skills necessary for this "multiskilling" through on-the-job training. Competency models have been developed that can be tailored to meet the specific requirements of a particular hospital; for example, Patient Service Associates in one hospital may perform food service delivery, may transport patients, and may stock medicines. In another facility, this function is called "Patient Care Associate," with functions of housekeeping, light maintenance, food tray delivery, and transportation as responsibilities.

The leadership structure of Integrated Service consists of a vice president or director of Integrated Service (DIS). The title is dependent on the scope of responsibility: large hospital systems might require a title that is consistent with other hospital or system leaders of similar accountability. Along with this position, every Integrated Service site has an Integrated Service Organization Effectiveness Consultant (OEC), an OD professional who is a key member of the IS leadership cadre. The OEC has overall responsibility for design and process consultation for the culture change initiative. His primary role as an internal practitioner is, as author Warner Burke suggests, is to serve as "guardian of the new culture."[7] Others in the leadership cadre are a finance director and the directors who will lead the changes in the overarching functional areas of hospital services, technical services, and materials logistics. Table 1 illustrates the varied functional areas that can be included in each of these service areas based on the tailoring process used at the facility.

Table 1. Integrated Service Program Spectrum

Hospitality Services	Technical Services	Materials Logistics
• Housekeeping	• Clinical Equipment Management	• Materials Management
• Food Service		• Purchasing
• Retail Food Operations	• Facilities Engineering	• Warehouse
• Clinical Dietetics	• Grounds and Landscape Management	• Distribution
• Patient Service Associate	• Energy Management	• Patient Transportation
• Valet Services	• Asset Management	• Central Supply
• Laundry/Linen	• Safety	• Print Shop
• Meeting Room Scheduling	• Technical Service	• Mail Room
• Rapid Response Team	• Property Management	
• Security	• Facility Planning	
	• Construction	
	• Telecommunications Management	

ServiceMASTER has over 25 Integrated Service locations, ranging from single hospital operations to large, complex multihospital healthcare systems. The approach relies on a strong partnership between ServiceMASTER and the hospital, a model that is notably different from the vendor-supplier transactional nature that characterizes most outsourced service arrangements. This partnership is cultivated initially in the sales process. Once the ink has dried on the agreement, cementing the relationship, the cultivation of a strong, seamless relationship between ServiceMASTER and the hospital leadership is essential for a smooth operation. Financially, the relationship is characterized by a performance-based fee structure that may include a shared risk-shared savings arrangement. Although there are different methods used at different sites, fees and shared savings are usually dependent on results of a jointly decided evaluation process by members of both ServiceMASTER and the hospital or healthcare system leaders. These leaders form an advisory board, created to manage and guide the integration and to evaluate the success of the endeavor. The IS leadership cadre serves as resources to the advisory board. At the outset of the relationship, the board usually meets every two weeks; once implementation is underway, the board meetings are established on a monthly or quarterly basis. The board is a visible feature of the collaborative nature of the IS relationship.

Integrated Service Multiphased Approach

A multiphased approach is utilized for implementation of the Integrated Service organization:

1. Exploratory, when the culture of the organization and opportunity for improvement of service is explored
2. Confirmation, when the business-oriented details are agreed upon
3. Design, when the architecture for the new organization is established
4. Startup and Implementation

Initially, the sales executive chartered with pursuing opportunities for Integrated Service sets up the engagement that explores the "fit" for Integrated Service within a hospital or healthcare system. Organizations that are most inclined to pursue this option as a way to increase performance while increasing savings are often organizations that are concerned with the cultural dimensions that support employee involvement and "empowerment" in the workplace.

An organization development professional, the organization effectiveness consultant (OEC), works with the sales executive at the outset to introduce the prospective healthcare organization to the role of OD in the entire implementation process. (*Note:* On occasion, the OEC consulting on the preliminary phases of Integrated Service may become the candidate for the permanent OEC position, in which case their familiarity with the site, staff, and issues is invaluable in designing the implementation strategy.) Initial discussions to explore the strategic outcomes that the hospital or system is pursuing as well as to gain understanding of the thinking that supports this initiative are conducted between the OEC and key executives. The main approach is to gather information that will assist both the partners-to-be in the subsequent stages in formulating implementation steps.

Successful implementation requires engaging workforce members already in place and incorporating them in the process. The OEC plays a vital role in this phase, leading the development of the communication plan that explains, step-by-step, the action agenda for impending changes. Hospital leaders deliver the message to the entire organization and clearly describe their vision for how they believe this change initiative is necessary and how they hope it will improve the organization.

ASSESSMENT

The pre-start up phases provide the OD consultant the opportunity to gather significant information about the current climate of the total healthcare organization. In the Exploratory stage, the OEC meets primarily with the healthcare executives to address the strategic outcomes that are desired through the integration of the support services. Several questions are addressed here:

1. What do the senior leaders want to accomplish through this change?
2. What strategic business initiatives will be supported or achieved through Integrated Service implementation?
3. What do they believe will be different, better, or the same?

Once the organization's leaders have made the commitment to move forward with the initiative, a more comprehensive assessment is conducted as part of the Design stage. At this point, several research questions are leveraged to drive the assessment process:

1. What is going on in this organization that will enable or hinder successful implementation of this organizational change?
2. What can we do to achieve the delivery of excellent service?
3. What do we need to do to work well together in this partnership?
4. What affects readiness in this organization to address change?

The information is gathered from all strata of the organization from senior leadership to the worker level following Schein's Process Consultation approach.[8] Process Consultation advocates the perspective that the consultant is in a "helping mode" to collaboratively address and design the change intervention. It is not a prescriptive approach that suggests "I know more than you about your own organization." Rather, the OEC engages the client or partner to become involved in the diagnosis and the design to enable joint ownership of the cultural change strategy.

Various modes are used to get indepth data: one-on-one interviews, focus groups, examination of climate survey data (if available) and human resource records, and unobtrusive measures (for example, observation of work patterns, patients, and their families in the facility). The assessment process can take several days or weeks; in reality, this assessment phase begins the ongoing assessment that continues through implementation and daily operations in a continuous process improvement approach. Depending on the size of the organization implementing Integrated Service (or the number of facilities integrating services into one department and size of facilities), a SWAT (Special Weapons and Tactics) team approach is implemented. In a SWAT team, 3 to 4 OECs are placed on-site to conduct the assessment. This approach yields significant amounts of information about the current organizational state.

As the data is collected, it is processed utilizing Weisbord's Six-Box model[9] of organizational diagnosis. The Weisbord model facilitates understanding of organizational systems in six organizational diagnostic areas: Mission/Purpose, Structure, Rewards, People/Relationships, Helpful Mechanisms, and Leadership. This diagnostic process provides information regarding cultural characteristics that assist the change process as well as understanding those artifacts, attitudes, and assumptions that impede change. This data is shared with the *Service-MASTER* staff responsible for guiding structural and work change as well as the hospital/healthcare leadership vis-à-vis the advisory board. The data creates a common understanding of the current culture at the facility. In addition, it serves as a baseline as in the case of formal survey data that illustrates current climate. Lastly, the data provides a guide for the development of the strategic implementation plan and business plan for implementation (Table 2). With joint agreement on the assessment data, the establishment of key steps for improvement sets the stage for the initial steps to address readiness and start implementation.

In addition to gathering information from hospital staff, the assessment process provides an opportunity to explain the Integrated Service process, answer questions, and gather initial inputs for organizational improvements from workers and internal hospital customers. The individual interview process provides a relatively safe environment to interact one-on-one with an OEC and ask questions that one might withhold from large-group interviewing experiences. The questions usually include, "How will this affect me?" and "Is my job going away?" since reorganizations have come to signify lost jobs and position displacement. In some cases, jobs may be consolidated, but the process of restructuring also involves changes in position, opportunities to learn new skills, and job expansion (increase in levels of responsibility).

Typical information from the overall assessment process includes:

(a) Identification of issues facing the service workforce that would influence learning new skills: literacy, previous learning/training experiences, work loads, English language proficiency, morale

(b) Current relationships that exist between functional areas both within and external to the service departments

(c) Other change initiatives that may be currently underway or completed. (These initiatives usually manifest themselves as organization-wide training programs or external consulting organization programs such as task forces, process teams, and so on, that might contribute to a sense of enthusiasm or cynicism depending on perceived success of those initiatives.)

(d) Political dynamics that exist in the healthcare organization that could influence strategy alignment and agreement over purposes of Integrated Service.

It is essential that the assessment phase not be regarded as a step that leads to a prescriptive analysis of the hospital system. Rather, it is a joint identification of what areas may need attention and which areas can facilitate the implementation and ongoing success of Integrated Service. The more that the service partners are considered as resources to not only be tapped into for information but enlisted to

Table 2. Sample from Initial Organization Development Plan

St. Elsewhere's Hope Hospital

Key Issue	Strategies	Expected Outcomes	Timing of Initiatives
Lack of understanding of mission and purpose of hospital and role of service functions	Engage all service workers in understanding of hospital mission and purpose through information sessions, employee meetings, and training.	Clarity of purpose as demonstrated by attention to needs of patients and customers.	Information sessions within 3 weeks, meetings in intact groups within 1 month, training within 90 days.
Lack of demonstrated personal commitment and understanding of patient service chain	Engage all service workers in mission development and commitment to patients.	All service employees will be able to describe how their personal contribution affect patient and customer satisfaction.	Employee team meetings; We Serve,* and Ready! For Healthcare**; training within 90 days
Consistency, quality, and timeliness of Support Service work are poor.	Engage leader cadre and work teams in defining scope of service and performance standards.	1. All service area teams will meet with customers to develop shared expectations. 2. Service area teams develop standards of performance. 3. Work teams increase skills, modify work processes to increase service delivery.	Within first 6 months

* We Serve is a *ServiceMASTER* Customer Service training program.

** Ready! for Healthcare is a *ServiceMASTER* training program preparing hospital environments on leading changes in healthcare.

change those items that they themselves believe will improve performance, the faster sustainable change will take place.

PROGRAM DESIGN

Each Integrated Service site has unique characteristics that differentiate it from the other partnership sites. These changes run from minor changes as to the terminology used at a particular site (such as "Consolidated Services" versus "Integrated Service Support") to major differences in number of services and how they are configured. Features that are consistent among the sites include:

- A centralized service center that becomes the main conduit for delivery of services, a "one-stop" center for customer interface
- An organizational effectiveness consultant (OEC) who designs and facilitates the growth of the partnership strategy and the culture change process
- Specialized training for the leadership cadre that prepares them for leading in a partnership mode
- A workforce that works in multiskilled team structures
- Utilization of a proprietary software system, Integrated Service Information System (ISIS), that provides sophisticated electronic tracking and record keeping (Figure 2)
- Measuring performance through the use of an internally developed continuous value improvement process (CVIP), which assesses the organization against Baldrige and Joint Commission on Accreditation of Healthcare Organizations (JCAHO) criteria
- Use of consistent dress identifying one's membership in the service organization

These are the outward and structural manifestations of actions taken to implement the necessary changes. Additional, less tangible changes fall into 4 specific arenas:

1. Strengthening the partnership between the healthcare leadership and the leaders of the new Integrated Service organization
2. Preparing leadership to guide and facilitate more participation
3. Overcoming resistance to change and learning anxiety on the part of the service partners
4. Increasing the skills and capabilities of the collective IS membership to improve work processes

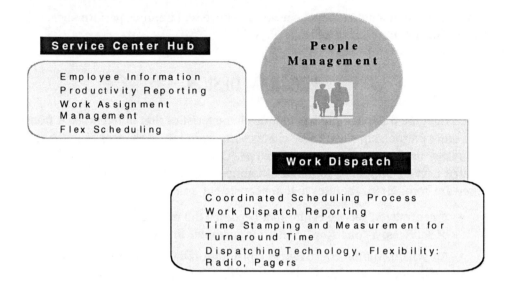

Figure 2 Application of ISIS Improves Service Delivery

Accomplishment of these 4 is within the scope of responsibility of the OEC—not to specifically perform all the tasks required to achieve these outcomes but to develop the methodology and implement steps to achieve these goals.

Of the entirety of relationship-building interaction between the healthcare organization and *ServiceMASTER,* the one process that focuses on creation of a strong working foundation is the Partnership Retreat. This off-site meeting occurs within the Confirmation stage and provides an opportunity for the senior leaders of both the healthcare organization and *ServiceMASTER* to strengthen the relationship necessary to move into implementation. The participants are often those who will be members of the Advisory Board. The agenda has the components of an intergroup intervention. The healthcare and *ServiceMASTER* participants both identify their own expectations, expectations they believe the others hold, shared perceptions of each other, desired outcomes, and models for success. The end result of the "mirroring" process is a collaboratively built model for success. They identify the norms present in their own organizations (which are usually borne out in the assessment information; hence, this becomes an additional data point for the OEC) and collaboratively build a model for the partnership success. Through specific elaboration of agreements on how they will work together, this becomes the foundational norms for board interaction.

Development of the Relationship Principles often appears to be as routine as the establishment of "ground rules" or "guiding norms" in meeting management parlance. However, for the board to have a deep and sound commitment to the partnership, it is important for the group to move beyond the mundane (such as agreeing to speak openly and honestly) and agree to principles that will stand the test of stress and tension as well as serve in the "good times" when all is going along to plan. One board adopted Glenn Kiser's Change Facilitation Principles:[10]

1. We commit to provide access to the people and information necessary to understand this hospital system.

2. We commit to personal change as we model change for others.

3. We commit to visible support of this change initiative by providing physical resources, financial resources, by being present at board meetings, by being active, and by allocating others if we are unable to be here.

4. We agree to consider changing any aspect of the system that is a barrier to the success of Consolidated Service (Integrated Service).

5. We support and hold accountable other team members and their efforts to change.

A *ServiceMASTER* organizational effectiveness consultant, who can provide any required follow-up at subsequent advisory board meetings, leads the relationship-building process.

The OEC also plays a major coaching and resource role in the creation of a leadership cadre that will not only espouse the principles of an empowered workforce but can successfully practice the skills that underlie a participative culture. The competencies for leadership in Integrated Service specifically indicate the traditional leadership skills in financial and technical areas but also articulate a need for change leadership, flexibility, adaptability, and excellent interpersonal communications skills (Table 3). The leaders of IS are selected jointly by an interview team of hospital and *ServiceMASTER* staff using a behavioral interview approach.

Three-Step Leadership Development Model

Once selected, the leaders participate in a 3-step leadership development model for Integrated Service. This model has been created to provide a common framework for IS operations and to quickly orient leaders to the core elements of the approach. The first element is attendance at the Integrated Service Institute, comprising a 2-day training class that provides leaders with a full understanding of IS, including the following components:

1. Essential information on the capabilities of Integrated Service

2. Role and responsibilities of the director of IS, the OEC, and the directors of the 3 technical areas

3. Understanding of organization development as the "glue" in creating one integrated organization

Table 3. Common Core Competencies for Integrated Services Leader Positions

Relational Experiences

Leadership	Servant leadership, visioning, coaching, mentoring, delegating work, supporting teams, self-awareness, personal development
Interpersonal Relationships	Personal integrity, respect, values diversity
Communication	Information sharing, listening, feedback, appropriate use of critique
Continuous Improvement or Development	Development of managerial skills, improving work process skills
Problem Solving	Information gathering, problem identification and definition
Decision Making	Effective decision making and evaluation, risk taking

Management Experiences

Business Management	Expands existing business, negotiated solutions, monitors competition, designs business plans
Financial Management	Developed budgets, managed budgets, interpreted financial information, cost controls, managed inventory
Contract Management	Monitoring contract specifications, writing proposals, estimating work for special projects
Personnel Administration	Hiring, staffing, job documentation, payroll system, provides performance feedback and reviews, trains employees
Quality	Insuring quality, managing audits and inspections
Safety	Remains updated on safety policy regulations and laws, implements safety programs, conducts inspections

Computer Experiences

Word Processing	Word or WordPerfect
Spreadsheet	Excel or Lotus 123
Database	Access, Filemaker Pro, Oracle
Telecommunication	Fax, e-mail, Lotus Notes, Web Browser

4. Overview on the Integrated Service Information System (ISIS)

5. Key issues related to startup and implementation such as communicating to the workforce, gathering data on current baselines, maintaining timelines in sourcing, and staffing for positions

6. Elements related to partnership building

7. Support to IS from regional *ServiceMASTER* People Services (human resources support)

8. Quality tools and benchmarks

9. Introduction to the Continuous Value Improvement Plan (CVIP), a key Integrated Service tool

10. Completion of a personal competency and development tool called "Feeding the Roots"

The new leaders of Integrated Service become familiar with the wide *ServiceMASTER* catalog of training, in both technical areas and personal development. This is a densely packed overview that relies on subsequent post-support from the network of established IS managers.

The second element is participation at a Leadership GRID(tm) seminar. This seminar is an Organization Development learning laboratory based on the seminal work of Blake & Mouton.[11] The GRID™ seminar links personal attitudes and behaviors to teamwork and the achievement of an excellent organizational culture. Although thirty years old, the seminar is especially relevant as the movement toward creating Learning Organizations[12] gains momentum. The week-long seminar is a vehicle for self-awareness and development of critical reflection—skills that are vital leadership competencies.[13] It also provides the foundation that increases managers' ability to "learn how to learn."[14]

Through the seminar design, participants are encouraged to examine their behavior in "double-loop" learning mode.[15] By examining their actions in their small learning team, the practice of critique is used to reflect upon action and resulting outcomes and develop new action. Participants gain first-hand awareness of how their actions may not be those intended or espoused. They gain insight on their defensive routines, those behaviors and attitudes that block their ability to learn. Through repeated practice in examining inquiry, advocacy, and approaches to conflict solving, the managers learn how to improve their personal effectiveness to positively impact their teams and overall culture.

The leadership cadre follows up their GRID™ learning experience with team-building as an intact leadership group. The team-building model, dependent on having a common understanding of the shared vision and common application of effective communication skills in initiative, advocacy, and conflict resolution skills, links team performance to an action learning approach of improving business operations. The team must identify an actual project as a vehicle for learning, a criterion for action learning.[16] Other areas covered in the 3-day team-building are exercises that explore levels of commitment, approaches to decision making, and relationship issues between the team members. Use of critique focuses on the practice of reflection and improvement of personal behavior. The OEC is a participant in the team-building as a member of the site leadership team; however, the OEC is also a resource for ongoing cultivation of the learning organization.

The use of other team-building approaches are also available for the participants to gain more awareness of the importance of group dynamics, working together, and getting to know each other. Ropes training is often used as a kickoff to the Integrated Service team working together; as such, it can prepare the group for the deeper intervention work that GRID(tm) organization development represents.

The third phase of Integrated Service leadership development is field site visitation. New directors and OEC consultants have an opportunity to visit at least two established IS sites to learn from others already installed in their positions. The visiting leader has an opportunity to spend two to three days at the visited site, participate in meetings, and engage in inquiry as to "what worked, what didn't."

Continuous Learning for Leaders

Leaders continue learning experiences as part of their role requirements. One method is through an ongoing process established in the "Feeding the Roots" self-managed development plan. "Feeding the Roots" is a *ServiceMASTER* program that provides the individual manager with a structure for self-assessment on the leadership competency areas (to include technical skill proficiency), a strategy for development, and support from others within one's leadership chain. Through a self-diagnostic workbook, the manager evaluates the degree to which she has attained competency in both leadership and technical arenas associated with her particular position. Once the self-assessment is complete, the manager completes a plan for how to improve the skills over the next year. Among the resources to meet learning plan objectives are the many formal courses offered through People Services. The *ServiceMASTER* Intranet called Network to Knowledge offers a source of on-line training and it is available to all employees. Once established, the plan is shared with the manager's superior for support and discussion relative to ways the senior manager can support the training plan.

Another tool for professional development and learning to new managers in Integrated Service is the *ServiceMASTER* Management Academy. This 2-week program is a core tool to transfer knowledge of the *ServiceMASTER* culture and values. The 9-day curriculum (Table 4) covers general management knowledge, safety management, financial management, and ISIS training through varied adult education formats: mini-lectures, small group exercises, and case study practice.

Table 4. Management Academy Curriculum

Welcome to the Academy and Getting to Know You	Employee Relations, Sexual Harassment
Just the Facts . . . About SM	Labor Relations
Travel	Risk and Loss Control Management
Safety Management	How to Use the STK
SM and Its Family of Companies	Hazard Assessment
How to Transfer Our Culture and Values Into the Workplace	Asbestos Awareness
Safe Behavior Management	Hazard Communication and Hazardous Materials
Safety Support Programs	Control of Hazardous Energy
Network to Knowledge	Lotus Notes
Goals of Business Organization	Purchasing
The Income Statement	Diversity
Billing, Labor, and Related Expenses	Balance Sheet
Supplies and Other Expenses	Cost of Capital
Employee Motivation Through Innovative Management	Calculating Margin and Mark-Up
Exceeding Standards	Pursuing Excellence
ISIS Training	Measuring Quality and Delivering Value

Learning Interventions for Service Partners

Supporting the ongoing development initiatives of Integrated Service leaders is an OEC's major role in guiding the establishment of development plans for the service partners. This is an important step in preparing the workforce for participation. At the outset of the implementation phases, there is often much confusion, anxiety, and concern among the service worker population. The OEC must determine what factors affect these dynamics and work with the leadership team at the site to create a learning strategy for the service partners. This learning intervention addresses the readiness for involvement and participation.

Among the tools used to increase the readiness of the workforce is the application of Future Search technology.[17] At Integrated Service at the Central Iowa Health System, the OEC trained housekeepers and customer service center staff to facilitate[12] small groups of service workers through a one-day Future Search. The day started with some reticence on the part of the workers to describe how they felt about the organization in which they worked. However, by the end of the day, after some facilitated "breakthrough," honest statements were expressed by the small groups and individual workers who stepped up to microphones with their group's recommendations for improvements, and thus volunteered follow-up actions. The groups are actively working on changes, seven months later.

At some of the sites, the initial skill building designed to develop individual and team skills are more classroom-training oriented. At one Integrated Service site, the OEC created a Leadership Academy for service workers. The basics of self-management skills are presented to workers who have had a variety of educational experiences, mostly nonmemorable. The OEC introduced video and group learning exercises into the classroom, building upon the hands-on technical skill training that the students receive on the floor. The classroom training has encouraged confidence in participants' abilities to learn: The adult education technologies used break through participants' mental models that school is boring or that they aren't bright enough to succeed. They succeed in learning at work and several Leadership Academy graduates have used their experience to move into supervisory and management positions.

Employee confidence is further supported as the multiskilled worker engages in the traditional technically oriented training that *ServiceMASTER* has refined. The training provides the job "know-how" that is essential to doing a job correctly. At the Bakersfield, California, site of Integrated Service, for example, a Service Liaison employee would receive the following training:

Hospital Orientation	Integrated Service Essentials (Mission,
Basic Departmental Orientation	Customer Service, Teamwork)
Housekeeping Processes	Transport
Laundry/Linen	Orientation Lab/Imaging/ER/ER Admit
CPR Certificate	Clinical Expectations with Triage Staff
"Grace Under Fire"	ER Liaison Shadowing

The Service Liaison employee undergoes 96 hours of training in this program, on the job with additional customer service training as required. The interface with the clinical staff is an important component of building trust with the nursing staff in the ability of the Service Liaison to work successfully supporting the patient.

Literacy is an issue for many of the service workers. The OEC has an opportunity to demonstrate adeptness in modifying the interventions and training delivery to meet a variety of language challenges. An example of how creativity plays a role in communicating with non-English-speaking workers is demonstrated in the OEC use of drawings in an employee satisfaction survey for those who could not read or speak English.

The importance of training as a tool to increase readiness for change is commonly practiced especially as it relates to team development training. Some of the training is developed internally by the OEC. Some is acquired from within the *ServiceMASTER* toolkit of courses. Two of these resources are the Self-

Directed Toolkit, a library of materials that can be used to educate on team processes leading to self-directed work teams. Another tool is a program entitled *Ready! For Healthcare,* developed by a *ServiceMASTER*'s affiliate, International Learning Systems, Inc. Ready! is a modularized series of workshops designed to increase awareness of the changing face of hospital environments. Content of the course covers world of change, self-management, communication, customer service, and coaching.

If the hospital or healthcare system is engaged in training employees on the impact of change, Integrated Service aligns the service partner change training to be consistent. Several of the hospitals have initiated in-house programs based on William Bridges's model of change18 and this training is often delivered to the Integrated Service staff by the OEC.

An approach that supports the learning attained through the use of the GRID(tm) organization development technology is available for supervisors and nonexempt staff members. Gridworks" is a 3-day team skill building that encourages learning through critique and reflection as well as personal awareness in team interactions. Like the GRID(tm) seminar and team building, Gridworks provides the individual team members with self-knowledge and essential skills needed to work in team environments. This training is essential as it focuses the Integrated Service staff on how to deal with conflict and how to problem solve in a collaborative manner. Gridworks also provides the foundation upon which the zone team building can occur. The focus of the zone team building is work-related: What will enable our team to better meet our customers' needs? How do our interactions affect service delivery? The team building may also extend to engaging clinical staff in an intergroup team building in order to improve interaction.

Development plans are an important part of the leadership's plan for ongoing learning; the same is true for the service partner. The OEC has the responsibility for leading the directors through a process to mentor and develop their staff as an essential dimension of performance management. Each service partner is scheduled for a prescribed amount of training each year. This can take the shape of any adult education format: classes outside the IS organization, community-learning opportunities, or computer-based training provided by *ServiceMASTER*. Others may participate in IS-sponsored learning, like the aforementioned corporate courses such as Ready! or We Serve. Newer innovations in training for service partners, such as the Toastmasters group that meets every Friday morning at one site, create opportunities for development.

The critical emphasis on developing oneself as a means to increasing self-esteem is understood and appreciated by the service partners. As one employee stated to an OEC as he was signing up for classes, "I'd like to take more of these classes . . . my wife said she can see I'm finally getting smarter!" On the demonstrable side, there is an increase in the numbers of service partners who indicate that they are interested in promotions and in preparing themselves for growth opportunities.

Learning Transfer

The implementation of Integrated Service promises to transform the service delivery by transforming the service culture through several change initiatives:

1. Eliminating work redundancy and reducing costs
2. Improving patient satisfaction through patient-focused employees
3. Increasing employee satisfaction and reducing turnover
4. Improving quality through more effective work processes

At each Integrated Service partnership, specific measurements are used to gauge the ongoing achievement of the culture change and the desired organizational improvements. Hence, the changes that occur as a result of the technical and structural redesign and through the effective utilization of organizational development tools and processes receive continual focus to ensure that they are maintained. If organization development is instrumental in creating the culture that operates more effectively, then there are both qualitative and quantitative measures that can demonstrate OD's value. Among the measurements are increases in patient, employee, and internal customer satisfaction, as well as the requisite desired financial savings that an efficient Integrated Service organization can yield.

Key focus indicators are one way to translate learning to everyday action on the part of the Integrated Service team. Work teams ideally establish the baselines of performance. As part of ongoing team activity, work teams establish targets for improvement with dates and goals. Examples of potential areas for measurement are presented in Table 5. The continuous focus on increasing overall performance is seen in work teams taking on the challenge of finding new ways to deliver service. Technical innovation from *ServiceMASTER* such as implementation of Floor Care/Carpet Care 2000, Palmtop menu ordering, bed-tracking software, spoken menu and automated diet offices continually challenge workers to become more "high tech" and incorporate the latest technology.

This creates new interaction opportunities with internal customers as well as increases the service partner's confidence in keeping up with change.

In the practice of everyday work, evidence that the Integrated Service organization development is changing work methods can be seen in the ways that service workers deal with the crises that arise. At one Midwest system hospital, a dispute broke out between several Patient Service Associates (Integrated Service multiskilled workers who serve on the medical floors in housekeeping/transport/food tray delivery roles) and the nurses on the floor. One of the PSAs tried to mediate the disagreement that was escalating into a power battle with orders and refusals. Recognizing that she was at the upper limits of her skill sets

Table 5. Possible Key Focus Indicators

Customer Service (Hospitality Service)
Cost Per Meal
Production Man Hours Per 100 Meals
Patient Contacts Per Clinical Dietetic Staff
Laundry-Pounds Per Patient Day
Processing Cost Per Pound
Replacement Cost Per Pound
Production Housekeeping Man Hours Per 1,000 Sq Ft
Daily Inspection Scores
Weekly Inspection Scores
Quarterly Inspection Scores

and not having much success, she negotiated a "timeout" and called the OEC to ask for assistance to resolve the dispute. The nursing staff was agreeable to a joint meeting and three hours later, the floors were cleaned, patients were tended to, and all were pleased to have resolved the conflict through collaborative discussion. The entire way the dispute was handled was so very different than previous situations that one nurse wrote a poem describing the event and how the end result was mutual respect. The poem was published in a hospital newsletter and became the subject of conversation through the facility.

EVALUATION

Implementation of Integrated Service can yield significant organizational improvements that are of critical importance to those who look at quantitative measurements to demonstrate value. There are various tools utilized to measure the efficacy of the organization development work as well as the overall performance of Integrated Service. The measurements established by the Advisory Board at the initiation of the IS partnership are most widely used as the measurement tool for performance; success in creating a customer-focused culture is one of the measures.

The most common way that the cultural climate is measured is through the use of employee satisfaction surveys. When a hospital or healthcare system utilizes an organization-wide employee survey, the Integrated Service workers participate. Data is broken down into the 3 technical areas in addition to the overall feedback of the entire IS group. Action plans are put into place to address issues identified. The scoring is evaluated against the numerical targets that were established in the outset of the partnership. Combined with two other measures, overall patient satisfaction and customer satisfaction, a composite evaluation is established for the Integrated Service partnership. Fee structure and shared savings are determined by the successful attainment of the partnership measurement targets.

In addition to the 3 most common measures (employee, customer, and patient satisfaction), other measures in use at various Integrated Service sites are measures of overtime usage, specific measures of time and money savings, reduction in turnover and absenteeism, responsiveness of Service Center and response teams, and employee participation in off-duty training or community involvement. Overall success has been quantified as follows:

- Nine months into the partnership, a total operational savings of $3.3 million, along with improved employee morale and productivity
- A 30% reduction in support service cost per adjusted patient day
- Payroll and benefit reductions of over $1 million in one system
- Service partner turnover reduced from 83% in 1993 to 20% in 1997
- A reduction through development and reassignment in job classes from 13 to 9, job positions from 33 to 18, and leadership full-time equivalents from 22 to 12
- Joint Commission Accreditation with commendation at a system of 7 hospitals that reflected improvement over a previous inspection that had noted over 30 "Type 1" violations in environmental care

The use of the Continuous Value Improvement Plan (CVIP) provides another quantitative measurement of the performance of the IS organization. The CVIP is a *ServiceMASTER*-developed assessment tool that integrates both Baldrige Quality Award Program for Health Care Organizations criteria and the accreditation standards established by the Joint Commission on Accreditation for Health Care Organizations. The overall outcome is to gain a snapshot of the organization in several categories: leadership (see Table 6), information and analysis, strategic planning, human resources and development, process management, organizational performance results, and patient satisfaction. Led by the OEC, the CVIP assessment is undertaken by the entire Integrated Service leadership team. Since it is time-intensive, the tendency is to perform the assessment once a year. It is an absolute that the team critique their performance with candor and trust to gain a true perspective. If the leadership group is not working well, the process of self-assessment surfaces issues that may be impacting the team's performance. In this way, engaging in the CVIP becomes a team development tool.

The result of the assessment is a numerical scoring that establishes a self-diagnosed level of performance. Once complete, the Integrated Service leadership team has an awareness of shortfalls in performance for which they can create an action plan.

Table 6. Sample Assessment Category From the Continuous Value Improvement Plan (CVIP)

No Evidence	Plan Written	Approach Developed with Timelines	Approach Success- fully Deployed	Measurable Results Acted Upon	JCAHO Standard: LD 1.1; LD 1.2; LD 1.3.1 There is evidence to indicate that:
					The management team has defined the mission and future vision of the department based on a review of market, customers and their needs, and an assessment of its own capabilities and updates as the business environment changes.
					The mission and vision is realistic and understandable to all team members and has been clearly communicated.
					The management team has proactively pursued opportunities for future growth by reviewing possible partnerships, acquisitions, new markets, new products and services, and other avenues of expansion.

Category: 1.1 Leadership
The management team provides effective leadership, taking into account the needs and expectations of all key stakeholders; includes how the team sets its direction and seeks future opportunities to provide service.

Quantitative performance measures are convincing but they are certainly not the only indicators of changes in the service culture. Significant changes are also evident in interactions among team members, in group norms and performance standards, and in espoused values—true indicators of culture.[19] There is a noticeable difference in how the Integrated Service partners have been engaged and connected to their work. At one site, where there was a concern that Integrated Service would be eliminated after a hospital merger created a giant healthcare system, one service worker raised a hand in an employee meeting and asked, "Does this mean that we have to go back to working the way we used to? We don't want that to happen!" A woman who had been a house-keeper started attending Toastmaster's (through the encouragement of the OEC's "You can do it!"). This inspired her to take a course at the local community college on Speech Communication. One semester and an "A" later, she has enrolled for 12 hours en route to her associate's degree and she has received a promotion into a position in the Service Center as a customer representative.

In a Houston facility, the Integrated Service newsletter regularly features profiles on the achievements of the service staff. When the laundry at the IS site in Cedar Rapids was shortstaffed due to illness and vacation, others in IS, including a manager, showed up in time to ensure that diapers and sheets were folded and all hospital floors had their clean linen distribution as expected. This is an environment that supports teamwork and a "one for all" spirit.

At a Texas location, the Integrated Service department created a "Clothing Closet" for patients who were ready for discharge and lacked a clean set of clothing with which to go home. This meant that discharged patients would not have to wear "scrubs" on departure (which represented savings to the hospi-tal). For some of these patients, selecting a set of clothes represented "over and above" customer service. When over half the names on the hospital's Adopt-a-Family Christmas Tree were taken by the staff from Integrated Service, a hospi-tal patient advocate was overheard to say, "I guess our service staff knows just how important it is to share."

The stories go on and on from sites all over the country, adding credence to the statement of Bill Pollard, chairman and CEO of *ServiceMASTER*: "The story will be told in the changed lives of people."[20]

Endnotes

1. *Fortune,* vol. 139, no. 4, March 1, 1999.

2. Pollard, C. William, *The Soul of the Firm,* New York: Harper Business, 1996.

3. Greenleaf, Robert K., *Servant Leadership,* San Francisco: Jossey-Bass, 1977.

4. Carlozo, Louis R., "Masters of Service," *The Life@Work Journal,* vol. I, no. 6, Nov./Dec. 1998.

5. Herzlinger, Regina, *Market-Driven Health Care,* Reading, MA: Perseus, 1997.

6. Morrison, Ian, *The Second Curve,* New York: Ballantine, 1996.

7. Burke, W. Warner, *Organization Development: A Normative View,* Reading, MA: Addison-Wesley, 1987.

8. Schein, Edgar, *Process Consultation Revisited,* Reading, MA: Addison-Wesley, 1999.

9. Weisbord, Marvin, *Organizational Diagnosis: A Workbook of Theory and Practice,* Perseus Press, 1978.

10. Kiser, A. Glenn, *Masterful Facilitation,* New York: Amacom, 1999.

11. Blake & Mouton, *Managerial Grid*, Gulf Publishing, 1964.

12. Senge, Peter, *The Fifth Discipline*, New York: Doubleday, 1990.

13. Bennis, Warren and Goldsmith, Joan, *Learning to Lead: A Workbook on Becoming a Leader*, Reading, MA: Addison-Wesley, 1997.

14. Argyris, Chris, "Teaching Smart People How to Learn," *Harvard Business Review*, May-June 1991.

15. Argyris, Chris, *Reasoning, Learning, and Action: Individual and Organizational*, San Francisco: Jossey-Bass, 1982.

16. Yorks, Lyle, O'Neil, Judy, and Marsick, Victoria J., ed. "Action Learning: Successful Strategies for Individual, Team, and Organizational Development," *Advances in Developing Human Resources*, no. 2, 1999.

17. Weisbord, Marvin, *Productive Workplaces*, San Francisco: Jossey-Bass, 1991.

18. Bridges, William, *Transitions*, Reading, MA: Addison-Wesley, 1980.

19. Schein, Edgar, *Organizational Culture and Leadership*, (2nd ed.), San Francisco: Jossey-Bass, 1992.

20. Pollard, C. William, *The Soul of the Firm*, New York: Harper Business, 1996.

ABOUT THE CONTRIBUTOR

Dr. Sandy Wells (sjwells@earthlink.net) has over 20 years of experience in the field of organization development. Prior to joining *ServiceMASTER* Integrated Service as national director of organization development, she consulted with leaders at Northrop, Lockheed, Applied Materials, CSC, and Columbia/HCA to improve organizational performance through leadership, collaboration, and the development of healthy work environments. A graduate of the U.S. Army Organizational Effectiveness School, Wells completed her doctorate at North Carolina State University and is the author of *Women Entrepreneurs: Developing Leadership for Success* (Garland, 1998).

CHAPTER FOUR

SmithKline Beecham

An organization development initiative that leverages cultural, management and behavioral analysis tools, competency modeling, and team-building activities to successfully merge two distinct healthcare organizations.

INTRODUCTION

Until recently, within the last decade, it was widely believed that a true merger of two organizations, especially large companies, was nothing more than a fantasy. Acquisition, yes; merger, absolutely not. The coming together of SmithKline, based in Philadelphia, and Beecham, headquartered in London, in the summer of 1989 was touted as a merger of equals. As it turned out, this proclamation was not a fantasy. Four other characteristics of this merger contributed to its unique nature. It was:

1. The first of what later became a string of consolidations in the pharmaceuticals industry in the 1990s

2. The first to deliberately come together around a vision of "integrated healthcare"

3. At the time the largest trans-Atlantic equity swap in business history

4. A hitch-free approval process, despite the financial and legal regulatory systems of two countries.[1]

The purpose of this chapter is to tell the story of this successful merger and attempt to explain some of the key reasons as to why it worked. The story will follow the 6-phased sequence of diagnosis, assessment, design, implementation, support, and evaluation.

Diagnosis

In the late 1980s, the worldwide pharmaceutical industry was highly dispersed. The top five companies, for example, represented only 15% of the global market. SmithKline Beckman in the United States, headquartered in Philadelphia, was ninth in the pharmaceutical industry and Beecham in the United Kingdom was number 23. While each of the two companies was surviving reasonably well, they were not high-performing businesses and were seen by many as prime candidates for takeovers by larger "predators." It was also believed that a worldwide consolidation was forthcoming. This belief turned out to be true.

Although Beecham had been a high-flying company in the United Kingdom for many years, especially with its over-the-counter products, by the mid-1980s it began to flounder. New leadership was sought and after a long exhaustive search, Bob Bauman, an American formerly with General Foods and at the time vice chairman of Textron, was hired as CEO. He came on board in June 1986. After about a year, Bauman became convinced that Beecham as it was would not be a major player in the pharmaceuticals industry and he began to "look around." In Philadelphia, Henry Wendt, the CEO of SmithKline Beckman (SKB), was coming to the same conclusions about his company. Bauman's search finally led to SKB, and he and Wendt arranged a meeting. During the following year, the two men met many times, each flying across the Atlantic, and they finally agreed that a merger of equals seemed feasible as both companies were about the same size (employees and sales) and about the same age—150 years old.

Beecham was known more for its over-the-counter products, such as Tums, and less for its prescription pharmaceuticals. It was strong in marketing and sales (its sales people were competitive and known as "street fighters") yet not so strong in research and development, in long-range planning, and international market development. SmithKline Beckman was known for its R&D, its good reputation in the industry, and for having a strong technology and product focus. In short, SmithKline was strategic while Beecham was operational. The companies had different cultures, yet they were similar in terms of being paternalistic, risk averse, and being viewed by the financial community as "one-product companies." For example, SmithKline's blockbuster drug, Tagament, was a highly dominant product in its product portfolio. For a more comprehensive summary of the two companies' cultures, see Table 1.

After the due diligence and legal matters were taken care of, the merger became official on July 26, 1989, meaning that not only were documents signed but the new stock became available on both the City of London and New York stock exchanges. Also on that day, huge banners were positioned over the main entrances of the former SKB headquarters building in Philadelphia and the Beecham headquarters building in London that declared in bold new-company letters, "Now We Are One." The banners were largely symbolic, of course, but Bauman and Wendt, along with their senior team, wanted to send a clear message that from day one every effort would be made to bring the two companies together.

This would not be easy because from the outset everyone was looking nervously to the new organizational chart. Typically under such circumstances, organizational members want to know where they "are going to land." They begin the process of "score keeping," that is, how many SKB people get important jobs as compared with the placements of Beecham people. Bauman and Wendt took great care in this regard and made certain that a balance was achieved. About a year later, people stopped keeping score. They no longer asked when a new position change was announced whether the person was a former Beecham or SKB individual. Although subjective and anecdotal, this change in behavior is one sign that the merger has been completed successfully.

As noted earlier, SKB had strength, for example, in R&D and Beecham had strength in marketing and especially sales. The merged company would need to bring these two strengths to the entire company. Turf (or "patch," as the British call it) issues would have to be addressed. These issues are businesslike

Table 1. A Comparison of the Two Companies' Cultures (July 1989)

SKB Culture (150 Years)	Beecham Culture (150 Years)
"Pharmaceutical"/Strategic • Long product cycles and planning horizons	**"Brands"/Operational** • Short cycle, "retail" environment
Strategic/Visionary	**Pragmatic/Tactical**
Elitist—"Club" • Attention to form, style, tradition	**Elitist—"Status"** • Attention to hierarchy, "one's place," chain of command
Multinational (Multidomestic) • Country autonomy • Minimum corporate control	**International (Centrist/Regional)** • More centralized at corporate and sector
Vision—"Good for Mankind" • Improving quality of living • Higher purpose orientation	**Vision—Performance/Financial Results** • Bottom line and value added
People-Oriented • Respect for individual (but paternalistic)	**Numbers—Oriented** • "You're only as good as today's results."
Technology/Product Orientation • Hold and "milk" assets • Diversify asset base	**Market Orientation** • Fight for shelf space and market share
Emphasis on Scientific Excellence • Input focus	**Emphasis on Product Development** • Line extensions, output focus
Inertia/Bureaucracy • Inward focus • Many levels	**Rigidity/Formality** • Chain of command • High-control orientation • Rules and procedures

Both

Paternalistic
• Disempowering
• Creative dependency

Risk averse
• SKB—"Don't look bad."
• Beecham—"Don't make a mistake."

"One Product Companies"
• As viewed by the financial community

in nature and are common to the process of bringing two organizations together. Compounding the merger issues, however, were the differences surrounding nationalities. While Americans and British speak the same language and much American heritage is linked to the United Kingdom, the cultures of the two countries are nevertheless quite different. Modes of communicating and relating with one another do indeed differ. One small example: At the outset of a business meeting, Americans typically leap to the agenda and the task at hand. British employees spend at least some amount of time at the outset socializing, discussing a new restaurant or a recent cricket match. So, not only did differences in business practices have to be addressed, but strange and "foreign" behavioral differences did as well.

Both Bauman and Wendt believed that: a) many of the right people were not in the right jobs, particularly at the senior management level, b) there was a need for a new mission and strategic business plan, and c) a new organizational structure was needed. And, of course, they realized that a new culture had to be forged.

Assessment

Assessments of the changes needed for mission and strategy were fairly informal. Wendt and Bauman had many discussions with their colleagues in senior management. Assessment with respect to corporate culture was quite another matter, one that was rather amorphous and complex. An external consultant was brought in to help with this more complicated assessment. The consultant argued that culture should be assessed within a larger organizational context and he presented a model for framing an overall organizational assessment (see Figure 1.)

While a number of questions regarding culture were composed for the survey, items assessing the other 11 categories in the model were also developed. For a summary of questions organized according to the model and used with the newly merged company SmithKline Beecham (SB), see Exhibit 1.

Also assessed were management practices and behavior, starting with the top team, including the chairman (Wendt), CEO and president (Bauman), and the CEO's direct reports for a total group of 12 people. Assessment tools used were 1) individual interviews based on questions about how well the merger was going, how well they thought they were working as a team, and what would they change if they could change anything they desired; 2) the Myers-Briggs Type Indicator (MBTI), used to assess individual personality types; and 3) multirater feedback, comprising ratings on nine primary leadership practices by the individual executive and by his or her boss, peers, and direct reports. Eventually, the assessments cascaded down through the hierarchy but in proper, role-model fashion, began with the top 12 people.

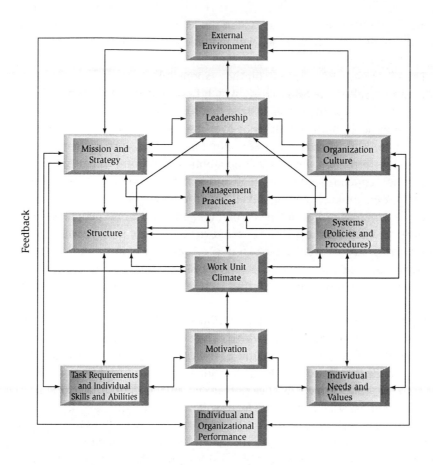

Figure 1 Burke-Litwin Model for Organizational Assessment.

The company used other assessments, for example, to monitor the external environment, but with respect to managing the merger, the assessment tools mentioned above were the primary ones—organization-wide survey, interviews, the MBTI, and multirater feedback.

Design

A key design element of the SB merger was the creation of the "merger management committee" (MMC). Bauman chaired this group of 7 with close to equal composition from both SmithKline and Beecham. The MMC's job was to take care of merger matters so that all other managers and executives could take care of the daily business. A critical task of the MMC was to match the right people with the right jobs. Another task was to work with external consultants on strategy and structure.

The chairman, Wendt, took on the responsibility of mission and he drafted a document called the *SB Promise,* which became the new company's mission statement. The statement emphasized that SB was a global healthcare company (not just ethical pharmaceuticals or over-the-counter drugs) that relied heavily on science, high standards of commercial practice, and a strong set of five values—performance, customer, innovation, people, and integrity.

Bauman concentrated on strategy and structure and Peter Jackson, the head of personnel, concentrated on developing the new culture.

Three hundred project teams involving more than 2,000 people were formed to work on local business strategies and structures. As noted earlier, an organization-wide survey was constructed to establish a beginning benchmark for assessing merger progress and overall employee opinions, attitudes, and perceptions. Top team-building activities were also initiated early on in the merger process.

In the next section, a brief description of certain aspects of team building with the top group of SB is provided. The work of this group cascaded down through the management structure of the company. These activities followed the sequence that Beckhard (1972) has advocated—to focus first on team goals, next on roles and responsibilities of team members, then on working processes and procedures, such as how the team will make decisions, and finally on interpersonal relationships. The two tools used primarily were the Myers-Briggs Type Indicator (MBTI) and 360-degree feedback. The MBTI helped the teams to gain greater clarity and effectiveness on working processes and procedures and on interpersonal relationships. For example, if the team consisted of a heavy majority of intuitive types and perceiving types (go with the flow and keeping options open), then it meant that some members must deliberately take on roles of keeping the group data based and decisive to counter the dominant styles and maintain a better balance of working relationships.

The 360-degree feedback process helped to instill the SB values and provide congruent leadership behavior to move the larger system toward its new culture. Conducting this process at the team level helped to a) provide mutual support to one another as the group members dealt with their feedback and b) instill the behaviors at the most appropriate level in the organization—the local work unit. At the individual level, the process would lack sufficient support and, at the larger system level, the process would be too unwieldy and logistically complex.

The top half of the Burke-Litwin model (external environment, mission and strategy, leadership, and culture) represents transformational factors or large-scale aspects of organization performance and change. The lower half of the model represents transactional factors (the day-to-day operational aspects of organizational performance and change.) See Burke and Litwin (1992) for a comprehensive examination of the model. The point, then, is this: When change such as the merger of SmithKline and Beecham is undertaken on such a large-scale, total system basis, the effort must begin with the transformational, not the transactional, factors. Thus, it was highly appropriate for SB senior management to concentrate at the outset on purpose (the *SB Promise*), business strategy (focusing on becoming a global healthcare company), leadership (getting the right executives in the right jobs), and culture (determining a set of guiding values). The next steps involve getting the loftier goals and values into the daily behaviors of employees, especially executives and managers.

Implementation

Key executives were selected, predominantly from within the company, for key jobs. The *SB Promise* was finalized and distributed throughout the company. Global business plans were implemented by business category but within the context of a healthcare company. The new structure consisted of 5 major categories—business sectors, as they were called—and 4 businesses and corporate headquarters. The businesses were:

- pharmaceuticals
- consumer brands (over-the-counter, nonprescriptive drugs)
- animal healths
- clinical laboratories

Each of these business sectors was further organized to serve global markets and was essentially functionally structured, with each business having its own marketing and sales, personnel, MIS, operations, and so on. Finance and R&D were the more centralized functions.

At a significant, early off-site meeting of the top executive group, known as the Executive Management Committee (EMC), the hard work of identifying the core values for the company was initiated. The team-building meeting was a combination of hammering out the values and taking a look at themselves as a work group of top executives.

While Bauman pointed out flexibility regarding what the values were to be, he insisted that there be no more than five. He believed strongly that 5 was an easy amount to remember and to have more would complicate the process. After debating them at this initial meeting and then discussing them some more at future meetings, the group finally settled on performance, customer, innovation, people, and integrity.

Using the results from individual interviews conducted by an external consultant, combined with administration of the MBTI, the top team took a good, hard look at themselves as a working body. The group did agree that to move the merger forward and define the new culture would have to start with them. The MBTI results, for example, showed that personally they were more intuitive than they cared to admit and great at generating ideas but poor at following them through. It was as if once they had spoken an idea, they considered it done and then moved on to the next challenge. The implications for the organization were far-reaching: No sooner would employees be given one task than another would come hurtling toward them. The explanation of the test findings created a forum that was nonthreatening and nonevaluative as EMC members tried to gain insight into the collective impact of the simple team-building tool. The MBTI data was incidental to its true purpose: providing a legitimate opportunity to talk through their differences.

The EMC gained two important insights from the results. 1) Given the chance, they would try to tackle everything at once. 2) There would have to be a more definitive decision-making process to ensure that each proposal was completely thought through. To cooperate more effectively as a team, they would have to work harder at setting priorities and be more focused and consciously disciplined about their demands on employees. As a simple first step, members agreed that future EMC meeting agendas would be limited to 10 items (compared with the present average of 18), permitting greater focus and more discussion time.[2]

Values to Behavior

It was understood that value statements could be one thing and behavior another. With the help of the external consultant, a set of behaviors was identified as manifestations of the 5 values. Again, Bauman insisted on this set of behaviors, called *leadership practices* being comparatively small in number; ultimately the number agreed on was 9—2 behavioral practices for each of 4 values and 1 practice for the fifth (see Table 2). Multirater feedback was used to instill these practices into daily behaviors. The EMC started the process, and at another key team-building session they received their feedback reports. With Bauman taking the lead, slowly but surely they began to share their individual results with one another.

For a statement of rationale and theory about the importance of this linkage between values and behavior for purposes of organizational culture change, see Burke (1994).

Shortly after this top team-building initiative and the launch of the value statements and leadership practices, the first SB organization-wide survey was conducted in the summer of 1991. The survey, consisting of 105 items, was translated into ten languages and was administered to all managers worldwide, nearly 4,900 people. The total population of SB at the time was around 50,000.

Table 2. The Nine Leadership Practices According to the Five Values in the *SB Promise*

Value	Leadership Practice
Customer	• Identify and continuously implement improved ways to anticipate, serve, and satisfy internal and external customer needs. • Stress the importance of developing and implementing more effective and efficient ways to improve SB procedures, products, and services through quality analysis.
Innovation	• Initiate and display a willingness to change in order to obtain and to sustain a competitive advantage. • Reward and celebrate significant and creative accomplishments.
Integrity	• Communicate with all constituents openly, honestly, interactively, and on a timely basis.
People	• Develop and appoint high-performing and high-potential people to key positions. • Help all employees to achieve their full potential by matching their talents with the jobs to be done and through quality performance feedback and coaching.
Performance	• Find opportunities for constantly challenging and improving his/her personal performance. • Work with his/her people individually and as a team to determine new targets and to develop programs to achieve these higher standards of performance.

The return rate was 73%, a very high number. In brief, the results showed, for example, that according to the 5 values:

- performance was the most highly rated
- customers were rated second-highest
- integrity and people were rated at about an average level
- the biggest problem was innovation

This last point got top management's attention. They are a science-based company with creativity and innovation being absolutely necessary for success, yet in the eyes of management, they were not doing well. Obviously the survey results helped to focus attention on where the action was needed. Some other key findings from the survey were that managers:

- believed SB was a good company
- liked their work and were motivated
- thought that SB had high standards and was ethical

yet they also perceived that

- SB was not sufficiently customer-driven
- employees were underutilized
- there was considerable waste, bureaucracy, and inefficiency
- SB did not allow for feedback

The survey itself was a step in the direction of doing something about the last point—feedback.

Support

While many examples of support for the merger and culture change process could be listed, 4 stand out.

1. *Communication*—always a problem, particularly in times of change. Activities used by SB were a) annual meetings of 2 days involving the top 150 managers and executives, followed by systematic dissemination of the meetings' outcomes down through the hierarchy (attendees, for example, were given notebooks with guidelines for communicating these outcomes), b) a new company magazine, *Communiqué*, to keep employees informed, specifically about the culture change effort, and c) other media—videotapes, bulletin boards, and so on.

2. *Symbols and language*—used judiciously, these support mechanisms can help a change effort considerably. The abbreviation for SmithKline Beecham is SB, but SB also became known as "Simply Better," the company's slogan for continuous improvement. The "Now We Are One" banner was another example of a slogan or motto.

3. *Business sector strategies*—cascading down what had begun within the EMC. The emphasis of the process was on matching word with deed.

4. *Performance management*—managing against clear goals with the use of specific measures and installing a pay-for-performance system.

It should be pointed out that these examples of support for change may seem obvious and taken for granted. Rarely, however, do organizations undergoing change pay sufficient attention to communication, to how the subtleties of language and symbols can either help or undermine the effort, to how the business should relate to and reflect the company's core values, and to measurement and reward systems.

Evaluation

A time 2 (post-implementation) survey in 1994 was conducted with a stratified random sample of all SB employees, about 13,600 people. The results were encouraging, showing far more gains than setbacks. Management, for example, was perceived as better in rewarding people, using people's skills and abilities more effectively, and being more customer-driven. Also, employees were more aligned with SB's mission and overall goals. The problem with innovation remained, however, as did the problem of bureaucracy and inefficiency. Finally, more attention was paid at time 2 to working on the issues identified from the survey results.

By the end of April 1994, both Wendt and Bauman had retired.* Jan Leschly, the former head of pharmaceuticals, became the CEO and the transition was a smooth one.

---

* For the year ended December 31, 1995, SB's trading profits had increased 7 percent over 1994, to £1.4/$2.2 billion on sales that had grown 16 percent, to over £7.0/$11.1 billion. The company employed more than 52,000 people worldwide—the target number it had set at the time of the merger in 1989. Geographically, its businesses were spread over 100 countries, with 34 percent in Europe, 48 percent in the United States, and 18 percent in the rest of the world. It was growing its global presence, exemplified by its effort in China, where SB was now that country's second largest foreign pharmaceutical company, and its initiation of a pioneering community healthcare partnership in Eastern Europe. Its total investment in research and development had increased to £653 million/$1.03 billion, which was double what it had been at the time of the merger and nearly eight times what Beecham Group's had been ten years earlier. (p. 278)

For a more comprehensive coverage of the SB story, see the work by Bauman et al. (1997) and see a recent interview with Bauman and the chapter on SB in Burke and Trahant (2000).

Finally, for a review of the literature on interorganizational relations, including mergers and acquisitions and ending with implications for practice, see Burke and Biggart (1997).

Exhibit 1. Sample Survey Items According to the Dimensions of the Burke-Litwin Model

External Environment	Do managers monitor the external environment on a regular basis, i.e., learning more about customers, competitors, technological advancements, regulatory bodies, and communities?
Mission	Is SB a customer-driven company?
Strategy	Is SB effective at selling its diverse line of products globally?
Leadership	Is senior management consistent in word and deed?
Culture	Is challenging the status quo what life in SB is all about?
Structure	Does the way we are organized and structured facilitate rather than hinder business performance?
Systems	Do our management systems and processes make it difficult to meet customer needs?
Management Practices	Can managers be counted on to express appreciation for a job well done?
Climate	Do people in my work group have the freedom to take whatever actions are necessary to achieve results?
Task Requirements and Individual Skills and Abilities	Is talent fully utilized in the company?
Individual Needs and Values	Does my work give me a sense of accomplishment?
Motivation	Is the real reward the work itself?
Individual and Organizational Performance	Do we compare our financial performance with that of our major competitors in judging how well we are doing?

Note: Each item begins with "To What Extent . . . "

Endnotes

1. Bauman, Jackson, & Lawrence, 1999, p. 2.

2. Bauman, Jackson & Lawrence, 1997, pp. 159–160.

Bibliography

Bauman, R. P., Jackson, P., and Lawrence, J. T. *From Promise to Performance: A Journey of Transformation at SmithKline Beecham*. Boston: Harvard Business School Press, 1999.

Beckhard, R. "Optimizing Team-Building Efforts," *Journal of Contemporary Business*, 1(3), 23–32, 1972.

Burke, W. W. *Organization Development: A Process of Learning and Changing* (2nd ed.) Reading, MA: Addison-Wesley, 1994.

Burke, W. W. and Biggart, N. W. "Interorganizational Relations." In D. Druckman, J. E. Singer, and H. Van Cott (Eds.) *Enhancing Organizational Performance*. Washington, DC: National Academy Press, 1997.

Burke, W. W. and Jackson, P. "Making the SmithKline Beecham Merger Work," *Human Resource Management*, 30, 69–87, 1991.

Burke, W. W. and Litwin, G. H. "A Causal Model of Organizational Performance and Change," *Journal of Management*, 18(3), 532–545, 1992.

Burke, W. W. and Trahant, B. *Business Climate Shifts: Profiles of Change Makers*. Boston: Butterworth Heineman, to be published 2000.

ABOUT THE CONTRIBUTOR

W. Warner Burke (wwb3@colombia.edu) is a professor and chair of the Department of Organization and Leadership at Teacher's College, Columbia University. Burke is the author or editor of more than 100 articles and 13 books. He has been recognized for his book, *Organization Development: A Process of Learning and Changing*, in Addison-Wesley's OD Series. In 1990, he received the Distinguished Contribution to Human Resources Development Award and in 1993 the Organization Development Professional Practice Area Award for Excellence. He is a diplomate in industrial-organizational psychology, American Board of Professional Psychology.

CHAPTER FIVE

Westinghouse

A change management model for creating a world-class safety culture or leading other large-scale improvement initiatives that leverage internal audits, employee testing, extensive training, job analysis, and cultural change interventions

SUMMARY

This change management case study describes the systematic approach used by the Westinghouse Waste Isolation Division to successfully create a world-class safety culture at the U.S. Department of Energy's Waste Isolation Pilot Plant located near Carlsbad, New Mexico. The plant is the world's first deep-underground repository for defense-generated nuclear waste.

Under the leadership of a visionary general manager, the organization redrew the change management circle, enlisting all employees as safety change agents, and tapping previously untapped change management resources. Using bench-marked tools and the power of symbolic acts, the division melded 4 distinct sub-cultures into a unified culture that makes safety its top priority. The division went on to establish a sterling safety record, achieve many safety "firsts," and win numerous safety awards.

The lessons learned by the Westinghouse Waste Isolation Division are important for any organization undergoing a major change initiative where success of the entire organization rides on the outcome of the effort.

INTRODUCTION: THE OTHER CHERNOBYL FALLOUT

According to an apocryphal story, a Russian scientist was showing an American scientist the first picture he took upon entering the cement tomb encasing the remains of Chernobyl Unit 4. The snapshot showed a large sign with Russian words on it. "What does that mean?" asked the American scientist. The Russian scientist sighed and answered grimly, "SAFETY FIRST!"

Following the Chernobyl accident and the end of the Cold War, the United States Congress, environmental groups, and the American public itself demanded that the nationwide nuclear weapons complex clean up its act. Long accustomed to focusing on production and secrecy, the complex was not a poster child for environmental protection, industrial safety, and worker health. The change management mission for the complex was clear: Create a complex-wide culture that "walked the safety talk."

This challenge caused many sleepless nights for leaders in the complex. The nuclear navy and power industry had created such cultures after the Thresher and Three-Mile Island accidents, but those change management efforts required a major amount of resources and time. Many of the smaller organizations in the complex, such as the Westinghouse Waste Isolation Division, had neither of these. So, the question became *could leadership create a world-class safety culture with limited resources and time?*

DIAGNOSIS: WE AREN'T THERE YET

In 1989, the 800-employee Westinghouse Waste Isolation Division was preparing the Carlsbad, New Mexico, Waste Isolation Pilot Plant to be the world's first deep-underground nuclear waste repository. Once operational, the plant would store low-level radioactive waste generated in the production of nuclear weapons in ancient salt beds located 2,150 feet below the surface. After touring the facility and talking to employees, the customer, regulators, politicians, and citizens, the new general manager declared that the opening and success of the facility would depend on the division living and breathing safety. "And," he added, surveying the room full of managers through narrowed eyes, "We aren't there yet."

Organizational Challenge

During his tours, discussions, and review of the plant's industrial safety performance, the general manager quickly realized that the division did not have one unified safety culture, but several safety subcultures. Employees of this new division came from many different work environments. Some employees valued production over safety; others valued safety over production. Some employees advocated strict adherence to written safety procedures; others saw written procedures as an affront to their intelligence and experience. Many were used to working under a shroud of secrecy ("What safety incident?"); others had worked in fishbowls where even the most minor safety incident was likely to turn up the next day on the front page of the local newspaper. The general manager made it quite clear to his management team that their mission was to transform those safety subcultures into a unified, "walks-the-talk" safety culture.

Drivers for Change

The general manager was not acting solely out of personal preference. As he said at the time, "The bulldozer has hit the pile."

Regulatory expectations—Congress, the Environmental Protection Agency (EPA), state regulatory and oversight groups, and the Department of Energy (DOE) required that the facility meet all safety standards before the facility would be allowed to open. In reality, all of these organizations expected the division to significantly *exceed* all safety standards. Standards ranged from the typical (adhering to ladder safety regulations) to the unique (ensuring that the waste is safely encapsulated in salt until it no longer poses a threat to humans or the environment—in 2000 A.D.).

Stakeholder expectations—The public, environmental groups, local communities, politicians, and the press demanded that the facility be operated in a completely safe manner.

Profitability—The fee that the division earned for management and operation of the facility was contractually contingent upon safety performance.

Budget pressure—The facility cost some $250,000 a day to maintain; it needed to open as soon as possible.

Clearly, "SAFETY FIRST!" had to be more than just words.

Change Objectives

In a series of onsite and offsite meetings, the general manager led his staff in defining safety change objectives. The senior management team committed to transforming the division into an organization that performs the following:

- Values safety as the number-one priority
- Follows good safety practices in all work endeavors
- Communicates safety concerns in an open manner; addresses safety concerns quickly and efficiently
- Maintains a sterling safety record
- Becomes the safety leader in the DOE complex

To ensure that everyone knew his expectations, the general manager conducted six hour-long meetings over a 2-day period, meeting with every divisional employee. To the surprise of many employees, this new general manager religiously continued to meet with all employees in this manner every 5 weeks. Safety was always the first topic of these meetings. Although the general manager was promoted out of the division over 6 years ago, employees still fondly reminisce about him and his employee meetings.

APPROACH

Working with organizational and employee development specialists, the senior management team came to realize that employing the traditional change management approach would not work. Historically, change management efforts were performed in-house by a small group of DOE complex veterans. These efforts tended to move slowly and have minimal impact. The general manager declared that a new era had dawned in the complex. To succeed, said the general manager, the division would need to redraw its change management circle to include resources not previously tapped. Specifically, the general manager called for the division to use the following model (see Exhibit 1):

- Leverage the knowledge, skills, abilities, and experience of a core group of employees who came from a world-class safety culture outside of the DOE complex to develop an effective change management program.
- Adopt and adapt the change management tools of world class safety cultures from outside of the DOE complex.
- Include departments, individuals, and tools not always fully tapped during change management efforts.

This new model was not without critics. Some managers resented the idea of using a nontraditional approach and resources. The general manager replaced some of these managers quickly after taking the helm. Seeing this, many of the resisters quickly adapted.

ASSESSMENT: A TALE OF FOUR CULTURES

Although a preliminary organizational diagnosis had been made, it was clear to the division's organizational development manager that a thorough assessment was needed to establish a safety culture baseline and identify knowledge, skill, abilities, and attitude gaps. The term *assessment* conjured up bad memories for many of the division's managers because of failed attempts to perform assessments using the traditional change management model. "Mark my words," warned one manager, "we are going to suffer paralysis through analysis." "Brother, can you paradigm?" snorted another. "Let's just skip this assessment stuff and go right into training," advised one senior manager. With the support of the general manager, the organizational development manager was able to include the resistors in a multicomponent, division-wide assessment. "Much better to have them bringing up the rear than sniping from the bushes," the organizational development manager said.

Participants

The assessors consisted of the organizational development group, the training group, the division's management team, and external auditors. The organizational development group led the assessment, conducting surveys and focus group sessions. The training group tested employees' knowledge of safety, and conducted needs, job, and task analysis. With the assistance of external auditors, the division management team conducted safety audits. The rest of the division's employees were involved in one way or another, completing surveys, participating in focus groups, and assisting in the audits. Even DOE got into the act, participating in audits and surveys. "This place is a zoo!" marveled one employee. The massiveness and inclusiveness of the effort had captured employee attention.

Instruments

The assessors used the following instruments:

- *Surveys and Focus Groups*—A university professor who is an internationally recognized expert in organizational communication helped the assessment team conduct employee and managerial communication surveys and focus groups. These were used to determine if and how safety was being communicated. Operations managers administered "conduct of operations" surveys to help establish a baseline for employee safety behavior and knowledge (see Exhibits 2 and 3).

- *Audits*—Internal assessors and external auditors from regulatory groups, other Westinghouse units, and the DOE conducted audits using government operational readiness review material, Malcolm Baldridge-style criteria, and homegrown audit tools (see Exhibits 4 and 5).

- *Employee Testing*—The training group conducted general employee and management examinations to define organizational safety knowledge. *Every employee was required to take at least one safety examination.* Managers were required to take multiple examinations covering safety and other subjects. Safety quizzes were featured in the division's weekly employee newsletter. "I take more tests here than I did in school," laughed a supervisor. Despite some initial trepidation about examinations, most employees grew to accept and even look forward to these examinations. "This is one way I can show management that I have the right stuff," said an employee. (See Exhibit 6.)

- *Needs, Job, and Task Analysis*—The division obtained wonderful needs, job, and task analysis tools from the U.S. Navy and the commercial nuclear power industry. However, there was a problem—the tools were too complex and labor intensive to administer. Training group personnel modified these tools so line personnel could administer them with only a small amount of training (see Exhibits 7 and 8).

Feedback

How many times are American workers asked to complete a survey or assessment, but never see the results? The division's change agents made sure that all participants received the results of the assessments. Detailed reports were presented to the management team at all manager meetings and in one-on-one sessions. The general manager presented a summary of assessment findings to employees during his regular all-employee meetings. Auditors held closeout sessions with managers to encourage open discussion. The training group provided immediate one-on-one feedback to employees on safety examination performance, reviewing each missed question to ensure that employees knew the correct safety practice.

Issues and Use

The assessment showed that the division had four distinct safety subcultures: bomb, commercial nuclear, navy nuclear, and mining. Safety knowledge, skills, abilities, and attitudes varied considerably among the subcultures:

Bomb Subculture—management and professional employees from Cold War era nuclear weapons production facilities such as Hanford, Washington, and the Idaho National Engineering Laboratory; very production-oriented; used to working in secrecy; placed a low value on formal safety training and procedures

Commercial Nuclear Subculture—management and professional employees from the commercial nuclear power plants; safety-oriented; used to working in a fishbowl; placed a high value on formal training and procedures

Navy Nuclear Subculture—management and professional employees from the U.S. Nuclear Navy; safety-oriented; used to working in secrecy; placed high value on formal safety training and procedures

Mining Subculture—Hourly employees from local potash mines; production-oriented; used to working with limited regulatory oversight; placed low value on formal safety training and procedures

The change management mission had become clear: meld the 4 subcultures into one safety culture. However, the division did not have massive resources—innovation would have to carry the day. The major assessment findings were entered into a user-friendly tracking system and used to design the intervention.

DESIGN: THE GANG OF 10+

The organizational development group and senior management designed the intervention. With assessment data in hand, this design team quickly determined that the commercial nuclear culture was the one to emulate. The team identified a core group of 10 or so employees from the commercial nuclear industry to address the training and procedural needs identified during the assessment. The design team directed the core group to beg and borrow commercial nuclear training courses, procedures, guidelines, regulations, and good practices and customize them for division use. Customizing meant streamlining these materials to accommodate budget and time constraints.

From the success of the "get-everybody-involved" assessment, the design team enlisted the support of departments and individuals whose resources were available during change management efforts to help address safety attitude gaps:

Employee communications group—feature safety in each edition of the division's weekly newsletter; write workplace safety scripts for managers; ensure that safety is featured in each all-employee meeting; ensure employees making significant contributions to safety are recognized; develop and use a communication matrix to ensure the safety message is sent out a regular basis using a variety of media (see Exhibit 9).

Safety group—conduct safety contests; give out freebies promoting safety; present safety awards; and coordinate good cop/bad cop safety audits.

Customer (Department of Energy)—provide safety quotes for newsletters, press releases, and meetings to bring home the importance of this change effort to employees.

Project management group—maintain, monitor, and report current organizational performance data against baseline safety data (assessment findings, goals, objectives, and safety record) to measure intervention effectiveness and keep the effort on track.

In hindsight, the critical success factors of this approach included:

1. Leveraging the knowledge, skills, and abilities of the core employee group
2. Streamlining borrowed processes
3. Continuing to redraw the change management circle to be more inclusive

INTERVENTION: KEY ELEMENTS

The general manager kicked off the intervention with a series of meetings (senior staff, all-managers, all-employees) describing his safety vision and what the division had to do to get there.

The division immediately began an effort to ensure that safety status was updated in *each* major communication with employees, the customer, and the public: every employee newsletter; every senior staff, all-manager, and all-employee meeting; every report to the customer; every press release, conference paper, and presentation. Every employee freebie (mugs, hats, pens, T-shirts, jackets) carried a safety message.

While the core group of employees from the commercial nuclear industry developed cost-effective safety procedures and training, a cross-section of employees from the other divisional subcultures reviewed, approved, and implemented the new procedures and training. This approach led to some heated conflict but, in the end, showed the groups that they could work together and reach common ground. One of the bomb subculture managers later remarked, "At first, I thought we would never get anything done. The commercial nukes came across as arrogant know-it-alls. But after a few audits by the Defense Nuclear Safety Board and other groups, it became clear these guys knew what they were talking about . . . well, most of the time." A commercial nuclear subculture manager recalls, "I had a lot of preconceived notions about the miners and folks from other DOE facilities. What I came to learn is that those groups include some pretty sharp folks. I got the opportunity to train some of them to be trainers and procedure writers and they were among my best trainees."

One of the intervention's most critical elements was the implementation of a mandatory, comprehensive safety-training program to cover the gaps identified during the assessment. To show that the division was serious, exemptions were not granted to any employee, including the general manager. All safety courses required employees to pass examinations. The safety-training program consisted of the following elements:

- *5-day general employee training course for all new hires.* This course covered not only safety specifics, but also the division's safety philosophy (see Exhibit 10).
- *1-day annual safety training refresher course for all employees.*
- *Formal on-the-job training and classroom training.* Line trainers conducted the on-the-job training and the training group conducted the classroom training. Designed for operators and technicians, this training covered dozens of areas, including confined space safety, forklift safety, hazardous materials handling, and advance radiation safety courses.
- *31-module self-study training program for all managers.* This program included modules on industrial safety, radiation safety, conduct of operations, and environmental and waste management (see Exhibit 11).

The division instituted an extensive safety awards and recognition program. Employees completing safety training and/or contributing to the safety change effort received certificates, gifts, awards, cash; recognition in written communication; and, most important, timely individual and team recognition by senior managers in regularly scheduled meetings. For example, the general manager made a habit of recognizing safety contributors at all employee meetings without contrived hoopla. He just called out the employee's name, cited her or his contribution, asked her or him to stand, and led a round of applause. Even the most cynical employees came to appreciate this sincere, unadorned form of recognition. A number of employees cried when they were recognized, having never received this type of recognition in their lives.

Other key elements of the intervention included the following:

- Brought audit teams in on a regular basis to give the division report cards on progress toward achieving safety goals and objectives.
- Linked a significant portion of employee compensation to divisional safety performance.
- Empowered each employee with the authority to stop work if unsafe work conditions were found.
- Established an anonymous telephone hot line for employees for employees to identify safety issues that arose during the intervention. The concerns were addressed immediately by the management team and the safety group.
- Celebrated major safety milestones (such as achieving 3 million safe work hours) with parties, lunches, dinners.
- Retained intervention learning for future use by developing presentations, papers, and reports.

Critical Success Factors

The elements that contributed the most to intervention success were 1) the "no exception" approach to training; 2) the safety-in-every-communication approach, instilling in employee, customer, and public minds that the division "eats, breathes, lives" safety; 3) the recognition of employees by senior managers during regularly scheduled meetings; and 4) the general manager's "walk the talk" approach. Together, these elements helped overcome the inevitable pockets of internal skepticism and resistance, as well as other program obstacles.

"No exception" training not only ensured that employees possessed the knowledge, skills, and ability to perform their jobs safely, but it sent a clear message to skeptics, resisters, and critics that the division was, as one manager said it, putting its "resources where its mouth is."

The safety-in-every communication approach helped the division overcome external and internal perceptions created in the nuclear weapons complex during the Cold War concerning secrecy.

The employee recognition approach helped overcome the preconceived notion held by some employees that management would "take credit" for any positive changes without "recognizing the little guy."

Finally, the general manager's contributions to the success of the intervention are legendary within the division. At an all-managers meeting, the general manager said in a soft voice, "You know, these management and supervisor training modules are pretty good. I've completed the first one and passed the test. How many of you have done the same?" The next day, nearly 50% of the division's managers took the test for first module.

In another incident, the general manager entered the training building, obtained a copy of the examination for the management safety-training module, and casually seated himself in the testing room next to technicians and operators taking examinations for other safety training programs. Word of this spread like wildfire through the division. "That dude is dead serious about safety," said a miner.

ON-THE-JOB SUPPORT: REINFORCING THE REINFORCEMENTS

As the intervention proceeded, an external consultant advised the change agents to reduce the intensity of the safety campaign. "Back off or your employees will get sick of hearing about safety and choose to ignore the message." This consultant was not invited back to the facility.

To the contrary, the change agents found that the more the division talked and walked safety, the more the division's morale and safety record improved. To reinforce the safety message on the job, the division took the following measures:

- Institutionalized nearly all of elements of the intervention processes— communication, recognition program, celebrations, stop-work-for-safety empowerment, pay-for-safety performance, training, audits, and issues handling system
- Disciplined employees who chose to ignore safety rules up to and including termination
- Provided managers with materials to conduct on-the-job safety meetings and demonstrations
- Conducted annual "stand down for safety" days. Required all employees to inspect and correct unsafe working conditions in their areas— challenged them to raise the safety bar

EVALUATION

To determine the effectiveness of the change management effort, the change agents compared baseline data collected during the assessment phase to data collected at regular points during and after the intervention. Specifically, the change agents looked at the following measures:

- Safety record (using measures such as OSHA lost-time accidents)
- Audit results
- Annual customer evaluation of performance
- Employee examination results
- Survey results
- Focus group results

Results and Impact

Safety had improved dramatically and continually using all measures. OSHA lost-time injuries dropped dramatically: The division posted a no-lost-time, three-million work-hour record in 1992, and one million safe work hours in 1993. Auditors made fewer findings during safety audits, indicating that employee safety attitudes and work practices improved. "We were very impressed," a safety program said after his team interviewed over 100 employees to stringent criteria (see Exhibit 12). Another auditor lauded the division as a "model of safety." "The only people who will ever really know how much things changed around here are the people who lived through [the safety change initiative]," recalled a division manager. "It is the difference between night and day."

The division transformed the four distinct safety subcultures into a single safety culture. According to follow-up surveys, audits, and safety analysis, the new safety culture:

- Values safety as the number-one priority
- Follows good safety practices
- Communicates safety concerns in an open manner
- Maintains a sterling safety record

The division met and exceeded all safety requirements for facility opening. With all safety questions resolved and expectations met, the facility opened on March 26, 1999, receiving its first shipment of nuclear waste.

The division has become a DOE complex *and* a world leader in safety as indicated by the following:

- Received a National Safety Council award for safe operations
- Became the first DOE contractor to achieve Voluntary Protection Program star status
- Became the first DOE contractor to achieve Voluntary Protection Program re-certification

- Became the first DOE facility to earn ISO 14001 registration
- Received the State Inspector of Mines "Operator of the Year" award for 10 consecutive years
- Maintains an outstanding Mine Safety and Health Administration inspection record—went from numerous inspection findings in the pre-intervention period to zero findings in the post-intervention period
- Shares safety training courses, assessment tools, and other intervention materials with hundreds of requesting organizations worldwide
- Changed the hearts and minds of stakeholders concerning the safety of the facility. For example, in 1989, U.S. Representative Bill Richardson (D-NM) was one of the facility's most vocal watchdogs, vowing to keep the facility from opening until all safety questions were addressed. In 1999, U.S. Secretary of Energy Bill Richardson declared the facility safe and opened it.
- Continues to astonish safety experts during audits. One such expert noted that employees said the following to him in one-on-one interviews during a recent audit:

"If I am concerned about safety, I can stop anyone's work—even if it is the general manager."

"WIPP is the safest place I ever worked."

"Safety is our way of work. If you aren't safe, you don't work here."

LESSONS LEARNED

Lesson #1—Redraw the change management leadership circle. It should include more than the organizational development practitioners and senior management.

Lesson #2—Borrow from the best. Because the best usually have more resources than you do, streamline their tools, training, and practices to match your organization's schedule and resources.

Lesson #3—Establish a simple, user-friendly tracking system. This will ensure the likelihood that assessment findings are used in the design and evaluation phases (instead of being lost or ignored during the shuffle).

Lesson #4—One of the executive's most important roles during a change management effort is to perform symbolic acts. The general manager taking an examination along side a technician during this change effort was one such symbolic act. Pave the way for your executive to act upon these opportunities.

Lesson #5—Simple recognition of contributors by senior management during regular meetings is a powerful tool. It will motivate employees to participate in and support change.

Lesson #6—Hang in there. They say change takes a long time, but sometimes the time between the end of the change effort and the ultimate desired impact is much longer. In case of the Westinghouse Waste Isolation Division, the creation of a safety culture took three years—the ultimate desired impact (opening of the facility) took another seven.

Exhibit 1. The Change Management Circle

New Circle

New knowledge, skills, abilities, and people from a world-class safety culture located outside of the DOE complex

New change management tools from outside of the DOE complex

Expand to include in-house people, tools, and departments not traditionally tapped during change management efforts

Old Circle

- In-house effort
- Same people
- Few people involved
- Same tools

Exhibit 2. Survey Samples

The following is a sample of selected survey questions.

Managerial Communication Survey

8. When a new Department of Energy order is issued, how much relevant information do you typically provide to your employees?

    a. I provide a lot of relevant information
    b. I provide some relevant information
    c. I provide little or no relevant information

9. After you've discussed a safety initiative with your employees, how often to do **you** follow up with a memo to clarify who will do what by when?

    a. Always
    b. Usually
    c. Sometimes
    d. Almost never
    e. Never

15. Two division managers share a joint process that isn't working well. They've had frequent discussions on the fix but have been unable to reach any consensus. What communications typically occur?

    a. They stop communicating
    b. They enlist support for their positions from peers
    c. They send memos to each other to confirm their positions
    d. They let their employees work it out
    e. They involve their bosses to solve the problem
       Other (please describe): _____

16. You're in a casual conversation with the customer. The customer expresses concern about a safety practice in another division department. What do you typically do with this information?

    a. Tell the cognizant manager about it
    b. Tell your boss about it
    c. Do nothing because the cognizant manager probably already knows about it
    d. Do nothing because it's outside the scope of your responsibility
    e. Write a memo documenting what you've heard and send it to the cognizant manager
       Other (please describe): _____

Employee Communication Survey

23. Do you know what the **Open Door Policy** is?

    _____ Yes _____ No

(Countinued)

Exhibit 2. Survey Samples (*Continued*)

24. If you had a safety concern that you could not resolve to your satisfaction with your supervisor, how likely is it that you would use the **Open Door Policy** to take your concern directly to upper management? (Circle one answer; skip this question if you answered "no" to question 23.)

    a. 0% likelihood
    b. 25% likelihood
    c. 50% likelihood
    d. 75% likelihood
    e. 100% likelihood

22. A variety of information is discussed at the all-employees meetings. Rate each of the topics below with respect to the degree to which the information presented at these meetings is **helpful** to you. Respond by circling the response category to the right of each topic that best approximates the percent of time you find discussion of the topic helpful.

Topics Discussed at All-Employees Meetings	Percent of Time You Find These Discussions Helpful:				
a. Work priorities/schedules	0%	25%	50%	75%	100%
b. Safety issues	0%	25%	50%	75%	100%
c. Westinghouse corporate issues	0%	25%	50%	75%	100%
d. Dept. of Energy issues	0%	25%	50%	75%	100%
e. Total quality	0%	25%	50%	75%	100%
f. Productivity improvement	0%	25%	50%	75%	100%
g. Human Resources information	0%	25%	50%	75%	100%
h. Recognition of employees	0%	25%	50%	75%	100%
i. Budget information	0%	25%	50%	75%	100%
j. Organization/management changes	0%	25%	50%	75%	100%

Conduct of Operations Survey

22. A visitor to your facility asks you, "Tell me about the safety pre-planning requirement for operations activities. You know, the role of safety analyses, and the handling of safety matters." How comfortable would you be in answering the question?

    a. Uncomfortable—I know few of the details
    b. Somewhat comfortable—I know some of the details
    c. Comfortable—I know all of the details

23. Does your manager hold you accountable for your operating performance?

    a. Always
    b. Usually

Exhibit 2. Survey Samples (*Continued*)

   c. Sometimes

   d. Almost never

   e. Never

   f. I don't know

30. Which of the following statements reflect your field practice concerning instrument readings?

   a. I believe instrument readings and treat them as accurate

   b. I occasionally ignore readings of some instruments are known to be faulty

   c. I ignore many readings because many instruments are out of calibration

31. While you are working out in the field, a circuit breaker for a piece of equipment trips. What typically occurs next?

   a. The breaker is reset to see if it trips again

   b. The circuit breaker is written up for maintenance and the job suspended

   c. The cause of the trip is investigated

Exhibit 3. Focus Group Agenda

1. Introduce yourself, the topic, and why we are conducting focus groups

2. Cover the focus group ground rules

3. Field questions and answers

4. Discuss communication methods and sources

5. Discuss communication with managers and supervisors

6. Ask participants to assess the information they receive

7. Discuss group and intergroup communication

8. Discuss the relationship of communication, quality, and effectiveness

9. Solicit feedback to improve the next focus groups

Exhibit 4. Audit Criteria Sample

1.1 Line Management Involvement in the Safety-Training Program

(Note: In this assessment, the term "line management" refers to all managers in the organization outside of the technical training section.)

Line management ownership, commitment, and accountability are the foundation for our organization's safety-training program.

Line management is responsible for ensuring that our safety-training program will produce competent personnel.

The commitment to the training of personnel in this organization includes participation of line management in all phases of the safety-training program.

Line management ensures that resources are available to support the safety-training effort, including assigning personnel from within the line organization to coordinate implementation of the safety-training program.

Line management mandates attendance at safety training sessions.

Line management is thoroughly knowledgeable of all aspects of the safety-training programs in which personnel participate.

Line management-approved policies and procedures are implemented that promote a systematic approach to training.

Line management policies and procedures adequately describe the duties, responsibilities, and authorities of line and training management, and detail the interfaces involved in implementing the safety training of personnel.

Exhibit 5. Malcolm Baldridge-Style Criteria Sample

Describe your approach, implementation, and results for each of the following:

1.0 Customer Orientation

1.7 Public Safety and Health

- *Appropriate formal safety program for customers and the community. Clarity and completeness of safety documentation (i.e., safety manuals, warnings, and training, etc.)*
- *Collection and use of safety-related data from the customer. Timeliness of responding to customer complaints about safety*
- *Compliance with federal and state safety regulations (i.e., CPSC, DoT, FTC, etc.)*

2.0 Participation

2.1 Management Involvement

- *Meetings: staff and workplace; regularly planned and scheduled; results communicated; judged effective; all functions represented*
- *Managers visibly involved and committed; open door policy exists*
- *Managers lead by example: hands-on; daily involvement; up/down/peer participation*
- *Decision making is at the lowest practical level in the organization*

Exhibit 6. Safety Examination Items

1. Indirect costs of an accident usually are

   a. greater than the direct costs of an accident
   b. less than the direct costs of an accident
   c. about the same as the direct costs of an accident

2. A manager tells his employees, "Our building is due to be inspected next week. If a deficiency is found in our area, the building landlord will see that the deficiency is corrected." Is this statement correct? Why?

   a. YES—The landlord is responsible for ensuring that audit shortcomings and inspection deficiencies are corrected in a timely manner.

   b. NO—The party who inspects the building is responsible for seeing that deficiencies are corrected in a timely manner.

   c. NO—If a building inspector finds a deficiency in a WIPP structure, Industrial Safety is responsible for correcting the deficiency in a timely manner.

   d. NO—If a building inspector finds a deficiency in your area, it is up to you—not the landlord, not Industrial Safety—to correct the deficiency in a timely manner.

Exhibit 7 Needs/Job Analysis Sample

Assessors Guide Sheet

Instructions:

- Review all of the tasks on the survey form, deleting any that do not apply to your organization.

- Have each employee in your organization complete a survey form. Be sure that each employee receives the participant's guide sheet.

- Collect all of the analysis forms. Go through each form scoring each task. Example:

Task	Difficulty	Importance	Frequency
Conduct formal safety inspection of work area	(1 2 3) 4 5	1 2 3 4 (5)	D W (M) Y N

$$2 + 5 + 3 = 10$$

- Note that frequency is scored as follows:

   D = 1
   W = 2
   M = 3
   Y = 4
   N = 5

- After you have scored each task on each form, determine the mean score for each task. To calculate the mean score, add all of the individual scores together for a given task and divide by the number of employees who completed the analysis. The mean scores should be = 3.0 and = 15.0.

- Order the tasks from highest mean score to lowest mean score. You have just created a prioritized list of general employee training needs using a systematic approach to training.

- Use the following guide to determine the best type of training:

Mean Score

3–7   *No formal training necessary—address specific needs through informal on-the-job training (OJT)*

8–11   *Initial formal training necessary (train one time)*

12–15   *Initial and on-going formal training necessary*

Exhibit 8. Task Analysis Sample

TASK:	RESPOND TO SEVERE WEATHER
AREA:	EMERGENCY OPERATIONS
JOB:	FACILITY OPERATOR

Step #	Step	Required Knowledge, Skill, and/or Ability (KSA)
1.	Determine severity of threat. If severe, proceed to step 2.	1a. KSA necessary to identify weather that represents a threat to personnel or property
2.	Call central monitoring room operator.	2a. Knowledge of emergency telephone number and channel 2b. KSA necessary to operate telephone or hand-held two-way radio
3.	Notify central monitoring room operator of threat.	3a. Knowledge of emergency information reporting requirements 3b. Knowledge of formal communications protocol
4.	Verify "take shelter" alarm and message.	4a. Knowledge of different site alarms 4b. Knowledge of proper "take cover" message
5.	Assist in evacuation of personnel to hard-sheltered buildings.	5a. Knowledge of hard-sheltered building locations 5b. Knowledge of nonhard-sheltered building locations
6.	Assistant in accounting for personnel.	6a. Knowledge of accountability system
7.	Assess the facility for damage after the threat has passed.	7a. KSA necessary to walk down the surface facility and inspect equipment and buildings for damage

Exhibit 9. Communication Matrix Sample

Area of Focus	All-Manager Meetings	All-Employee Meetings	TRU News—Weekly Newsletter	Workplace Scripts	Letters, Periodicals to Home	Bulletin Boards	GM Memos
Industrial Safety	Every meeting	Every meeting	Every issue	4 per year	2 per year	Always featured on boards, update monthly	Upon attainment of milestones
Environmental Safety	Before and after audits	Before and after audits	Monthly	As needed	Upon attainment of milestones	Feature quarterly	Upon attainment of milestones
Employee Health	As needed	As needed	Every issue	As needed	Monthly	Always featured on boards, update monthly	As needed
Conduct of Operations	Quarterly	Quarterly	12 week series	14 per year	As needed	As needed	As needed

Exhibit 10. Safety Curriculum in General Employee Training

1. Radiation Safety—nuclear physics basics, health risks, protective measures, signage, regulatory requirements

2. Industrial Safety—hearing, eye, and foot protection, material safety data sheets, equipment operation safety, ergonomics, signage, regulatory requirements

3. Environmental Safety—RCRA, NEPA, CERCLA responsibilities and regulatory requirements

4. Emergency Preparedness—tornadoes and other natural phenomena, bomb threats, warning sounds, evacuation procedures

5. Employee Health—blood-borne pathogens, AIDS

Exhibit 11. Industrial Safety Training Module for Managers—Table of Contents

A. INTRODUCTION

B. REGULATORY REQUIREMENTS

C. SAFETY AND ACCOUNTABILITY

D. MANAGER AND SUPERVISOR RESPONSIBILITIES

E. LANDLORD RESPONSIBILITIES

F. FIRE PROTECTION

G. SUBCONTRACTS AND SAFETY

H. WHAT YOU CAN DO TO PREVENT ACCIDENTS

I. INCIDENT REPORTING REQUIREMENTS

J. HOW TO ANALYZE TASKS FOR HAZARDS

K. ELECTRICAL SAFETY

L. HAZARDOUS MATERIALS

M. HOUSEKEEPING

N. WORK IN HIGH PLACES OR CONFINED SPACES

O. SAFETY MEETINGS

P. MONITORING THE SAFETY PROGRAM

Q. SAFETY GOALS

R. SMART MOVES—WHAT YOU CAN DO NOW

S. MODULE REFERENCES

T. PRACTICE TEST

U. ANSWERS AND FEEDBACK FOR THE PRACTICE TEST

V. APPENDIX

Exhibit 12. Safety Program Evaluation Criteria Sample (*Continued*)

From the Department of Energy's Voluntary Protection Program (STAR Program):

1. Management Leadership. Each applicant must demonstrate top-level management commitment to occupational health and safety in general and to the specific requirements of DOE-VPP. Management systems for comprehensive planning must address health and safety. (a) Commitment to Health and Safety Protection. As with any other management system, authority and responsibility for employee health and safety must be integrated with the management system of the organization and must involve employees. This commitment includes the following: (1) Policy. There should be a clearly stated policy on safe and healthful working conditions that is communicated to employees at all levels, so they understand the priority of safety and health protection in relation to other organizational values. (2) Goal and Objectives. There should be an established and communicated goal and related objectives for the safety and health program so that the desired results and the planned measures for achieving those results are clearly understood. (3) Planning. Planning for safety and health must be part of the overall long-term management planning. b. Written Safety and Health Program. All critical elements of the safety and health program, including management leadership, employee involvement, worksite analysis, hazard prevention and control, and safety and health training, must be a part of the written program. (1) Adequacy. All aspects of the safety and health program must be appropriate to the size of the worksite, the complexity of the hazards, and the nature of the industry. (2) Responsibility. Responsibility for all aspects of the safety and health program must be assigned and communicated so that all managers, supervisors, and line employees know what is expected of them. (3) Authority and Resources. Responsible personnel must have adequate authority and resources to perform the desired tasks. Commitment of necessary resources for workplace health and safety must be documented and must address staffing, space, equipment, training, and promotions. Budget and capital expenditures for health and safety improvements must also be included. (4) Line Accountability. Managers, supervisors, and employees must be held accountable for meeting their assigned responsibilities, as demonstrated through evaluation of employees at all levels. A functional and operational system for rewarding good performance and correcting deficient performance must be in place. (5) Visible Management Involvement. Top management involvement in health and safety related activities must be apparent to all employees. This involvement should include establishing clear lines of communication with employees; setting an example of safe and healthful behavior; ensuring that all employees (including subcontract employees and vendors) and visitors in the contractor's controlled spaces have a safe and healthful workplace; and being accessible to employees for health

Exhibit 13. Safety Program Evaluation Criteria Sample (*Continued*)

and safety concerns. (6) Site Orientation and General Accountability. There must be documented programs for orienting and holding accountable all persons operating in contractor-controlled spaces, including subcontractor employees, vendors, consultants, students, and visiting scientists. (7) Subcontractor Employee Coverage. (a) Applicants must be able to demonstrate that they have considered the health and safety programs and performance of all subcontractors during the evaluation and selection process, especially for operations such as construction. (b) Records of the hours worked and the injuries and illnesses incurred by subcontractor employees while working in the applicant/participant contractor's controlled spaces must be kept. Rates calculated for such work are expected to be at or below the most appropriate industry average, as reported by the most recent BLS publication. (c) Contracts must (1) specify authority for the oversight, coordination, and enforcement of safety and health programs by the applicant and provide documentary evidence of the applicant's exercise of this authority; (2) provide for the applicant's prompt correction and control of hazards, however detected, in the event that contractors or individuals fail to correct or control such hazards; and (3) specify penalties, including dismissal from the worksite, for willful or repeated noncompliance by contractors, subcontractors, or individuals. (d) The applicant/participant must be able to demonstrate that the above contract provisions have been carried out. (8) Safety and Health Program Evaluation The applicant/participant must have a system for evaluating the success of the safety and health program in meeting the goal and objectives, so that those responsible can determine and implement any needed changes. (a) The system must provide for an annual, written, narrative report, including recommendations for improvements and documented timely follow-up. (b) The evaluation must assess the effectiveness of each element and sub-element described in Section II.E of this document (c) The evaluation may be conducted by competent corporate or site personnel or by a third party from the private sector.

ABOUT THE CONTRIBUTOR

Bill Keeley (keeleyb@wipp.carlsbad.nm.us) is intellectual capital manager for the Westinghouse Waste Isolation Division in Carlsbad, New Mexico. He is responsible for leveraging organizational knowledge to improve divisional performance and for leading change initiatives. Previously, Keeley served as an organizational development manager, human resources development manager, training manager, and training consultant for Westinghouse and other organizations. He is the author of many organizational and employee development tools, including the Leadership Development Needs Assessment (LEADNA), the Management Training and Development Analysis (MTDNA) tool, and the Work Obstacle Metric (WOBRIC). Westinghouse shares these and other tools with thousands of organizations worldwide through a federal knowledge-sharing program. Recipients include NASA, Intel, Harvard University, the United Nations, Cornell University, and Motorola. To obtain these materials at no cost, visit the program Web site (http://www.t2ed.com). A graduate of Eastern Illinois University, Keeley is currently working on a master's of science in organisational behaviour at the University of London, England. He is a recipient of his company's highest recognition, the George Westinghouse Signature Award.

CHAPTER SIX

CK Witco

An innovative 5-month project to redesign work at a plant site that incorporates such change management tools as balanced scorecard, strategic analysis, process redesign, competency-based training, and performance gap analysis to improve operations

This case study discusses a work redesign project for CK Witco, a technologically sophisticated specialty chemicals manufacturer. Using an innovative "fast cycle" change process, the plant created a new business strategy and their first ever balanced scorecard to communicate a new direction for their 175 employees. Additonally, the entire plant was then redesigned around its core processes into a series of self-directed, problem-solving, and cross-functional teams to optimize responsiveness to the market. Unlike many theoretical approaches, the entire design and implementation process took approximately 5 months to complete with both revenue generation and cost-cutting benefits accruing shortly thereafter. The Houston plant is now widely considered within CK Witco as the prototype of their "starship factory of the future."

INTRODUCTION

In 1920, David and Julius Tumpeer and Robert Wishnick formed the Witco Chemical Company that was later renamed Witco Corporation. Witco is a specialty chemicals company with operating plants located throughout the world, it has sales of almost $2 billion dollars, and employs approximately 6,000 people. Witco's products are largely intermediates used in the polymer additives and initiators, petroleum specialties, resins and refined products, oleochemicals, organosilicones, and industrial surfactants markets.

Over the years the company grew largely by acquiring such companies as Sonneborn Chemical and Refining, Golden Bear Oil, Argus Chemical, Kendall Refining, Retzloff Chemical, Continental Carbon, and several other companies or divisions of companies. Witco's products are sold to a variety of major corporations or distributors such as Dupont, Dow, Merck, Union Carbide, Novartis, Andrew Jerkins, and Monsanto.

The Houston site is a 175 person, nonunion plant that operates 24 hours a day, 365 days a year with most of the employees working 12-hour rotating shifts. It manufactures industrial surfactants via oxylation or sulfonation processes that are run in both batch and continuous modes. The final products are used as emulsifiers or deemulsifiers for oil field businesses; as soaps or soap-related products for personal care uses; and as carriers or bases for various agricultural applications. The Houston site also manufactures stearate materials which are primarily used in the manufacture of PVC piping. Additionally, the plant is currently undergoing a major expansion which will double the plant's capacity and enable Houston to pick up some product lines from other plants that are being closed or sold as part of the asset consolidation initiative or as part of the merger with Crompton & Knowles (CK). The challenge is to at least double the plant's output without any significant increase in our headcount.

Key Business Issues

Like the corporation, the Houston site has also undergone many significant changes over the past few years. The principal changes were in the management and organizational structures of the site. Prior plant management was very traditional. Information and decision-making were held tightly and controlled at the top. In January 1997, a new management team was brought in to run the Houston site. Changes were made to flatten the organizational structure and disseminate information and decision making to the lower levels of the organization. These changes included a plan to redesign how the work was to be done. The goal was to evolve the operation to what many describe as self-sufficient, self-directed, high-performance work teams. The approach used is described in the pages that follow. One of the key obstacles faced was past history. The Houston site had unsuccessfully tried to redesign work 2 years earlier. The earlier attempt failed for several reasons.

1. The plant did not have a clear design/implementation plan.
2. Management did not provide strong sponsorship.
3. The organizational systems (reward, recruiting, and so on) were not modified to support teams.
4. Limited effort was expended to align the culture.
5. Not enough training was provided to bridge competency gaps that the new structure required.

The Witco Corporation, including the Houston site, came under considerable pressure to find ways to enhance both the top and bottom lines of the profit and loss statement. Revenues needed to increase while also managing and controlling cash outflows. In addition, Witco needed to focus on establishing business systems that were standard across the corporation and then having the discipline to uniformly use them. The organization's strategy focused on safety, quality, customer service, and improving productivity by working in a team-based work environment. These were the keys to moving the corporation forward and improving overall competitiveness.

In 1999, the corporation made several more changes to further streamline its business vision and portfolio of product offerings. Consequently, several business lines and plants were sold or put up for sale. At the same time, Crompton & Knowles and Witco announced plans to merge the 2 corporations into a new entity to be called CK Witco.

This new entity, CK Witco, would then be able to leverage its resources and capabilities in the various markets that the former corporations served independently. These synergies should be very powerful to the benefit of all parties involved. In addition, when the merger has been completed, many of the redundancies that currently exist can be eliminated, thereby saving significant cost in the process.

The new vision of CK Witco is to grow shareholder value by driving both the top and bottom lines. The goal is to be one of the best specialty chemical companies in the world. This will be attained not by being the biggest company, but rather by delivering superior results in the areas of quality, safety, customer service, and financial performance.

CURRENT STATE ASSESSMENT

In an effort to better understand the opportunities facing the Houston plant, the Catalyst Consulting Group was engaged to conduct a 1-week assessment to:

1. Identify the plant's strengths and weaknesses at both an aggregate and function-by-function level.
2. Propose a blueprint for transforming the plant that would incorporate the principles of empowerment and high-performance work teams.
3. Present a high-level implementation plan to achieve the desired results.

Data instruments were then customized to collect information on a far-ranging set of dimensions including:

1. Business strategy
2. Workforce characteristics
3. Information and production technology
4. Environmental demands and constraints
5. Management practices
6. Performance metrics
7. Organizational structure
8. Stakeholder needs and concerns
9. Stakeholder sources of satisfaction and dissatisfaction
10. HR systems
11. Business processes
12. Physical layout
13. Administrative policies

The methods used to collect this data included:

1. Direct observation
2. Reviewing various documents (such as business strategy and historical performance records)
3. Interviewing key stakeholders
4. Conducting focus group meetings with a cross section of all employees
5. Administering a short targeted survey to a sample of employees

Exhibit 1 shows an example of the focus group protocol that was utilized.

The lists below document the results of this organizational assessment, which were then presented to the senior management team using a workshop format. This was done in order to foster discussion and further understanding of the critical items needing to be addressed by the Houston plant. Exhibit 2 shows a data table illustrating the survey results.

Most Strategic Plant Strengths and Weaknesses

Plant Strengths

- Employees are committed to the success of the plant and have pride in their work
- Strong leadership
- Operators are willing to learn, accept additional responsibility, and accept ownership for the decisions they make
- Good labor and management relations exist
- Operators long tenured and highly skilled
- Management is dedicated to raising expectations of performance
- Workforce is flexible and able to multitask

Key Performance Gaps

- Communication across the organization (top down and across functions) was weak, especially regarding the strategic direction of the plant
- Not enough integration occurs between the plant and the business team
- Limited use of metrics exists to effectively drive the business
- Workforce is excessively internally focused—not enough employees are involved in associations, trade groups, and so on
- Not enough customer or market knowledge
- Organizational structure has redundancies in several areas

- Need to integrate more of the support functions and responsibilities into the line
- Plant has a "doing vs. planning" orientation
- Personnel have limited understanding of process improvement and world-class manufacturing principles
- Not enough accountability for deadlines and commitments by plant personnel
- HR systems need to be better aligned to support the plant's focus, especially in the areas of reward and recognition
- Too much variation exists in manufacturing processes
- It is difficult, if not impossible, to identify root causes of problems or errors because quality function is focusing on detection, not root cause analysis and prevention
- Limited understanding of finance so management team can clearly understand the link between financial and operational performance and their individual efforts
- Limited understanding of the services each function delivers to its internal customers

STRATEGIC DIRECTION SETTING

One of the most critical plant shortcomings was a lack of strategic direction. Therefore, one of the first activities undertaken was the development of a plant-wide business strategy and balanced scorecard.

In an effort to minimize the cycle time to develop the strategy, a fast-paced, 2-day workshop was developed for the senior management team of the plant. Prior to the workshop, the attendees were provided some pre-reading to familiarize them with the strategic planning process that they would complete. This also included examples of how other similar companies approached strategic planning along with examples of strategic planning deliverables (for instance, e-scans, performance gap analysis, competitor and market assessment, and so on). Each attendee was asked to think about and prepare some data that ranged from an analysis of specific market segments and identification of industry trends to a competitor analysis in order to identify sources of competitive advantage and/or vulnerabilities. This prepared the participants for the rigors of the data-based strategic planning approach and it was the basis to facilitate discussions during the workshop itself. Table 1 lists those external opportunities and threats that the group identified as having the highest likelihood of occurrence and the largest impact on the organization.

Table 1. The Most Strategic Opportunities and Threats

Opportunities	Threats
Trend toward long-term contracts and supply chain management will ensure cost stability	More difficult to manage younger workforce's expectations
OPEC policy regarding pricing is likely to increase, positively impacting revenues	Competitors reducing price to gain market share
Major customers business is very synergistic. This creates opportunities for joint ventures or alliances.	World-wide chemical regulations more stringent
Substitute products (R&D)	Institutional investors have large stake and can influence decision making
Utilize Electric Data Interchange (EDI) whenever possible	Risk management plan (new legislation) may create considerable backlash from community
	Forward or backward integration from either suppliers or customers
	Tight job market for contractors, operators, and professional
	Competitors recruiting away best sales people

The data from this analysis became important when considering the other items needed to help us set the strategic direction for the plant. Data from the performance gap analysis, the environmental scan, and the corporate or SBU strategic plan were also key inputs into the formulation of the plant-wide business strategies. The Houston plant selected a five-year planning horizon over which the strategies and supporting initiatives would be executed (see Table 2).

Balanced Scorecard

Under the leadership of Bob Lucas, plant manager of the Houston site, the senior management team realized that the strategy could not be attained without aligning the culture of the plant to promote specific key employee behaviors. Thus, it was determined that the plant would develop their first balanced scorecard of measures to facilitate the desired cultural change. A balanced scorecard is a series of measures that cascade from the business strategy and align functions, processes, individuals, and teams. Unlike the traditional measurement systems, a balanced scorecard typically contains leading and trailing measures and tracks

Table 2. The Business Strategy and Supporting Initiatives

Key Strategies and *Initiatives*	Yr 1	Yr 2	Yr 3	Yr 4	Yr 5
Strategy: Build supplier and customer relationships					
Initiatives					
• Develop supplier alliances	×				
• Visit key suppliers	×				
Strategy: Optimize skills and knowledge of organization					
Initiatives					
• Create competency model for all employees	×				
• Establish resource center					
• Establish formalized training and development program		×	×		
• Establish me ntoring program	×	×	×		
Strategy: Better understand our markets					
Initiatives					
• Design and conduct training on plant products	×				
• Establish monthly meetings with sales and marketing to educate plant personnel on the market and competitors			Y		
• Establish regular meetings with R&D to educate plant personnel on new products in the pipeline			×		
• Each function head will develop a report and provide a presentation on best practices relative to their function and what competitors are doing relative to their function				×	
Strategy: Error-free delivery					
Initiatives					
1. Zero complaints					
– Root cause investigation training	×				
– Corrective action implementation	×				
– Ears program		×			
– Create specialized training for logistics personnel			×		

Table 3. The Business Strategy and Supporting Initiatives (*Continued*)

Key Strategies and *Initiatives*	Yr 1	Yr 2	Yr 3	Yr 4	Yr 5
– Coordinate sales, marketing, customer plant programs				×	
2. On-time shipments	×				
– Obtain Class A implementation		×			
– Complete EDGE implementation					×
– Implement equipment reliability program					×
3. Document errors					
– Improve interface with CSOM				×	×
– Cross-train plant and CSOM					×
– Define interface procedure for plant, CSOM, WWH logistics, sales, and WWH purchasing					×
4. Quality waved shipments					×
– Spec rationalization cost				×	
– External spec pruning				×	
– Internal spec pruning					

activities, results, and behaviors so that you know whether you are making progress towards your desired goals and objectives.

The process used to develop the scorecard was as follows:

Identify major categories of key performance measures (KPMs) that can be used to evaluate progress toward achieving the strategy. The Houston plant identified 6 KPMs. Each KPM was then defined to ensure uniformity of understanding by all.

Each KPM was then broken down into 1 or more indicators. An indicator is the dimension you will measure within the category. For example, if a KPM is organization effectiveness, potential indicators could be job satisfaction and/or company satisfaction. For each indicator, it is important to identify what data you will collect, who is responsible for the data collection, and how often the data will be collected. Establish and define a baseline for each indicator. The utility of the scorecard is maximized by comparing a baseline for each indicator against its optimal target. In a well-constructed scorecard, some of the measures can be leading or predictive, enabling the organization to forecast performance based on cause-and-effect relationships.

Exhibit 3 shows the balanced scorecard the Houston plant developed. Since this scorecard contained desired behaviors and was linked to key HR systems (performance management, compensation, recruiting, and so on), it was an invaluable tool for communicating the business strategy in more operational terms. It also helped when allocating resources and fixing accountability.

WORK REDESIGN

The work redesign effort started with a kick-off meeting of the Steering Committee, when a plant charter was created that began to articulate how work would likely change and teams would evolve at the Houston plant. Unlike most redesign efforts, the Steering Committee decided to empower each team to design itself but clearly specified the constraints or boundaries teams could and could not address in their redesign efforts. The Steering Committee also created a vision statement so that each team would be aligned across the Houston plant.

The Vision Statement for Teams at the Houston Plant

To create a safe environment where empowered, multifunctional work teams are responsible to decide how best to meet their work requirements, thereby meeting our customers' need for a high-quality product, delivered on time and at the agreed upon price. To do so, our organization will be run by a set of guiding principles focused on meeting our commonly held business objectives. Key to this is our ability to create an environment where communications are open, honest, and frequent. Respect and mutual trust amongst all employees are expected. Every person must continue to learn, grow, and improve.

This vision was then translated into a number of technology, organization, and process design principles which could provide further assistance to each team as they progressed in their efforts (see Table 3). A team-based balanced scorecard was developed at a plant-wide level to focus efforts and gauge performance. Lastly, a commitment strategy was created to identify sources and causes of resistance, as well as to develop a plan for obtaining and cascading commitment throughout the plant. The loop was closed through the specification of a communication plan that identified milestones throughout the project lifecycle, targeting specific messages for *each* key stakeholder and utilizing feedback mechanisms for soliciting employee feedback. This feedback could then be incorporated into the overall design plan.

With the Steering Committee providing a good framework for work design, each team embarked on the detailed work redesign. The data from the readiness assessment strongly indicated that in order for the plant to realize its optimal performance, it should be reorganized away from its current silo orientation into 4 distinct process teams: sulfonation, oxylation, kettles, and stearates. Each of the teams comprised 4 sub-teams that were organized along

Table 3. Examples of Technology, Organization, and Design Principles

Technology Principles	Organization Principles	Process Principles
Aggressively use technology to reduce costs.	Minimize the layers of management.	Ensure the physical layout supports the work processes.
Select technology that is state of the art and has a long life expectancy.	Knock down silos whenever possible.	Eliminate cost-adding activities.
Use Internal Rate of Return (IRR) calculations to guide technology decisions.	Create a culture that is conducive to teams.	Optimize processes cross functionally.
Coordinate technologies and applications across teams. Ensure they adhere to corporate standards.	Give employees the authority and responsibility to make decisions.	Integrate support functions and/or support processes whenever possible.
Do not create islands of technology.	Use metrics to guide efforts and hold people accountable.	Use customer requirements to drive the process.

shift lines. Since the first 3 processes were all high volume with high levels of interdependence, it was decided to configure these teams as fully functioning high-performance work teams (see Figure 1). The focus of each of these teams was to redesign the way work was completed and integrate support functions into the team where applicable. Since the stearates process was part of a different business group, had lower product volumes, and was a stand-alone unit, it was decided to design these teams as problem-solving teams. Unlike the other work teams, problem-solving teams focus the majority of their efforts on identifying and solving operational problems. They were not designed to be self-sufficient.

Once the 4 process teams were established, they completed a curriculum of training including a team design workshop. The training curriculum consisted of several courses required for all employees, specific to the roles that employees had to perform as part of the team (see Exhibit 4). In the team design workshop, each work team was introduced to Catalyst Consulting Group's Technology, Organization, and Process (TOPS) model for implementing change. According to the model, all organizations comprise 3 distinct but interdependent elements of architecture. The technology element comprises the information technology and equipment that enables the business to deliver its

From This:

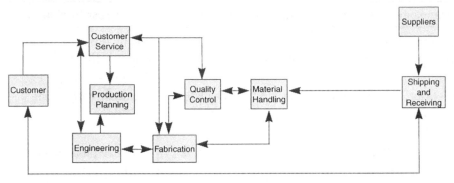

To This:

Customer Service → Production Planning → Engineering → Fabrication → Quality Control → Material Handling → Shipping

Figure 1 Concept Diagram of Sulfonation, Oxylation, and Kettles Teams

core product or service. It also involves how data is stored and accessed, as well as other IT applications. The organization element comprises the people systems: organization structure, culture, human resource systems, and administrative policies. Lastly, the process architecture comprises the physical layout of the work environment and the work processes. In order to ensure the success of the redesign efforts, each team needed to utilize a balanced approach that took into consideration the technology, organizational, and process issues.

Since a large percentage of the work redesign and teaming efforts fail, each team was strongly encouraged to create a well-defined charter and set of operating principles. This enhanced each team member's buy-in while significantly reducing role ambiguity. With the charter being used to guide the efforts of each team, the team then focused their attention on defining the technology, organizational, and process changes they wanted in order to ensure that their team was successful. This iterative process produced several new ways of completing their day-to-day work while also identifying new projects that could reduce cost, enhance efficiency, or improve safety. One of the key deliverables of the team design workshop was the creation of a team charter and operating principles for each subteam (see Table 4). This also included a roles and responsibilities matrix. This matrix identified who was responsible to complete each task, who needed to be informed after a decision was made, and who provided key input into making each decision (see Table 5).

Table 4. Roles and Responsibilities Matrix

(R = RESPONSIBLE, I = INFORM, C = CONSULT, NA = NOT APPLICABLE)

STAKEHOLDERS

Process/Task	Now	Later	Opera-tors	Team Ldr.	Eng.	Maint.	Mtrls Mgt.	Steering Comm.
Housekeeping								
Identify needed tooling	×		R	C	C	I	C	I
Identify optimal location of tooling	×		R	C	C	C	CL	NA
Identify consumable supplies	×		C	C	C	R	C	I
Develop standard operating procedures		×	C	R	C	C	NA	NA
Share with other shifts		×	NA	R	NA	NA	NA	I
Build storage lockers		×	R	NA	C	NA	C	I
Footprint tooling		×	R	I	C	NA	NA	NA

Table 5. Team Competency Matrix

Competencies

L = Low, M = Medium, H = High

	Meeting Management	Just in Time	Project Management	Process Improvement	Four Function Math	Writing Skill
Requirements	H	H	H	M	M	L
Team Members						
Tom	L	L	M	L	L	L
Michelle	H	L	H	H	H	M
Harry	H	M	L	H	H	L
Frank	M	L	L	M	M	L
Jenny	M	L	M	H	L	L

Components of the Team Charters and Operating Principles

Team Charter Components

- Team mission
- Products and services produced
- Customers served
- Processes owned
- Team structure
- Roles and responsibilities matrix
- Team-balanced scorecard
- Key interfaces (IT systems, other processes, and so on)

Operating Principles

- Values
- Desired and undesired behaviors
- Decision-making process
- Meeting management elements (such as when meetings occur, what will be discussed, guidelines for meetings, and so on)
- Conflict management process
- Communications elements (for example, who is responsible for communications and when and what will be communicated, and so on)

As each of the teams finalized their charters, a team and competency matrix was created. Technical and nontechnical competencies were identified on the top of each vertical column. The strength or level of sophistication of each skill was then determined. The most important skills identified for the team were meeting management and just in time. The matrix was helpful in selecting individual team members. Key competency gaps were addressed through individualized development plans or through training seminars.

During the latter stages of the team implementation efforts, the Steering Committee was instrumental in helping the teams to continue to "think outside the box" and align all elements of architecture. They also helped to evaluate each team's planned projects and authorize capital funding to make these projects happen. If conflicts arose between teams or functional areas, the Steering Committee was the final arbiter of all disputes. As changes occurred, the Steering Committee was responsible for identifying that revised goals were communicated to the various work teams. This ensured that all necessary and appropriate changes were made to the work teams' balanced scorecard targets.

EVALUATION: BENEFITS AND IMPACT

The progress of the work redesign efforts can be measured at 2 levels—plant-wide performance and by a project-by-project basis. Plant-wide performance is measured largely on a monthly basis by comparing the baselines and targets in the plant-wide balanced scorecard. Listed below are several essential results attributable to the work redesign efforts:

Customer Service: Line fill rate improved from 50% to 94%. On-time shipments improved from 50% to 94%.

Safety: Reportable incidents rate decreased from 4.5 to 0.5.

Quality: Customer complaints decreased from 192 per year to 48.

Productivity: Performance to schedule improved from 50% to 85%. Inventory record accuracy improved from 62% to 92%.

Cost: Demurrage cost decreased from an average of $10,000 per month to $1,500 per month. Unplanned overtime decreased from 20% to 10%.

People: Turnover decreased from 15% per year to 3% per year.

Additionally, several qualitative benefits have been realized as measured by focus groups. Employees are very proud of the site and its accomplishments. There is a spirit and sense of comaraderie. Employees are more enthusiastic, work well from a cross-functional perspective, have a high dedication to excellence, and better understand the business as a whole.

Employees have taken on more responsibility and are generally held accountable for issues relating to personnel matters. Teams have become the gatekeepers of administrative items like attendance control and time keeping. Teams also determine whether to call out additional labor to supplement their shift when people are absent from work.

In addition, teams participated in employee disciplinary contacts for errors or problems occurring on their team. Should the latter occur, they were responsible for conducting the root cause analysis and identifying corrective actions in order to prevent reoccurrence in the future. Another major task that the work teams became responsible for was the training and skills development of their co-workers. They were responsible to work cooperatively to evaluate each other's skill level and help each other learn, grow, and improve. If they did not possess the needed skills internally to their team, then they had to arrange with others in the plant to help. This also included any contract or temporary employees who were working along with the team. Since they were responsible for the training of any workers on their team, they also participated in any recruiting that needed to take place in order to fill vacancies on their team. Accordingly, they conducted interviews of prospective candidates for employment along with others from the site (such as site HR, production management representatives, and so on). In addition, they were asked to recommend and justify team member promotions based on demonstrated skills and contribution to the team. These "people-related" matters were previously performed by their shift supervisor or facilitator. These resources were then redeployed to other areas within the plant. They were available to assist the teams if and/or when they requested such assistance. Another task that the work teams took over from the shift supervisor was in the area of customer interaction. Team members now routinely participate in customer visits. They are asked to make presentations on various subjects, take visitors on plant tours, or go to the customer's plant for assistance.

Teams are also more cognizant of the impact they have on costs than they ever were. They have agreed to be held accountable for realizing the key dimensions in their balanced scorecards. Some of these include such items as scrap or rework items, overtime costs, and truck demurrage. Each team also looks for ways to reuse materials whenever possible in order to save costs.

Teams have begun to reuse drums (sometimes they are used to transport product) whenever possible instead of merely disposing them at a cost of $22 per drum. In addition, the work teams are continually looking for ways to minimize or prevent demurrage costs on incoming or outgoing trucks. Demurrage costs have been reduced by at least 50% by focusing on having racks open when needed, lines and tanks cleaned and ready, and finished products staged in advance of shipment.

Since the teams are responsible for operating costs, they periodically identify and develop proposals for projects to enhance plant performance. First, each team is required to inform the other work teams when they have an idea they wish to implement. After receiving input from their colleagues, the team then documents the idea for presentation to the Steering Committee. This presentation must include the pro's and con's of the proposed change along with information relative to the funding and savings to be derived. The information is then translated into financial terms so that a rank order of projects by rates of return can be established. This is important because projects are competing for limited funds. This is the same process that the plant manager follows to receive funding from the corporation. It should be noted that many of the teams' projects were process improvement projects not requiring any funding. They merely looked for ways to optimize a given process in order to improve yields or reduce cycle times.

Over the last two years, many different projects have been approved by the Steering Committee. These projects have tended to be broken down into one of three types: safety-related projects, logistics projects, and process or product improvement projects. One such project implemented was for a material recovery system that reduced the disposal costs for spent materials and the reuse of some of the spent materials (this reduced raw material costs). The team first consulted with engineering and quality control to determine the feasibility of the idea. After this was determined to be acceptable, the other teams were consulted for their input. Progressing next to the Steering Committee, $8,500 in funds was requested to acquire the needed equipment. Projected savings for this project are expected to be approximately $100,000 per year, one-third coming from raw material purchase avoidance and two-thirds from disposal cost avoidance.

Another project initiated was tank-swapping. The essence of this project was to dedicate raw material storage space closer to where to materials would be used in the process. This meant that materials would not have to be carted or transferred across the plant and thereby consuming finite labor time. The team also identified several places where diaphragm pumps could be installed to make the process safer or easier for the operators. It was estimated that these changes, essentially no-cost changes, would create revenue opportunities of 35 hours per man per year on average. This idea also got other teams looking for similar ideas where they could identify ways to make their job easier, safer, and cheaper. One example was to dedicate 2 tanks for high-moving raw materials previously held in drop trailers. The drop trailers were costing the plant approximately $100,000 per year in fees. Now by having the raw materials stored in a dedicated tank large enough to store several trailers, drop trailer fees have been eliminated and the job is safer and easier for the operator.

Another project was from a team that chose to work on process improvement issues. They focused on identifying optimal conditions and set points for a high-moving product that is made in a continuous run mode. "Clearly, this project will save in the amount of off-spec materials we make and have to dispose of as well as the raw materials we consume in the process," said one team member. The team worked with a group of resources including engineering, quality control, process assistance, and maintenance to run a statistical process controlled (SPC) experiment. From this, the team determined and documented the critical parameters and optimal sequence of events required to manufacture this product. This project yielded annual savings of approximately $20,000 per year and had a cycle time improvement of 25%. Another team took up this banner and designed a controlled experiment to identify cycle time reductions for a critical intermediate that is shipped to a sister plant. They, in turn, use it in a very profitable product that is sold to a major agricultural manufacturer. In essence, this group reduced product cycle time from 25–26 hours down to 19–20 hours by applying process redesign and problem-solving tools. The cycle time reductions mean that the plant has additional capacity to produce more product with the same amount of resources (including both people and equipment). All teams continue to look for additional opportunities to make product or process improvements in all areas of the plant.

Exhibit 1. Organization Assessment Focus Group Protocol

I. Build rapport and project orientation (15 minutes)
Provide a brief overview of the project and assurance of confidentiality. Review the objectives of the project, the role of the consultants, and the expected project benefits.

II. Administer employee survey (30 minutes)

III. Understanding employee needs (60 minutes)
- Think about the best job you ever had in your life. What were the **qualities** of that job you liked the most?
- In your **present** job what do you like **most/least**?
- Think about the **key tasks you perform as part of your job.** What causes you the **most frustration**?
- What gets in the way of you **doing your job most effectively**? **Why**? What do you recommend to **eliminate** these issues?
- What creates the **greatest dissatisfaction**? What do you recommend to **eliminate** this dissatisfaction?

IV. Goal setting: Collect data on how well employees understand and are committed to the strategy.
- What is the **strategy** of the plant? **How** was it communicated to you?
- How well is the company performing? **How** do you know? Do you specifically understand how you individually contribute to the plant's performance? How?
- What **input** do you have in setting your performance expectations?
- Who are the **customers** of the product or service you deliver? What are their **requirements**?

V. Adaptation: Determine if there is silo or cross-functional orientation in the plant.
- What are the **critical areas** this plant needs to focus on to be competitive?
- In the past how well has the organization **implemented change**? What can you recommend to improve the way the organization introduces change in the future?

VI. Integration: Assess how well the disparate functions and departments work together.
- How well do interdependent functions and departments **work together**? Where does the most conflict **originate** from? Why? What can be done to **enhance cooperation**?

VII. Long-term development: This defines management's emphasis and the degree to which management provides opportunities for new skill acquisition and career progression.

Exhibit 1. Organization Assessment Focus Group Protocol (*Continued*)

- Do you feel you are adequately trained for your **current job**? What type of development did you complete last year? Does management provide enough development opportunities to prepare you for **future** jobs?
- What **types of behaviors** does management reward? Does management **reward cross-functional cooperation,** teamwork **within each** department? **Initiative? Risk taking? Flexibility relative to job assignment and responsibilities?**

Exhibit 2. Organizational Assessment Survey Results

Employee Needs (1–5 scale)	Impor-tance MEAN	Satisfac-tion MEAN	+/−
1. A supervisor who listens to my concerns and suggestions	4.8	2.8	
2. Increased job challenge	3.3	2.9	
3. A supervisor who recognizes employees for teamwork	4.1	2.5	
4. High levels of trust and mutual cooperation between management and employees	4.9	2.0	−
5. Being treated with respect and dignity	4.8	2.8	
6. Open, honest, unfiltered communications	4.4	2.4	−
7. A job that provides a variety of things to do	3.6	3.3	
8. Regular feedback from your supervisor and customers	4.1	3.0	
9. Competitive salary and fringe benefits	4.9	2.0	−
10. Pay increases that are based on merit	3.8	2.4	−
11. Completing a whole product or complete a whole service	3.4	3.1	
12. Having input in decisions that affect your job	4.0	2.9	
13. A supervisor who doesn't accept mediocrity	3.5	2.8	
14. Job security	4.0	3.8	−
15. The ability to express concerns and issues	4.3	3.5	−

The Work Environment

	Strongly Agree/ Agree	Neither Agree/ Disagree	Strongly Disagree/ Disagree	+/−
16. I know who my customers are.	20%	40%	20%	−
17. I know what this plant's strategy is.	31	25	44	
18. The existing information system provides timely and accurate data.	28	39	32	
19. I understand how I will be evaluated.	19	48	33	
20. Management is very participatory.	32	40	28	
21. Management shares performance data.	43	33	24	

Exhibit 2. Organizational Assessment Survey Results (Continued)

	Strongly Agree/ Agree	Neither Agree/ Disagree	Strongly Disagree/ Disagree	+/−
22. I receive regular feedback on my performance.	21	39	40	
23. This plant does a good job of promoting the most competent people.	10	15	75	−
24. Most employees here are highly motivated.	31	28	41	
25. Policies and procedures are applied in a fair and consistent manner.	29	29	42	
26. If offered the **same** job (by another company) with the **same** pay and benefits I would not leave my job.	28	39	33	
27. Management encourages:				
a) Risk taking	19	31	50	
b) Employee empowerment	59	31	9	
c) Cross-functional cooperation	55	25	20	
d) Innovation	30	30	40	

Exhibit 3. Plant-Wde Balanced Scorecard

Key Performance Measure: People
Definition: The effective application and growth of human capital

Indicators	Data Source	Frequency of Data Collection	Responsibility	Baseline	Targets (T = Trailing, L = Leading)
Employee satisfaction (will use serveral key questions from survey and track over time)	Employee survey	Annually		• Job satisfaction • Confidence in management • Same job with the same pay • Honesty and dignity	80% outstanding and excellent L 80% outstanding and excellent L 80% outstanding and excellent L
Voluntary turnover rate	HRIS	Annually		7%	< 3 % by 2nd Q99 T
Cycle time of new hires	HRIS	Quarterly		92 days	< 60 days by 2nd Q99 T
Salary competitiveness	Internal/external salary surveys	Annually		No baseline	Pay at or above average rate per job class. Year 1 focus on salaried workforce, year 2 all nonexempt L

Exhibit 3. Plant-Wide Balanced Scorecard

KPM: Productivity
Definition: Ratio of inputs to outputs

Indicators	Data Source	Frequency of Data Collection	Responsibility	Baseline	Targets (T = Trailing, L = Leading)
% uptime	Uptime database	Monthly	Alan L.	93%	95% L
Yields (across all products)	Material resource planning (MRP)	Monthly	Al N.	85%	95% T
Due date (manufacturer's adherance to schedule)	MRP	Weekly	Al N.	94%	98% T
Cycle times (need to break down by process, product family, or specific product)	Batch records, SPC info, MRP	Monthly	Al N.	30 hours	25 hours T
Pounds produced per man hour	MRP	Monthly	Sissy	8,000/man/hr	8,800/man/hr T
Pounds shipped per man hour (includes contractors)	MRP	Monthly	Sissy	7,000/man/hr	8,000/man/hr T
	360-degree assessment				**Behaviors** • Job flexibility • Challenging paradigms • Calculated risk-taking

KPM: Cost
Definition: Prudent application of finite resources

Indicators	Data Source	Frequency of Data Collection	Responsibility	Baseline	Targets (T = Trailing, L = Leading)
Operating costs	Profit & Loss Statement (P&L)	Monthly	Keith/Dennis	None	Reduce Operating costs by at least $2 million by 12/99 T
Demurrage costs	P&L	Monthly	Sissy	10%	2% T
Unplanned Overtime • Production • Maintenance	Payroll	Weekly	Team Leaders Scott M.	10% 12.5%	5% T 8% T
Plant budget	P&L	Monthly	Dennis	1991 budget	Zero deviation from budget L
	360-degree Assessment				**Behaviors** • Sense of urgency • Results focus

KPM: Customer Service
Definition: Error-free delivery (EFD)

Indicators	Data Source	Frequency of Data Collection	Responsibility	Baseline	Targets (T = Trailing, L = Leading)
Shipments	Z020 (Company-generated report)	Daily	Customer service	92%	96% T
Complaints	Complaint log	Daily	QA	15/month	5/month T
EFD	Customer service order management Logistics 360-degree assessment	Daily	QA	94%	98% T
					Behaviors • Empathy • Listening

Exhibit 4. Curriculum of Work Team Education

For Steering Committee
- Management's Role in Leading Change
- Executive Overview on Self-Directed Work Teams

For Facilitators/Team Leaders
- Overview Self-Directed Work Teams
- Coaching
- Team Facilitation
- Group Dynamics
- Understanding Your New Role In a Team Environment
- Team Assessment/Intervention
- Communication Skills
- Conflict Management

For Team Members
- Overview Self-Directed Work Teams
- High-Performance Work Teams
- Group Dynamics
- Team Assessment/Intervention
- Communication Skills
- Conflict Management
- Performance Measurement/Goal Setting
- Meeting Management
- Interviewing and Selection
- Problem-Solving Skills
- Process-Improvement Skills
- Project Management
- Change Management: Tools and Techniques
- Self-Directed Work Teams: Design and Implementation

ABOUT THE CONTRIBUTORS

Keith Montgomery (montgke@witco.com) is the production manager at the Houston plant of CK Witco. Prior to this, Montgomery was a regional human resources manager for Witco's Texas locations. In his current capacity at the site, he is an essential member of the senior management team. He also continues to provide the organization with internal consulting and human resources support in addition to his responsibilities as the production manager. Prior to joining Witco, Montgomery worked for several years for Dupont in a series of human resources positions. These included both specialist and generalist assignments in various plant and/or staff work sites. These also included union as well as union-free operations. Montgomery received his BBA and MBA degrees from Temple University, where he majored in human resources. He also received his JD degree from the Delaware Law School of Widener University. Montgomery is a licensed attorney and he is certified as a senior professional in human resources.

Ronald Recardo (RRecardo@aol.com) is the founder and managing partner of the Catalyst Consulting Group, LLC, which specializes in strategy, operations improvement, and change management. Recardo works with Fortune 500 organizations to assist them in designing and implementing transformational change that addresses technology, organization, and process issues. Prior to founding the Catalyst Consulting Group, Recardo worked for Arthur Andersen's Strategic Change Management practice where he had a lead role in developing their firm-wide organization change methodology. He also started up an internal consulting department for a multinational financial services company and was responsible for worldwide consulting for a pharmaceutical company. Recardo's book, entitled *Teams, Who Needs Them and Why* (Gulf Publishing), was selected by the Institute of Management Studies as their Book of the Month selection. He is currently in the process of writing his third book, which discusses business strategy, performance measurement, and organization alignment. He has also presented a number of speeches before such groups as *Inc. Magazine, Business Month*, the Association for Quality and Participation, the Association for Manufacturing Excellence, the Conference Board, American Production and Inventory Control Society, and the Society of Human Resource Management. He is a member of American Mensa Ltd., the Institute of Management Consultants, and is listed in the *International Who's Who of Professionals and the Who's Who of Entrepreneurs*. Recardo received his formal education at Southern Connecticut State University where he earned a bachelor of science degree; the University of Maine where he earned an MBA degree; and at the University of Hartford where he earned a master's of science degree in organization development. Additionally, Recardo is a certified Baldrige Examiner, certified in Just-in-Time, and he is a certified management consultant.

CHAPTER SEVEN

Xerox

An organizational development initiative that transformed a traditional work culture into an entrepreneurial, self-managing, productive work community, dedicated to increased customer satisfaction and levels of decision-making authority, and enabling employees to develop a better understanding of organizational business objectives

INTRODUCTION—"POWER TO THE PEOPLE"

"Our ultimate goal is to organize the entire company into self-managed work teams—or what we call '[Empowered Work Groups].'"

Paul Allaire, "The CEO as Organizational Architect"
Harvard Business Review, September/October 1992.

It's fair to say that in 1995, Xerox, The Document Company, was on a roll. From its beginnings in 1906, in Rochester, New York, as a fledgling "start up" by the name of the Haloid Company, Xerox had grown into a global corporation of 05,000 employees. A Wall Street favorite, income was up 36% from the previous year and earnings per share rose 38% during the same period. Xerox products dominated their traditional markets, light lens copiers and duplicators. Things were poised to get even better as the company moved away from traditional products and committed fully to a digital future. But this move brought with it a whole new set of competitive challenges that required the installation of a new work model to meet them. Implementing this new model would not be easy, and in truth Xerox had already been trying to do just that, but with limited success.

For years Xerox had been dedicated to creating "empowerment" within the workplace culture. The oft-stated company goal was to "unleash" the full potential of their employees through this empowerment process. But after years of effort, this cornerstone of the new Xerox culture was still more fantasy than fact. Why all this concern over empowerment? Simple. An empowered workforce, consisting of "Empowered Work Groups," or EWGs, has been shown to be quicker, more creative, and more flexible in response to customer needs. That in turn leads to higher customer satisfaction with Xerox products and services, which means more sales.[1] In short, empowerment equals sales equals profits. If Xerox was going to repeat the success it was accustomed to in the cut-throat digital world, it needed to find a way to maximize profits and productivity. Empowerment was the way.

Empowerment is the practice of enabling people at all levels of the organization to take responsibility for and ownership of company functions, especially satisfying their customers' requirements, solving their customers' problems, and continuously improving their work processes. EWGs are self-managed, productive, and entrepreneurial work communities consisting of various numbers of empowered workers. Creating a corporation composed of EWGs was Xerox's goal, but it was, so far, unrealized. Clearly, based on its poor results to date, an exciting new initiative was needed to create the empowered workplace culture the company had been searching for.

DIAGNOSE BUSINESS—"SO WHERE DO WE GO FROM HERE?"

"We are facing a crisis of opportunity. On the one hand, we see attractive markets and we have superior technology. On the other hand, we won't be able to take advantage of this situation unless we can overcome cumbersome, functionally driven bureaucracy and . . . become more productive."

Paul Allaire,
CEO, Xerox Corporation

With Xerox entering the burgeoning new digital market for the first time, they needed to find an effective, efficacious way to enhance service and responsiveness to increasingly demanding customers, or risk losing them to a slew of new competitors ranging from computer giants like IBM to large numbers of local equipment networking companies. Any of these companies would be eager to pick up the ball and run with it if Xerox dropped it.

This new market is known for its lightning-fast product cycles. Digital customers not only demand high-quality traditional services but also "value-added" solutions that increase their productivity. The current system was too inflexible to allow workers to effectively manage the growing volume of information they needed to use to run the business day to day. Employees wanted and needed more decision-making authority and control to enable them to deliver the best results. The current system was being bogged down by many factors; chief among them were:

- Limited program integration—Stand-alone programs didn't link with other initiatives.
- Inflexible work design—Assumes a "one size fits all" approach, which has slow response.
- Controlling, inflexible human resource practices that focused on the individual and inhibited teamwork.

- Overly specialized, narrowly defined jobs that caused stagnation and discouraged learning.

- Ambiguous requirements—Unclear boundaries lead to employee confusion and mistakes.

- Highly controlled work rules and regulations that require expensive, unresponsive work environments.

Finally a change was needed if the company hoped to motivate employees enough to create more value for their customers and bring their customer satisfaction ratings up to "benchmark levels" for the industry. (See Exhibit 1 for additional information.)

A study conducted by Wilson Learning, a recognized consulting and research group, of 25,000 workers in 14 different industries concluded that there was a statistically significant correlation between employee satisfaction and work performance. Xerox, in its own study, demonstrated that there was also a statistically high correlation between an "Empowering" style of management and employee satisfaction, and subsequently between employee satisfaction and customer satisfaction.[2] From these studies it was clear to even the most die-hard "top down" manager that an empowered workplace was directly linked with consistent, high-performance marketplace results (see Exhibit 2). It was clear that senior management find a way to deliver on the "Empowered Workplace" promise or risk losing out on their best chance to win big in the digital market.

Xerox had been pursuing empowerment for years, long before most companies had ever heard the term. In 1983, the company identified "employee involvement" as one of the key facets of their new total quality strategy. One of its first actions to that end instituted "Teamwork Day" in a cafeteria at the Webster, New York, site. Teamwork Day is an annual event that showcases self-directed and empowered work teams and their best practices to internal and external customers (see Exhibit 3). The event has since spread to every Xerox site around the world. In 1991, Xerox made "Employee Motivation and Satisfaction" one of their four corporate priorities. "Empowerment" was a central theme at the Xerox Senior Management Summit in 1993. At the 1994 Senior Management Summit, empowerment was designated one of the 10 areas of the Xerox Management Model to be focused on that year. Yet for all this attention, the idea of empowerment far outpaced the reality and this was cause for concern.

The question was, why was the "empowered employee" still more fiction than fact? After much collective corporate soul searching, conducting research, and, most important, listening to what the people were saying, the company developed "High Performance Work Systems Vision 2000" to finally address the problem and serve as the blueprint for their change management initiative.

Xerox organizations worldwide consist of empowered team-based work environments where people, work, technology, and information are effectively integrated. These teams use state-of-the-art systems to deliver customized Document Solutions, resulting in world-class productivity for our customers and Xerox."—High Performance Work Systems Vision 2000.

Incorporating empowered work environments, team-based work, integration, technology systems, and customized document solutions, "Vision 2000" was to be the roadmap to finally, fully implementing the "Empowered Workplace." (Please refer to Exhibit 4.)

ASSESSMENT—"DO AS I SAY, NOT AS I DO"

"We have to recognize a new paradigm: not great leaders alone, but great leaders who exist in a fertile relationship with a Great Group. . . . The leader and the team are able to achieve something together that neither could achieve alone. . . . The leader finds greatness in the group."

Bennis and Biederman, *Organizing Genius: The Secrets of Creative Collaboration (1997).*

Just how were management and employees to finally make this quantum leap together?

The first step in any management change initiative is to find out where you stand currently. What are the greatest weaknesses to be addressed? Are any elements of your program already in place? So, in 1994, the corporate office performed a business assessment to determine where the company stood on empowerment issues at that time. The assessment, consisting of several different surveys on empowerment, was administered to CSEs and other employees throughout Xerox. In addition, several studies on the topic were undertaken by outside consultants. The results and conclusions drawn from these were surprising and clear. (Please see Exhibit 5.)

- They showed that Xerox senior managers were "talking the talk," but weren't "walking" that talk. Their communications were less than open and honest and they had not linked their empowerment strategy to business results.

- As a management team, they were delegating "empowerment" issues to staff but had no cohesive, shared vision of where they were heading with it.

- Lack of clear vision led to employee confusion and failure to act proactively.

- Management was still resistant to the idea of delegating authority down through the organization.

The assessment also indicated that less than half (46%) of all Xerox employees felt empowered, while an equal number felt that they worked in an empowered environment. Despite all their efforts over the last 16 years, Xerox senior management had to admit that much of the responsibility for the lack of creating an empowered workplace or tapping the anticipated productivity of empowered employees rested with leadership and the lack of leadership it showed toward empowerment issues (Exhibit 6).

Three interrelated core elements necessary to creating empowerment were identified:

- Direction and communication—Work groups (WGs) need to understand where they are going and have open channels of communication with management.
- Ownership—WGs needs to develop a sense of "ownership" of company vision and problems.
- Group dynamics—WGs need to be created by the employees, based on needed skills.

With respect to "direction and communication," four elements were necessary. First, a vision that was inspiring and motivational. Second, employees needed to be given knowledge of the corporate direction and their work group's direction. Third, there needed to be alignment of all organizations to this vision. Fourth, managers and individuals both needed to understand how objectives and tasks are linked to each other and how they support the vision and direction. The assessment indicated that once these factors were implemented, Xerox employees would began to see themselves as part of the shared vision of the group and could articulate its meaning.

In terms of "ownership," the assessment found that it was lacking, that employees did not feel ownership of company policies and principles. This was a strong barrier to empowerment and to foment this feeling of ownership four factors had to be fostered:

1. There needed to be an environment where employees were genuinely valued, where diverse perspectives, styles, and opinions were encouraged.
2. Participation and involvement would also be encouraged, as well as employee participation in defining work process and priorities.
3. Employees needed to have the resources and information necessary to get their work done, while achieving business goals and satisfying customer needs.
4. Employees need to have the freedom to work within negotiated boundaries-responsible freedom. Responsible freedom is what is

sometimes referred to as setting clear boundaries and then "getting out of the way." In other words, let them act like the responsible adults they are.[3]

Other Issues

It was clear that within Xerox, in contrast to the corporate vision of a creative, empowered work force where people are members of productive work communities, the predominant work design continued to be managers as decision makers and employees as doers. Customer support was still provided by individuals, with defined territories or tasks, who took direction about day-to-day operations from their managers. The vision of individuals on functional teams sharing work group accountability and responsibility for satisfying customer requirements while others provided back-up support was not the norm. In addition, current business processes were often bureaucratic and were not customer-oriented. There was a lack of perceived empowerment at the customer-decision level. The outcome was inadequate customer and employee satisfaction and unimpressive business results.

DESIGN/IMPLEMENTATION—"WITH A GOOD FOUNDATION . . . "

"I envision a time when this company will consist of many, many small groups of people who have the technical expertise and the business knowledge and the information tools they need to design their own work processes continuously as business conditions change. These work groups will be tied directly to the customer. They will be working in a much less supervised environment. And they will have the resources they need to design their work environment and modify their behaviors as needed to achieve their objectives in the marketplace."

Paul Allaire, "The CEO as Organizational Architect"
Harvard Business Review, September/October 1992.

When implemented effectively, the results attributed to empowered teams are remarkable. For example:

- General Electric's Salisbury, North Carolina, plant increased productivity by 250% compared to other GE plants producing the same products.

- Corning's specialty cellular ceramics plant decreased defect rates from 1,800 parts per million to 9 parts per million.

- Semco S/A in Brazil went from near financial disaster in 1980 to a 10% sales profit margin in 1988 by flattening the organization and implementing teams. In one year, sales doubled, the inventory cycle improved 300%, and productivity and defect rates drastically improved.[4]

For Xerox to match such lofty results from its change management plan, the management team needed to play a critical part in the organizational redesign effort. Therefore, a Design Team was created to support the design and implementation of the strategy. Membership included representation from all levels of the organization. Every member of the team had operational experience and high credibility with their peers. A network of empowerment "experts" still functions as the Empowerment Design Team.

The implementation of EWGs was designed to change the very nature of how the business was managed and outputs were delivered, so it was essential for the organization's leaders to truly understand and be committed to making the required culture changes. To this end, the key steps in the implementation plan for the management team were as follows:

1. Document their direction regarding EWGs for the organization.
2. Develop and agree on a plan to communicate the direction.
3. Develop a plan for being personally involved.
4. Plan "next steps" with regard to their own education in order to champion and drive the required culture change.
5. Develop and agree to a plan for creating tension in the system with regard to the required culture change.[5]

By reiterating and articulating these points frequently and inspecting and maintaining the integrity of the plan as it became systemic during the deployment of EWG strategies and tactics, the senior management team was able to keep the implementation process on track. This diligence began to pay off in short order. Within the first six months after the implementation began, signature elements of employee satisfaction (commitment to goals, having common goals, and empowerment ratings) had all increased significantly. There were corresponding improvements in customer satisfaction ratings as well.[6]

In addition to and possibly more important to the plan's success, two other areas were to be addressed to ensure the successful implementation of the EWG process—education and communication.

Education Plan

Education and training needed to play a central role in the cultural change that was being made. The new roles and job definitions for management and front line employees needed to be clearly defined and taught. All employees needed to be given a clear vision of how they fit into the big picture. The education, training, and reinforcement associated with the implementation of EWGs was extensive and required a long-term strategy in addition to a short-term plan.

Participants included team members and managers at all levels of the organization (see Exhibit 7). Built around simulation exercises and extensive practice time, the curricula provided information and skills on both sides of the "socio-technical" equation, and included such topics as:

- Managing Change
- Empowerment
- Situational Leadership
- Elements of Group Dynamics
- Group Observation and Intervention Skills
- Resolving Operational Issues as a Team
- Systemic Change
- Total Quality Management (TQM)

Communication Plan

Keeping people well-informed about the direction the organization was heading, in addition to giving them detailed information about current and future change, was essential if management was to be part of the solution rather than part of the problem. Clear communication and frequent updates enabled people to be excited rather than frightened by the prospect of a major organizational change. Managers and executives would be required, through the use of frequent meetings, e-mail updates, and printed reports, to keep all members informed of any information on the progress of the "change" program. They were also required to create a feeling of "ownership" among all employees of the company (see Exhibit 8).

These two areas were vital to implementing the High Performance Work Systems vision. If EWGs would now consist of small groups of employees whose members were to be highly interdependant (the members have complementary skills and must rely on each other's competencies in order to achieve their business objectives), then education is imperative to ensure and maintain a consistently high level of technical acumen. Education and open communication are the natural prerequisites to team building.

ON-THE-JOB SUPPORT—"WHERE THE RUBBER MEETS THE ROAD"

Grandiose plans, training seminars, and workplace assessments are all vital elements in the creation of an empowered work environment. But after the last overhead slide is shown and the last training class is held, there needs to be tangible support for EWGs in the workplace. In terms of "empowerment," the desktops of employees is the point where the "rubber meets the road." That's why specific measures need to be taken to keep the process moving and growing after it is implemented and all the consultants have gone home.

Xerox used several different methods to keep their process on track:

Post-Implementation Surveys

Prior to implementing their Empowered Work Group Strategy, Xerox surveyed the company as a whole to define where it stood at the time and to ascertain where it needed to go to be successful. This process was carried out within every group and across the entire enterprise. Surveys were administered prior to the start of the process, nine months later, and then on a continuing basis, to assess the progress and enable adjustments to be made. Included in these surveys were Employee Motivation and Satisfaction, Empowering Work Environment, and an Organizational Empowerment survey. These are completed on a regular basis in order to track and adjust the implementation process on an ongoing basis (see Exhibit 9).

Shared Solutions and Best Practices

Groups are encouraged to create systems, usually databases and Web sites, through which they can share solutions to business problems that they have faced and resolved. This enhances the free flow of ideas and diverse points of view within groups and across the company. At the same time they improve efficiency through easy access to proven solutions and faster problem resolution. Xerox has taken this idea enterprise-wide with several on-line "best practices" and "solutions" database products designed to be used by everyone in the company. A good example being the "Eureka!" and "Eureka II" solutions databases.

Reward and Recognition Programs

No culture change initiative can succeed without strong reinforcement from a solid Recognition and Reward system. To "keep the pedal to the metal," Xerox installed an R&R system that would reinforce the virtues of its new management style. The system recognizes individuals who contribute to team performance and rewards empowered teams based on performance results, both essential factors to the long-term success of any empowerment effort.

Other key attributes of Xerox's Recognition & Reward program include:

- There is recognition for demonstrated desired habits, continuous improvement, and skill development.
- Rewards are earned and are contingent upon team performance.
- Rewards provide a clear link between the work group, as well as team and organizational performance.

- Recognition and reward should be timely and tied to the events that warranted it.
- Recognition and reward will be based on both results and continuous improvement (see Exhibit 10).

Documented Work Processes

In order to foment and facilitate the growth of "interdependence" among the members of the new EWGs, managers began to formalize and document the work processes within their groups. These work processes focused on the groups' core tasks, with particular emphasis on processes that enhance customer satisfaction. This "process management" benefits the EWGs in several important ways:

- They give groups a consistent set of common processes that ensure consistent, repeatable results.
- They allow decision-making authority to be spread more easily throughout the group.
- They enable continuous improvement by providing a "benchmark" against which work quality can be judged.[7]

EVALUATE RESULTS—"SEA CHANGE"

Because of the cultural "sea change" that was required, implementing Empowered Work Groups was not easy. Without the required support, it was virtually impossible. In addition, it is an ongoing process, not a "magic pill" that will suddenly solve all of an organization's woes. However, if implemented thoughtfully and maintained studiously, EWGs and the High Performance Work Systems will deliver the results promised and expected. In a 1995 report entitled "Empowered Work Groups, Pre-Post Implementation Assessment" done by Xerox Canada to evaluate the results they got from the "change management process," it was learned that after the initial implementation of EWGs:

- Of those reporting, there was greater understanding of the organization's vision and direction.
- Levels of decision-making authority significantly improved.
- There was a large increase in the "perception" of empowerment.
- All business units reported a significantly greater involvement in key business decision making.
- Levels of decision-making authority at the "group" level greatly increased (see Exhibit 11).

It is also significant to note that, when surveyed about the access to empowerment support structures such as Management Support of work groups and Performance Feedback from management, the results were much more ambivalent. This would indicate that the original obstacle to full implementation—lack of leadership support—had not been fully resolved; more work in this area was needed (Exhibit 12). However, these are minor "dips in the road." Customer Satisfaction is the true test of the new system and here the results are unmistakable. From 1996 to the present, customer satisfaction with Xerox has improved significantly. In fact, as EWGs took hold and became increasingly effective, Customer Satisfaction ratings rose approximately 15% relative to "pre-empowerment" levels.[8]

Since Customer Satisfaction is the final arbiter of EWG effectiveness, then Xerox's experience can only be looked at as a success. The mixed results on leadership issues should be seen as problems of perception and procedure that will work themselves out as the process continues and the new culture takes root.

Despite its initial problems with implementation of EWGs and High Performance Work Systems, Xerox has become the "empowerment benchmark" for corporations worldwide, with the successful implementation of the concept across its entire 85,000-person organization. Given the sea change in management style and work culture that was undertaken, it's amazing to look back at what was accomplished. In short, all of the roles shifted to focus on adding value. Self-management assumed many of the traditional management responsibilities. Managers became leaders who then provided a clear vision and direction, while ensuring it was meaningful to their people and aligned with the greater good of the company. Participative management built trust and respect. Empowered individuals learned how they fit into the broader Xerox vision and direction, and they became engaged and committed to the new work process. Teams shared vision and goals and managed the work processes and practices. The empowered team became a model for organizational learning. As leaders, Xerox managers began the transition to the empowered leader profile by increasing communications, delegating authority to the work groups, and taking responsibility for codifying work processes and ensuring that everyone developed "ownership" of Xerox's vision.

Finally, EWGs began providing the structure to allow independent employees to become interdependent groups able to manage their day-to-day operations effectively and efficiently. As a result, members of EWGs learned to share responsibility and accountability for providing their customers with innovative products and services that would delight them.

Exhibit 1. Xerox Customer Satisfaction vs. Competition

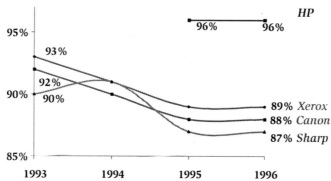

- Overall industry declining vs. expectations
- Xerox slightly better than traditional competition
- HP achieving benchmark performance

Why Customer First?

Source: CBS Survey.

Exhibit 2. Summary: Relationship Between Employee Satisfaction and Performance Results

Employee Satisfaction (OSI)	Customer Satisfaction	Weighted MIF	Work Group Module (WG)	Customer Satisfaction	Weighted MIF
Low	8.22	54.3	Low	8.22	54.5
Medium	8.29	55.1	Medium	8.31	56.4
High	8.33*	58.5*	High	8.32*	57.7*

Key Message: Districts that have high employee satisfaction (OSI) and work group effectiveness (WG) have significantly better (*p < .05) customer satisfaction and weighted MIF performance than districts with low employee satisfaction and low work group effectiveness.
Source: District ESMS Study 1994.

Exhibit 3. Teamwork Day

"Teamwork: Share the Knowledge"

What Is Teamwork Day?

Teamwork Day is a celebration by the people of The Document Company—Xerox of our commitment to knowledge sharing, teamwork, and customer satisfaction. Since the first *Teamwork Day* event in 1983, the event has grown into an international celebration attracting thousands of participants in many worldwide locations. Teams of empowered Xerox people, representing every organization within the company, join together and share their successes and best practices with co-workers, customers, suppliers, partners and other special guests.

What To Expect On Teamwork Day

Learning Sessions! Interactive Displays! Colorful Exhibits! In a festive-like atmosphere, teams showcase their use of quality processes and tools to ensure customer and employee satisfaction and to achieve superior results. The energy and enthusiasm of participating teams are contagious as they share what they have learned with others. Satellite connections enable a worldwide celebration of teamwork and the Xerox commitment to quality.

Each organization within the Xerox Group develops its own team selection process that best meets its needs. Team exhibits and presentations provide our people with a unique opportunity to meet co-workers from a variety of Xerox locations and to learn from each other through practice sharing.

Purpose of Teamwork Day

The purpose of *Teamwork Day* is to share and celebrate quality, to recognize teams, and to provide a forum to reinforce the Xerox commitment to Leadership Through Quality. It serves as:

- *A knowledge-sharing forum. Participating team members and visitors to* Teamwork Day *learn how quality processes and tools help us satisfy customers and improve results. By sharing these practices, we all gain increased knowledge, become more productive, and grow revenue.*

- *An outstanding recognition vehicle. Teamwork Day provides an excellent opportunity for teams to be recognized for their achievements, to feel pride in their accomplishments, and to share in the excitement of the celebration.*

- *An opportunity to demonstrate the Xerox commitment to quality. At* Teamwork Day, *our people, customers, suppliers and partners can experience first-hand the Xerox commitment to continuous quality improvement and customer satisfaction.*

- *A reminder. We are reminded that the customer is at the center of all we do. "Serving the customer is the responsibility of every Xerox employee." (Joseph C. Wilson)*

(Continued)

Exhibit 3. Teamwork Day (*Continued*)

What Happens at Teamwork Day '99?

This year's theme is "Share the Knowledge." It symbolizes that we all need to share our successful work experiences with others as a way to capture business opportunities in the market place and to become more productive. It also reflects how teamwork and the effective use of the Leadership Through Quality processes and tools have helped people take Xerox and quality to new heights. Teamwork '99 provides excellent opportunities to showcase teams that have shared their learning's and practices and have achieved excellent results. This year's event also features learning sessions, awareness booths, and team-sharing forums. Xerox Chairman—Paul Allaire, Xerox CEO—Rick Thoman and Xerox Canada Chairman and CEO—Kevin Francis will be the keynote speakers during a **LIVE BROADCAST.**

Teamwork Day: Better Than Ever

Today, *Teamwork Day* is better than ever before. The first event in 1983 was a small gathering of quality teams in one location. Today, it is a major communications event shared by Xerox people around the world. Teamwork has changed and grown just as the use of Quality processes and tools has become part of the Xerox culture. The first event featured 44 team display booths and presentations in a Xerox cafeteria in Webster. Today, **over 12,000 people attend** *Teamwork Day* activities at several locations in the United States, Canada, and via satellite to many other Xerox sites around the world. Teams from all parts of the corporation participate in the event, as do Xerox suppliers and customers, to enable the quality-sharing experience. In short, *Teamwork Day* has become an integral part of Xerox culture.

Who Organizes Teamwork Day?

The *Teamwork Day* International Design Team, with representation from each local team, coordinates and plans activities such as the satellite broadcast, collaterals, and the feel of the event. The local Design Teams, groups of committed Xerox volunteers representing many Xerox organizations, spend several months planning and organizing *Teamwork Day*. The sponsorship of *Teamwork Day* is rotated annually across the various organizations in Xerox, making *Teamwork Day* an example of teamwork in action.

This year Head Office will be hosting a **Career Day** alongside of *Teamwork Day*. Information on this can be obtained by contacting: through:
Judy Dahm
or
Jenny Johnston.

To further enhance the day, customers and employees are invited to attend two **Knowledge Forums** being held from 10:30 to 11:30. Please contact Gord Neis for more information.

Exhibit 3. Teamwork Day (*Continued*)

Mark your calendars now and plan to participate either with your team or as an attendee in our celebration of *Teamwork Day*! Remember **this year in Canada,** we will be participating in the **LIVE BROADCAST** that will be beamed to Rochester and Los Angeles!

Xerox Canada Ltd. *Teamwork Day* will be at **Toronto Head Office, Concourse Level** from 10:00 a.m.–4.30 p.m.

Teamwork '99 Canada
    Co-Chairs: Cathy Tait & Chris Venneri
    Communications: Sue Anderson
    Customer Engagement: Nick Lisi
    Document/Information Management: Robert Allison & Marty Jefferies
    Knowledge Forum: Gord Neis
    Logistics: Thane Sinclair
    Quality Assurance and XQS: Jim Barron
    Team Liaison: Violette Lareau & Lisa Greatrix
    Career Day Project: Jenny Johnston & Judy Dahm

Teamwork '99 East
    (Chairperson, John Lawrence)
    Riverside Convention Center
    Rochester, NY

Teamwork '99 West
    (Co-Chairs, Jesse Mathus & Don Philips)
    El Segundo Complex
    El Segundo, CA

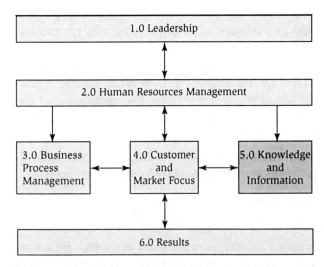

(Continued)

Exhibit 3. Teamwork Day (*Continued*)

If your team is interested in displaying at XCL's Teamwork Day—contact Cindy Moulton for information and details or check out the **Teamwork Day 1999** *Canadian Intranet Home Page* http://xww.xc.xerox.com/teamworkday

Or the USCO **Teamwork** *Intranet Home Page at* http://xww.mcse.world. xerox. com/twd. *Don't miss out on this exciting all-day event!*

Exhibit 4. High Performance Work Systems Vision 2000

Vision 2000

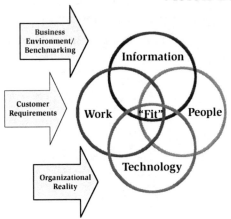

Xerox organizations worldwide consist of empowered team-based work environments where people, work, technology, and information are effectively integrated. These teams use state-of-the-art systems to deliver customized Document Solutions, resulting in world-class productivity for our customers and Xerox.

Exhibit 5. CSS Empowerment Survey

1. What is your definition of "empowerment?"

2. Based on this definition, how empowered are you in your current job? (Check *one*.)

Too little			Just right			Too much
1	2	3	4	5	6	7
○	○	○	○	○	○	○

3. Listed below are potential contributors to empowerment. In Column A, please mark those items that you feel contribute to your *current level* of empowerment, then rank-order the top 10 from most to least important. In column B, please mark those items which you believe, if true, *would increase* your level of empowerment, and again rank-order the top 10 from most to least important.

Potential contributors	-A- Contributes to my CURRENT LEVEL of empowerment	Rank order top 10	-B- Would INCREASE my level of empowerment	Rank order top 10
Knowing my work is important	○	___	○	___
Knowing my manager believes my work is important	○	___	○	___
Knowing my work contributes to my organization's success	○	___	○	___
Knowing I have "ownership" of my job	○	___	○	___
Knowing I am accountable for the outcomes of my work	○	___	○	___
Knowing what is expected of me in my job	○	___	○	___
Having the technical expertise to do my job	○	___	○	___
Having confidence in my ability to do my job	○	___	○	___
Having the business knowledge needed to do my job	○	___	○	___
Having the tools/resources needed to do my job	○	___	○	___
Being able to work with minimal direct supervision	○	___	○	___
Being able to decide how I do my work	○	___	○	___
Being able to set my own priorities	○	___	○	___
Being able to change my work processes as needed	○	___	○	___
Being able to negotiate boundaries for assignments	○	___	○	___
Being able to contact customers and suppliers directly	○	___	○	___
Being able to make decisions to satisfy customer requirements	○	___	○	___
Being able to implement decisions in a timely fashion	○	___	○	___
Being able to influence decisions that affect my work	○	___	○	___
Being able to influence what happens in my department	○	___	○	___
Being able to provide input to hiring decisions	○	___	○	___
Being able to provide input to promotion decisions	○	___	○	___
Being able to give candid feedback to my peers	○	___	○	___
Being able to share ideas and best practices with others	○	___	○	___
Being able to share task-related information with my workgroup	○	___	○	___

Thank you for completing this CSS Empowerment Survey!

Exhibit 6: The Leadership Continuum

Low	*Relationship Quality*		High
Management by Exception	**Laissez-Faire**	**Transactional**	**Transformational**
Wait for things to go wrong before taking action	Absent when needed	Clarify what outcomes are expected	Promote self-development
Focus on mistakes, complaints, or failures	Fail to follow-up requests for assistance	Deliver what is promised in exchange for support	Inspire & motivate
			Provide intellectual stimulation

Key Message: Transformational behaviors are necessary for developing high quality relationships. To achieve the process and performance gains associated with high-quality leadership relationships, leaders should emphasize transformational behaviors.

Exhibit 7. Education Model

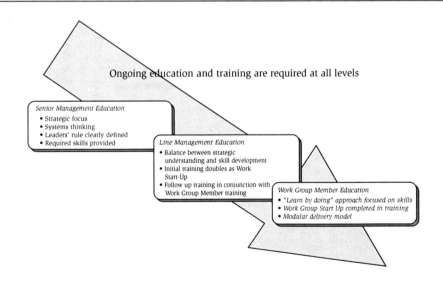

Ongoing education and training are required at all levels

Senior Management Education
- Strategic focus
- Systems thinking
- Leaders' rule clearly defined
- Required skills provided

Line Management Education
- Balance between strategic understanding and skill development
- Initial training doubles as Work Start-Up
- Follow up training in conjunction with Work Group Member training

Work Group Member Education
- "Learn by doing" approach focused on skills
- Work Group Start Up completed in training
- Modular delivery model

Exhibit 8. Communication Model

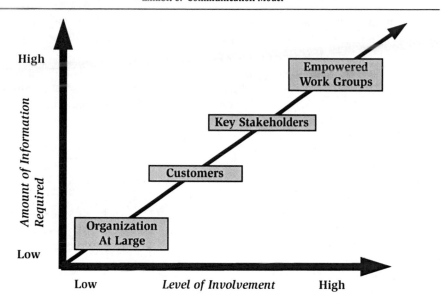

Exhibit 9. Empowered Teams—Pre-Post Implementation Survey

When you are answering the questions on this survey, please base your answers on your current experiences. Please answer every question as candidly as you can.

	Strongly Agree	Agree	Neither Agree Nor Disagree	Disagree	Strongly Disagree
1. Members of my team . . . dearly understand our organization's vision . . .	☐	☐	☐	☐	☐
are well informed about our business objectives . . .	☐	☐	☐	☐	☐
understand what we can do, day-to-day, to make our organization's vision a reality . . .	☐	☐	☐	☐	☐
clearly understand our district's objectives . . .	☐	☐	☐	☐	☐
clearly understand the goals of this team . . .	☐	☐	☐	☐	☐
have common goals that we all support . . .	☐	☐	☐	☐	☐
have a Mission Statement that we all support . . .	☐	☐	☐	☐	☐
willingly work together to achieve our objectives . . .	☐	☐	☐	☐	☐
are responsible for determining the best way to satisfy our customers' requirements . . .	☐	☐	☐	☐	☐
are responsible for deciding how to achieve our goals . . .	☐	☐	☐	☐	☐
are responsible for deciding how to organize our work . . .	☐	☐	☐	☐	☐
have a great deal of freedom in deciding how we will do our work . . .	☐	☐	☐	☐	☐

(Continued)

Exhibit 9. Empowered Teams—Pre-Post Implementation Survey (*continued*)

are accountable for the outcomes of our work . . .	☐	☐	☐	☐	☐
are afraid to implement a decision without our manager's approval . . .	☐	☐	☐	☐	☐
have dearly defined boundaries regarding out decision authority . . .	☐	☐	☐	☐	☐
are committed to the achievement of our organization's objectives . . .	☐	☐	☐	☐	☐
feel that our performance has a direct impact on customer satisfaction . . .	☐	☐	☐	☐	☐
feel that our performance has a direct impact on profit . . .	☐	☐	☐	☐	☐
feel that we contribute to the success of the organization . , ,	☐	☐	☐	☐	☐
are proud to tell people we work for Xerox . . .	☐	☐	☐	☐	☐
have an effective process for communicating with each other throughout the workday . . .	☐	☐	☐	☐	☐
share good ideas . . .	☐	☐	☐	☐	☐
learn from each other . . .	☐	☐	☐	☐	☐

Exhibit 10. Impact of Team Rewards On Performance

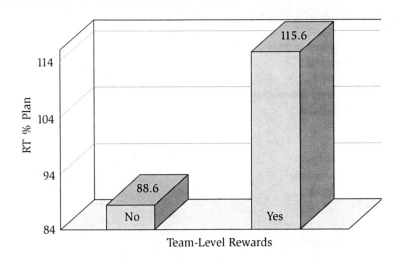

Key Messages: Teams that have team-level reward systems have significantly better Response Time performance (115.6% plan) compared to teams with individual-level rewards (88.6% plan).

Source: Critical Success Factors Study 1995.

Exhibit 11. Summary: Work Group Perceptions

Dimension	XCL	BC	Great Lakes	North-west	Atlantic	Quebec	Toronto
Common Goals	↑	↑	↑	↑	↑	↑	↑
Commitment to Organizational Goals	↑	↑				↑	↑
Norms and Roles	↑	↑	↑	↑	↑		↑
Current Decision Making	↑	↑	↑	↑	↑	↑	↑
Future Decision Making	↑	↑					↑
Perceived Empowerment	↑	↑	↑	↑	↑	↑	↑
Willingness to Challenge Authority	↑	↑		↑		↑	↑
Trust	↑	↑			↑	↑	↑
Cooperation	↑	↑				↑	
Teamwork	↑	↑	↑	↑	↑	↑	↑

Exhibit 12. Summary: Support Structures

Dimension	XCL	BC	Great Lakes	North-west	Atlantic	Quebec	Toronto
Coaching: Availability of Expert Coaching	↑			↑		↑	
Honesty and Respect	↑			↑		↑	
Acts as Work Group Motivator		↓				↑	
Supervisor as Supporter of WGs	↑	↓				↑	
Training Access							
Information Availability	↑					↑	
Performance Feedback	↓	↓		↓			
Recognition and Reward		↓				↑	
Process Management	↑	↑	↑		↑	↑	↑
Quality tools	↑				↑	↑	↑
Material Resources							

Endnotes

1. "Critical Succesors Study." Xerox Corporation, 1995.

2. "Critical Success Factors for Work Group Strategy Advancement," Xerox Corporation, 1995.

3. "High Performance Work Systems Vision 2000," Xerox Corporation, 1995.

4. "Fisher, Kimball. *Leading Self-Directed Work Teams*, New York: McGraw-Hill, 1993.

5. "Empowered Work Groups, Leadership Study." Xerox Corporation, 1998.

6. "Empowered Work Groups Pre-Post Implementation Assessment," Xerox Corporation, 1996.

7. "High Performance Work Systems Vision 2000," Xerox Corporation, 1995.

8. "The Impact of High Performance Work Systems on Organizational Performance Outcomes," Xerox Corporation, 1996.

ABOUT THE CONTRIBUTOR

Fernan R. Cepero (Fernan.Cepero@mc.usa.xerox.com) is a human resources operations manager for Manufacturing Support at The Document Company, Xerox. His responsibilities include recruiting, employee development, and ensuring effective succession planning. Prior to assuming this position, he served as employee development manager for Xerox, where he was responsible for the development and implementation of a People Development Strategy. He developed and maintained, at all levels, a pool of management talent to meet the companies' long-term needs. He has also served as a training analyst and consultant and marketing support manager and contract specialist with Xerox before assuming his current position.

Cepero has a master's of science in human resource development from Rochester Institute of Technology, a master's degree in foreign studies from American University, and a bachelor's degree from Fordham University. He maintains certifications from Mager Associates in both Instructional Development & Criterion Referenced Instruction. He is certified to administer Consulting Psychologist Press, standardized psychological profiles, the Kirton Adaptation Innovation instrument, and he is a certified consultant for the 360 PROFILER Instrument.

This case was created in collaboration with Xerox, XSERV Creative Group.

LEADERSHIP DEVELOPMENT

THE FIELD OF LEADERSHIP DEVELOPMENT: AN INTRODUCTION BY JAY A. CONGER

This is a remarkable time for the field of leadership development. In some ways, I think of it as a "golden age." I say this for two reasons. One, most of the major Fortune 1000 companies in the last few years either are or have undertaken some initiative toward leadership training and development. In the end, it has spawned a billion-dollar leadership development industry. The second reason is the equally remarkable amount of innovation in the field. Think back to the 1980s when the terms "360-degree feedback," "personal coach," and "action learning" would have been quite novel. At the same time, we are finally realizing that a one-time training event is insufficient to truly develop leadership talent. As a result, we are seeing experiments in deploying systems to help facilitate leadership development on an on-going basis, such as adapting rewards and performance measures, providing coaching on call, or focusing succession plans on leadership needs.

A singular insight has driven this flowering of leadership development: Most organizations realize they have a serious shortage of leadership talent. In the face of intense competition, a global marketplace, and new opportunities opened up by advances in technology and science, it is a shortage that few can afford. The CEO of Johnson & Johnson comments: "Leadership is the biggest single constraint to growth at Johnson & Johnson, and it is the most critical business issue we face." As a result, leadership development has become a high priority for most companies. In a few companies like J&J, it has become an essential part of their business strategy. Yet as Beth Benjamin and I showed in our recent book, *Building Leaders* (1999), many leadership development initiatives end up at best with a limited impact. Some are simply a waste of money.

In the cases that follow, we will look at three companies that have dedicated serious time and resources to leadership development. Their initiatives hold great promise. For one, they have moved beyond simple training initiatives to multiple-pronged programs that increase the chances of leadership "taking hold." At Sun, for example, leadership issues are a part of the company's succession planning. All three companies' initiatives are supported by senior management. Before the first executive leadership program was held at Johnson & Johnson, CEO Ralph Larsen and his direct reports received 360-degree feedback and coaching on themselves. Sun has a Leadership Council comprising senior executives who undertake special leadership initiatives every year, initiatives whose outcomes are then tracked. Company executives at Boeing are involved in the action learning projects. In addition, all three of the company cases make extended use of competency models, 360-degree feedback, and action learning.

In this overview, I will focus on these latter three components—competency models, 360-degree feedback, and action learning. All of them have now become standard tools in leadership development initiatives. Yet few have questioned their universal effectiveness. I believe there are important lessons to be learned about their application.

The term *competency* gained popularity after the publication of Richard Boyatzis's book *The Competent Manager* (1982). In it, Boyatzis defined a competency as "an underlying characteristic of a person—a motive, trait, skill, aspect of one's self-image or social role, or a body of knowledge which he or she uses." Within the leadership field, however, competencies typically refer to behavioral dimensions of leaders. Competency models as such provide a catalogue of the leadership traits desired by the organization in its managers. These traits in turn become the key attributes to be developed.

The advantages of these models are multiple. First, they are often constructed around tangible dimensions—either behaviors, outcomes, or activities. They can be visibly measured. Second, they send a clear message to an organization about the specific attributes that are considered valuable at this point in time. As the Sun case points out, they establish a common language around what leadership really means in that particular organization. If they are linked to rewards and performance measures, they can establish clear expectations. In the case of Johnson & Johnson, attributes are also tied to the company's long-standing core values and the global nature of the J&J's operations. The third advantage is that they provide a framework or checklist for both individual managers and their organizations to benchmark themselves—in other words, to see which competencies are strong or weak within the individual and within the management ranks of the organization. In Boeing's case, they smartly used the lowest-ranked competencies of the company's top 200 executives as a guide in developing their next generation of leadership programs. Competency models can become a powerful design tool.

Before we fall too much in love with competencies, however, it is important to recognize their shortcomings. There is often a strong tendency to use them as "universal" criteria. By this, I mean that their intended audience must somehow live up to possessing most or all of them. A manager must be "an agile learner," "empowering," "reflective," "team-building," "able to develop their people," "able to understand marketplace trends," and the list goes on. We forget that many of these competencies are derived from "ideal types" of leadership. In other words, if this were an perfect world, this is what the ideal leader would look like. It is doubtful that many managers can in reality possess all or most of the qualities that are commonly identified. Organizations need to be thoughtful about prioritizing the competences that an individual manager needs to focus on in their own development.

By employing a universal set of criteria across management levels, competency models can fail to recognize that leadership requirements vary by level and by situation. The leadership skills demanded at senior executive levels are vastly different from those at frontline levels or even the middle levels. In addition, it is taken as a given that these models apply across functions and operating units. In reality, different units may demand different leadership styles given their unique requirements. For example, a more directive style may be necessary in an operating unit that has minute-to-minute delivery demands versus a strategic planning unit where a consultative approach is often the norm. Yet many models do not provide for this level of differentiation.

There are other problems. Competency models tend to "stabilize" in the sense that, like a paradigm, they become well-established. For example, many of the leadership competencies we see today have been in use for practically a decade. For this reason, the Sun Leadership Council periodically reviews its competences. Oftentimes, competency models are derived from research comparing high and low performers within an organization, the high performers creating the benchmarks. While today's high performers may tell us about today's essential skills, they may or may not tell us about what is needed in the future. In a rapidly changing business environment, these models may simply reinforce behaviors that are soon to be outdated. Organizations must continually ask themselves whether their competency lists are still appropriate given changes in company marketplaces and in the organization.

Finally, there are the issues of integration. Many organizations use these models in their training programs but in isolation from the actual reward and performance measurement systems of the firm. So while the competencies draw attention to behaviors such as "empowering others," a manager in organization X may in reality be rewarded solely on his or her performance outcomes, not on actual behavior. As long as an individual delivers on his or her budget or revenue goals, there may be no penalty for being ineffective at building collaborative teams. Competency models need teeth—they need to be embedded in both an organization's rewards, promotion criteria, and performance measurements.

The second of our tools, 360-degree feedback, builds upon research in training that shows that feedback is an essential element in any successful learning experience.[1] The better designed development initiatives employ structured 360-degree feedback based on responses from workplace colleagues. As important, this survey feedback is tightly aligned to the course material. In other words, it focuses on the very dimensions of leadership that participants will soon be taught or rewarded for. Interestingly, few human resources tools have achieved such popularity so quickly as the 360-degree feedback tool.

As I discussed in my book *Learning to Lead* (1992), the impact of formal feedback surveys varies dramatically by individual. Some are prepared to use them as a source of real learning and insight, others react more defensively. It is completely person-dependent. The only potential to increase feedback's impact over the long term is to support it with ongoing coaching and follow-up. At Johnson & Johnson, for example, participants in their program had several forms of follow up assistance: 1) mini-surveys held 6 months to a year after the initial feedback survey to check progress, 2) telephone coaching to provide personal assistance, and 3) 4 sets of correspondence focusing on their progress, especially around areas of improvement. What such devices do is provide a discipline and source of accountability over time. At J&J, they found that the process proved to be the most powerful element contributing to a perceived increase in an individual's leadership effectiveness.

Despite the popularity of 360-degree feedback, there have been some criticisms.[2] First of all, it can be very time-consuming. A boss might have to fill out a dozen or more forms on his or her peers and subordinates. On the other hand, technology will eliminate some of this burden with assessments conducted over company intranets. Given that behavior is driven by what is measured and rewarded, organizations must be very clear on what behaviors they are seeking to reinforce and whether these directly tie to company goals. Raters themselves may not see a link between an individual's behavior and systematic problems facing the organization. For example, in one organization I studied, the company was experiencing a significant downturn in their market share due to its failure to understand changing customer needs. Surprisingly, 360-degree feedback surveys of the company's managers showed very high ratings across the organization on dimensions relating to individual managers having an intimate understanding and sensitivity to customer needs! Remember, however, that the raters were all company insiders. This is a good example where outside customers would have provided more reliable data. There is also the possibility that the frequent use of the same feedback questionnaire may diminish its impact if responses fall into a similar pattern during each application. We know from research that raters themselves may commit common types of rating errors—either rating too harshly or too leniently or playing it safe with mid-point ratings. It is important that raters receive some form of guidance beforehand. In addition, certain organizational cultures are highly autocratic or conflict-averse, which may inhibit candor with respondents providing positively biased feedback instead of actual perceptions.

I personally believe that the selective use of 360-degree feedback is appropriate simply on the grounds that learning is enhanced whenever individuals have some form of behavioral feedback. It provides an opportunity for the individual to benchmark themselves against the very dimensions being taught in a program. Participants can gauge the extent to which they need to focus their energies on developing certain weaker competences. At a minimum, they will be alert to their shortcomings and find ways of compensating for them. The key is to effectively and tightly align competencies to course learnings and then align reward, promotion, and performance measurement systems to include those competencies.

The final of our three key elements—action learning—has also achieved enormous popularity in the leadership development field. Two forces have been behind the widespread use of these learning formats. First of all, companies want to see their investments in education turn into tangible outcomes. Learning experiences therefore revolve around projects that address key issues facing the company. The second force is a growing appreciation for the learning requirements of adults. Research has shown that adults are most motivated for learning when it is immediately applicable to their lives. Action learning usually can meet both of these needs. The problem with many action learning programs is that they typically have several design flaws that hinder their impact. For example, the sponsors for projects may have only a half-hearted commitment to the program, which in turn leads them to provide "make-work" projects with few significant learning opportunities. Since much of the learning is team-based, skills development is crucial. I have witnessed a number of action learning groups fail largely because of dysfunctional team dynamics. Expert coaching and facilitation is a critical ingredient. Follow-up is another common problem. In many companies, the process ends the moment participants present their findings and recommendations. The Boeing program, on the other hand, teaches us about some of the critical design elements that need to be in place for programs to have a real impact. For example, participation in the program is selective to ensure the best use of limited resources and a great need for talent. The projects are based around the intersection of real needs felt by both the company and individual managers who would be participating. There is also a wonderfully clear and official contract around expectations. The total experience is spread out over an extended time period and is supplemented with education, exposure to executives, seminars, special projects, and personal feedback. This type of design ensures multiple opportunities for individuals to revisit learnings and to reflect more frequently. Finally, it incorporated a measure of follow-up after the program ended. The more that programs contain similar design elements, the more likely action learning will produce tangible payouts for both the individual and the company.

In closing, the greatest challenge facing the leadership development field is to continually remind ourselves that leadership has a long developmental cycle. It is one of those investments that pays off over the long haul. My fear at times is that leadership development will become simply another management fad, that in a few years, we will have moved on to the next thing. In the end, that would be a tragedy. Our challenge is therefore to continually remind those who support our initiatives that talent takes time and experience to be nourished and developed. We must expect, at a minimum, decade-long developmental cycles for junior people to become extraordinary leaders later down their career paths. However, it is up to us to provide an organizational soil that is rich and fertile with opportunities and education in order for them to grow.

Endnotes

1. Conger, J.A., *Learning to Lead.* San Francisco: Jossey-Bass, 1992.
2. Waldman, D.A., L.E. Atwater, and D. Antonioni. "Has 360-degree Feedback Gone Amok?" *Academy of Management Executive,* 12 (2), 86–94, 1998.

Jay Conger (jconger@sba.usc.edu) is the executive director of the Leadership Institute at the University of Southern California. Dr. Conger has authored more than 60 articles and 4 books on the topic. One of his books, *Learning to Lead,* is the culmination of a 2-year research effort examining leadership training. *Fortune* calls the book "the source" for understanding leadership training. Conger's most recent book is entitled *Building Leaders: How Successful Companies Develop the Next Generation* (Jossey-Bass, 1999).

CHAPTER EIGHT

Boeing

A leadership development program designed to broaden identified successors to executive positions and prepare individuals for a variety of new assignments while delivering solutions to top management through action learning and personal development

INTRODUCTION—THE VISION

The Executive Development Program (EDP) was established in 1995 by Harry Stonecipher, while he was CEO of the former McDonnell Douglas Company (MDC). Upon announcement of the Boeing/McDonnell Douglas merger in 1997, several programs, initiatives, and processes were identified by synergy opportunity teams as best practices and worthy of expansion into the newly merged company. (*Note:* During the merger transition period, over 100 small teams were chartered to find and assess synergy opportunities among the three companies and recommend common best practices for implementation after the merger was consummated.) MDC's Executive Development Program was one of the programs selected and has evolved to become a premier development strategy for targeted executive potentials. EDP alumni have been rotated to key assignments throughout the company; project sponsors have rated business solutions from project teams as excellent; program nominee quality has increased and the wait list is long; top executives speak at weekly breakfasts and in other venues and strongly support the program in both words and action. This chapter provides an account of the evolution of this program from its startup through merger transition and redesign into full implementation across The Boeing Company.

BUILDING THE BUSINESS CASE
FOR LEADERSHIP DEVELOPMENT

When Harry Stonecipher arrived at MDC as the new CEO, he was disappointed with executive successor development processes. He often remarked that the fact that MDC had to bring in an outsider to fill the CEO position was indicative of a systemic problem in internal leadership development. His lengthy experience at General Electric with disciplined, sophisticated executive succession and development programs was a catalyst for the development of MDC's EDP. He was determined to build "one company" and was concerned about the lack of horizontal movement of executives among the various business units and geographic regions, a key factor contributing to separate organizational cultures. The "one company" initiative was launched when Stonecipher and his executives recognized that, since 1967 the two companies (McDonnell Aircraft and Douglas Aircraft) had not completely merged, but that additional business unit silos had emerged, creating a fractured set of company cultures, practices, and processes. Creating "one company" was a number-one priority. Stonecipher and his top executives were convinced that several executive successors must be taken out of their siloed jobs and placed in full-time, enterprise-level, project-based situations. These situations would provide top executives with a bigger perspective of the company and opportunities to broaden at an accelerated pace, and they would foster movement of individuals across the company. This would accelerate Boeing's "one company" culture, grow future leaders, and surface best practices company-wide. They began the process of reviewing their succession plans, targeting individuals for placement in this program, and surfacing business challenges for project teams.

After McDonnell Douglas and The Boeing Company merged in 1997, executive assessments were conducted on the top 200 senior executives of the newly formed company. Nineteen competencies were identified as required for future leaders of Boeing and the competencies assessed as lowest-ranking among the current top leadership involved attracting and developing employees, aligning the organization, thinking globally, driving execution, applying financial acumen, and a few others. It was clear that the company needed to focus more attention to these leadership characteristics, especially in the development of executive successors. The Executive Development Program was selected as one of the key opportunities to accelerate this development. The program was already in place, and expansion of the participant base was seen as a cost-effective way to increase executive development. The action learning experiences were redesigned to achieve greater impact. Senior management provided more in-depth projects and challenges to the participants, thereby accelerating the cycle time for acquiring improved leadership competencies. Project teams were encouraged to surface best practices from within (and external to) The Boeing Company and accelerate the transfer of these practices among the various business segments. The resulting improvements in process quality are seen as significantly offsetting the cost of the development program. Nominations to the program are directly linked to the succession plans, thereby assuring quality candidates and targeted development of future leaders.

PROGRAM OVERVIEW

The EDP is a full-time development opportunity that provides a broad array of experiences through team approaches to solving real-time business challenges facing The Boeing Company. This is an action learning program—i.e., participants learn by doing, managing team-based projects that are targeted to address their development needs while delivering recommendations that can be implemented throughout the company.

Target Population

Twice a year, middle managers who are near term or ready-now successors to E-series positions (Boeing's terminology for executive positions) are nominated by top executive management to participate full-time in the program. Program duration is intended for an 18-24 month period. To maximize the experience, participants co-locate with their teams, thus developing a familiarity with the geographic and business unit diversity of the company. A minimum 1-year participation commitment is critical for both program process analysis performance and individual development. Participants are exposed to new career options as they experience the EDP. It is anticipated that they will exercise one of these options to explore a significant job change upon completing the program.

The Benefit of the Program Is Twofold

The key benefits of the EDP are leadership development and process analysis. Each is critical to the ongoing success of The Boeing Company. The leadership development aspect provides participants an opportunity to broaden their organizational and functional exposure and experience. The second aspect of the program design, process analysis, provides a mechanism for examining critical processes across the corporation and identifying and sharing the "best practices" for implementation enterprise-wide. Key developmental experiences include the following:

- Exposure to key management and business issues and decision processes through participation in cross-functional, cross-regional EDP Project Teams addressing major enterprise-wide, high-leverage processes or problems

- Presentations of recommendations based on business case analysis to project sponsors and other process owners for review, approval, and implementation

- Attendance at external executive development programs recognized for excellence and leading-edge expertise (e.g., Stanford, Michigan, MIT, Wharton)

- Development of personal leadership skills through highly focused individual analysis (e.g., the Leadership Development Intensive at John Scherer & Associates)

- Opportunity for executive exposures, including mentorship arrangements

- Other special projects, seminars, and unique individual opportunities

- Opportunity to work in several regions of The Boeing Company, nationwide

Projects are identified and sponsored by senior executive leadership. EDP participants team together in a boundary-free environment to assess actual and substantial business issues using various process analysis techniques. The "customer" for the process analysis provides a general description of the business concern and the affected processes, including the key issues, scope, and potential benefits resulting from enterprise-wide implementation or resolution. The team is responsible for analyzing the issues, developing recommendations, and presenting these recommendations to management. This requires extensive travel, often working virtually from laptops and cell phones, on the following monthly schedule:

- One week spent in company headquarters in Seattle, Washington
- Two weeks spent in locations supportive of the project requirements (could be anywhere)
- One week spent at the home Boeing facility working virtually with team on project

Participants work a 10-hour day, 4 days a week, and travel home each weekend on their own time (e.g., Thursday night, Friday morning, Sunday evening) to ensure quality time with family and friends.

THE REDESIGN PROCESS

Influencing the Evolving Infrastructure

As a result of the merger of three aerospace companies, human resource policies and processes were evolving during the first few years, taking advantage of the best practices of all three firms. It was imperative that the EDP processes were aligned with key HR processes to ensure effective selection, training and development, compensation, and exit strategies. Since the new HR processes were under construction and were somewhat of a "moving target," the implementation of the modified EDP was difficult. Succession planning was the key process supporting both entry to and exit from the program. The formal, company-wide succession planning process was not in place until much later in the transition period and required the EDP to use interim processes for about 2 years. The Boeing-wide leadership development curriculum was also in transition, with a new chief learning officer hired 1 year after the merger. Company-wide compensation systems as well as job classification structures were also in development at this same time. The executive management of human resources was aware of the need for strong alignment and was extremely supportive of the EDP. They made an effort to include EDP management in various committees and policy decisions as these processes evolved. EDP project teams were requested to work on some of these HR process improvements. The EDP was seen by human resources development (HRD) specialists as a unique development opportunity that required nurturing and alignment with current and future training and development strategies. It was not seen as competing with any development initiative.

Surfacing Executive Expectations

As part of the marketing of the program, the design team requested the assistance of an internal communications specialist. The corporate communications department provided the team with a writer/editor and support from the graphics organization. The communications specialist conducted face-to-face and telephone interviews with several key senior executives, asking them about the program, their ideas on developing leaders, and their expectations of the program. Executive perspectives were documented during these interviews and utilized to revamp the program. Senior executives genuinely felt that they were influencing the reshaping of the program and knew that they had a direct influence on its success. The quotes from these interviews were used in subsequent news articles and a brochure. Also, during this same period, The Boeing Company developed a set of leadership competencies that would become the foundation for future development programs (Exhibit 1). Once these competencies were established, the top 200 senior executives participated in an extensive assessment process to surface the summarized "as is" condition of their own behaviors and skills. The summarized list was shared widely with management throughout The Boeing Company, indicating the highest, middle, and lowest-ranking competencies of the current top executives. Most of the newer leadership development programs were designed to meet the lower scoring competencies. These competencies were also a focus of the EDP and assisted in the redesign of the program. Special attention was given to developing and coaching others, giving and receiving feedback, displaying business acumen, and maintaining teamwork competencies.

Assessing the Current Program

Soon after the merger, the program office requested the assistance of the Organization Development group. They were asked to put together an assessment process that would gauge viewpoints of various stakeholders and assess several aspects of the current program (the McDonnell Douglas original design). The OD group and the program office created a process model/hierarchy that provided an architecture around which to formulate questions. A set of specific questions was created for each process (e.g., soliciting candidates, obtaining projects, developing participants, developing and managing exit strategy, managing projects, marketing the program, etc.). Stakeholder categories were created (e.g., current participants, alumni, project sponsors, nominating sponsors, senior executives, internal audit management, etc.) and a random list of names from each category was identified. For approximately two months, OD consultants interviewed the randomly selected individuals, asking them the specific set of questions, obtaining additional comments for each process, and ending with the standard, "What would you like the program to start doing, stop doing and continue doing?" The responses were summarized in an extensive report to the program office, internal audit management, and the participants themselves. Ideas for process improvements were solicited in a two-day offsite meeting with the participants and so began the redesign process.

KEY ELEMENTS OF THE NEW DESIGN— DEVELOPMENT STRATEGIES

Development Needs Assessment

Upon acceptance to the program, participants discuss their development needs with their nominating sponsor and document them prior to entry. The Nominating Sponsor's Proposal (Exhibit 2) is prepared jointly, signed, and forwarded to the EDP office. Leadership competency development needs are selected from the list of The Boeing Company competencies. These are the development needs that the participant hopes to have addressed while on the program for 18 to 24 months. These development needs are the basis for future project assignments, optional training programs, external executive program selection, personal development coaching, feedback requests, and so on. These development needs are dynamic and are often modified during the program. They are the focal point for career development planning, which will be discussed below.

The Nominating Sponsor's Proposal also shows commitment to development and provides a "safety net" (described in the following paragraph) thereby minimizing the initial concern regarding placement upon graduation:

> We expect that Joe may be exposed to new career options as he experiences the Executive Development Program. It is anticipated that he may exercise one of these options and explore a significant change in job upon completing the EDP. We agree to assist him in exploring these options and will arrange the appropriate executive exposures in support of Joe's career development. However, at a minimum, we will assure Joe that he will be returned to our organization in an equivalent position upon completing the EDP, to minimize any risk associated with this development assignment.

Also, upon entry to the program, participants are requested to provide names of peers, customers, superiors, and subordinates from whom feedback on leadership behaviors will be requested. Within one month of entry, a 360-degree feedback tool (*Acumen Leadership Style Inventory*) is sent out to people on the list and the responses are summarized for future use in the Leadership Discovery—LDI offsite described next.

Developing Career Planning and Management Skills

As participants join the program, they are immediately aware of the prospect that the next 18–24 months will provide them with insights into new career options. They also realize that they are now teamed with individuals from all over the country, different product divisions, and different functional disciplines. They are no longer a part of a traditional organization with a management hierarchy, siloed job families, well-defined tasks and deliverables, processes with boundaries, and people who are familiar with each other. The infrastructure is not set up to manage the careers of individuals—rather, individuals decide to take advantage of various development opportunities and must take charge of their own careers. Entry into this program really brings this point home, especially as participants become further removed from their nominating organization. In addition, the merger created significant changes in the organization—nominating sponsors changed jobs or left the company, organizational structures and alliances changed, new faces appeared in the new management structure, geographic locations and associated businesses/products changed or were even eliminated. This event gave participants insights as to their responsibilities to manage their own career. They realized that they had to quickly take the time to create a career development plan and self-manage to that plan. They had to keep their development needs in perspective, get on projects that addressed those needs, develop networks that provided them with new insights and perspectives, regularly share their needs with others, deal with the insecurities presented by being on the program and not in a "real job," and become well-versed in career management techniques.

To assist the company in the development of a curriculum that addresses these needs for self-managed career development plans, the design team partnered with a recognized outplacement firm. Together, the outplacement firm and the design team created and continuously improved a mandatory curriculum to supplement the individual development needs. Exhibit 3 contains the career management curriculum as it is delivered today. At first, participants viewed the curriculum and remarked, "I already know how to do this." However, attendance at the first class moved these "nonbelievers" from dubious to a believer in the need for improving their skill sets. In a company the size of Boeing, individuals who can master the skills listed and do not assume that someone else will manage their careers have the advantage of spotting opportunities and capitalizing on them.

Leadership Discovery—Leadership Development Intensive

As a key element of effective leadership, discovering and knowing who you are and what your values are is critical. In the old program, participants attended a traditional 5-day offsite meeting, using several assessment tools, teaming to surface unwelcome leadership behaviors and reinforce individual improvement efforts. They usually return from a good bonding experience with a thick note-book full of assessment data to contemplate. During the assessment of the program processes, this experience was questioned and the company began to search for a deeper, more meaningful experience. Program developers were anxious to help the participants look more inwardly to adapt a more flexible style of leadership and a more resilient identity and purpose. The Leadership Development Intensive (LDI) was selected, designed, and delivered by John Scherer and Associates from Spokane, Washington. Their approach is to "expand the mind, stretch the body, deepen the spirit." They are a small firm, willing to accommodate new requirements and ideas, genuinely interested in making a difference in the lives of the participants. The offsite experience challenges the participants' current thinking, relaxes and strengthens the body with yoga and aikido, and deepens their connection to that which is most important in their life. They can count on the following outcomes:

- Unhook yourself from counterproductive reactions and patterns
- Resolve unresolvable conflicts with courage and grace
- Know the difference between problems to be solved and polarities to be managed
- Produce extraordinary results in the face of obstacles and resistance
- Integrate body, mind, and spirit by making significant lifestyle changes
- Turn your work into a powerful vehicle for rich, lifelong development
- Become a communicator who can hear and be heard
- Work with a greater sense of purpose

The EDP director attended a public seminar and experienced the program first hand. Her assessment was very positive and the customization began. The customized approach provided the project teams with a new opportunity for participants to get "below the waterline" in their depth of understanding of themselves. The first group attended the offsite in a wooded, secluded meeting center and the response was overwhelmingly positive. The EDP was commended for taking a risk and offering something out of the ordinary. The changes in behavior and bonding among teammates were outstanding. The same results have been seen in subsequent groups. While the LDI doesn't necessarily offer new ways to self-assess and explore oneself, the combination of techniques and the orderly transition through the exploration are most effective. Comments like "this has been a life-changing experience," "I have never experienced this depth of understanding before," "my life will never be the same," and "all Boeing executives must go through this program" are not uncommon. One of the primary outcomes of this program is the development of a "purpose worthy of who you are." When participants return from the offsite, they share these purpose statements with several stakeholders in their development and their careers. The purpose statement becomes part of their career development planning process and the foundation from which they will make future decisions regarding potential permanent assignments. Most come to the conclusion that if they leave the EDP to take a permanent assignment that does not align with the "purpose worthy of who they are," they will not be motivated to succeed. This purpose statement process is key to leadership discovery.

Leadership Discovery—Executive Exposures

Prior to the merger, The Boeing Company had a 15-year-old leadership development program, also managed by internal audit, called Management Control Systems Audit (MCSA)—Loaned Auditor program. First-level management candidates are targeted to enter this program for 12 months in an action learning experience, conducting internal audits of various processes throughout the company. This program continues today and has been expanded to include all business units of the newly merged Boeing Company. This leadership development program is managed by the same EDP office staff. An element of the loaned auditor program that was adapted for EDP was the weekly executive breakfasts. Each Wednesday, a senior executive comes to talk informally with EDP participants and Loaned Auditors for an hour about their business challenges, leadership philosophies, and backgrounds. The questions from the audience make for a lively discussion. The executive speaker is often impressed with the depth and breadth of the participants, and follow-up discussions are not uncommon following the breakfasts. In addition, luncheons with executives are arranged for EDP members. Most of the senior executives have given them an open invitation to attend weekly staff/business meetings and process council events. Project sponsors provide significant exposures to EDP project teams while they are working in the region.

Leadership Discovery—Development Coach

Within three months of joining the program, EDPers are provided with a personal development coach to assist them in behavior change, career management, or life planning. These coaches are outside consultants, well-versed in executive coaching techniques and are brought together quarterly to share trends, concerns, and improvement ideas. The assignment of a development coach coincides with the attendance at the LDI so that coaching can reinforce the learnings from the intensive experience. The discussions between coach and EDPer are confidential and are not shared with The Boeing Company. This is relatively new process (10 months) and EDPers are not sure how to utilize the coach, what the roles should be, how much to share, who to trust, and so on. In the last group meeting with the coaches the design team decided to get 3 more months of experience and then try to formalize the expectations, roles, and responsibilities and improve the process as necessary. The use of external development coaches is very limited in The Boeing Company and only used at the top levels of the organization in a structured program context. The company's experience with this development strategy is minimal and the evolution is inevitable.

External Executive Education

Each participant is afforded an opportunity to attend 2 weeks at a recognized executive education institution during the program. MIT, Harvard, Wharton, and Stanford are but a few of the schools that EDPers select in fields ranging from finance for nonfinancial managers to developing a global operations strategy. EDPers are encouraged to discuss their options with a wide range of executives throughout the company (those from their sponsoring organization as well as those in new parts of the company who might be interested in the EDPer when he/she graduates from the program). EDPers then prepare a briefing when they return from the executive education program and share it formally with other participants and members of internal audit as well as the executives who encouraged them to attend. This increases the networking opportunities for the EDPer to be viewed as a resource to the organization. Briefings and the extensive notebooks of materials received at the external executive education programs are filed (electronically and manually) in the central EDP library for all to use. A database of who has gone where is kept for future reference.

Team/Project Assessment Processes

As projects are kicked off, a formal "norming and storming" session is facilitated to develop the teamwork required on the project. These norms are addressed periodically in facilitated sessions at least twice more throughout the project. Individuals receive direct, honest, and authentic feedback from their teammates in a nonthreatening, low-risk environment. The feedback is not shared outside of the team and the individual is responsible to use the feedback to accelerate their development. Development coaches are notified after a team assessment session has been completed and are encouraged to contact their "client" to see how it went, reinforce behaviors, coach new behaviors, and so on. The program processes are ripe with opportunities to give and receive feedback, a key learning objective of the program. At the end of the project, the team identifies key stakeholders in the project and a third party conducts an interview with the stakeholders and prepares a written report of findings. These are shared with the team, summarized quarterly, and trends are identified. Exhibit 4 is the first page of the report issued by the consultants and describes the process.

Building Teamwork/Networking Among Participants

One of the advantages provided by this program is the extraordinary opportunity to team build and to develop new networks of people who are a resource to each other while on as well as following the program. All efforts in this area are focused on changing attitudes about networking and teaming to ensure that common interests can surface and contributions to each other can be achieved. To be in the service of each other is a common theme. Many events are held to assist in accelerating teambuilding and networking. For example, each Wednesday, communications meetings and peer reviews are held (face-to-face or virtually) with all EDPers. Every quarter, an all-hands, face-to-face, two-day event is held—one day of social gathering (golf, community service, etc.) and one day of training/process improvement discussions. Every Tuesday in Seattle (at the corporate apartment complex where apartments are maintained for EDPers), a social gathering (pot luck, dinner out, sporting event, etc) is scheduled. Project teams travel together whenever possible. Random events occur and the EDPers themselves set up opportunities to get together. With so much travel, it helps to continually develop the relationships that are supportive and nurturing.

KEY ELEMENTS OF THE NEW DESIGN—SELECTION AND ORIENTATION PROCESS

Selection Criteria/Program Familiarization Briefings

While senior executives manage the selection process, the EDP office validates nominations by review of succession charts, rate progression, current and prior job assignments, and nomination forms and résumés. To ensure quality nominations, presidents review all nominations and down-select finalists. The commitment to the program is significant, given the 24-month assignment, the extensive travel, the impact on family and friends, and the apprehension caused by working out of the comfort zone of expertise and familiarity. Therefore, a program familiarization briefing is held 2 weeks before the program start date. Nominees are invited to a 5-hour briefing, a roundtable discussion with either the COO or CEO, and are given material to take back (e.g., Frequently Asked Questions—see Exhibit 5) and discuss with their stakeholders. Following the briefing, nominees are given 1 week to fully commit to the program. These briefings include program details, expectations, what the program is, what it isn't, and a panel discussion (including Q&A) with randomly selected current participants.

Managing Expectations/Orientation Program

When management nominates individuals to the program, they may inadvertently raise expectations of the nominee beyond what the program can provide (e.g., alleging promotion opportunities at the end of the program is inappropriate). Nominees may develop misconceptions as to program details and offerings and what to expect upon graduation. Often, nominees set unrealistic expectations with their spouses and/or significant others as they enter the program. To ensure that clear expectations are set early in the process, both the familiarization briefing and the first-week orientation process are full of reinforcements. The program is positioned as an accelerated development opportunity that is deployed to broaden individuals in ways that their current assignment cannot. It provides participants with opportunities to work all over the nation, in functions and business units in which they need familiarity. It is a chance to build an entirely new network and become a resource to more people. It is expected that upon graduation, participants will make a major shift in their career patterns—changing job function/discipline, geographic location, or business unit, resulting in a significant change in roles and responsibilities. The expectation that someone else will arrange this successful exit is quickly dispelled. A dependence on the infrastructure to ensure that development occurs over the 24 months and that a permanent assignment awaits upon graduation is also dispelled early in the briefings and orientation. The program *does* commit to providing opportunities to develop superior career management skills that will last a lifetime, thus eliminating the dependence on others. It is up to the participant to take advantage of what the program offers. During orientation, 2 days of project management skill training is provided by a specialized consultant firm due to its criticality to the success of the EDP projects.

During the orientation, spouses and/or significant others are brought to Seattle and given a full day of transition training, dealing with concerns, fear of the unknown, frequently asked questions, and their commitment to their partners' career development. Often spouses create a support network among themselves during this session. Expectations are made clear in this meeting as well and partners are brought together at the end of the day to share insights. Social interactions are planned twice during the orientation week, with current participants invited as well.

KEY ELEMENTS OF THE NEW DESIGN— PROJECT NOMINATION AND SELECTION PROCESS

Solicitation of Projects

Three times per year, the program office sends out a written request for projects, carefully outlining the criteria for selection. Exhibit 6 is the Project Nomination form used by management to describe the business issue and indicate benefits of this project to the company and the participants. This takes approximately 6 weeks from start to finish. Executive assistants to the business unit presidents usually handle this solicitation and down-select process. They work closely with the EDP office during the process, validating the alignment of their proposed projects with the objectives of the program, as well as ensuring that the top business issues are being considered. Project Nominations are prioritized by each business unit president and submitted to the EDP office for consideration.

Company-Wide Down-Select Process

Once all project nominations are received, internal audit directors participate in rating each project against the established criteria (e.g., potential cost impact, enterprise-wide impact, new business opportunity, applicability to development needs of the EDPers, impact on managing for value, etc.). Projects are plotted on a process map to assess functional area coverage (e.g., manufacturing problem, business development issue, finance process improvement, etc.). Business unit and regional coverage are also considered. The top 10–20 projects (depending on available EDP resources ready for new projects) are presented to the CFO, treasurer, and controller to validate that key business issues are being addressed. Once priority is set, business unit presidents are notified of selection and asked to have focal points on hand on project kickoff date. Projects not selected fall off the list and usually do not reappear during subsequent solicitations since working projects that have a sense of urgency and high-impact potential take first priority.

Matching EDPers and Forming Teams

As development needs are met and/or changed throughout the program, EDPers modify their personalized development plans to reflect status. Exhibit 7 is a sample development plan that shows how projects are meeting the development needs of the EDPer as well as other development opportunities of which the individual has taken advantage. Prior to each new cycle of projects being started, one-on-one discussions between the EDPer and the program office management are conducted to surface outstanding development needs (e.g., exposures needed to business units, regions, functions). A matrix is created that lists these outstanding needs. Projects are assessed as to what development exposures they offer and the matching begins. Every effort is made to get a diversity of region, function, and business unit background on each team. EDPers are not placed on teams with prior teammates whenever possible to enhance learning and networking opportunities. Every EDPer is afforded an opportunity to lead a project team—this is another key development experience, leading a cross-functional, cross-cultural, cross-business unit team of peers over whom you have no authority. To minimize changes and eliminate undue influence, the team-matching process (including the identification of the lead) is handled by program office management behind closed doors until teams are firmly set, EDPers are notified of their teammates, and new projects are announced in a facilitated project kickoff session. To date, the design team has been very successful in meeting outstanding development needs and EDPers are very excited and energized by their projects.

KEY ELEMENTS OF THE NEW DESIGN—
PROJECT MANAGEMENT PROCESS

Project Kickoff

An entire day is dedicated to a facilitated session where team "norming and storming" is accomplished, projects announced, scoping and consulting strategies discussed, and initial phone calls to project sponsors are planned and executed. Consulting skills and strategies are reinforced during this session in as much as EDPers are acting as internal business consultants during their projects. Travel schedules are developed for the next 3 months to assist the program office in space planning and setting up the first set of peer reviews. EDP project teams begin working on the project the very next day, setting up meetings and scoping the project.

Managing the Projects—A Disciplined Approach

Analysis of a process or problem typically requires the following:

- Study of the issues
- Data collection at various business units and regions
- Comparable data collection from benchmarking other companies
- Coordination with key executives
- Analysis of the gathered data
- Preparation and presentation of data findings and recommendations to appropriate company-wide process councils and other stakeholders
- Follow up on recommendations

Rather than spending time in this business case on this process, which is extensive, suffice it to say that all teams follow this basic project management flow (see Exhibit 8). It continues to be improved as a model that will accommodate the future vision of the internal audit function, which intends to change its support mix from predominantly traditional audits to more internal business consulting. An element of this process that is being improved significantly in 1999 is the follow-up process. Once recommendations are made, it is incumbent on internal audit to follow-up to see what has been implemented, especially where risk of not implementing is significant. It is anticipated that business unit senior management will be advised of significant risks in failure to execute recommendations, with potential notification to the board of directors, should the lack of action be deemed irresponsible. In an effort to provide the reader with a sense of projects, Exhibit 9 reflects a breakdown of a recent cycle of projects by region, business unit, and function. The projects provide an enormous diversity of exposures for the EDPers. Projects are closely linked to internal audit projects and information is shared across all regions. Often, internal auditors join EDP project teams to provide subject matter expertise. Project team coaches also are assigned from internal audit management to ensure alignment with process, business issue resolution, resource support, and increased executive exposures during the project. The increased involvement of permanent auditors and management has enhanced their own development and improved the sharing of best practices across the company.

EXIT MANAGEMENT

Networking

Throughout the 24-month program, every effort is made to shift participants' perspectives on the purpose and value of networking. In addition to including this skill in the career management curriculum, speakers are brought into the quarterly meetings to reinforce the principles. One such resource is Donna Fisher, author of *Power Networking* (1999). She has had a tremendous impact on the participants in reshaping their use of networking as a continuous opportunity to be a resource to others so that when you need to periodically engage your continually growing network as a resource for yourself, it will be there. Many people view networking as a one-way event—Whom can I network with who will do something for me? The design team is shifting the EDPers' attitudes to see themselves as resources to others, especially their fellow EDPers. The social skills associated with networking are critical and strongly emphasized. If an EDP participant is successful at building networks by being a resource to others, his or her exit strategy will be greatly enhanced. The leadership development program design team encourages them to build their networks early in the program and utilize the skills for life.

Succession Planning Exposures

Twice a year, The Boeing Company conducts succession planning. The EDP office takes advantage of this periodic process by creating detailed information regarding the current EDPers and sharing it widely with executive management. The EDP Web site contains this detailed information, including résumés and project description and results. The leadership development program team makes this information readily available for management to assess to meet their future needs. Management is encouraged to achieve diversity of function, geography, and business unit among their succession candidates, and the EDP pool is a great source for several different jobs.

Executive Support

For those EDPers who have successfully built an extensive network over the 24-month period (and before entry to the program), the executives in their network are very willing to guide them in targeting a job opportunity and facilitating a meeting with the organization. EDPers can engage their own network to provide support to another EDPer in gaining quick access to an executive who might have a future opportunity for a challenging assignment. Without exception, the program has not had to resort to top management *directing* placement of any individual graduating from the program. Undoubtedly, those EDPers who have taken advantage of the career management skills training, practiced the techniques, built an extensive network particularly among each other, and shown exceptional ability throughout their projects will be most successful in identifying their exit opportunities. The uncertainty in the exit process often affects the emotional stability of participants during the program. Their ability to deal with this uncertainty and turn to their network for ideas and support continues to be a competitive advantage.

EVALUATION—RESULTS TO DATE

Placement Results

The following reflects the career changes that have occurred for the program graduates:

- 65% have changed job function/discipline
- 44% have changed geographic locations
- 44% have changed business units
- 50% have been promoted

Exit Interview/Survey Results

Exit surveys and interviews reflect the overwhelming satisfaction of participants with all program elements:

- Development opportunities—"Outstanding," "Was able to immediately apply learnings."

- Project experiences—"I learned more about the company than I ever knew existed."

- Peer relationships and networking with each other—"Could be the best part of the program—The networks we developed will be used throughout the year."

- Met expectations—"Far exceeded my expectations—Never knew what was possible."

Customer Satisfaction (Project Sponsors/Stakeholders) Results

The third-party interview reports have been summarized each quarter and the results are very positive. Negative trends, minor to date, are surfaced and process improvements made to mitigate concerns. A few quotes are included below to illustrate the sense of satisfaction with project work:

- Communication—"The team did an excellent job of keeping us informed—They had a disciplined approach to status reporting and were able to engage all stakeholders."

- Collaboration—"Lots of teamwork displayed—A real can-do group— Very respectful of each other—The interaction was positive—Ideas were always flowing."

- Project recommendations (quality)—"Their recommendations were right on the mark—I was amazed how much was accomplished in so little time. We intend to implement all ideas."

- Making a difference—"The out-of-the-box perspectives took us to a new level—Our processes are already improved. Just having them in our organization got us thinking in different, more productive ways."

The Boeing Company is pleased with the results that this program has achieved. With only 4 years of experience, the program is well-positioned to face the new millennium, looking forward to the continuous challenge that leadership development brings. The company plans to share this program extensively among other companies, thereby perpetuating action learning, job rotation, career risk-taking, and positively influencing and reshaping future leadership development strategies.

Exhibit 1. Executive Competencies

Thinking Factor

Using Sound Judgment: Develops and applies broad knowledge and expertise when addressing complex issues; identifies interrelationships among issues and identifies the implications for other parts of the business; takes all critical information into account when making decisions; makes timely tough decisions.

Shaping Strategy: Understands the organization's strengths, weaknesses, opportunities, and threats, external developments and trends, customer and market needs, and competitor actions; develops strategies to achieve sustained competitive advantage; identifies critical goals and success factors; pursues initiatives based on fit with broader strategies.

Demonstrating Vision: Has a clear vision for the industry, business, or operation; maintains a long-term, big-picture view; foresees obstacles and opportunities; generates breakthrough ideas.

Applying Financial Acumen: Understands the meaning and implications of key financial indicators; manages overall financial performance (current results and long-term value); uses financial analysis to evaluate strategic and opportunities; balances risks versus rewards in investment decisions.

Management Factor

Aligning the Organization: Translates broad strategies into specific objectives and action plans; creates or modifies structures, processes, and systems to support strategic priorities, integrates efforts across functions and locations; obtains and allocates needed resources; assigns clear authority and accountability.

Driving Execution: Monitors performance against key operational and financial results; provides resources and support to ensure that key strategies and results are achieved; improves the operating effectiveness of the business; holds people accountable for achieving their goals; tackles problems before they become crises and resolves them efficiently and effectively.

Leadership Factor

Leading Courageously: Maintains and projects confidence in all situations; projects credibility and poise even when challenged; shows a willingness to take risks and act independently; takes personal responsibility for actions.

Inspiring and Empowering Others: Creates a climate that fosters personal investment and excellence; nurtures commitment to a common vision and shared values; gives people opportunity and latitude to grow and achieve; sets high expectations and conveys confidence in others' ability to achieve them.

Influencing and Negotiating: Promotes ideas and proposals persuasively; provides compelling rationales for arguments; builds a broad base of support among key stakeholders; negotiates win/win solutions.

(Continued)

Exhibit 1. Executive Competencies (*Continued*)

Attracting and Developing Talent: Identifies the competencies needed in the workforce; attracts high-caliber people; accurately appraises the strengths and weaknesses of others; provides constructive feedback and coaching; develops successors and talent pools; addresses career development and work environment issues that impact retention.

Fostering Teamwork and Collaboration: Promotes collaboration and teamwork across organizational boundaries; breaks down polarized perspectives and builds consensus; collaborates as a team player.

Interpersonal and Communication Factor

Building Relationships: Cultivates an active network of relationships inside and outside the organization; relates to others in an approachable manner; responds to the needs and concerns of others; accepts and accommodates a variety of interpersonal styles.

Inspiring Trust: Establishes open, candid, trusting relationships; treats all individuals fairly and with respect; maintains high standards of integrity; places organizational success over personal gain.

Fostering Open and Effective Communication: Promotes a free flow of information and communication throughout the organization (upward, downward, and across); listens actively; encourages open expression of ideas and opinions; expresses ideas clearly, concisely, and with impact.

Motivation and Self-Management Factors

Driving Stakeholder Success: Sets and pursues aggressive goals; drives for results; demonstrates a strong commitment to organizational success; works to do what is best for all stakeholders (e.g., customers, shareholders, employees); pursues both short- and long-term success.

Adapting: Maintains composure in stressful situations; works constructively and resourcefully under pressure; demonstrates flexibility and resilience; seeks and accepts constructive criticism.

Breadth and Depth Factor

Working Cross-Functionally: Works effectively across internal organizational and functional boundaries to provide integrated solutions; utilizes the full capabilities of each management function; demonstrates the ability to access resources and capabilities across the system; leverages cross-disciplinary knowledge; understands general management principles necessary to improve the profitability of the business.

Thinking Globally: Keeps abreast of important international trends that impact the business or organization; understands the position of the organization within a global context; understands the pro's and con's of doing business in various global regions; demonstrates sensitivity to cultural norms, local customs, and taboos; pursues opportunities for global expansion; ensures that initiatives do not focus only on home market.

Focusing on Quality and Continuous Improvement: Creates an environment that supports innovation, continuous improvement, and risk-taking; leads efforts to improve or streamline processes; investigates and adopts best practices.

Exhibit 2. EDP Nominating Sponsors' Proposal

Nominee:_____ Org No _____ SSN: _____ Date:_____

Group: □ BCA   □ CO   □ A&M   □ S&C   □ SSG   Business Unit/Org Title_____

Nominees to the Executive Development Program are high performing managers with near term E-series and long-term vice president potential. The program targets individuals with relatively deep and narrowly based backgrounds who are in need of a broader set of developmental experiences. These experiences are primarily obtained during a full-time assignment of 18 to 24 months to the program, working in cross-functional/business unit teams on high-leverage, enterprise-wide projects. To this end, the following are proposed:

I. We have targeted the following **Development Needs** to be met while _____ is on EDP assignment:

Functional exposures needed:	Leadership/Managerial Competencies to be developed:

Boeing Organizational exposures needed:	Other development needs:

II. We will provide a workspace for _____ at our locations where he/she will work "virtually" with his/her team approximately one (l) week a month. During these one-week residencies (and other times as appropriate), we will continue to involve _____ in our organization, providing higher level exposures to business issues and concerns as appropriate to his/her accelerated career development.

(Continued)

Exhibit 2. EDP Nominating Sponsors' Proposal (*Continued*)

III. We expect that _____ may be exposed to new career options as he/she experiences the Executive Development Program. It is anticipated that he/she may exercise one of these options and explore a significant change in job upon completing the EDP. We agree to assist him/her in exploring these options and will arrange the appropriate executive exposures in support of _____'s career development. However, *at a minimum*, we will assure _____ that he/she will be returned to our organization in an equivalent position upon completing the EDP, to minimize any risk associated with this development assignment.

IV. In collaboration with the Executive Development Program Office, we will review _____'s involvement, development, and performance at 6-month intervals to assure continued growth and appropriateness of program assignment.

We are committed to _____'s development and career growth through participation in the Executive Development Program, and we actively support his/her involvement in it. We have discussed the above with _____ and he/she concurs.

_____   _____

Nominating VP Sponsor   Nominating Senior Executive Co-Sponsor

Exhibit 3. Career Management Curriculum

Identifying your Career Assets (4 hrs) (Before LDI)

- Current work trends and implications on career
- Identifying your career assets, priority values, and motivators
- Defining your ideal work preferences

Portfolio Development & Development Needs Planning (4 hrs)

- Determining your work competencies, skills, and knowledge
- Proactively developing a career portfolio

Communication/Networking (4 hrs) (fifth month)

- Identifying your communication style and adapting to others' styles
- Building relationships and exploring the landscape
- Ins and outs of networking

Executive Behavior (4 hrs)

- Polishing appropriate behavior
- Identifying and improving inappropriate behavior

Creating a Power Resume (8 hrs)
Interview Skills Building (4 hrs)

- Types of interviews and how to prepare
- How to field the tough questions
- Putting your best foot forward

Exhibit 4. Sponsor/Stakeholder Project Assessment

Introduction

A key element of the Boeing Executive Development Program Critical is the project work done by program participants. These projects, which are sponsored by executive leadership, focus on issues critical to the success of the organization. EDP projects serve many purposes including addressing issues critical to the future of The Boeing Company, identifying and sharing best practices, and providing an opportunity for EDP team members to receive valuable developmental experiences and opportunities for action learning in the context of real and meaningful work.

In order to assess the extent that these projects produce these desired outcomes for both sponsors and participants several feedback mechanisms are in place. These include:

- A *Sponsor/Stakeholder Survey* to determine the degree to which the project team accomplished the results agreed to in the team's charter and to evaluate the effectiveness of the processes used to execute that charter
- A *Team Effectiveness Survey*, which is a self-assessment by team members to gauge how well the team itself executed its charter during the life of the project
- A *Team Member Survey* that provides each participant with feedback regarding how well he/she executed the roles and responsibilities of a team member or team leader

This report provides a summary and analysis of the data from the Sponsor/Stakeholder Survey. The report is provided to the program's leadership team. The results of the both the EDP Team and EDP Team Member Surveys are provided directly to the members of each EDP team in a facilitated process.

Data Collection and Analysis

Data for this assessment was collected through individual interviews with sponsors and advisors of the Company Health Metrics Project using a structured questionnaire. Interviews were conducted between August 6 and September 3, 1998. A total of 5 people were interviewed. An additional sponsor has expressed a desire to participate in an interview; however, that interview has not as of yet been completed. These interviews, while brief, provided a wide range of feedback for both the subject EDP Team and for EDP Management.

Report Structure

The findings of the assessments are reported in the following sections of this report:

- Project Management
- Results Delivered
- Making a Difference
- Feedback for Program Management

The first three sections focus on the project and project team related data. The final section is feedback applicable to all project teams and the EDP in general.

Exhibit 5. Frequently Asked Questions

1. What are the objectives of the Executive Development Program (EDP)?

The program is intended to expose high-performing managers to a broader set of developmental experiences and provide opportunity to learn about various aspects of company operations. Through participation on cross-functional teams, the participants are expected to accelerate change in business processes and share best practices throughout The Boeing Company.

2. Why was my partner selected?

Twice each year, senior executives nominate high-potential managers for this program. Your spouse/partner has shown an interest in accelerating career growth and has exhibited leadership potential.

3. What are the primary program elements?

- *Cross-functional project teams*
- *Meet and/or work with company executives*
- *24-month career management skills curriculum*
- *2-week external executive development program*
- *Formal mentors*
- *Opportunity to work in various facilities, organizations, and disciplines*

4. What are the risks associated with this assignment?

The program is designed to minimize risk. Once a nominee commits to this program, nominating sponsors will prepare a proposal that ensures: 1) Nominee specific development needs will be addressed during the program; 2) A connection to point of origination (home work site) will be maintained; 3) Upon program completion, at minimum, participants will be returned to the originating organization in an equivalent assignment. It is anticipated that a significant change in job assignment will be made upon completion of the program (see question #17).

5. How long is this program?

The EDP assignment will last 18–24 months. Participants will be participating in at least three team projects and one special assignment. Often, due to the exposure received from working on projects and assignments, EDP employees are frequently pulled out of the program to fill key positions within the company. This may happen at any time during the program, but generally during the last six months.

6. What will the work schedule be?

Teams will collaborate on weekly and monthly work schedules according to the following guidelines: 1) Work weeks will be Monday through Thursday for 10 hours each day; 2) Employees will travel home each weekend (for a Friday, Saturday, and Sunday three-day weekend); 3) Each month, participants will spend 1 week in Seattle, 2 weeks at the project required location, and 1 week at the home work site. Required travel will be accomplished on off-hours for weekend visits home and return to work site.

(Continued)

Exhibit 5. Frequently Asked Questions (*Continued*)

7. Why one week in Seattle?

The week in Seattle will further program objectives by facilitating camaraderie among all EDP participants. Portions of the 24-month training curriculum will be delivered during this monthly 1-week stay. The EDP administrative staff is located in Seattle; therefore, this guarantees once-a-month, face-to-face contact with the program office and other EDP participants. Also, the majority of company senior executives are located in the Puget Sound area and executive exposures and mentor relationships will be enhanced.

8. How much travel is involved?

For a participant not living in Puget Sound, whose project is not at their home work site, the most *that person would be away from home would be 12 work days per month. (This is the "worst case scenario.") Some variations to the normal monthly travel will occur as teams conduct benchmarking, take advantage of developmental opportunities, etc. Travel requirements are project-driven and vary based on where traveling to and from, and will change as each person begins new projects or assignments during the 18–24 months. As individuals are assigned to new projects, efforts will be made to equalize and/or minimize the travel based on development needs and past project requirements.*

9. Is there any guidance or advice for those of us with children on how to adapt to a single-parent role during the week while my partner is away?

You will be invited to an "on-boarding" seminar, presented by professional consultants, to discuss these and other related issues (see attached agenda "Boeing EDP Partner Program").

10. Will my partner still get vacation time off?

As in any assignment, vacation will be earned, scheduled, and used according to standard heritage company policy. EDP participants will coordinate specific vacation days with his or her current team members as well as the EDP office.

11. What do I do in case of emergencies?

Each participant will have a beeper or cell phone. In addition, office administrators will be available to receive your call, then locate your spouse. While on travel, employees will be able to phone home as required. Each participant will also have a laptop computer to be used as a virtual tool.

12. Will we be able to visit some of the Boeing locations where my partner is doing work?

Family visits, which includes spouse/significant other and children, will be provided every 6 months. The purpose of these visits is to familiarize you with work locations that your partner might select for permanent assignment upon graduation. Boeing will pay the cost of transportation, meals, and lodging for the 3-day weekend. If the participant is assigned to a Puget Sound-based project and does not live in Puget Sound, he or she will be provided with an apartment that the family will be able to use for the family visit.

Exhibit 5. Frequently Asked Questions (*Continued*)

13. Will this assignment cause financial hardship for us?

Consistent with Boeing policies, reasonable expenses associated with this assignment (e.g., travel, lodging, weekends home, family visits) will be paid for by the company. For income tax purposes, some of these expenses qualify as income (e.g., weekend visits home and family visits). Boeing will provide tax assistance to partially offset this increase in income.

14. Will there be a regular opportunity to meet and talk with other EDP spouses and significant others?

There will be a formal opportunity during the January "on-boarding" seminar (see question #9). Informal opportunities may occur as each EDP team works on their projects. Additionally, during family visits, opportunities for informal gatherings may also occur.

15. What can I expect to go through emotionally during my partner's assignment?

As with any change, there is uncertainty. To assist partners, this will be discussed at length during the "on-boarding" seminar in January that addresses this issue and provides ways to develop a strategy to deal with this type of change.

16. What happens to my partner's benefits and salary?

Employees will retain all current heritage benefit plans while on this program unless the heritage programs are changed by the company. Participants will remain on heritage payroll and accounting systems until those systems merge. Salary progression will occur during the program at the same time as all other salaried employees receive their raises. All participants will receive the same percentage increase based on a common EDP pool. Annual salary pools are created based on company business performance and equity factors.

17. What type of permanent assignment will my spouse get at the end of the program?

Participants will be exposed to many new career options as they experience the EDP. It is anticipated that they will exercise one of these options and explore a significant change in jobs upon completing the program. This may involve a change in functional discipline, business unit, leadership role, work location, etc.

18. If my spouse chooses to exercise an option at another work location, what relocation benefits will the company provide?

Boeing has a standard set of relocation benefits. Detailed information is available on the Boeing Intranet.

Exhibit 6. EDP Project Nomination Request Form

(maximum 2 pages)

Project title:
Description of business issue/condition:

Business Units/Programs and or processes/functions potentially impacted by this project:
(check appropriate box)

☐ **All Boeing**	☐ **All BCAG**	☐ **All A&M**	☐ **All Phantom Works**
☐ *(indicate specific program/function)*	☐ Single Aisle	☐ *(indicate specific program/function)*	☐ *(indicate specific program/function)*
☐ *(indicate specific program/function)*	☐ Twin Aisle	☐ *(indicate specific program/function)*	☐ *(indicate specific program/function)*
	☐ Customer Services		
☐ **All Boeing**		☐ **All SSG**	☐ **Company Offices**
☐ *(indicate specific program/function)*	☐ *(**indicate specific**) program/function)*	☐ *(indicate specific program/function)*	☐ *(program/function)*
☐ *(indicate specific program/function)*	☐ *(**indicate specific**) program/function)*	☐ *(indicate specific program/function)*	☐ *(program/function)*

Affected Process Councils: *(check appropriate box)*

☐ Program Management	☐ Communications	☐ Sales & Business Development
☐ Finance	☐ Engineering	☐ Support
☐ People	☐ Operations	☐ Shared Services
☐ Legal Contracts/Ethics	☐ Quality	☐ WDC
☐ Administration	☐ Supplier Management	☐ Phantom Works

Proposed project will provide team with exposure to the following Boeing work locations and/or regions:

☐ Puget Sound   ☐ So. California   ☐ Wichita   ☐ St. Louis   ☐ *Other*

Anticipated duration of project (range is 3–5 months only): _____ **months**
Anticipated size of team (range is 1–5 team members only): _____ **team members**

Expected Deliverables:

Benefit to Company:

Benefit to Participants on Team:

Points of Contact: *(names and phone numbers of individuals who can help provide immediate insight into business issue as to scope of project)*

Name   Phone Number

During this project assignment, we will support the development of EDP team members by providing significant **exposures to company executives** and their issues. In addition, we will provide a **workspace** (both individual and collaborative), **subject matter experts,** and some

Exhibit 6. EDP Project Nomination Request Form (*Continued*)

administrative support for teams as they work in project locations. We will become familiar with the capabilities of team members and **assist them in their career development**. We understand that while the team will work primarily on our project, they plan to follow the following monthly schedule guidelines to take advantage of various program attributes:

- 1 week/mo in Seattle company offices
- 2 weeks/mo in project required locations
- 1 week/mo at home work site working virtually with team
- Most teams will be working a 4/10-hour work week, traveling on off hours.

The assigned EDP team will coordinate these logistics and a milestone schedule early in their project work with us.

_____	_____
Nominating Project Sponsor	Senior Executive Nominating Sponsor/ Company-wide Process Council Member

Exhibit 7. Personal Development Plan

Information Technology (Puget Sound)	SSG Wichita	BCAG, WD Engineering (Product Definition)	BCAG, WD Operations			Projects					Classes				Self-Study				Program / Project				
Leadership and Managerial Competencies						Documentation Architecture	Integrated Logistics Strategy	Financial Strategy Activities	TBD	TBD	Competitive Advantage Through Operations (Harvard)	Worldwide Lessons in Leadership (8 hr)	TBD	TBD	APICS - CPIM	Birds of Prey (book)	TBD	TBD	Project Management	Leadership Development Intensive (LDI)	DBM (Composite)	TBD	TBD
H	H	H	H		Drive for Results / Action Orientated	L				L									H	M			
H	M	M	M		Planning / Assigning / Managing Work	L	M						L						H				
M	M	M	M		Managing Vision & Purpose	M	M	M			H			L				L	H		L	
M	M	M	M		Priority Setting	L					L							H	M			
H	H	H	H		Business Acumen	L	H	H			L			L	L						L	
H	H	H	H		Leading Courageously													M				
H	M	M	L		Thinking Globally					M	L		H									
Skills and Knowledge																							
M	M	H	H		Lean Concepts					M			L									
M	M	H	H		Value Chain Management		M			M			L									
H	H	L	H		Contract Management					L			M									
M	M	M	M		APICS - CPIM								H									
H	M	L	L		Microsoft Certified Professional (MCP)																	

Information Technology (Puget Sound)	SSG Wichita	BCAG, WD Engineering (Product Definition)	BCAG, WD Operations		Development Needs																	
					Job Objectives — Development & Exposure — Opportunities — Experience & Exposure Needs																	
Functional																						
M	M	H	H		Production and Operations	M	L			L			H									
M	M	M	L		Program Management													M			
H	H	H	M		Product Development	M	L						L									
H	H	L	L		Information Systems / Services	M	L						L									
Organizational																						
M	H	H	H		BCAG Wichita	L	L	L					H									
M	M	M	H		BCAG Operations	L	L						H									
M	M	H	M		BCAG Engineering	L	L						L									
H	M	L			BCAG Information Systems		L						M									
M	H				SSG Outside of Wichita	M	L						L									

Exhibit 8. EDP Project Management Process

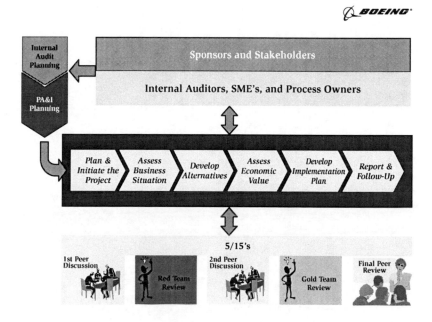

Exhibit 9. Breakdown of Recent Projects

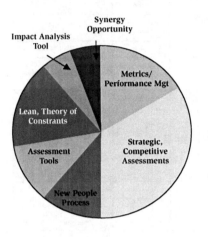

Subject Matter

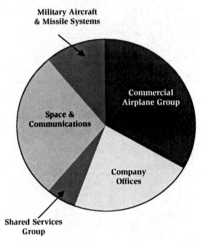

Business Units

ABOUT THE CONTRIBUTOR

Suzanne Browning (suzanne.s.browning@boeing.com) is the director of process analysis and improvement at the Boeing Company. Browning manages two enterprise-wide leadership development programs. She and her staff are responsible for handling all elements of the program office ranging from project management, leadership development opportunities, targeted selection of participants and projects, and general administration of program guidelines. Browning's background is uniquely matched to this current assignment. With more than 30 years experience in management positions within large organizations, she has become a progressive business-oriented executive in both human resource management and line management functions. Earlier in her career, Browning's, experience included management of traditional human resources functions, while providing leadership and support to staff and management engaged in improving the organization's culture and business results through major initiatives. Later in her career, she held assignments such as a line executive managing information systems and services in Southern California. In this position, she displayed her strong ability to directly apply techniques of team-building, participation, performance management, quality improvement measurement, work centers, production control processes, cycle time analysis, employee/ management relations, and employee/management development.

She served as adjunct professor at the UCLA School of Business—HRM (Strategic Planning). She has held several leadership positions on the Boeing Management Association and is a member of the Human Resource Planning Society, ASTD, and AMA. Browning is also an alumni of the Brookings Institute and has consulted and lectured at various institutions and conferences. Suzanne received her bachelor's degree in English/Business from California State University Long Beach in 1977 and her MBA from Claremont Graduate School, Peter Drucker Center, in 1990.

CHAPTER NINE

Johnson & Johnson

A global leadership development program that leverages 360-degree feedback, action learning, and one-on-one coaching to drive change in the business and develop a global leadership pipeline

> *Progress is impossible without change; and those who cannot change*
> *their minds cannot change anything.*
>
> George Bernard Shaw

INTRODUCTION

This article illustrates a highly integrated organizational intervention developed to grow leadership talent at multiple levels within Johnson & Johnson and leverage the cross-functional global talent of its leaders in solving complex business issues. The outcomes are that leaders at Johnson & Johnson not only learn how to individually become more effective leaders, they learn how to own and lead strategic change for their organizations. The results speak for themselves and the learning surrounding the critical levers for success in this highly decentralized, global organization is insightful. In this case, leadership development is at center stage with a keen focus on accelerating business strategy and results through action learning.

An essential part of any intervention is an evaluation of its outcomes. Assessments that tell you the outcomes only after things have already gone wrong, or after a program has run its course, are limited in their utility. Executive Conference III was assessed while in implementation and prior to launching the next generation of its sort, providing valuable information needed by program users to understand the conference's positive outcomes and problems, demonstrate the value of its methodology and techniques, and identify areas for possible influence or improvement. This case study offers an overview of how Johnson & Johnson demonstrated the value of this leadership development experience and identifies the critical success factors for Johnson & Johnson in delivering a high-value leadership development intervention.

Company Background

Johnson & Johnson is the world's largest and most comprehensive manufacturer of healthcare products. With 94,000 employees operating in 180 companies and selling products in 175 countries, its 1998 sales reached $23.7 billion. These figures were allocated across three business segments (see Figure 1).

The *Consumer Franchise* focuses on the following segments: skin and hair care, sanitary protection, wound care, oral care, baby care, and over-the-counter pharmaceuticals. Popular brand names include Tylenol, Neutrogena, Band-Aid, o.b. Tampons, Stay Free, Mylanta, Pepcid AC Acid Controller, and Motrin.

The *Pharmaceutical Franchise* is responsible for the development and sale of prescription pharmaceuticals. Within this franchise, there is a diverse array of products in the following categories: family planning; psychiatry, mental illness, and diseases of the nervous system; gastroenterology; oncology; immunotherapy; cardiovascular disease; dermatology; pain management; allergy; antifungals;

1998 Sales By Business Segment

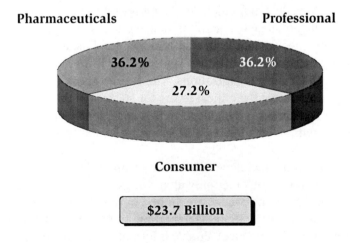

Figure 1 Net Trade Sales (By Segment)

antihistamines, anti-infectives, antiparasitic drugs; and biotechnology-derived products.

The *Professional Franchise* develops and markets products, which are commonly found in hospitals, clinics, and physicians' offices. Medical professionals use them for surgery, patient care, wound closure, diagnosis, blood testing, and related medical purposes.

The glue, which holds this highly decentralized organization together, is the Credo (see Exhibit 1), a statement of values created by Robert Wood Johnson in 1943. The Credo describes the organizational responsibility to the key stakeholders, who include the customer, the employees, the community, and the stockholder. It was Johnson's belief that by putting the customer first and focusing on the employees and the communities in which we operate that the interests of the stockholder would be well taken care of. When he wrote and then institutionalized the Credo within Johnson & Johnson, Robert Wood Johnson never suggested that it guaranteed perfection. But its principles have become a constant goal as well as a source of inspiration for all who are part of the Johnson & Johnson Family of Companies.

Building the Business Case for Change

When you examine the financial results of Johnson & Johnson, whether it is over a period of 5, 10, or 20 years, the term that best describes its achievements is *consistent performance*. This performance is reflected in the fact that there have been:

- 66 consecutive years of sales increases
- 55 continuous years of dividend payments
- 36 consecutive years of dividend increases

While in any single year there may be fluctuations, Johnson & Johnson has historically grown at double-digit rates in terms of sales and profits. Looking forward, the corporation is well-positioned for future growth.

In September of 1996, in a report to the Johnson & Johnson management team, Chairman of the Board Ralph Larsen stated, "As you look at our growth projections over time, we're going to need more and more leaders. Leadership is the biggest single constraint to growth at Johnson & Johnson, and it is the most critical business issue we face." While the current leadership supply had effectively met the needs of today's business, strengthening the Johnson & Johnson leadership pipeline, in order to realize future growth, became a key business imperative. Meeting this challenge has become the joint responsibility of line management, who are the owners, and the Human Resources community, who are charged with deploying systems and processes that attract, develop, and retain a high-performing talent pool.

ASSESSMENT

Standards of Leadership—Foundations for Growth

With 180 operating companies and a highly decentralized mode of operation, a critical step in strengthening the leadership pipeline was to first define the organization's expectations regarding leadership and then gain a shared understanding across the global organization with its cultural and regional differences.

The Standards of Leadership reflect what is and will be expected of those who aspire to leadership positions within Johnson & Johnson (see Exhibit 2). At the outset of its development there was a clear understanding that the leadership behaviors, which have driven the organization to its current level of excellence, may not be sufficient to achieve the success in the future. A second tenet or belief was that developing a set of competencies or behaviors without providing a series of guiding principles would significantly hamper the ability to gain alignment across the global organization. The competencies reflect the "content" aspects of leadership while the guiding principles mirror the "contextual."

A task force of line leaders developed the Johnson & Johnson Standards of Leadership. In addressing its challenge, the working group focused on six key objectives:

1. *Build on Johnson & Johnson core strengths*—Central to the success of Johnson & Johnson has been its value system. It would be essential that the leadership model be aligned with the beliefs contained within the Credo.

2. *Make it globally applicable*—The company's business and markets are global. Sales outside of the United States account for 47% of the Johnson & Johnson business. Many of its businesses are structured as global franchises. If the leadership model was to have impact, it had to reflect concepts that could be embraced by the worldwide organization.

3. *Make it situationally adaptable*—Effective leadership is a dynamic process that adapts to the critical needs of the moment. Likewise the leadership model is a framework for operating and not a generic prescription for success.

4. *Make it simple but not simplistic*—A key challenge was to develop a leadership model that captured sufficient detail to achieve shared understanding while at the same time not present itself as an oppressive maze of definitions or descriptions.

5. *Focus on positively changing the behavior of current and future leaders*—The charter of the task force was to develop a projective model of leadership, which would define behaviors that would drive success in the marketplaces of today and tomorrow.

6. *Make it central to Johnson & Johnson leadership development process—* Once defined, the Standards of Leadership would become a base from which individuals and organizations could assess their current levels of effectiveness and then put in place action plans for improvement.

The task force utilized the following process (Figure 2) in developing the Leadership model for Johnson & Johnson.

The Johnson & Johnson Standards of Leadership have seven primary components. The graphic representations reflect a dynamic, interactive model and not a collection of stand-alone independent variables.

Building on the core strength of Johnson & Johnson, at the center of the leadership model are Credo values. This reflects the organizational belief that "the Credo is the heart of Johnson & Johnson and without a heart, you can't exist." Flowing from adherence to Credo values are the business results and these results are realized through a focus on the five major standards:

- Customer/Marketplace Focus

- Innovation

- Interdependent Partnering

- Mastering Complexity

- Organizational and People Development

Each of these major segments is then defined in terms of core competencies and defining behaviors

Leadership Development Principles

In addition to defining the competencies associated with effective leadership, the task force also described the seven critical success factors for leadership development within Johnson & Johnson.

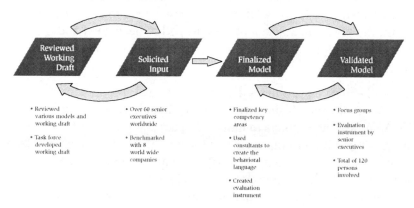

Figure 2 Assessment and Development Process

1. *Leadership Development Is a Key Business Strategy*—Leadership development needed to move from an issue of "importance" to one of criticality. The business units had to address this issue with resolve and in the same manner as if they were developing strategies to launch a new product or gain market share of an existing brand.

2. *Leadership Excellence Is a Definable Set of Standards*—For development to take place there needs to be clear understanding of what is required for success. These standards then serve as the guideposts for development.

3. *People Are Responsible For Their Own Development*—They must accept the responsibility for seeking feedback and committing to ongoing improvement. This does not suggest that individuals are in this alone.

4. *J&J's Executives Are Accountable for Developing Leaders*—The business strategies of an organization are owned by its leaders. Likewise, the plans for developing a leadership pipeline and the resulting outcomes are a key measure of management effectiveness.

5. *Leaders Are Developed Primarily on the Job*—The complexities and variability of real-world challenges cannot be truly experienced in a classroom. While the classroom can provide a base of understanding, growth is a result of experience and assimilation.

6. *People Are an Asset of the Corporation*—Since people are developed primarily on the job, one unit can not provide the totality of experiences that individuals may need. The corporation as a whole is capable of providing the wide diversity of developmental opportunities.

7. *Human Resources Support Is Vital to the Success of Leadership Development*—With the goal being success on an organization-wide basis, the people management systems had to be aligned and integrated with the business goals in order to achieve maximum leverage.

With the leadership competencies defined and critical success factors outlined, the next major challenge was moving the leadership model from concept to practice. An established vehicle to initiate this direction was the Executive Conference, which had been in place for five years. In the past, senior-level leaders would come to the corporate headquarters to participate in a week-long exercise focusing on strategic corporate issues. While this was an effective process for exposing individuals to the strategic challenges of the enterprise, what was needed was a framework that could focus on change at a personal and organizational level.

DESIGNING THE INTERVENTION

Leadership Development Through Action Learning

Companies are finding that the best learning occurs in problem-solving situations rather than the more traditional classroom teaching. Executive Conference III (Exhibit 3) is an action learning leadership experience whose targeted population is the senior management team of Johnson & Johnson. The action learning methodology for the Executive Conference III focuses on learning while working on real business issues. As the name "action learning" implies, participants expect to achieve tangible progress on a business issue as well as to advance their learning on the three Executive Conference III.

During the past three years there have been 26 conferences conducted in the four regions of the world. The objective of this process is to have participants experience leadership on three levels:

1. *Leadership on a Personal Level*

   a. Develop a personal improvement plan vis-à-vis gaps against the leadership model (360-degree/multirater feedback)
   b. Follow-up meetings with boss and others
   c. Follow-up a year later with second 360-degree survey focused on targeted areas
   d. Assimilate individual leadership development feedback while working on a multi-disciplinary team comprising individuals from dispersed geographies

2. *Leadership Development on an Organizational Basis*

   a. Both leading "my management team" and leading across organizational boundaries
   b. Practice personal leadership in a business context
   c. Develop a team action plan that addresses a business issue while applying the leadership model
   d. Achieve a measurable result within 90 days

3. *Leadership Development Through Credo Values and Culture*

   a. Led by top executives
   b. Reinforces Credo values
   c. Provides critical decision-making "guideposts"
   d. Supports today's new realities of doing business across boundaries

The Business Change Process

Executive Conference III employs action learning, a methodology that focuses on learning while working on real business issues. Action learning takes place as each team addresses an important business issue selected by the conference sponsor. Typically, the team is not a natural or intact work team, but one chosen expressly to work across organizational and geographic boundaries. Each team confronts a different, strategic business issue and is tasked with presenting a solution to address the challenge at the end of the team workshop experience. The sponsor, in addition to selecting the ECIII participants, must make several key decisions related to the teams. Those decisions include:

- What business issues will the teams address?
- Who will be the team leader?
- Who to select as the other members of the team?

The sponsor sets an overall theme for the conference; for example, "Achieving Profitable Growth." Additionally, he or she establishes the tone of the conference through messages conveyed in various forms before, during, and following the week in which the participants are together as a group.

The Executive Conference process is not a singular event but rather a process, which has four distinct phases (Figure 3).

1. *Pre-session*

   - Identify the critical business issue to be addressed
   - Identify participants
   - Form business project teams
   - Initiate the 360-degree survey process
   - Perform initial research of best practices surrounding each business issue

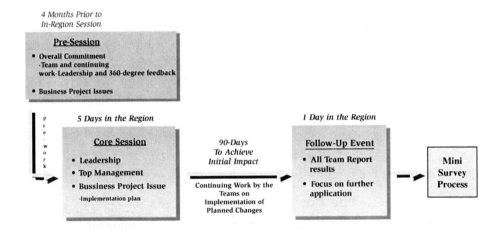

Figure 3 Executive Conference III Overall Flow

2. *Core Session—5 day in region conference* (4 months from Pre-Session)
   - Standards of Leadership & Personal Leadership Development
   - Credo values
   - Creating substantial business change
3. *Follow-up Event* (3 months following the core session)
   - Business project teams provide feedback on initial impact of their recommendations
4. *Mini-Survey Process* (9–12 months from core session)
   - Participants survey and receive feedback on identified developmental areas

Leadership Development on an Individual Level

Within Executive Conference III, the 360-degree feedback process has been the primary vehicle utilized in achieving the goal of leadership development on a personal basis. Early on it was realized that to launch a 360-degree process as a stand-alone tool would doom it to the long list of organizational initiatives that fall short of their desired outcomes. In order to effectively position this critical developmental vehicle, the feedback process became a core component for not only the Executive Conference process, but also all enterprise-wide leadership programs.

Before the first Executive Conference was conducted, CEO Ralph Larsen, his direct reports, and their global management teams participated in the Standards of Leadership 360-degree feedback and action planning process. They received feedback and coaching on an individual basis and then as a management team. Improvement plans were developed by the management team and each individual. Participation of the management team created an effective sponsorship for the initiative and enrolled the senior management team as role models for the desired behaviors.

The 360-degree feedback process was anchored in the behaviors contained within the Standards of Leadership. Keilty, Goldsmith & Company constructed behavioral inventories (see Exhibit 4) to provide individuals with feedback in the defined areas. The primary objective of the process was to create a positive measurable change in behavior that is consistent with the Standards of Leadership. Key operating principles built into this 360-degree feedback process were:

1. This was a tool for development and not performance or assessment.
2. Three cuts of data would be presented to the individual.
   - Self ratings
   - Direct reports feedback

- Feedback from peers and others (supervisor ratings not disclosed but included in this breakout)

3. Since development was the focus, the data belonged to the individual; no one in the organization had access to individual data.

The inventories were not for general distribution but only to those certified in the 360-degree process. This certification process was targeted for three primary populations:

- Human resources managers supporting the individual operating companies
- Learning Services, the Internal J&J Organizational Effectiveness consulting team
- External consultants supporting operating units in specific leadership change efforts

The 360-degree certification process was designed to assure that there was a clear working knowledge of the critical elements for a successful deployment, which included:

Organizational Readiness/Orientation

- Organizational commitment to the development process
- Current levels of trust and openness
- Effectiveness and value of the current processes for providing feedback
- Risk and Benefit analysis of deploying another process
- Definition of how the process will be utilized

Implementation Fundamentals

- 360-degree administration process
- Data interpretation and giving feedback
- Coaching and the follow-up process
- Working with intact team
- Working with functional groups

The two-day certification process was conducted in North America, Europe, Asia Pacific, and Latin America. From the corporate perspective, the key issue was not controlling the process but rather providing guidance to ensure integrity and to enhance the likelihood of successful implementation.

IMPLEMENTATION

Moving from Awareness to Action

The 360-degree process, utilized within the Executive Conference process, is segmented into four major phases (see Exhibit 5):

Pre-conference

- Instruments are distributed, returned for processing via an outside organization and reports generated

Conference

- Feedback reports distributed
- Workshop on understanding the data
  Identification of themes or patterns
  Identification of gaps
  Understanding strengths as building blocks of change

Post-Conference (30 days)

- Phone coaching to review potential themes and action plans for change

Post-Conference (180 days to 1 year)

- Mini-survey to assess the degree of change

Within the executive survey there are 74 itemized feedback questions, along with open-ended questions for written commentary. When a participant receives their feedback report, the amount of information is initially overwhelming. A clear goal of the process is to help participants navigate through the statistical sea of data and set a clear course for change and improvement. In order to accomplish this, the first segment of Executive Conferences focuses on supporting participants in understanding the data, identifying themes, and developing an action plan for improvement. The action plan for long-term meaningful behavioral change through encouraging feedback (Exhibit 6) was developed and presented to the executives.

This eight-step process entails the following steps:

1. *Ask*—This simply entails gathering input from individuals in order to answer the question, "How am I doing?" This sends a message that you value their opinions and that you would consider making changes based on their input.

2. *Listen*—Listening means that you accepting their opinion as their perception. Your objective is to understand and not to take an evaluative or defensive position. Listening reinforces continued dialogue, and through continued dialogue understanding can be achieved.

3. *Think*—This is a process that requires the individuals to put their brains in gear before their mouths. By doing this, you think about the input before reacting, which helps filter out defensive reactions.

4. *Thank*—Giving feedback requires courage and by expressing your appreciation, you acknowledge their risk taking and keep the door open for future feedback.

5. *Respond*—Here you close the loop with the individual who provided input. You provide a concise summary of what you have learned from the feedback process, highlighting the positive learnings and plans for development.

6. *Involve*—In this phase, the participants solicit the involvement of those who provided feedback by asking for suggestions for improvement as well as a point of contact for ongoing support in the development process. This reinforces personal commitment as well as trust and partnership.

7. *Change*—Focus on the one or two identified behaviors and keep them a priority. Monitor your behavior periodically.

8. *Follow-up*—Check back with the co-workers you have involved in your development to solicit feedback on your progress and any additional recommendations. Follow-up is the single most important variable in impacting employees' perceptions.

This process provides the participant with a simple model for taking action. The steps for success are well within the current skill set of the participants. There is no new jargon to learn or complex communications skills to master. It focuses on talking to and involving others in the development plan.

ON-THE-JOB SUPPORT AND FOLLOW-THROUGH

Follow-up—The Critical Success Factor

As mentioned previously, the Executive Conference is as an action learning leadership development process. At the conclusion of the fifth day in-region core session, a significant degree of excitement has been generated regarding the business case proposed strategies. In addition, there is high commitment to the insights gained from the leadership feedback process and the personal action plans for improvement. Once the participants return to their operating units, they have to determine how best to balance the new directions and action plans with that which was already on their plate before the conference. In the process of prioritization, very often what falls to the bottom of the list are those issues, which are concerned with personal development. While many would say that improving the effectiveness of one's leadership is important, it seems to lack the sense of urgency required for holding a position of primary attention.

If the participant's level of personal commitment was measured at the end of the workshop, you'd see their buy-in reading off the scale. Continuing that measure over the next several months would reveal a curve with a sharp downward trend. The key to success is to provide supporting systems, which keeps the process alive while not transferring ownership for the change away from the individual.

The follow-up process has two major components, which include a series of correspondence (refer to Exhibit 7) from Keilty, Goldsmith, and the mini-survey process.

Initial Follow-up Letter

- 3 months following the close of the in-region core session
- Directs participants to engage survey participants in the development process and provide ongoing progress reports

Follow-up Letter #2

- 6 months from core session
- Focus = "a check-in"
- Asks participants to do a self-assessment of progress in "areas for improvement"
- Asks participants to continue to do progress check with direct reports and co-workers

Follow-up Letter #3

- 9 months from core session
- Asks participants to continue to do progress check with direct reports and co-workers
- Highlights the trend linking follow-up and the impact on degree of improvement
- Importance of teamwork and peer relationships for leaders of the future

Follow-up Letter #4

- 1 year from core session
- Final "check-in"
- Reflection on "areas for improvement"
- Invitation for ongoing support

The Mini-Survey Process

The objective of the mini-survey process is to determine if there has been any change in leadership effectiveness as a result of the survey, the feedback, and the coaching process. After a period of six months to a year, the participants solicit additional feedback from those who provided the initial input. The mini survey focuses on four areas:

- Whether or not the individual responded to the feedback
- The degree to which the individual followed up
- The degree of change in leadership effectiveness
- The degree of change in the "areas for improvement"

The survey measures effectiveness and improvement on a scale from −3 to +3

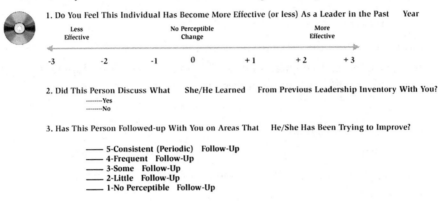

1. Do You Feel This Individual Has Become More Effective (or less) As a Leader in the Past   Year

| Less Effective | | No Perceptible Change | | More Effective | | |
| -3 | -2 | -1 | 0 | +1 | +2 | +3 |

2. Did This Person Discuss What   She/He Learned   From Previous Leadership Inventory With You?
    --------Yes
    --------No

3. Has This Person Followed-up With You on Areas That   He/She Has Been Trying to Improve?

    ——— 5-Consistent (Periodic)   Follow-Up
    ——— 4-Frequent   Follow-Up
    ——— 3-Some   Follow-Up
    ——— 2-Little   Follow-Up
    ——— 1-No Perceptible   Follow-Up

Figure 4 Mini-Survey

Sixty percent of the ECIII participants utilized the mini-survey process as a means for gaining additional insights and directions for improvement; 2,500 respondents provided valuable information not only to the individual participants but also to the organization in general. A review of their summary statistics revealed that the follow-up process was the most powerful variable contributing to the perceived increase in leadership effectiveness.

EVALUATION

Impacting Leadership Effectiveness—The Results

From the 2,500+ respondents who provided feedback on the mini-survey to the ECIII participants, clear trends became apparent in both the overall effectiveness ratings and the selected areas for improvement.

- Most of the graduates of Executive Conference III were becoming more effective as leaders (see Table 1A).
- 72% reported an increase in leadership effectiveness of the participants
- 5% see the participants as less effective
- The degree of increase in effectiveness correlates to follow-up (Table 1B).

Table 1A. Changes in Overall Leadership Effectiveness

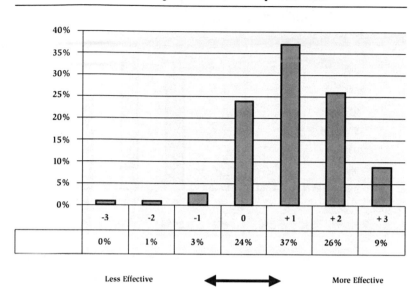

-3	-2	-1	0	+1	+2	+3
0%	1%	3%	24%	37%	26%	9%

Less Effective ⟷ More Effective

Table 1B. Increase in Effectiveness: Follow-up vs. No Follow-up

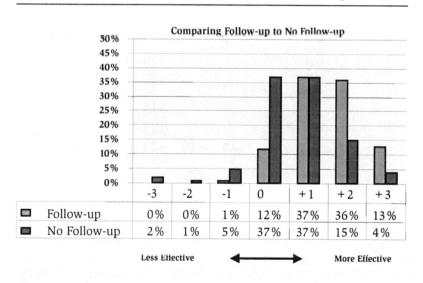

Comparing Follow-up to No Follow-up

	-3	-2	-1	0	+1	+2	+3
Follow-up	0%	0%	1%	12%	37%	36%	13%
No Follow-up	2%	1%	5%	37%	37%	15%	4%

Less Effective ⟷ More Effective

- When leaders were seen as following-up, 49% were rated at the +2 or +3 level of effectiveness.
- When leaders were not seen as follow-up, only 19% were rated +2 or +3.

The final set of summary data examined the degree of effectiveness regarding the self-selected areas for improvement (Tables 2A and 2B).

Table 2A. Changes in Self-Selected Areas for Improvement

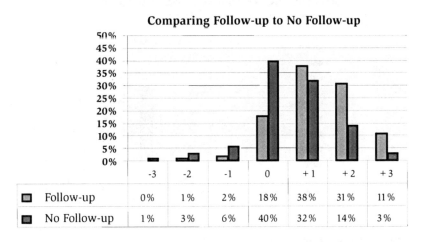

	-3	-2	-1	0	+1	+2	+3
	1%	2%	4%	29%	35%	23%	7%

Less Effective ←——————→ More Effective

Table 2B. Self-Selected Areas for Improvement: Follow-up vs. No Follow-up

Comparing Follow-up to No Follow-up

	-3	-2	-1	0	+1	+2	+3
Follow-up	0%	1%	2%	18%	38%	31%	11%
No Follow-up	1%	3%	6%	40%	32%	14%	3%

Clearly in both major categories, overall leadership effectiveness and the personal areas for improvement, the 360-degree process has demonstrated itself to be an effective means for driving personal and organizational change. The impact of this change process was significantly enhanced when the conference participants employed the model for encouraging feedback and made follow-up with associates a regular part of their developmental strategy.

Another factor, which had a significant impact on the degree of change realized, was the extent to which the senior executive sponsoring the conference demonstrated personal commitment to the feedback he or she received and the subsequent actions to bring about a personal change.

Assessing Action Learning

Executive Conference III is not only a notable personal leadership development experience, it is a significant event in developing organizational and Credo leadership capability in Johnson & Johnson. These critical domains of organizational leadership development are leveraged by Executive Conference III to accelerate change in the organization and contribute to business results. An undertaking of this magnitude raises the issue: Does it make a difference? In order to answer this question, Johnson & Johnson commissioned a major evaluation study by an independent party.

The evaluation of the leadership development framework and the action learning components of Executive Conference III was a perplexing challenge for Johnson & Johnson. Most fieldwork that has been done on program evaluation focuses on lower-level training initiatives, where it is easier to quantify learning. To evaluate leadership development programs and action learning approaches requires exploration of program outcomes—specifically learning outcomes, behavioral change, personal learning, and business impact. Designing a comprehensive evaluation to explore the effectiveness, the learning outcomes, and the perceived effect on the organization (i.e., business impact) of such a high-level development initiative as Executive Conference III demanded the use of qualitative research approaches in a field study.

The Approach

The assessment of the action learning components of Executive Conference III was based on Kirkpatrick's Four Level model for conducting program evaluations. This model, captured in Table 3, follows the following framework:

Table 3. The Classic Four Levels of Assessment in Corporate Education

Level I	*Reaction.* Level I assessment is defined as measures of participant satisfaction. Usually, the idea of "participants" is limited to those considered learners in the course.
Level II	*Learning.* Level II assessment is defined as measures of course outcomes in terms of learning and attitude. What is assessed or measured then is increased knowledge or and/or attitudes before and after the program. Did the training (learning) change the attitudes, increase the knowledge, or improve the skills of the participants?
Level III	*Behavior.* Level III assessment is defined as measures of on-the-job behavior that might be due to the effects of the education. Are they using their new knowledge, skills, and attitudes [learnings] on the job?
Level IV	*Results.* Level IV assessment is defined as measures of the effects of changed behavior on corporate goals and performance. What effect does the training have on the company? (Be satisfied with evidence if proof is not possible).

Kirkpatrick, 1994.

Guided by this four-level model, the field study aimed at two goals:

1. Design a comprehensive evaluation delivering useful findings as to the effectiveness of the custom-designed executive leadership development and team action learning program.

2. Better understand the learning outcomes of the program, explore the changes in on-the-job behavior that might be due to the effects of the development experience, and gather information on business impact. The results of the evaluation were used to demonstrate strengths and drive changes to Executive Conference III and the next generation of action learning approaches.

As noted above, the central question was: Does ECIII make a difference? This field study addressed this question on three different levels of analysis related to the conference's goals:

- Business impact
- Skill enhancement, behavior, and mind-set shifts
- Learning about leadership

Additionally, the researcher examined the quality of the conference's structure and methods in relationship to achievement of the stated goals.

The study consisted of 42 interviews in a two-phase process. The first set of interviews was conducted with 12 stakeholder members of the program's key constituency groups including selected ECIII sponsors. This step was designed to set the evaluation framework and to clarify the desired ends or goals of the Executive Conference III experience (see Exhibit 8). The results of these interviews stand on their own as well as provide the context for the second round of interviews.

A second round of interviews of 30 Executive Conference III participants across six conferences was the data-gathering mechanism to evaluate how effectively the conference goals were achieved experience (see Exhibit 9). A second purpose was to assess Executive Conference III outcomes on the three levels of analysis indicated above. At the time the study was conducted, 12 groups had completed the entire ECIII cycle—pre-conference activities, the week conference experience, and post-conference activities ending with the business review. From these 12, conference directors selected the six groups to be examined in the second phase of interviews. The chosen groups are representative of the business and geographic diversity of the total Executive Conference III population.

- Consumer Asia-Pacific
- Consumer Europe
- Pharmaceutical North America

- J&J Medical worldwide
- Ethicon Endo-surgery worldwide
- Information Management worldwide

From each group the directors identified five participants to be interviewed. Again, participants were chosen as representatives of the diversity of the group, always including a team leader as well as other team members.

The Interview Results

Interviews were transcribed verbatim and stored on computer disks. Data were analyzed using coding techniques to arrive at shared categories of outcomes and identifying incidents applicable to each category. This analysis involved the process of breaking down, examining, comparing, and categorizing data. This process was facilitated and managed by computer analysis using a qualitative data analysis software tool. Further, the interviews surfaced rich anecdotal data from participants. The following demonstrates some of the most salient findings across the categories.

Learning (Level II)
Individual Leadership Learning

- Leaders learned how to work and lead cross-functionally within a global organization.
  "I found it a marvelous learning experience to gain insight into European perspectives and the issues from different parts of the world, such as Malaysia. It really broadened my scope of understanding to more of a worldwide focus."
- Leaders learn to shift their focus from functional to big-picture thinking. Participants commented on how instructive ECIII was around cultural and business issues facing the corporation and companies.
  "I learned a lot about cultural differences in terms of the impact it has on leadership."

  "ECIII really made me realize the responsibility and initiative that top management and myself need to take in order to create needed change on a consistent basis. We are the real driver and engine for change."

Team Leadership Learning

- Participants learned the importance of a team perspective and cross-geographic teams for breaking the limits in perspective that a single-country focus can generate.

"I gained so much from the experience that was shared on the team from different people from other countries. It was very valuable."

"I feel I learned the importance of being a better team player, not just in a country but also across boarders—a better international team player."

"ECIII helped me learn how to be a better team player, not just in a country, but across borders—to be a more international team player."

"The action learning segment was a reinforcing exercise for me around the power of diversity and the good thoughts that result when getting a powerful, diverse team together."

- Participants learned that team-based problem solving is an effective way to both develop ownership in people, by sharing in the company's goals and issues, and align senior management toward a common vision.

"It was simply a team approach and everybody felt responsible and dedicated."

"The ECIII action learning experience aligned areas that we were previously doing in a vacuum. Prior to ECIII we spent more time internally focusing on resolving our issues of difference—it was almost an exchange of point counterpoint. ECIII helped us arrive at agreements we could execute in the marketplace in the business."

"We all got to know each other on the team, we had the full diversity of thought, so it became a reliable way to galvanize folks around some key issues with the business."

Organizational Leadership Learning

- The Standards of Leadership (SOL) provided the "glue" to the organization by becoming the primary focus of training, communications, and actions. Research supported that a key learning outcome of ECIII was how the organization defines leadership.

- ECIII has reduced resistance to change in the organization.
  "All senior executives have gone through this process, or the SOL, and therefore I think we have a lot less resistance to change today than we had two years ago. Having gone through this meeting, people understand that change is coming and there is tremendous opportunity if we change as a result. I think large change processes are more accepted now."

Skills Learned or Strengthened

- Participants learned to listen more carefully to people and create the space to listen. They strongly associated listening in order to be an effective team contributor with successful leadership.

"One of the skills that was reinforced, learned, or strengthened was to create the field to listen."

- Another skill improved upon was the process of asking for and receiving feedback and the importance of follow-up to this process.
  "Rather than just spending time with the folks that work for me, I now try to get more feedback from them regularly."

  "People like it [referring to the entire 360-degree feedback experience] because it is learning. It's looking at yourself in the mirror."

Knowledge Gained

- Greater knowledge of the Johnson & Johnson business systems.

- A significant understanding of the need for interdependent partnering across functions and geographic locations.

- Knowledge of the standards of leadership as a personal leadership compass.

Changed Attitudes and Mindsets Fostered

- Recognition that individuals absolutely must have a strong understanding and appreciation for the business issues that drive change.
  "I really learned the importance of change and the need for the vision for change to be directed by top management."

  "The ECIII process made me realize that the real driver and engine for change needs to be top management."

- Confidence in one's ability to make a difference in the community of J&J.

- Growth of "big picture" and open-minded thinking.
  "Grappling with the business issues forced me to grow a broader perspective—a CEO perspective."

  "I found the participants from other companies and disciplines to have very, very different input into the discussions and to come at it from perspectives I would never have thought of. ECIII cements an open-minded approach and gets you to think beyond your own affiliate."

Evidence and Outcomes of Behavioral Changes: Integration of Leadership Learnings, Skills Strengthened, Mindsets Fostered (Level III)

- The application of the Standards of Leadership: The SOL have been integrated as the only behavioral assessment criteria used for performance management appraisals. It is currently being used to evaluate individual and group strengths and assess where opportunities for improvement lie.

Management development programs are being designed targeting the identified gaps in individual and group performance vis-à-vis the SOL. The Standards of Leadership are actively being used for leading recruitment decisions and as a communication tool. The six clusters of the SOL are consciously being communicated and reinforced in day-to-day conversations with team members and subordinates. In some cases, the SOL have been incorporated into the succession planning process or directly used as competencies for identifying and developing high-potential employees. These SOL applications all cite examples of how learning around the SOL has impacted on-the-job behavior and has become a useful management tool on a day-to-day basis. A supporting artifact of this is the desk caddie (a pen/pencil holder) one organization developed to capture the six SOL focus areas as a daily, visual reminder for employees.

- A shift in role from being carriers and communicators of the vision to now being the ones who are the implementers of this vision.

"I discuss with my own management team what are we actually doing? Are we just managing the business or are we trying to be leaders in this business?"

Business Results Attributed to ECIII
(Level IV: Anecdotal and Concrete Evidence)
Business results attributed to the action plans

- Resulting from a conference project piloted in Europe, the business has grown by 30% YTD against a plan that called for a 10% growth across the entire region. While the region is performing at the 10% target, those two countries are performing at a 30% growth over the prior year. The company estimates $20 million in cost reduction that will be realized as the programs are further implemented.

- The outcomes of ECIII resulted in uncovering a weakness in our R&D organization. This drove the team to look at the whole internal R&D structure with a very positive impact in a movement toward a new business model. It resulted in a smaller R&D organization internally with an improved business model. The bottom-line business result was the team was able to take 50% of the cost out of product line, delivering cost-effective products for the future.

Results of Personal Leadership Development

- Competency centers have been started across Europe to further leadership development activities.

- Increased diligence in asking for feedback and then following up with others to improve one's behavior.

"I can say that the people who work directly for me have changed their behavior dramatically (from a leadership perspective) as a result of the 360-degree feedback process."

Results of Team Leadership Development

- Leaders of planning sessions have utilized the ECIII team action learning approach in the planning sessions within their organization in Europe.

  "Changes are taking place."

- An increased awareness of the value of implementing regulatory and clinical input early in the product development process.

  "Throughout various aspects of the organization, there is a greater sensitivity to including regulatory and clinical input early in the process of new product development and potential acquisitions."

Results of Credo Leadership Development

- A situation occurred almost immediately following ECIII where there was an issue with the packaging seals of an out-sourced product. While there was no hard evidence indicating any implications to sterility, the decision was made to recall the product. Guided by the Credo and the decision-making process, it was the right thing to do.

  "I doubt whether we would have had an FDA issue, I doubt whether we would have had a liability issue, but we would have had a Credo issue."

Results of Organizational Leadership Development

- A common language to support a more standardized way of approaching individual's leadership capabilities assessment. Johnson & Johnson now has the ability to look at professional planning across markets.

REFLECTIONS

Leadership Development

The Standards of Leadership have provided the organization a framework, which defines the leadership expectations of the 94,000 leaders who work at Johnson & Johnson. It reflects the values of the corporation and provides a profile of the critical success factors, which must prevail, if we as an organization are to achieve our long-term goals. To achieve this future state, there are things we as a corporation need to do better. Individuals who make personal commitments to learn and grow will bring about this change. The 360-degree feedback process has been a strategic vehicle for providing individuals and the organization the opportunity to learn and grow.

Action Learning Reflections: Six Key Lessons Learned

1. Arriving at and setting the context for the business issue is an important activity that builds participant buy-in, facilitates team problem solving, and ensures a successful outcome.

   - Defining the business issue may be an early opportunity to begin building participant buy-in to the case for change. Incorporate input from participants in defining or shaping the business issues.

   - Prior to solving the business issue, provide more input to teams on the front end. Greater clarification on acceptable bounds for creative solutions or debriefing any preconditions is necessary before solving the assigned business issue. Participants indicated they feel let down when their business solution is not picked up or implemented. It is disempowering to get so energized around a sanctioned set of initiatives to have it later blocked—and it may be counterproductive to the leadership development intent.

2. Timely sanctioning of the business issue is critical to sustaining enthusiasm and energy for driving change generated during the ECIII experience.

   - In order to maintain increased participant output of excitement and productivity, timely sanctioning or rejection of team business solutions is preferred. When too much time lapses, energy dissipates, momentum is lost, and participants fall back into the responsibilities of running the business and "old" ways of thinking.

   - Assist the sponsor in being clear on his or her role, responsibility, and authority in sanctioning and supporting the approved business solutions.

3. More planning and attention to follow-up events is needed to drive success.

   - Build in accountability for implementation of sanctioned initiatives and associated tasks and roles of action items. Recognize the time and effort it takes to implement the action plan initiatives. Team leaders, sponsors, and team members must follow up with teams and team members.

   - Acknowledge the ECIII participants, the team's outcomes, and their learnings in some sort of ceremony, perhaps a ceremonial dinner or reunion one year after the experience. Participants feel strongly about reconvening as a team at least one more time after the entire conference experience. This provides an opportunity to further leverage the leadership resources that are built through interdependent partnering.

- Report back to participants the outcomes of their ECIII team initiatives, such as what happened with each. Research indicated that sending a report out to all ECIII participants regarding what happened across other ECIII conference events would be helpful and informative. Share the successes of the action plans initiated and the learnings from them; additionally, share the critical learning success from teams whose action plans were either unsuccessfully implemented or not sanctioned. This leverages the outcomes and learnings across companies and fosters a leadership learning forum rather than, possibly, a competitive situation. Additionally, it may help to build in motivation and a sense of connectivity (across teams and within teams), and it provides closure.

4. Plan ahead for successful leadership development outcomes.

- Be sure to involve the influential decision makers needed to lead the change initiatives in the ECIII process. Participants indicated the importance of ensuring that key decision makers needed to implement a particular business issue are involved in the development exercise. The only people who change their thinking and expand their view creatively around solving the business issues are those involved in the process. Participants indicated solutions presented can meet with the constraints of unchanged thinking. Therefore, if other key decision makers are needed to implement a change initiative, either involve them in the conference experience (or post-conference activities), assist the team in managing the possible frustration, or get them out of the way.

- Prioritize initiatives. Select and focus on 2–3 key business solutions out of (or before) the ECIII conference and implement them. Participants felt it would be far more beneficial to the organization and as a leadership development experience to focus on those few critical issues and drive them to completion.

5. Expand the conference team presentations to include discussion.

- Build in time for reflection, dialoguing, challenging, and questioning the business solutions or plans presented. Make it less ceremonial and more a discussion about the viability of each presentation, defining next steps, ascertaining commitment, and establishing accountability.

- The time allocated for the team presentations is also a "training" opportunity to model and facilitate what you are advocating in this experience: i.e., being open to others' perspective, demonstrating listening skills, use of dialogue toward problem solving—reinforcing the learning in the action learning format. Use the opportunity for dialogue, questioning, and challenging in ascertaining and developing the viability of each business solution in a positive individual leadership and/or team leadership developmental way. People are learning how to be leaders by how they are being led.

6. Leverage the leadership resources you are harnessing.

- ECIII capitalizes on the power of team action learning in a decentralized organization as a mechanism for coalescing, aligning business strategies, and building interdependent partnering between individuals across functions, disciplines, and companies. This being the case, it is critical to have some facilitation or methodological approach to facilitating the implementation and follow up on activities of the meeting and even deeper, the processes involved in intercompany partnering.

Executive Conference III was a significant event in developing leadership capability in Johnson & Johnson and accelerating strategic change throughout the organization. Learning from the Executive Conference III experiences has since been leveraged forward and enhanced to contribute to the next generation of Leadership Development experiences and action learning approaches within Johnson & Johnson to further contribute to business results.

Exhibit 1. Our Credo

We believe our first responsibility is to the doctors, nurses and patients,
to mothers and fathers and all others who use our products and services.
In meeting their needs everything we do must be of high quality.
We must constantly strive to reduce our costs
in order to maintain reasonable prices.
Customers' orders must be serviced promptly and accurately.
Our suppliers and distributors must have an opportunity
to make a fair profit.

We are responsible to our employees,
the men and women who work with us throughout the world.
Everyone must be considered as an individual.
We must respect their dignity and recognize their merit.
They must have a sense of security in their jobs.
Compensation must be fair and adequate,
and working conditions clean, orderly, and safe.
We must be mindful of ways to help our employees fulfill
their family responsibilities.
Employees must feel free to make suggestions and complaints.
There must be equal opportunity for employment, development,
and advancement for those qualified.
We must provide competent management,
and their actions must be just and ethical.

We are responsible to the communities in which we live and work
and to the world community as well.
We must be good citizens—support good works and charities
and bear our fair share of taxes.
We must encourage civic improvements and better health and education.
We must maintain in good order the property we are privileged to use,
protecting the environment and natural resources.

Our final responsibility to is to our stockholders.
Business must make a sound profit.
We must experiment with new ideas.
Research must be carried on, innovative programs developed,
and mistakes paid for.
New equipment must be purchased, new facilities provided,
and new products launched.
Reserves must be created to provide for adverse times.
When operated according to these principles,
the stockholders should realize a fair return.

Exhibit 2. Standards of Leadership

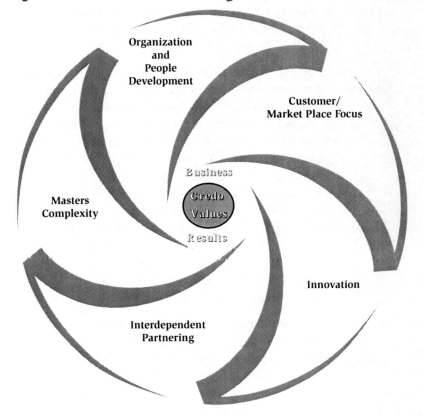

Exhibit 3. Executive Conference III

 Johnson & Johnson

Target Audience	• **Senior Executives** • **Management Boards**
Purpose	• **Communicate and Review Standards of Leadership** • **Individual Leadership Development** • **Company Action Plans**
Content	• **Leadership Standards and Principles** • **Credo Values** • **Interdependent Leadership**
Special Features	• **Natural Work Groups** • **Executive Committee Involvement** • **Delivered in Regions**

Exhibit 4. Advanced Manager Inventory

STANDARDS OF LEADERSHIP

DIRECT REPORT

Feedback for:

Confidential: Do Not Sign Your Name

(Continued)

Exhibit 4. Advanced Manager Inventory (*Continued*)

Johnson & Johnson Standards of Leadership
The Johnson & Johnson Leader . . .
. . . Lives Johnson & Johnson Credo Values
. . . Focuses on the Customer and Marketplace
. . . Encourages Innovation
. . . Builds Interdependent Partnerships
. . . Masters Complexity
. . . Develops Organizations and People

Instructions for Completing the Johnson & Johnson Advanced Manager
Leadership Inventory

The person named on the cover of this inventory will be participating in a process that focuses on their own individual development. As part of that process they will receive feedback from you and several other co-workers in the *immediate* future. This person will receive a consolidation of responses from all of the people who have been asked to provide feedback. You will not be identified in any way. To assure complete anonymity, *you should not identify yourself or make reference to anything that would identify yourself on this form.*

As you consider the behaviors of this individual, please circle the response which best describes **how satisfied you are with their performance.** The more honest you are in your responses, the more useful the feedback will be to the person being rated. The summary report will enable the individual to understand how her or his behavior is perceived by others.

While some items may appear to be similar, treat each item separately. No two items are the same. Although you may not have complete information concerning this individual's practices, try to provide a rating based on the information you have. **If you feel unable to answer a question, use the "Not Enough Information" category.** This response will not be calculated in the summary results. Please do *not* use the "Neither Satisfied nor Dissatisfied" response if you feel unable to respond to an item.

After responding to the questions, turn to the back page of the Inventory. This "Written Comments" section is for you to provide information about areas where the individual is especially effective and where he or she could be more effective. Finally, please supply and additional comments you would like the individual to be aware of, particularly regarding items which may not have been covered in the questionnaire portion.

Your responses will be combined with those of others into a summary report which is tabulated by an independent processing center. *No one in Johnson & Johnson* (other than the individual named on the cover) will see this feedback

Exhibit 4. Advanced Manager Inventory (*Continued*)

report unless she or he chooses to share it. The information in the report will be used by the individual for his or her own development.

Please seal this completed inventory and return it *within three days* to the individual named as "Collection Assistant" on the cover memo. That person will bulk ship the sealed envelopes to the processing center in the U.S. We have enclosed a pre-addressed envelope for your convenience.

Thank you for your help!

(*Continued*)

Exhibit 4. Advanced Manager Inventory (*Continued*)

Instructions: As you complete this questionnaire, please note that each item is preceded by the question, *"How satisfied are you with the way this individual . . ."* You response choices are **HD-Highly Dissatisfied, D-Dissatisfied, N-Neither Satisfied nor Dissatisfied, S-Satisfied, 6-Highly Satisfied,** or **NI-No Information.** Please indicate your response by circling your choice to the right of each item.

Consider this individual's effectiveness in the following items. *How satisfied are you with the way this individual . . .*	Highly Dissatisfied	Dissatisfied	Neither Satisfied nor Dissatisfied	Satisfied	Highly Satisfied	No Information
LIVES JOHNSON & JOHNSON CREDO VALUES						
1. Demonstrates honesty and ethical behavior in all transactions	HD	D	N	S	HS	NI
2. Consistently treats people with respect and dignity	HD	D	N	S	HS	NI
3. Genuinely listens to others	HD	D	N	S	HS	NI
4. Successfully balances meeting the need to achieve results with meeting need of key stakeholders (e.g. employees, customers, the community and shareholders)	HD	D	N	S	HS	NI
5. Is willing to incur immediate costs to achieve longer-term success	HD	D	N	S	HS	NI
6. Effectively addresses concerns raised by Credo Survey results	HD	D	N	S	HS	NI
7. Coaches her/his staff on how to apply the Credo Values in decision-making	HD	D	N	S	HS	NI
8. Is a role model for "living" Johnson & Johnson Credo Values	HD	D	N	S	HS	NI
FOCUSES ON THE CUSTOMER AND MARKET PLACE						
Creates Value for Customers						
9. Passionately cares about serving her/his customers	HD	D	N	S	HS	NI

Exhibit 4. Advanced Manager Inventory (*Continued*)

Consider this individual's effectiveness in the following items. *How satisfied are you with the way this individual . . .*	Highly Dissatisfied	Dissatisfied	Neither Satisfied nor Dissatisfied	Satisfied	Highly Satisfied	No Information
10. Proactively encourages and listens to input from customers	HD	D	N	S	HS	NI
11. Clearly understands customers' expectations	HD	D	N	S	HS	NI
12. Makes realistic commitments (avoids over committing)	HD	D	N	S	HS	NI
13. Effectively measures customer satisfaction	HD	D	N	S	HS	NI
14. Ensures that his/her staff is well prepared to manage a customer relationship	HD	D	N	S	HS	NI
15. Ensures that commitments to customers are consistently met	HD	D	N	S	HS	NI

* In this inventory, Customers are defined as the people who use the products/services delivered by this person and her/his organization.

Focuses Externally*

16. Anticipates future customer needs (rather than just reacting)	HD	D	N	S	HS	NI
17. Successfully positions her/his organization to capitalize on opportunities	HD	D	N	S	HS	NI
18. Ensures that his/her organization seizes the advantage of leadership in its field (or market)	HD	D	N	S	HS	NI
19. "Benchmarks" against other leaders in the field to help create or maintain a competitive advantage	HD	D	N	S	HS	NI

(Continued)

Exhibit 4. Advanced Manager Inventory (*Continued*)

Consider this individual's effectiveness in the following items. *How satisfied are you with the way this individual . . .*	Highly Dissatisfied	Dissatisfied	Neither Satisfied nor Dissatisfied	Satisfied	Highly Satisfied	No Information
ENCOURAGES INNOVATION						
Forges a Vision for the Future						
20. Involves the team in creating a vision for his/her organization	HD	D	N	S	HS	NI
21. Ensures that the team's vision is aligned with the larger company vision	HD	D	N	S	HS	NI
22. Involves people in developing a strategy on how to achieve the vision	HD	D	N	S	HS	NI
23. Effectively sets priorities	HD	D	N	S	HS	NI
24. Ensures the effective implementation of the strategy	HD	D	N	S	HS	NI
Fuels Business Growth						
25. Creates a positive sense of urgency towards achieving results	HD	D	N	S	HS	NI
26. Finds and acts upon new opportunities	HD	D	N	S	HS	NI
27. Eliminates unneeded bureaucracy	HD	D	N	S	HS	NI
28. Effectively takes risks in letting others make decision	HD	D	N	S	HS	NI
29. Is a role model for encouraging creativity	HD	D	N	S	HS	NI
Promotes Innovation and Continuous Learning						
30. Challenges the status quo (when change is needed)	HD	D	N	S	HS	NI
31. Asks people what they need to do their work better	HD	D	N	S	HS	NI

Exhibit 4. Advanced Manager Inventory (*continued*)

Consider this individual's effectiveness in the following items. *How satisfied are you with the way this individual . . .*	Highly Dissatisfied	Dissatisfied	Neither Satisfied nor Dissatisfied	Satisfied	Highly Satisfied	No Information
32. Uses both formal and informal networks to obtain new ideas	HD	D	N	S	HS	NI
33. Recognizes that making mistakes is an important part of learning	HD	D	N	S	HS	NI
34. Finds new ways to do things better and faster	HD	D	N	S	HS	NI

BUILDS INTERDEPENDENT PARTNERSHIPS

	Highly Dissatisfied	Dissatisfied	Neither Satisfied nor Dissatisfied	Satisfied	Highly Satisfied	No Information
35. Fosters open, candid communication across organizational boundaries	HD	D	N	S	HS	NI
36. Actively participates in the team (effectively shares information)	HD	D	N	S	HS	NI
37. Avoids political or self-serving behavior	HD	D	N	S	HS	NI
38. Strives to help colleagues across functions, business units, and geographic boundaries	HD	D	N	S	HS	NI
39. Successfully clarifies roles and responsibilities with business partners	HD	D	N	S	HS	NI
40. Builds consensus and impacts decisions without having to have "line" authority	HD	D	N	S	HS	NI
41. Creates mutually beneficial ("win-win") relationships with business partners	HD	D	N	S	HS	NI
42. Unites her/his organization into an effective team	HD	D	N	S	HS	NI

(*Continued*)

Exhibit 4. Advanced Manager Inventory (*Continued*)

Consider this individual's effectiveness in the following items. *How satisfied are you with the way this individual . . .*	Highly Dissatisfied	Dissatisfied	Neither Satisfied nor Dissatisfied	Satisfied	Highly Satisfied	No Information
MASTERS COMPLEXITY						
Effectively Manages Complexity						
43. Thrives in uncertain circumstances (avoids over reacting in stressful situations)	HD	D	N	S	HS	NI
44. Effectively analyzes situations before making decisions	HD	D	N	S	HS	NI
45. Makes decisions in a timely manner (avoids over analysis or procrastination)	HD	D	N	S	HS	NI
46. Communicates complex ideas in a manner that can be easily understood	HD	D	N	S	HS	NI
Implements Positive Change						
47. Sees change as an opportunity, not a problem	HD	D	N	S	HS	NI
48. Appreciates the value of diversity (in perspectives, ideas, backgrounds, styles, and cultures)	HD	D	N	S	HS	NI
49. Discourages destructive comments about other people or groups	HD	D	N	S	HS	NI
50. Helps people remove barriers to change	HD	D	N	S	HS	NI
51. Helps team members constructively deal with differences	HD	D	N	S	HS	NI
52. Strives to see the value of opinions that may differ from her/his own	HD	D	N	S	HS	NI

Exhibit 4. Advanced Manager Inventory (*Continued*)

Consider this individual's effectiveness in the following items. *How satisfied are you with the way this individual . . .*	Highly Dissatisfied	Dissatisfied	Neither Satisfied nor Dissatisfied	Satisfied	Highly Satisfied	No Information
53. Supports the final decision of the team (even if it was not his/her original idea)	HD	D	N	S	HS	NI
54. Effectively leads the change process	HD	D	N	S	HS	NI
55. Evaluates and rewards people for positive changes in behavior.	HD	D	N	S	HS	NI

DEVELOPS ORGANIZATIONS AND PEOPLE

Creates an Achievement Environment

56. Asks people what he/she can do to improve	HD	D	N	S	HS	NI
57. Challenges and motivates people to reach their highest potential	HD	D	N	S	HS	NI
58. Makes sure objectives are clearly understood	HD	D	N	S	HS	NI
59. Gives people the freedom they need to do their job well	HD	D	N	S	HS	NI
60. Holds people accountable for results	HD	D	N	S	HS	NI
61. Effectively deals with performance problems	HD	D	N	S	HS	NI
62. Effectively deals with individuals whose behavior undermines teamwork	HD	D	N	S	HS	NI
63. Recognizes and rewards outstanding performance	HD	D	N	S	HS	NI

Develops People for Optimal Performance

64. Effectively recruits the "right" people for positions	HD	D	N	S	HS	NI

(*Continued*)

Exhibit 4. Advanced Manager Inventory (*Continued*)

Consider this individual's effectiveness in the following items. *How satisfied are you with the way this individual . . .*	Highly Dissatisfied	Dissatisfied	Neither Satisfied nor Dissatisfied	Satisfied	Highly Satisfied	No Information
Develops People for Optimal Performance						
65. Challenges people to expand their capabilities, knowledge, and skills	HD	D	N	S	HS	NI
66. Provides developmental performance feedback in a timely manner	HD	D	N	S	HS	NI
67. Treats people fairly (avoids personal bias in decision-making)	HD	D	N	S	HS	NI
68. Provides coaching and guidance when needed	HD	D	N	S	HS	NI
69. Ensures that people receive the training they need	HD	D	N	S	HS	NI
70. Helps people prepare for greater responsibilities in J&J	HD	D	N	S	HS	NI
71. Identifies and champions high-potential talent as a J&J resource	HD	D	N	S	HS	NI
72. Creates an environment that fosters continuous professional development	HD	D	N	S	HS	NI
73. Strives to improve people's performance from "acceptable" to "excellent"	HD	D	N	S	HS	NI

PLEASE TURN TO NEXT PAGE FOR WRITTEN COMMENTS

Exhibit 4. Advanced Manager Inventory (*Continued*)

WRITTEN COMMENTS: Please note that your written comments below will be typed verbatim and will be combined with all other written comments in a report to the person named on the front page. To ensure your anonymity, please avoid comments or references that might identify you.

What does this person do that you particularly appreciate? (Please list two or three *specific* items.)

_____

_____

_____

_____

_____

What *specific* suggestions would you have for this person on how she/he could become even more effective? (Please list two or three *specific* items.)

_____

_____

_____

_____

_____

Additional comments for this individual:

_____

_____

_____

_____

_____

Developed with Keilty, Goldsmith & Company for Johnson & Johnson
internal use only

IMPORTANT:

Please return completed form within three business days to:

The Individual Named in the Cover Memo as "Collection Assistant"

Exhibit 5. 360-degree Feedback Process's Four Major Phases

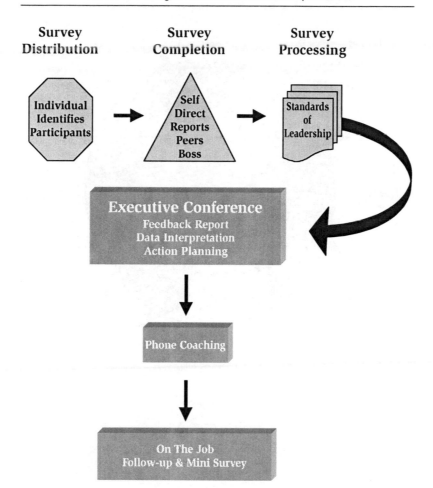

Exhibit 6. 360-degree Feedback Process—Encouraging Feedback

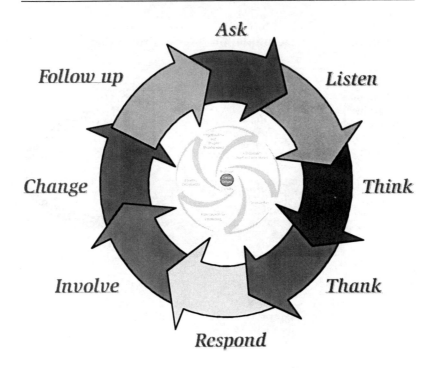

Exhibit 7. Series of Follow-Up Correspondence

Follow-Up Letter #1

Thank you very much for your active participation in the Johnson & Johnson Standard of Leadership Inventory process.

I had a great time working with your team. Feedback on the process was very positive and I appreciate your active involvement.

As we discussed, follow-up is the key to making the Leadership Inventory Feedback process work. Please take the time to briefly discuss what you learned from your feedback with your direct reports, your managers, and/or your colleagues. Please develop a follow-up schedule to help ensure that you get ongoing "progress reports" on people's perception of change in the areas for improvement that you have identified.

As a member of the Johnson & Johnson executive team, it is very important for you to be a role model on how to respond to feedback in a positive manner.

Please consider this as your first "reminder letter" from us. Please feel free to write or call us if you have any questions or if we can be of help in any way. My e-mail address is Marshall@kgcnet.com and I will be happy to respond to any e-mail questions.

Best Regards,

Marshall Goldsmith

P.S. Enclosed is a follow-up checklist to help remind you to conduct brief "progress checks" to help ensure that you successfully implement your plans for change.

Exhibit 7. Series of Follow-Up Correspondence (*Continued*)

Follow-Up Letter #2

It has now been about three months since our last reminder letter.

How is it going?

We have recently completed a research study involving several thousand people which reconfirms two trends: (1) leaders who follow up on their leadership inventory feedback tend to improve a lot more than leaders who do not follow up and (2) leaders tend to do a much better job of following up with their direct reports than following up with their peers.

Teamwork and positive peer relationships are very important success factors for the leader of the future. Please take a few minutes and follow up with both your peers and your direct reports on your leadership inventory feedback.

Please write or call if you ever want to talk.

Life is good!

Best Regards,

Marshall Goldsmith

(*Continued*)

Exhibit 7. Series of Follow-Up Correspondence (*Continued*)

Follow-Up Letter #3

It has now been more than three months since you received your last follow-up "reminder letter" us.

How is it going?

Now might be a good time to: (1) do a self-assessment of your progress in the "areas for improvement" that you selected (from your Leadership Inventory feedback) and (2) do a quick "progress check" with your direct reports and coworkers.

Please send me an e-mail with a report on your progress (Marshall@kgcnet.com) if you have a chance.

Life is good!

Best Regards,

Marshall Goldsmith

Exhibit 7. Series of Follow-Up Correspondence (*Continued*)

Follow-Up Letter #4

It has been a little over one year since you received your Leadership Inventory feedback.

Now might be a good time for reflection. How did the year go? Were you able to work on the "areas for improvement" that you selected? How would you rate your progress to date?

I hope that you found our leadership course and feedback process to be both thought provoking and useful. More important, I hope that you found that the process helped to produce a positive influence in your life.

This will be my final "reminder letter" to you. However, I still want you to feel free to write, call, or e-mail me (Marshall@KGCnet.com) if I can be of help or if you ever just want to talk (my address and numbers are enclosed).

Life is good!

Best Regards,

Marshall Goldsmith

Exhibit 8. Executive Conference III Program Evaluation—Interview Protocol #1

Interviewer: *Name A* supervised by *Name B*, Ph.D.

This interview is part of a larger evaluation study to explore both the effectiveness and the learning outcomes of the Executive Conference III experience. The study will be used to make meaningful improvements to ECIII and the next generation of development experiences and will additionally serve as the basis of my doctoral dissertation. The interview will take approximately 30 minutes to 1 hour and is focused on clarifying the desired ends of the ECIII program under study. The objective of the interview is to establish an understanding of shared program goals, expectations and outcomes across stakeholder groups for each phase of the ECIII program.

> Definition: When referring to the **ECIII program, process, or experience** please consider in your response the entire 6-month conference process:
> **Pre-conference work → the 6-day ECIII event → Post-conference activities**

In exploring the effectiveness of this program, specifying the criteria for evaluation is central and critical. Different stakeholders of a program will bring different criteria to the table; therefore, this step is designed to collect those different "sets" of criteria and collapse them down into shared categories of program effectiveness. Given your first hand experience in the ECIII process, your input is valued and needed in this step.

As a participant in this study, you are free to decline answering any question(s). You may also end this interview at any time should you feel the need to do so. In addition, should you feel the need, you may contact the study's sponsors *Name C* and/or *Name D* at Johnson & Johnson MED, (###) ###-####, or my supervisor, *Name B*. Her number is (###) ###-#### with her address as follows:

The California School of Professional Psychology

1000 South Fremont Avenue

Alhambra, CA 91803-1360

The risks of participation in this study are very minimal while the overall benefits are rich. As with any organizational research, risks to participant's confidentiality may be of issue and will be addressed by the researcher in the following manner. All information will be reported in an interim report, as well as a final report, in aggregate form only to maintain confidentiality of the information shared from each participant. Further, participant code numbers will be assigned to each participant to keep the information shared confidential. This interview will be recorded on audiotape. After the report is complete all tape recordings from this interview and note sheets will be destroyed. This research aims to benefit all participants of ECIII by contributing valuable information toward meaningful

Exhibit 8. Executive Conference III Program Evaluation—Interview Protocol #1 (*Continued*)

improvements to ECIII and the next generation of development experiences. Your input is highly valued and we appreciate your contribution to this study. If you wish, the results of the project will be forwarded to you as soon as the project is complete. Please feel free to talk about concerns that you may have with any of the topics discussed in this interview.

Based upon this information, do you agree to participate in this research study and have this interview audiotaped?   □ Yes   □ No

Interviewee's name_____ Code number _____

Date of interview _____

Note to interviewer: This document should be used as a guide, not a strict blueprint. Feel free to pursue conversations that seem relevant to the overall goal of the study.

(*Continued*)

Exhibit 8. Executive Conference III Program Evaluation—Interview Protocol #1 (*Continued*)

Questions

To begin, I'd like to gain a clear understanding, from your perspective, of the vision, goals, objectives, and desired ends for Johnson & Johnson's Executive Conference III process . . .

1. What do you believe the vision to be for the J&J ECIII conference?

2. What was your personal vision for the ECIII conference?

3. Please describe your [past] role in the design, development, implementation, and/or participation of the ECIII process?

4. How would you describe/define the ECIII experience?

5. In developing the ECIII process, what were the goals or objectives it was designed to meet? (Pre-conference, conference event, post-conference)

   • What results/outcomes are you trying to accomplish with the ECIII program?

6. What were your expectations for the ECIII team action-learning process?

7. Do you perceive ECIII's action learning approach to be a powerful learning strategy?

   ☐   Yes   Why and how?
   ☐   No   Why not?

8. What are the learning objectives (outcomes) designed for, or desired, in the ECIII experiences?

   • At the individual level?

   • At the team level?

   • At the organizational level?

Now, I would like to explore your perceptions of the actual outcomes of J&J's ECIII process to date . . .

9. Based on your experience, what are the outcomes of the ECIII experience? (Again, please respond across the three phases of the process.)

10. What do you feel are the most effective components of the ECIII process? Why?

11. What do you feel are the least effective components of the ECIII process? Why?

12. What do you feel are the important attributes of a successful ECIII conference experience?

13. In what way does ECIII's action learning process help executives learn more effectively from their experience?

Exhibit 8. Executive Conference III Program Evaluation—Interview Protocol #1 (*Continued*)

14. What knowledge, skills, and attitudes do you feel participants learn from the ECIII experience?

15. What, if any, processes do you feel participants learn or strengthen from this experience? (For example, perhaps executives are learning to leverage change in the corporation.)

16. Are there any other questions that you feel are relevant and wish that I had asked?

17. Do you have any other comments regarding the ECIII program that you would like to add?

Exhibit 9. Executive Conference III Program Evaluation—Interview Protocol #2

Interviewer: *Name A* supervised by *Name B*, Ph.D.

This interview is part of a larger evaluation study to explore both the effectiveness and the learning outcomes of the Executive Conference III experience. The study will be used to make meaningful improvements to ECIII and the next generation of development experiences and will additionally serve as the basis of my doctoral dissertation.

The interview will take approximately 1 hour and is focused on exploring the learning and business outcomes from the 6 month ECIII conference experience. The three objectives for this interview are: 1) to explore how participants have transferred conference learnings and outcomes to their jobs; 2) to explore perceptions and uncover anecdotal evidence of how ECIII has impacted business results, company goals, and/or performance; and 3) to understand what can be done to improve or enhance the program.

> Definition: When referring to the **ECIII program, process, or experience** please consider in your response the entire 6 month conference process:
> **Pre-conference work → the 6-day ECIII event → Post-conference activities**

As a participant in this study, you are free to decline answering any question(s). You may also end this interview at any time should you feel the need to do so. In addition, should you feel the need, you may contact the study's sponsors *Name C* (###) ###-#### and/or *Name D* (###) ###-#### at Johnson & Johnson MED, or my supervisor, *Name B*. Her number is (###) ###-#### with her address as follows:

The California School of Professional Psychology
1000 South Fremont Avenue
Alhambra, CA 91803-1360

The risks of participation in this study are very minimal while the overall benefits are rich. As with any organizational research, risks to participant's confidentiality may be of issue and will be addressed by the researcher in the following manner. All information will be reported in an interim report, as well as a final report, in aggregate form only to maintain confidentiality of the information shared from each participant. Further, participant code numbers will be assigned to each participant to keep the information shared confidential. This interview will be recorded on audiotape. After the report is complete all tape recordings from this interview and note sheets will be destroyed. This research aims to benefit all participants of ECIII by contributing valuable information toward meaningful improvements to ECIII and the next generation of development experiences. Your input is highly valued and we appreciate your contribution to this study. If you wish, the results of the project will be forwarded to you as soon as the project is

Exhibit 9. Executive Conference III Program Evaluation—Interview Protocol #2 (*Continued*)

complete. Please feel free to talk about concerns that you may have with any of the topics discussed in this interview.

Based upon this information, do you agree to participate in this research study and have this interview audiotaped? □ Yes □ No

Interviewee's name ____________________ Code number ____________________

Date of interview ____________________

(*Continued*)

Exhibit 9. Executive Conference III Program Evaluation—Interview Protocol #2 *(Continued)*

Questions

This first section of the interview is aimed at collecting information of those sustained outcomes, learnings, or behaviors being used "on the job" as a result of the Executive Conference III process.

1. I'd like to first understand a little bit about your conference experience. How would you describe your ECIII experience?

2. As a result of your ECIII experience, what are your key leadership learnings?

3. Considering how you encountered the Standards of Leadership in ECIII, what stands out?

4. How are you integrating the Standards of Leadership on the job?

5. ECIII attempts to reaffirm the Credo and foster Credo leadership development. How have you used your knowledge of Credo values and the Credo-based, decision-making process as a management tool back on the job?

6. ECIII attempts to assist participants in learning a leadership process. How have you helped your own people to learn leadership as a result of your learning from the ECIII experience? Please share an example if you can.

7. ECIII employs a change model for driving the action learning process. How have you integrated this change process and its associated tools to lead and drive change through your organization? If you can, please share with me an example of an event or experience where you have used this process.

8. While certain learning objectives are planned for ECIII, people learn unplanned outcomes as well. What skills, knowledge, and attitudes do you feel you learned or strengthened through the ECIII process? How have you integrated that learning back on your job?

9. Have you taken a leadership role in moving your team's action plans forward? How? If not, why not?

Now, I would like to explore perceptions and uncover anecdotal evidence of how Executive Conference III has impacted business results, company goals, and/or performance . . .

10. What do you perceive is generally different in your business as a result of ECIII? Can you ascribe any difference in the way your organization is being run to having been through ECIII? Please provide an example of an event or experience that would reflect this.

11. Was ECIII effective for launching or energizing an agenda for change? If so, how? Please provide an example if possible.

12. What business results can you attribute to the action plans developed at the ECIII 6-day meeting?

Exhibit 9. Executive Conference III Program Evaluation—Interview Protocol #2 (*Continued*)

At this point, I would like to get your input on how the Executive Conference III program can be improved or enhanced to deliver greater value to you . . .

13. Think about the ECIII experience—that is, the pre-work, 6-day meeting, post-conference—what worked well? What needs improvement?

14. Now that you have completed the full cycle of the ECIII experience, what 1–2 specific changes would make the biggest improvements to the pre-conference data gathering process?

    • What would be the biggest improvements for the on-site 6-day meeting?

    • For the post-conference follow-up process?

15. Having completed ECIII, what do you see as the next big step in leadership development?

16. Do you have any other comments to share regarding the ECIII program or this interview?

ABOUT THE CONTRIBUTORS

Charles J. Corace (ccorace@corus.jnj.com) is director of management education and development at Johnson & Johnson. Corace has responsibility for corporate-wide executive development products and services. In this role, he and his organization work closely with the senior management of Johnson & Johnson to define and implement experiences, which support the development of global business leaders. Prior to this assignment, he held the position of regional director, Learning Services. This organization was created as a shared service within J&J and provided organizational consulting support to the operating companies within North America. Over the past 14 years with Johnson & Johnson, Corace has also held positions in the areas of human resources and quality management. He is a member of the Executive Leadership Development Network and the Human Resource Planning Society.

Jodi Knox (jknox@executivedevelopment.com), is an Executive Director with Executive Development Associates based in New York. Holding a BS in Computer Engineering with an MS and Ph.D. in Organizational Psychology, Jodi focuses on emphazing Change Leadership activities with client organizations experiencing significant change in order to help them effectively implement new stratagies and achieve sustainable change and results. Her work includes focusing on leadership development/coaching activities, developing unique approaches to promote and leverage learning in teams and organizations for business results, implementing new and effective communications and dialogue approaches for action, and developing talent strategies and tactics to meet demands for business required talent. Using a collaborative consulting approach, Jodi's goal is to help clients achieve business objectives and behavioral change while transferring capabilities to effectively deal with ongoing change and learning on a sustained basis.With a strong bias toward results, Dr. Knox has conducted practical research with Fortune 50 companies on a global leadership development programs to measure and leverage the learning outcomes, knowledge transfer/behavioral changes, and the business impact of such initiatives. Jodi recently collaborated with world-renowned authors demonstrating the power of storytelling to convey learning, integraton of knowledge, and the application of wisdom in a new book entitled *Learning Journeys: Top Management Experts Share Hard-Earned Lessons on Becoming Great Mentors and Leaders* (Davies-Black). Prior to joining EDA, Jodi's experience includes manager with Deloitte Consulting's Change and Learning practice and consultant under the mentorships of Dr. Beverly Kaye, a world authority on career development and retention, and Dr. Marshall Goldsmith of Financial Times

Knowledge Dialogue. Jodi has consulted in multiple industries and to a variety of leading organizations including Johnson & Johnson, General Motors, Jones New York/Nine West Group, International Flavors & Fragrances, The MONY Group and Marsh, Inc.

CHAPTER TEN

Sun Microsystems, Inc.

An integrated leadership development and succession planning system designed for executives that leverage 360-degree feedback, a leadership skill/competency model, and individual development planning

INTRODUCTION

This chapter introduces the framework, processes, and tools currently used at Sun Microsystems, Inc. (SMI or Sun) for executive leadership development. The long-term goals of the strategy and programs Sun are currently implementing for leadership development are simple:

- To ensure that there are sufficient "ready now" candidates to backfill key executives

- To provide the necessary processes to grow the senior leadership pool for continued long-term success

- To maximize performance of executives in their current roles by increasing their capabilities

Company Background and Environment

Sun was founded in 1982 with the vision of open network computing: the ability for all computers to interoperate regardless of manufacturer, greatly expanding the availability of information for everyone. Since then, Sun has changed from a company that manufactured workstations for the scientific marketplace to a leading provider of computing product, service, and support solutions for building and maintaining enterprise-wide intranets and expanding the power of the Internet.

Sun operates in an industry where fast-paced, unpredictable change is a way of life. The information technology world is characterized by rapid innovations and applications of that technology in the marketplace. While Sun has long advocated that "the network is the computer," no one could have predicted the explosive growth fueled by the Internet. Companies that have succeeded in this environment have leaders who have learned to drive rapid change. In the Silicon Valley, California, where Sun is headquartered, people talk about operating at "Internet speed."

Coupled with this changing environment is rapid growth. Thanks to Sun's entrepreneurial culture and commitment to technical excellence, in 17 years it has grown from 3 employees and no revenues to 30,000 employees and approximately $12 billion in revenues in 150 countries. With 100% of Sun's revenue coming from products that are less than 18 months old, revenue and the number of employees are growing at 20% per year.

To ensure Sun survives and thrives in this environment, its leaders have had to nurture the agility, bias for action, and competitiveness it had as a start-up. Short-term results are imperative; longer-term thinking and planning often take a back seat. Frequent reorganizations in response to changing business needs eliminate and create jobs overnight. In addition, the content and scope of a job can change substantially from its original description over a short period of time. This means that executives must continually learn and grow or be left behind as everything changes around them.

THE CHALLENGE AND APPROACH

How do you develop executives in a company where long-range planning is measured in months, not years? Predicting what the business environment will look like, what jobs will exist, and what specific competencies will be needed in the future is practically guesswork.

Yet the development of executives is by nature a long-term process. There are no quick fixes or magic pills that will instantly transform an executive into a different and better leader.

The approach to implementing an executive development program linked to the company's strategy in this challenging environment must be adaptable to fast-paced change, but it should not be seen as the "program of the month." The process that has evolved, Sun's Executive Leadership Architecture, has the following features:

- A philosophy for executive development
- An architecture for development that integrates all the components that help executives grow
- A common language around leadership (the SMI Leadership Skill Profile) that is reinforced in multiple development processes and tools

A Competency Model As the Integrating Tool

Much has been written about competency models in recent years and many companies have invested significantly in their development. Sun's approach was to quickly develop a leadership competency model that fit the direction that Sun is heading and then invest in integrating that model into multiple tools and processes. The assumption is that more is gained by consistent and effective integration of the model into selection, performance management, and development processes than by a search for the perfect competencies.

The competency model, the SMI Leadership Skill Profile (shown in Figure 1) consists of 22 core leadership competencies that are considered most important

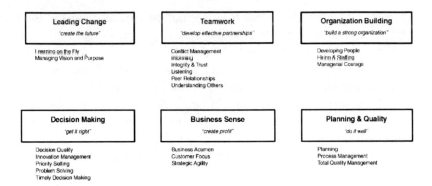

Figure 1 Leadership Skill Profile

to develop and master. It is not a complete list of the skills required to do executive jobs, and it does not describe the skills necessary for any one particular job. It is the set of skills that Sun's aggregate leadership should be strong in to ensure the company's continued success.

The SMI Leadership Skill Profile was created in 1994 with input from vice presidents, directors, and senior executives using the Lominger, Inc. Career Architect™ tool.

The goal is to develop a common language and understanding of leadership by reinforcing this model through an increasing number of processes and tools and events, as depicted in Figure 2. For example, various competencies from the model have been chosen as themes for annual leadership conferences for executives and are the focus of several leadership education programs. The profile is the basis of the 360-degree feedback instrument for executives and managers and for the Sun Leadership Award. The competencies are also used in the evaluation phases of the executive selection and succession planning processes. Most recent, the profile is being integrated into performance review processes for executives.

The profile has withstood the test of time so far; it has been reviewed several times by key leaders, but has not required change. Perhaps more important, the language of the competencies is being used by the most senior leaders in their speeches and other communications when they talk about what they expect of Sun leaders.

THE DEVELOPING ARCHITECTURE

With the SMI Leadership Skill Profile as a start, an architecture has developed to help drive decision making that is aligned with the business's medium and longer-term needs. The architecture is built around some fundamental beliefs and values:

™Career Architect is a registered trademark of Lominger, Inc. Copyright 1995. All Rights Reserved

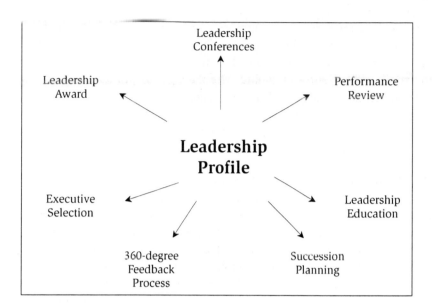

Figure 2 Leadership Profile Model

Beliefs About Leadership

- Continuity of Sun's executive leadership is critical to its ability to fulfill its mission to be number one in network computing.
- Sun's leadership as a whole needs to be strong in the competencies identified in the SMI Leadership Skill Profile.
- Both long-term employees, with their Sun specific expertise, and the fresh perspectives of outside talent will be needed for Sun to succeed, and selection processes should reflect this.
- Broad cross-organizational knowledge is essential to succeed in Sun's top jobs.

Responsibility for Development

The company has consistently maintained the view that development is a responsibility shared by the individual, the manager, and the company.

Individual Responsibility Employees are expected to take ownership of their careers, maintaining and evolving their skills so that they can continue to contribute meaningfully to Sun's success in the unpredictable future and strengthen the company's overall leadership capabilities.

Manager Responsibility Managers, particularly senior managers or executives, play a significant role in advancing the growth of Sun's leadership talent. They are responsible for encouraging ongoing development of their employees. However, in the constant overload of today's work environment and flat organizations where a manager is often also an individual contributor, how that responsibility plays out is changing. The manager as primary mentor/coach is not always realistic anymore. Sun's expectation is that managers do three basic things: convey the sense that development is important (e.g., ask how the development activities are going once in while), give effective feedback, and hold employees accountable for development.

The Company Is an Active Participant There are no career paths set in concrete, and Sun does not try to map out the steps employees should take to achieve long-term professional goals. At the same time, the company recognizes the importance of strong leadership to ongoing success and also strives to provide its employees an environment that will offer challenge and opportunities. So while Sun does not hand-hold employees through their careers, its role is to support personal career management with the development framework, planning processes, tools, and education that enhance the on-the-job developmental opportunities employees encounter regularly. Resources and opportunities are targeted for the best return on investment for both the individual and the company.

STRATEGY FOR SUCCESSION

Sun takes two approaches to succession planning. First, tools, processes, and programs are being put in place to ensure that a sufficient pool of candidates are developing basic general management and leadership skills. Second, traditional succession planning is done for a small number of the most senior jobs.

Figure 3 illustrates Sun's strategy for ensuring strong leadership continuity and how talent pool development fits into this plan. Sun's business strategy provides the direction for company growth and planning. Ongoing planning provides, to the extent possible, a picture of future talent needs that can help guide both internal development activities and a competitive external recruiting strategy. Sun provides resources and opportunities for all executives. At the same time, specific programs assure that individuals with the highest potential for succession to key jobs are identified and targeted for developmental opportunities.

As the figure indicates, the goal of these efforts is to enable the company to fill key senior executive positions with world-class leadership talent quickly and efficiently.

Recognizing Potential

There are certain key attributes that Sun looks at as indicators of high potential for future success in senior positions.

Figure 3 Strategy for Executive Development

Learning Agility Given Sun's rapidly changing environment, not only do individuals need to learn in preparation for future jobs, but incumbents need to grow to keep up with their current jobs. So the ability to learn and adapt is often more important than having all the skills necessary for a job at the start. In a business environment such as Sun's, highly learning-agile individuals provide a competitive advantage.

This skill is referred to as Learning Agility™ (Lominger), the ability and willingness to learn from experiences and successfully use that learning in new and different situations. Learning-agile people are more likely to learn on the job and grow enough to succeed in new jobs of greater responsibility in the future.

Sun's philosophy is that Learning Agility can be developed and improved just like other skills.

Established Track Record of Results Having a track record of delivering against goals and commitments is essential at Sun. It is a prerequisite to being viewed as a high potential. The ability to consistently deliver high-quality results is one of the primary factors evaluated when considering candidates for jobs and other developmental opportunities.

FRAMEWORK FOR EXECUTIVE DEVELOPMENT

The framework in which Sun is executing its executive development strategy establishes the key elements in the developmental system and how those elements generally integrate.

The model in Figure 4 shows two major sets of activities:

1 The cycle the company uses to manage, encourage, and support executive development to ensure continuity of Sun leadership (the outer circle).

2 The cycle of development that an individual typically experiences (the inner circle). The two sets of processes work together where the two cycles intersect on the model.

As the model shows, there is no beginning or ending point to the cycles; and the extent to which the processes work together determines the richness of the developmental environment that's created.

ELEMENTS OF THE EXECUTIVE DEVELOPMENT CYCLE— A CLOSER LOOK

To understand the model in more detail, start with the outer cycle in Figure 4 at "Developmental Experiences" and progress around the circle.

Developmental Experiences are everything that can be provided to employees for their growth. Challenging jobs, task forces, and other types of special projects can provide some of the best development experiences. For example, serving as chairperson of the Leadership Council or the Compensation Committee provides visibility to senior management, a new perspective, and the challenge of leading a cross-organizational team.

While learning on the job, performance is appraised formally through an annual *Executive Performance Review,* a process during which executives have an opportunity to critique their job performance with their managers. Performance reviews are intended to give executives direct feedback on their performance against goals and on their leadership. The process is simple. A 1-page form guides a discussion of specific achievements and shortfalls and a review of how the executive is rated on the 22 skills of the SMI Leadership Skill Profile. Goals for the upcoming year are also established at review time.

In addition, executives have the opportunity to get *Feedback* from direct reports and peers through other formal means, such as surveys and other specific tools. Coaching, mentoring, and frequent informal one-on-ones with a boss are other possible feedback methods, depending on the needs of the individual.

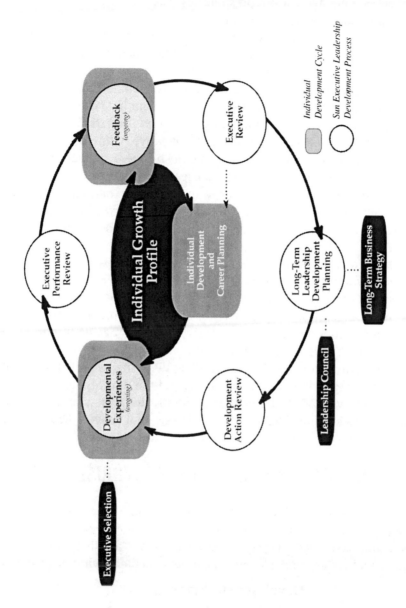

Figure 4 Executive Development System at Sun

Assessing executive talent is a continuous responsibility of senior management. To support this effort, an annual company-wide *Executive Review* provides a snapshot of Sun's executive talent for the senior executive team to consider in light of Sun's long- and short-term strategies. The review process also gives vice presidents and the senior executive staff members an opportunity to increase their awareness of individual development progress and upcoming development opportunities. Furthermore, they get the opportunity to review the strength of their organization's executive talent.

This review process better prepares executives to include *Leadership Development Planning* as part of the strategic business planning, which is the link between executive development and Sun's *Long-Term Business Strategy*. This link, while difficult to make, is critical; and the iterative nature of the development architecture is intended to help maintain the business strategy as the fundamental driver of the company's talent management processes.

To help ensure that the business strategy and leadership development strategies stay closely tied, Sun has created a *Leadership Council* composed of line vice presidents to drive strategic leadership initiatives (see more about the Council under "Executive Education Programs").

The action plans that come out of the Executive Review and Leadership Development Planning processes come alive when implemented. The *Executive Development Action Review* provides the accountability for development action planning. These meetings, held quarterly or at mid-year, provide senior management with the opportunity to compare their progress against action plans and update the executive talent snapshot.

An *Executive Selection Program* used for filling VP positions provides the link between the organization planning processes and the development needs of individual executives. With the help of this tool, the review and planning processes serve as key input for selection processes that provide *Developmental Experiences* for executives. And the cycle continues.

DEVELOPMENT CYCLE—THE INDIVIDUAL

The individual's leadership development cycle shown in Figure 5 occurs within the framework of the company's process for managing executive talent. The elements within the individual cycle are described below, together with some of the programs that are beginning to build the developmental environment at Sun.

Development Planning

Executives are encouraged to maintain an ongoing personal development plan. Sun provides information about what leadership skills and abilities are deemed most important for the company's executives to develop. As mentioned previously, the central tool for development planning is the SMI Leadership Skill

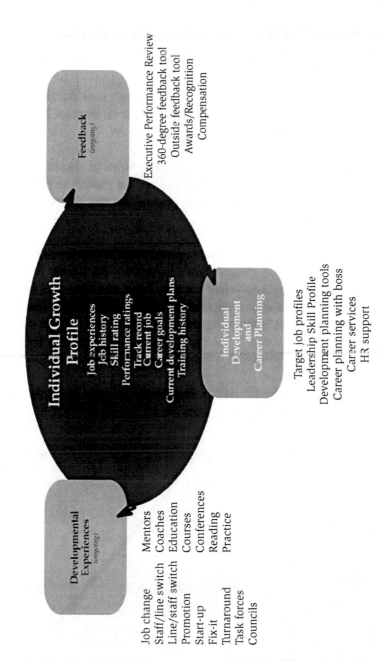

Figure 5 Individual Development Cycle

Profile (see Figure 1). Assistance and tools for development planning are available through various sources at Sun. Career counseling is an employee benefit provided by Sun's Career Services organization, and executives are supported by human resources professionals in their development planning. In addition, guides for development planning are accessible through Sun's internal Web site.

Developmental Experiences

Career planning links to opportunities for growth through new developmental experiences. These take the form of on-the-job experiences, internal and external educational programs, mentoring/coaching, and so on.

Jobs The absence of rigid job descriptions and boundaries to areas of responsibility at Sun provides an extremely rich opportunity for growth to those who seek it. Almost all jobs provide challenging opportunities and evolve uniquely depending on the incumbent.

Executive Education Programs The challenges of building an executive education curriculum at Sun are significant. Sun's executives are similar to executives at most modern corporations—they are very busy and very protective of their precious time. They are smart, successful, and readily accept change. In addition, the culture does not support top-down, mandatory programs as have been designed in other companies (a k a the "prison meal" approach to executive education.) So how do you build a curriculum in which smart, fast-moving, busy execs will participate?

Sun developed the Executive Education Framework (shown in Figure 6). At the base of the framework are two programs for transition into the executive

Figure 6 Executive Education Framework

levels: a program for executives hired or promoted into the director level and an assimilation program for new vice presidents. Approximately 2.5% of Sun's employees are at the director level and 0.5% are at the VP level. Programs timed to support career milestones are particularly useful and well received. They help employees jumpstart their transition; they are eager to learn because they recognize what they don't know.

The program for *New Directors Taking Charge* focuses on individual development, organizational leadership, and SMI business success. The 6 class days are separated into a 3.5-day module and a 2.5-day module approximately 30 days apart. This separation makes for more effective learning and it appeals to the executives' time constraints. The focus of Part 1 is "Building the Business," which covers Sun's vision, strategy, competition, and critical success factors for the director position.

These critical success factors include (from the SMI Leadership Skill Profile) managing vision and purpose, strategic agility, and business (financial) acumen. In this program, university professors are utilized to teach sessions on business strategy and finance. In addition, Scott McNealy, Sun's chairman and CEO, and Ed Zander, Sun's president and COO, visit each session to talk about Sun's vision and strategy and to interact with these new executives. "Leading Your Team" is the emphasis of Part 2, in which participants focus on their personal leadership styles: developing vision, leading, mentoring and coaching, and personal development. These "soft" skills cannot be taught by telling people rules and theories. It is necessary for participants to use all their senses to develop the self-awareness and understanding required to promote these leadership behaviors. To this end, this session utilizes experiential exercises to help executives learn these leadership skills. The program has been extremely well-received by new directors. Although the word "mandatory" is not used in the description, over 80% of new Sun directors worldwide voluntarily attend this program within 90 days of appointment to the director level.

The *Vice President Assimilation Program* is an individualized program that helps orient new vice presidents to Sun through a structured mentoring, reading, and meeting process. This customized program is presented to new vice presidents on their first day at Sun and is tailored to the specific job they have been hired to do. It does not utilize any classroom instruction.

The next tier of curriculum in the strategy is intended to provide an education program to build *General Management* capabilities. This program is in the planning stages and will be developed in the future.

The next tier, *Business Accelerators,* is a placeholder for short, rapidly developed programs that respond to specific, critical business issues. This is an evolving curriculum that will grow as significant business issues that can be supported with education programs are identified. Examples of Business Accelerators exclusively for executives are "Strategic Business Partnerships" and

"Maximizing Profitability at Sun." These are both 2-day programs, tailored to focused issues at Sun and all with a senior executive sponsor.

Strategic Business Partnerships Like most businesses, Sun is increasingly forming alliances and partnerships to meet the total needs of customers. When Sun first embarked on this business strategy, it was soon clear that the organization lacked the experience or skills to successfully manage partnerships. The Strategic Business Partnerships class was piloted 2 months after the need was identified. This program assists VPs and directors in selecting and managing complex partnerships, a key element of Sun's strategy. The program consists of instruction by external experts on strategic partnerships and management, as well as presentations by Sun internal executives. Because Sun has a unique approach to partnerships, it was not possible to benefit from public programs that were available on this topic. Instead, faculty was recruited from a successful program being taught elsewhere, and they were then educated on the specific aspects of Sun's strategy for partnerships.

Maximizing Profitability at Sun As Sun grows from a small, start up to a Fortune 200 company, the sophistication of its decision-making processes around investment opportunities must change from a "seat-of-the-pants" style to one that is based on financial analysis designed to produce the desired return to shareholders. Maximizing Profitability at Sun is a 2-day program that teaches a framework and methods to drive accountability for business decisions. In a customized business simulation, participants play the roles of executives on a team competing against other executive groups for market share, quality indexes, and product revenues. The program takes participants through 3 years of managing a multifaceted network computing business, allowing them to experience the impact of business decisions on the profitability. The teaching components of the program are the customized business simulation designed to Sun's business and financial operating environment and strategies, feedback sessions on the results of each period's simulation performance, and lectures tied to specific financial strategies of Sun.

At the top of the pyramid, programs for *High Potentials* take a variety of forms. The idea is that some programs would be made available exclusively to certain executives within the general executive population. The purpose is to make an extra investment in high-potential employees to accelerate their development, prepare them for more senior positions, and retain them at Sun. The company's Leadership Council program and the new Executive Development Program are two examples.

Sun Leadership Council The Leadership Council serves as an advisory board on leadership development at Sun for the CEO and the top leadership team. The

Council's role is to drive programs and policies that support leadership development and ensure that such programs align with the business. The Council is composed of 8 to 10 vice presidents selected by the CEO. Each member serves for 2 years. The company strives to select executives for the Council who have a broad understanding of Sun's business and are strong in the competencies of the SMI Leadership Skill Profile.

In addition to providing a valuable service to the company, members learn from their participation in several ways:

- Each quarterly meeting provides a learning opportunity through external speakers and practitioners in the area of executive leadership and development.

- Initiatives that are worked by the Council provide action learning opportunities.

- They learn from each other while broadening their internal networks.

Executive Development Program The concept of this program is to give high-potential executives intense and focused practice in a leadership role coupled with more quality feedback and coaching than they usually receive. The Executive Development Group, in collaboration with Assessment Solutions, Inc., runs a "development center" for high-potential executives in which they have an opportunity to test their leadership skills/style through simulations, role-playing, and other exercises tailored to the critical leadership challenges at Sun. The simulations are built around 7 of the most critical skills on the SMI Leadership Skill Profile. These skills were selected based on in-depth interviews with senior management and include conflict management, peer relationships, managing vision and purpose, strategic agility, and timely decision making. Throughout this 1.5-day program, participants receive in-depth feedback and coaching on development needs from professional executive coaches, as well as assistance in preparing a development plan.

Feedback

Feedback is an essential element of development that helps focus efforts to change. Seeking feedback from many sources besides the formal performance appraisal increases self-awareness and can accelerate growth. The dilemma in the Sun environment is that executives have very little time for self-development, feedback programs, and reflection. The Sun Executive Survey was designed with these difficulties in mind.

Sun Executive Survey The Sun Executive Survey is a 360-degree feedback instrument that executives are encouraged to use periodically as input to their development planning.

The survey is based on the SMI Leadership Skill Profile and is the primary tool for executives to benchmark their skills against the profile. The report format is simple and is intended to be presented by a skilled feedback coach who can engage the executive in a meaningful dialogue about the implications of the data and help him/her quickly focus on the improvement areas that will yield the most impact. The coach then provides guidance about developmental activities.

Individual Growth Profile

The Individual Growth Profile on the model represents the record of an individual's job and training experiences, performance record, and career goals and plans. This data is critical to the company's ongoing ability to understand its bench strength.

CONCLUSION

As to whether the executive leadership development strategy and programs are meeting their goals of ensuring "ready now" executive candidates and providing processes for strong leadership in the long term, it is too soon to tell. However, progress is being made.

On paper, this strategy may look highly integrated and systematic. The truth is that in reality, it is still evolving and somewhat chaotic. In spite of the need to make quick changes and deviations, the Executive Leadership Architecture has been helpful in maximizing the return on each piece of the development puzzle and in providing a framework to plan and introduce new leadership initiatives.

ABOUT THE CONTRIBUTORS

Jim Moore (jim.moore@corp.sun.com) is currently director of workforce planning and development at Sun Microsystems. He is responsible for executive development, which includes succession planning, executive selection, and executive development and for SunU, the company's corporate university. In addition, he is responsible for long-range human resource planning on workforce issues.

SunU provides learning initiatives to the 30,000 worldwide employees of Sun. SunU's education programs range from software engineering design to sales training to management and leadership development. SunU is a leader in utilizing network computing technologies for the desktop delivery of education. SunU is headquartered in Palo Alto, California, and has staff and facilities at Sun locations in 8 countries.

Prior to his current assignment, he was vice president of training and development for Northern Telecom Ltd. at their Washington, D.C., headquarters where he had corporate responsibility for global education programs for 57,000 employees. He has also led management and executive development organizations at BellSouth Corp., Bell Communications Research, and AT&T.

He spent the first 20 years of his career on the "doing" side of the business as a line manager in the former Bell System. He holds a master's degree in electrical engineering from the University of Louisville.

Ellen Johnston (ellen.johnston@corp.sun.com) is currently senior manager, executive development for Sun Microsystems, Inc. She is responsible for developing systems and programs to enhance leadership capability within the company.

Before Sun, she was director of human resources for Interactive Systems Corporation, a computer software company in Los Angeles, California, where she started and grew the human resources department. In more than 15 years of human resource experience heavily focused in the computer industry, she has had a variety of internal management, specialist, and consulting roles, and she has done selected external consulting.

She has a bachelor's degree in business administration from Bucknell University and an MBA focused on human resource management and organization development from UCLA.

RECRUITMENT AND RETENTION

RECRUITMENT AND RETENTION: AN INTRODUCTION BY DR. JOHN SULLIVAN

The world of work has changed dramatically in the last decade. With the advent of technology, telecommuting, globalization, and the Internet, most companies have found that the old approach to managing no longer works. High unemployment rates have forced companies to rethink how they treat their workers. Management tools that worked well in past decades are no longer effective now that the balance of power has shifted toward the worker. High-tech firms have implemented innovative new approaches such as relaxed work rules, an emphasis on teams, and by putting a significant portion of employee's pay at risk. Some firms have even had the audacity the try to make work fun! Unfortunately, most human resource practices were developed and refined during periods of high unemployment. Managers and workers are now finding that these legacy tools are becoming less and less effective. What has fundamentally changed is that the power pendulum has swung away from the employer towards the worker. The high demand for workers has led to the development of the concept of the worker as a "free agent." Free agents are more loyal to their profession and more committed to staying on the leading edge than they are to any job in any firm.

The human resources department has been slow to respond to this need for new set of tools for managers to deal with these free agents. Whether you are a manager, an employee, or a human resources professional, the time has come to rethink the way HR approaches recruiting and retention.

The biggest issues facing managers and organizations during the first decade of the twenty-first century will be the attraction and the retention of top performing employees. During the last 2 decades I have had the opportunity to work with some of the best high tech firms in the Silicon Valley. Leading firms such as Cisco, Intel, and Hewlett-Packard are developing and implementing some incredibly innovative strategies and tools which will allow them to maintain a significant competitive edge over other firms in their industry. For proprietary reasons I cannot divulge specific plans that these firms are using, but I can give a composite of the tools and strategies that will become best practices of all leading firms in the next century.

Attracting the Very Best

I know dozens of employment directors who claim they want their function to be "worldclass" or to become "an employer of choice," but few seem to have a plan on how to get there. If you are wondering why you are having difficulty recruiting talent, look no further than the tools you use. Just like you can't compete with Windows 3.1 software and an Intel 386 processor, you can't recruit the best using 1960 employment tools and strategies. Unfortunately, 90% of all employment functions are living in the "old" recruiting world of "placing ads, going to job fairs, and reading resumes." A few breakout firms (Cisco, Trilogy, and hire.com, to name a few) have broken the mold and moved into a higher plane, shifting to Web tools, continuous relationship recruiting, and focusing on the quality of the hire. If you are serious about shifting into "WOW" recruiting, here are the steps you need to take and the principles you need to adopt.

Winning Strategies in Recruiting

Employer of choice (EOC)—The most effective "big picture" recruitment strategy is becoming an "employer of choice." The focus of this strategy is to become well-known as a great place to work. The premise is simple if your company becomes known in the media as a "workers' paradise." Then the very best employees will seek you out and the job of the employment manager becomes little more than that of sorting out the best from the rest. The EOC strategy relies heavily on marketing and PR tools. The first step is to identify (through market research) which elements top performers expect in the job. With that data, adjust management practices and benefits to meet the expectations of the top performers. Then develop a marketing campaign to build the employment "brand." By getting managers and employees to speak at conferences and to the press, the word begins to spread about the company's "best practices." If you're successful, you'll be written up in one of the many "best places to work" lists published in popular magazines.

Hiring "passives"—Traditionally, when a firm placed in ad in the newspaper it would attract numerous qualified applicants. In times of high employment, that tactic no longer works because the very best are no longer unemployed and as a result they are not actively seeking new jobs. The percentage of "active" job seekers has dwindled as the unemployment rate has fallen. The new target is the passive jobseeker. Passives are defined as currently employed people who are doing well in their jobs. As a result, they don't read want ads and do not quickly respond to an offer of the new job. Passives are not "lazy"—it's just that they're doing well at their jobs and as a result they are well-treated and rewarded. The passive strategy focuses on "poaching" them away from other firms. Effective passive strategies include developing "answer guy" Web sites, which provide information that helps the passives do their current jobs better. The information brings them to your site and exposes them to what they might know if they work with your firm. A similar approach uses nonrecruiting events, such as wine tastings, to approach them and begin to build relationships that may someday result in a hire. It's a subtle approach but it's highly effective if you are patient.

Employee referrals—This is an old tool, but one that, when refined, can be the most effective of all recruiting tools. The employee referral strategy is based on the premise that "A" players (your top-performing employees) are the best recruiters available. By sending out your top performers to seek out other top performers, you dramatically increase your recruiting staff. In addition, many top performers (especially passives) will only talk to other professionals. By developing internal management systems that speed up the referral process, some firms have attracted over 60% of their hires using this process. An added benefit is that the quality of the hires is often the highest of any recruiting tool. Be forewared that slow processes with multiple restrictions will cause the tool to become ineffective.

WOWing them on the Web!—The growth of the Internet has opened up new approaches for recruiting top candidates from around the world. Many firms have found that the very top people in any field are the first to use the World Wide Web. Although large job boards have their role, the most effective tool is a great company Web page that uses multimedia and mass customization to excite the candidate. By offering a variety of options that answer the different questions an applicant might have, a firm can motivate a person in a way that is not possible in a brochure or newspaper ad. Firms like Cisco have pioneered tools that allow an applicant to apply for a job easily without a current résumé. By linking the company's site to other exciting sites, it can become a mini-portal, which attracts the top people in your industry, even those not looking for a job.

Relationship recruiting—"Someday you will work for us" is the slogan for relationship recruiting. This strategy takes a long-term approach to recruiting. Initially a firm builds a "Who's Who" database of the best in their industry. It then begins to build relationships with the top people through contacts at conferences and through a "friends of xyz" program. A friends program is where you develop connections through e-mail newsletters, product discounts, and invitations to company events. Over a period of months, you assess the candidates and build a sense of trust so that when they begin to job search, you are the first call.

The Next Steps in Recruiting

In addition to a great recruiting strategy there are other steps the firm must take in order to attract the very best. The first is to develop a series of measures or metrics that indicate which tools are the most effective. Metrics that look at the quality and the performance of the hire are the most essential. The next most important step is to reward managers and recruiters for great hiring. By providing incentives to managers who recruit top talent, you can dramatically increase their interest in recruiting. A final but essential step is to prioritize your jobs. Although all recruiting is important there is seldom time to do it all well. By identifying the key jobs and managers and by focusing your efforts, you can dramatically impact a firm's profitability.

Retention—Keeping the Employees You Have

Retention is one of the most misunderstood areas in management. It's an area that until recently received little focus. Firms seldom have retention departments; in many cases, no one is in charge of retention. Managers are usually not rewarded for retaining the best people. Until recently, causes for people leaving a job have been poorly researched.

The costs of turnover or the business impact of a "term" (a terminated employee, i.e. someone who quits or is fired) for a single software engineer averages $200,000. In some companies, it can exceed a million dollars.

When it comes to team leaders, the costs can escalate rapidly. One senior VP estimated the cost of losing a single product development team leader at $29 million, due to the necessity of getting a product rapidly to market. (The team leader subsequently got a $1 million "stay on" bonus.)

All "term" costs significantly escalate when the person is a "hi-per" (high performer), when he or she is in a key management position that impacts getting the firm's product to market, or when the former employee leaves and goes directly to a competitor.

The California Strategic Human Resource Partnership began studying the retention issue in 1995. In the last few years, some excellent retention work has been done by the McKinsey consulting firm and the Gallup organization. The results of these studies have been remarkably similar. Almost all show that turnover is directly related to how managers treat their workers. For the last decade, high unemployment rates and large-scale layoffs have allowed managers to treat employees "roughly" because employees had little choice but to take it. However, in times where employees act as free agents, managers must relearn how to motivate and support their employees.

Solving the retention riddle becomes relatively easy. First, you must identify and reinforce the positive aspects that cause employees to stay in their jobs. Second, you must counter or eliminate the "negatives" or factors cause people to quit their jobs. Both of these steps are summarized in what I call the "Big 6." They're are all controlled by an employee's direct supervisor or next-level manager. By providing employees with the "Big 6," voluntary turnover can be dramatically reduced to single-digit levels in a relatively short period of time.

The "Big 6" Causes of Turnover

Tell your workers they can expect *each* of the following things from their managers:

1. Honest, frequent, two-way communication, including rapid, constructive confrontation on issues. (Minimum standards—monthly "how am I doing?" meetings with every employee, rapid, proactive confrontation and resolution of issues, open-book access to relevant information.)

2. Challenging and exciting work. (Minimum standards—every employee has a challenge plan and is periodically asked to rate their degree of job excitement.)

3. Continual opportunities to grow and learn. (Minimum standards—every employee has a customized learning plan and the resources to carry it out.)

4. Recognition and rewards for their performance. (Minimum standards—every employee has at least 10% of their pay tied to output; forced ranking of all employees is done quarterly so all know where they stand and there are ample opportunities to ask managers how to improve their rankings; an escalation option for those who feel they are unfairly treated.)

5. Some degree of control over their job and life. (Minimum standards—8 hours a month of flexible time and one day a week "job rotation" possibilities, opportunity for dropping undesirable duties and a dream job list jointly developed with their manager; monthly more of/less of meetings with the manager.)

6. Knowing their work makes a difference. (Minimum standards—cross-functional opportunities to meet with the "up and downstream"

coworkers/customers; periodic reports on the impact of their work, as well as their team's work.)

The Next Steps in Retention

The first step in reducing turnover is measuring voluntary turnover rates and rewarding managers who keep the top performers. The next step is to identify why people stay and why some quit. You can identify this by doing "pre-exit interviews," no more than periodic surveys or a series of informal one-on-ones with each worker. The goal is to identify the factors that motivate them to stay and the factors that frustrate them and that might cause them to leave.

The third step is to identify the reasons why individuals who left the firm quit. Firms can easily accomplish this by using a "post-exit interview." Most exit interviews are skewed by the fact that the employee doesn't want to be overly critical for fear of impacting a positive reference. A supplemental approach is to follow up with the ex-employee 3 to 6 months after termination with a mailed (or e-mailed) questionnaire.

After identifying the root causes of turnover, the next step is to train managers on what they need to do to reduce frustration. However, if training fails, tough decisions need to be made as to whether this manager needs to be terminated or removed from the management ranks.

What You Will Learn in This Section

In this section of the book, you'll learn how three diverse companies tackled their retention and recruiting problems. Two of the firms are high tech (AMD and Cellular One), while another (Allstate) is in a more traditional industry. Both AMD and Cellular One focus on solving the hot issue of retention while Allstate takes a new look at the recruiting and selection processes. All three of the case studies use a scientific approach to identify which solutions have the most impact.

Allstate has demonstrated that even companies in "mature" industries can join the Internet revolution. Allstate demonstrates how it has made the jump from a classic paper-and-pencil testing system for applicants to one that uses technology and the Internet to both increase the speed and the effectiveness of the assessment. The "old" paper-based system resulted in significant delays in the hiring process, which slowed down the firm's capacity to grow in a highly competitive industry. Allstate used a very logical and scientific approach, which went beyond simply putting a paper system on the Internet. Instead, it undertook a systematic redesign that also increased the capability of the system to do things that were not possible under the old design. The results were impressive. Anticipated results include dramatic increases in the speed of hiring. Both managers and the candidate get instant results. The system has worldwide, 24-hour capacity, and it is designed to be able to track the effectiveness of each recruiting source and allow applicants to apply for jobs online.

Cellular One has developed a comprehensive retention and employee satisfaction strategy designed to pre-identify factors that cause turnover. Their strategic approach ties many of the HR functions together in a unified method. They began with baseline employee satisfaction data gathered from an online employee satisfaction survey. The survey helped them identify the basic issues that impacted employee satisfaction and retention. By comparing the results from their own multiple-year survey to nationally gathered "normative data," they were able to identify areas of strengths as well as areas where they needed to do additional work. Key aspects of the retention program included management development, policy improvement, companywide communication, and a series of continuous improvement metrics. One of the primary keys to Cellular One's success was the early buy-in by top management and their continual involvement throughout the 3-year period. Other contributors to the program's success included ensuring that employees believed in the change effort and a metric-based program of continuing follow-up and refinement.

AMD undertook an ambitious program to increase retention levels by targeting career development as the primary cause for turnover. After an initial needs assessment, AMD received top management buy-in and funding for a long-term effort to make increased career development a major factor in retaining employees. Both managers and employees were involved in the initial pilot study. Although this highly benchmarked processes is still ongoing, the early results have been positive. Their career development program has allowed workers to better understand the range of job and career opportunities they have within the firm.

Management participation has been mixed. Initially, employees were more excited about program than their managers. Only recently has AMD begun to make progress toward formally rewarding managers for developing their people. The lessons learned from this case include the fact that a pilot and an extensive needs assessment are necessary in order to "get the bugs out early." AMD also learned that career development can be easily confused with performance management and that internal "silos" and fixed cultures can impede any change effort.

All three of these case studies are worth examining because of their scientific methodology as well as their results. All are full of powerful "lessons learned" for those who are soon to begin a major recruitment or retention effort.

John Sullivan (JohnS@sfsu.edu) is a well known HR "guru," international speaker, author, and advisor to Fortune 500 and Silicon Valley firms. He has been featured in *Fast Company* magazine, as well as on ABC News and CNN. His solutions to management problems have been documented in *Fortune*, *Time*, the *Wall Street Journal*, *HR Executive*, *Workforce*, and *PC World*. He has provided management with "out of the box" solutions at such major leading-edge firms as Intel, Cisco, Hewlett-Packard, Sun Micro, McKinsey, and Nike. He specializes in making HR *the* competitive advantage and in developing worldclass recruiting and retention solutions. Dr. Sullivan is a professor of HR and the head of the Human Resource Management Program in the College of Business at San Francisco State University. He was called the "Michael Jordan of hiring" by *Fast Company* magazine.

CHAPTER ELEVEN

Advanced Micro Devices

A retention program designed to help employees align their interests, values, and skills with rapidly changing business needs through a set of integrated activities

INTRODUCTION

Background

With revenues of over $2.5 billion and 13,000 employees worldwide, Advanced Micro Devices (AMD) is a global supplier of integrated circuits for the personal and networked computer and communications markets. The company produces processors, flash memories, programmable logic devices, and products for communications and networking applications. Given a rapidly changing workplace where the demand for new skills is in an ever-accelerating state of flux, coupled with the highly competitive and lucrative nature of Silicon Valley, AMD was concerned about its ability to recruit, and most important, retain employees.

External factors affecting the organization included the complexity of living in an era of "Free Agent Nation." New and exciting development opportunities proliferated: sky-is-the-limit stock options; inflated salaries; enormous sign-on bonuses; the lure of start-up Internet-based companies with their own visions of the "Promised Land." Beguiling terms such as venture capitalists and angels were interwoven into the lexicon, luring employees in every organization.

How could AMD retain their employees with so many enticements? With limited intellectual capital competing for positions within a number of high-technology companies, what could AMD offer above and beyond the traditional recruiting and retention tools of yore? Where was the competitive advantage? Complacency relative to retention was clearly unacceptable, but with the traditional contract of guaranteed lifetime employment a relic of times long past, a new agreement was needed.

Complicating the picture were a number of internal factors within AMD that created a demand for "out of the box" thinking relative to recruitment and retention.

The convergence of external and internal drivers formed the strategic rationale for a new approach to recruitment, retention, and workforce development. Thus, AMD Career Partnership™ was born. It is defined as a set of integrated activities—a process to help employees align their interests, values, and skills with the rapidly changing business needs at AMD.

This chapter tells a story—born out of necessity—about curtailing anticipated hemorrhaging of outbound talent by proactively addressing development needs throughout the worklife cycle, beginning with recruiting and continuing through retention efforts. The attempt would be made to reduce outplacement by focusing on in-placement.

Equally challenging would be the task to ensure that a career development process would be an integral part of the way AMD conducted business on a daily basis. It could not be an event or an HR flavor of the month. Rather, the focus needed to be on a process that was sustainable with practices that could be replicated elsewhere in the organization. The importance of a strategic approach, built on a solid business, derived from both quantitative and qualitative data, could not be underestimated.

The Business Issues

In the early 1990s, both the Organizational Development and Learning and Development organizations at AMD prepared white papers addressing a need for new retention strategies. Both treatises cited early warning signals (see external factors cited previously) relative to the need for a new approach to recruit, retain, and develop employees. Both indicated that a formalized career development process, offering opportunities for employees at all levels of the organization to grow and develop new skills *within* the company, was becoming increasingly critical.

These early warning signals were validated by 2 separate employee surveys. The data that emerged from the internal surveys was powerful and compelling. Results from the 1992 survey indicated that well over 93% of employees cited career development opportunities as one of their top 3 priorities at AMD. In the 1994 survey, over two-thirds of the divisions placed career development or development opportunities on their list of top 3 priorities.

In addition to the employee surveys, other internal factors surfaced. Data gathered from exit interviews and discussions with AMD employees in voluntary departure situations indicated that many felt a strong affinity for the company and would have preferred to stay within the organization. Lack of development opportunity again surfaced as the top reason for people leaving, albeit reluctantly. Increasingly, employees who had been doing the same type of work for a number of years were expressing a need to develop in other directions within the company—directions that reflected their changing interests, values, passions, and motivations, as well as their skills. The turnover and replacement cost of these valued employees was beginning to mount.

Still another factor at AMD involved the recruitment and retention of young talent of Generation X. Every organization wishes to recruit the best and the brightest of the limited intellectual capital available. Nowhere was this pressure felt more intensely than in the heart of Silicon Valley.

Generation X is defined by Bruce Tulgan in *The Manager's Pocket Guide to Generation X* (HRD Press, 1997) as those born between 1963–1977. They are characterized as the proverbial latchkey kids, independent and entrepreneurial. They arrived at AMD demanding help with their careers. Clearly, they had learned the lessons of their elders: No job is guaranteed for life. Indeed, a relationship was only viable for the mutual time in which an employee and an organization both benefited. Generation X recognized that the old "loyalty" contract had long ago been broken—many of them saw the fallout from their parents who had been reengineered, reorganized, downsized, etc., after many years of dedication to a single company. In the eyes of many Gen Xers, the alignment of personal and corporate values was critical—especially relative to the premium that an organization placed on development opportunities in terms of interests, values, and skills. Baby Boomers, the generation born in the post–World War II years, share many of the same viewpoints, forcing organizations to increasingly respond to a critical mass demand for development opportunities.

Simultaneously, a similar theme was emerging in business plans across the United States as the demand to develop and align employees' skills with rapidly changing technological innovations was becoming viewed as a critical necessity. The demand became louder as pressure increased to recruit and retain best-in-class employees.

In some business plans, the term "career development" was specifically called out, but more often the "symptoms" emerged under the general heading of development. There was also an increasing shift from individual contributors to team-based projects. The extent to which AMD could get a jumpstart on anticipated changes and translate them into desired behavioral competencies (stated in specific, realistic, and measurable terms) could provide a clear and compelling competitive advantage.

Several issues needed to be addressed including an idealized "future perfect" vision of where the organization, a department, and a team or individual was headed in the next 2–5 years. This vision required that all employees think out of the box—that is, outside of the way business was traditionally accomplished or the way individuals usually succeeded.

At AMD, these internal factors, as well as the external issues mentioned earlier, were driving the company to react in rapid-response mode—and were forcing a new model of career development as a recruitment and retention tool.

As evidence of the organization's commitment to address the retention issue with a specific focus on internal career development as a key strategy, a new position was created with the sole focus dedicated to the assessment, design, development, implementation, and evaluation of the new approach.

NEEDS ASSESSMENT

Cognizant that a clear assessment of the current state versus the desired outcomes was critical to the success of the retention strategy, a needs assessment was conducted as a first step.

A multidimensional needs assessment incorporated a variety of approaches. Both quantitative and qualitative data were gathered from existing information, including employee surveys, business plans, and exit interviews. While it is generally agreed that a percentage of employees are reluctant to state the real reason for leaving a company at the time of departure, it was also felt that patterns and trends around lack of development opportunity clearly surfaced as a top issue.

Given this data that pointed to a proactive, internal career development strategy as key to positively impacting retention, a process was designed to ensure that additional insights could be obtained on the topic. Using different techniques and varied questions, a level of consistency was established with some questions such as:

- How is career development currently defined at AMD?

- Given the changing nature of the workplace—and the accelerating pace of change—what criteria would you use to judge if a career development strategy would have a positive impact on retention at AMD?

- What are the biggest obstacles to achieving a future perfect vision of career development as a retention strategy?

- What key milestones will need to be achieved to reach the desired state? How will the organization be impacted? Management? Employees?

Individual interviews were conducted with 8 key division vice presidents in both California and Texas. Approximately 8 directors were also interviewed. The senior vice president of HR and his entire staff also participated in the process.

Focus groups were conducted with managers and employees in both states. Additional interviews were conducted with managers and employees from the staffing, recruiting, organizational development, and learning and development departments.

Organization benchmarking, using internal career development processes as a retention strategy, was conducted. At the time the assessment commenced (late 1994, early 1995), few companies were aware of the approach. The seminal article, "Toward a Career Resilient Workforce" (*Harvard Business Review,* July/August 1994), had only begun to make the tremendous impact it would ultimately have on how organizations could create a career resilient workforce and influence retention in the process. However, 4 high-technology organizations in Silicon Valley had recently commenced efforts in implementing a career development process as a retention strategy. All were in early stages of evolution and thus proved invaluable as resources to be benchmarked. Interviews were conducted with the principals at all 4 organizations and information was shared relative to hard-won successes and lessons learned.

Findings from the multidimensional needs assessment included the following:

- Lack of development opportunity was the number one reason for voluntary employee departures. Many of these same employees did not want to leave the organization but saw no room for growth.

- Little consensus on what the term "career development" meant. There was enormous confusion between career development and performance development. Many thought that the little development box checked on a performance review or quarterly goal assessment form was career development.

- Confidentiality was deemed an essential component of success in the new initiative. While employees and managers ideally wished for a true partnership in the process, many employees expressed concern that their managers would either block them or view their career development interests as an expression of intent to leave AMD.

- Gen X development and expectations surfaced as an issue in both recruiting and retention. Specific techniques were needed to address them.

- Perceptions that this could be another HR flavor-of-the-month program.

- Concern that managers would resist the initiative due to a number of perceptions: that the initiative was fluff; that it was an additional burden due to the overload in numbers of staff reporting to them; interference from other priorities would be perceived as hard versus soft; that there would be no rewards or accountability for supporting efforts.

- Perceptions regarding employees included: they may be too comfortable and resistant to change; fear of letting managers know their career goals; concern that this was another box to be checked and was not real.

- Initial resistance was encountered from some senior executives who had achieved their positions in earlier years, when the workplace and career development emanated from a more traditional, hierarchical process of upward promotion. Validation of their past experience in the workplace was important. However, a process of evolutionary and educational dialogues combined with an increased pain threshold related to recruitment, retention, and workforce development eventually contributed to turning many of the initial resisters into somewhat reluctant supporters.

By applying the findings of the multidimensional needs assessment, guidelines for implementation emerged. These included:

- For a formalized career development strategy, a fundamental *culture shift* was needed to move the organization away from a traditional view that career development could only move on upward and parallel tracks. Some employees wanted to develop breadth and depth of skills in their current positions while others sought development opportunities across the organization.

- Horizontal movement was becoming increasingly as important as vertical progression in terms of job satisfaction. Several challenges were implicit in the desired state including the perception that:

  Managers will be the toughest group to shift from the "command/control" mode to enablers

  Silo blockage, resulting from fear of losing an individual manager's best and brightest employee, was contributing to an exodus of employees

  Horizontal movement or in-place expansion outside of current responsibilities was difficult to reward given the traditional vertical compensation system

- Learning activities would be critical to a) understand why and how a career development process is needed relative to recruitment and retention and, b) the evolving roles of the organization, management, and employees.

- Need for workforce development techniques, including integrating online tools, surfaced particularly if the initiative was to develop site-to-site over time.

- Both formative and summative data would be critical if the initiative is to be successful.

- Measurement and evaluation processes will need to be multidimensional in determining the impact of a career development process on retention. This was especially evident given the differing criteria for success according to each level of the target audiences, which surfaced during the needs assessment.

- Two fundamental challenges threatened the process:

  Lack of consistency perceived in initiatives driven from corporate to field

  Lack of systemic organizational linkages and a process to tie them together so that the initiative has sustainability

In summary, the results of the multidimensional needs assessment had a direct impact on all aspects of the career management retention strategy. The results were analyzed and summarized in a master design plan, which served as the blueprint for the project. A succinct extrapolation from the very detailed design plan served as an executive briefing presentation to the senior executives. This briefing tied the data from the needs assessment and the resulting recommendations for a career development initiative directly to the business case of recruitment, retention, and workforce development. The result? Top-down buy-in and support for the initiative, as well as the funding to execute it.

TARGET POPULATION

The target population for the career development retention strategy was to ultimately encompass all employees at all levels of the organization. Recognizing, however, that an undertaking of this magnitude could be cumbersome and that it would be difficult to maintain quality control, it was determined that the process could only remain feasible if a phased-in approach was used. The following components were established:

- Two demographically representative pilot groups (1 for managers, 1 for employees) would be selected from groups across the Sunnyvale, California, site. Attempts were made to include Austin, Texas, representation in both pilot groups from the beginning. HR representatives from each of the groups were asked to work with senior management in their respective areas to select and engage the pilot participants.

- Criteria for participation in the pilot groups included.

  An emphasis on high performers so that the process could become a model of excellence

  Inclusion from 3 different entities representing major areas of the organization: manufacturing, product divisions, and finance/administration

  Accurate representation of diverse groups and cultures

  A special emphasis on individuals who were not afraid to openly disagree with a concept but were willing to be part of a solution

- The objectives of the pilot were to engage participants in helping design and develop the career development retention initiative, eliminating as many major obstacles to it as possible, obtaining buy-in during the process, and, ultimately, ensuring a successful launch. Following completion of the pilot, the initiative and all related activities would be implemented site-wide in Sunnyvale. A second pilot, mirroring the first, would be held at the Austin site with the same goals and intentions.

- Plans for expansion of virtual services to remote sites—primarily sales offices in the United States—were also designed.

- Requests for international expansion to Europe and Asia were to be accommodated following the U.S. launch. A proposal for expansion to Europe was written.

DESIGN AND STRUCTURE OF AMD CAREER PARTNERSHIP

The AMD Career Partnership™ Design Plan, which resulted from the in-depth needs assessment, provided guidelines for a process that addressed issues representing a major culture shift in both the external workplace and internally at AMD relative to recruitment and retention strategies. All data pointed out that the number one reason that most employees left an organization was lack of development opportunities. With the traditional loyalty contract irretrievably broken, development opportunities were identified as the missing link in a multi-dimensional approach to recruit and retain best in class. It was not to be viewed as a panacea but rather as a key missing link in a more holistic—and realistic—approach.

Given the enormity of the culture shift from a traditional, hierarchical organization toward a more evolved partnership comprising 3 key components—the organization, management, and employees—it was clearly evident that a comprehensive design plan must encompass many systemic linkages throughout AMD. These linkages were required to create an infrastructure that would support and ultimately sustain the AMD Career Partnership™ initiative. The goal was to ensure that the process itself would be integrated into the way AMD conducted business on a daily basis.

The AMD Career Partnership™ Design Plan was produced as the blueprint to guide the culture shift, accompanied by a more detailed AMD Career Partnership™ Learning Activities Design Plan.

The AMD Career Partnership™ Design Plan included:

- Program Goals/Objectives
- Target Audiences
- Strategic Rationale (the business case)
- Benefits to the Organization, Management, Employees
- Conceptual Overview
- Resources
- Design Methodology
- Assumptions

- Prerequisites
- Key Materials
- Phased Implementation
- Marketing Communications
- Roles and Responsibilities
- Timeline
- Budget
- Issues and Challenges

The Learning Activities Design Plan included a description of learning activities for managers and employees addressing many of the same categories listed above on a module-by-module basis.

Incorporated into the design were examples of organizational issues that would be affected by the culture shift, including:

- *Compensation.* How does a traditional vertical compensation plan accommodate increasingly lateral movement or development of breadth and depth of skills in-place; how are managers rewarded and recognized for supporting their employees' career development goals, etc.
- *Diversity.* How do I address a variety of cultures where it is viewed as bragging to articulate one's value-add to the organization?
- *Integration.* How do I merge AMD Career Partnership™ concepts with existing efforts: management development, new employee orientation, succession planning, etc.?

The design plan was reviewed and revised by selected key players, including those experts both inside and outside AMD. It was updated throughout the design, development, implementation, and evaluation process. The importance and value of a systematic design plan cannot be underestimated.

"Companies are losing talent because they don't approach employee retention systematically," said Quinn Spitzer, chairman of Kepner-Tregoe, Inc., a Princeton, New Jersey, management consultant. "We're finding holding on to key talent is an increasing issue," he said, noting that replacing key people can cost 3 to 5 times their annual salary. Spitzer said businesses that were able to keep people did such things as:

- Monitor, analyze, and come to understand the underlying causes of voluntary turnover.
- Develop systems to retain key employees, including communication. The more informed executives and employees are, the less likely turnover is to occur.

- Ensure that workers have a clear idea of the company's future and the implications for them.
- Establish formal career development programs. When an employee believes a company is genuinely interested in his career, an unwanted departure is less likely. (Taken from an article by John Cunniff, Associated Press, *San Francisco Examiner,* May 30, 1999)

An executive briefing was derived from the design plan and presented to senior executives for review and buy-in. This presentation tied the data from the needs assessment and the resulting design recommendations for a career development initiative directly to the business case. One example of a business case includes an analysis of the reasons for voluntary departure of employees from an organization and the subsequent negative impact on the company's bottom line. Lost revenue can be measured in terms of the cost of turnover replacement (recruiting costs, hiring bonuses, relocation expenses, HR and hiring managers' time, etc.). Soft costs can be more difficult to measure but take a tremendous toll including time of assimilation for the new employee resulting in lost productivity, impact on morale, and so on. An investment in proactive development measures could help minimize such an impact.

It was recognized that individual learning activities for managers and employees would be implemented earlier than some of the more problematic systemic issues that would require a culture shift within the organization. This proved to be the case as the pilot and implementation phase of the learning activities occurred over a 6-month timeframe. The larger systemic issues related to compensation, rewards and recognition, and so on, are still in the evolutionary pipeline. There have been slow but steady movements to address them; but these issues reside at the very core of any organization's culture, beliefs, and values. They require much more time and focused dedication. A 3- to 5-year evolution is not at all unusual. However, these are the very factors that are critical to address if an initiative is to be sustained.

Sustainability, however, can be measured in the interim. One positive example relative to AMD Career Partnership™ is that the initiative *has* been sustained—even during downturns, which the organization endured periodically, in part due to the impact on recruitment and retention. The survival of the initiative over the next 5 years will depend on whether the more severe systemic issues can change with the times.

TRAINING AND LEARNING ACTIVITIES

The pilot process was key to successfully implementing AMD Career Partnership™ learning activities. The term "learning activities" is used, traditionally, as the word "training" implied something that was classroom-based. While the initial activities did take place in the classroom, emphasis was placed on the learning activities that would occur on the job.

Key guidelines for the pilot process included the following:

- A demographically representative range of high performers from both employee and management ranks were selected. High performers were chosen so that a model of excellence could be set for the initiative. The pilot went through several stages of refinement prior to implementation thus allowing for an AMD "best fit." One size does not fit all!

- Formative evaluations throughout the process helped avoid negative surprises.

- Emphasis was placed on the ability to recognize risks taken, mistakes made, lessons learned, and opportunities for improvement. The pilot process provided the latitude to do this.

- Multidimensional communications were essential to keep all employees apprised of the progress of the initiative and to both set expectations and recalibrate them when necessary.

- Simultaneously, as the pilot for the learning activities progressed through its various stages, efforts were underway to escalate the necessity for establishing systemic linkages throughout AMD. Efforts to do so were a bit premature at this juncture.

Based on the design plan recommendations, 3 phases of testing the viability of the learning activities occurred prior to site-wide implementation. These phases included:

Alpha

The Alpha test was essentially a top-line walk-through with the pilot participants of both managers' and employees' learning activities with examples of the exercises and materials to be used. Feedback from the Alpha test was then used to refine the design of the learning activities prior to the next and more involved stage of testing.

Beta

The Beta test mirrored the actual training activities as closely as possible with pilot participants involved in all aspects of both the 1-day AMD Career Partnership™ for Managers' learning activities and the one-and-a-half day Career Development at AMD™ learning activities.

Pilot

The Pilot represented the actual final phase of the testing prior to site-wide implementation. At this point, materials, exercises, tools, etc., had been refined extensively. There were still, however, revisions of a lesser nature that were needed.

Implementation

Site-wide Implementation was the next phase. All materials were finalized, packaged, and ready for the employees and managers. Plans for the launch included a division-by-division presentation during upcoming quarterly communications meetings. These sessions were brief and included a testimonial from 1 or 2 of the original pilot participants; a lively 6-minute video overview of AMD Career Partnership™; distribution of a AMD Career Partnership™ brochure as a take-away; and closing statements of support from the division vice presidents.

At the same time, a barrage of marketing communications had been underway for several weeks preceding the implementation including articles in the company paper, advertisements on AMD-TV, online notification on the AMD intranet, and flyers distributed to every key location on the campus. Surprisingly, the 2 most successful marketing communication strategies were the testimonials from the pilot participants and the flyers. This was determined through a question asked when managers or employees registered for learning activities.

CONTENT

The purpose of AMD Career Partnership™ is to help employees understand and align their interests, values, and skills with the organization's future workforce requirements and rapidly changing business needs.

AMD Career Partnership™ is a 3-way agreement among the organization, managers, and employees. AMD (the organization) provides the resources, environment, processes, and tools. Managers guide and enable employees by communicating business needs, supporting learning activities, and providing resources to help employees meet their career goals and increase employability within AMD. Employees are responsible to work collaboratively with the organization to complete learning activities to achieve their career goals at AMD.

Given the above tenets, 2 sets of learning activities were implemented. A one-and-a-half day program, with follow-on career coaching, was provided for employees. A 1-day set of learning activities was designed for managers.

Career Development at AMD™ for employees is offered monthly in different formats. One month it is offered in back-to-back days; in alternate months, it is offered in 3 half-day sessions. These alternative options were a learning gained from early trial-and-error scheduling. The employees' session is limited to a maximum of 15 participants due to the intense nature of career exploration. A career coach teaches all sessions.

Career Development at AMD™ comprises the following learning modules and support resources:

Self-Assessment—Before deciding on a career goal and plan, an employee completes a multidimensional personal assessment, which enables them to:

- Assess their interests, values, skills, and personality preferences using a variety of career development tools
- Articulate their value-add to themselves and to AMD

Identifying Business Trends—Having completed a thorough assessment, employees benchmark their interests, values, and skills to:

- Assess their marketability in their current position or across AMD
- Explore trends in the industry and the organization as well as in their fields or functions
- Analyze strengths and opportunities for professional development in current positions related to longer-term career goals.

Creating Goals—Short-term professional development goals are written relating to longer-term career goals. These goals represent actions that can be taken while in the current position in order to move toward a longer-term career goal.

Moving Forward—Employees identify barriers that may prevent accomplishment of goals, and identify activities to overcome them.

Plan of Action—Specific action steps, the support needed, timelines, and measurements of success are identified (see Exhibit 1).

Connecting—This entails realizing the importance of establishing relationships to assist one's self and others in meeting goals.

Career Discussions with Managers—Employees receive tips on how to initiate and conduct a meaningful discussion with a manager.

As part of the learning activities, employees have the option to use 2 private coaching sessions. Most often these sessions deal with synthesizing the assessment data and developing career plans. A few employees do plan to leave the organization to seek opportunities outside the company. In those situations, which comprise a distinct minority, employees are granted 1 hour of career coaching to determine if there is any opportunity to retain them.

General outcomes for employee learning activities include the tools and preparation to begin a career development plan and initiate and conduct a career development discussion.

Supporting Career Development at AMD: The Manager's Role™ is a 1-day session that enables managers to:

- Articulate the business case for Career Partnership™ at AMD and relate the critical role managers play relative to retention and the career development strategy in particular.

- Distinguish between career development and performance development discussions.

- Discuss issues and challenges managers may face in dealing with their employees' career goals. Using performance support tools and engaging in a series of interactive exercises, managers brainstorm solutions to the issues.

- Relate the key objectives and outcomes of Career Development at AMD™ to their own staffs.

- Prepare for their roles and responsibilities in a career development discussion—and learn follow-up actions that would be helpful to their employees. Managers understand that is not enough to simply check the box by "holding a career development discussion"; it is the follow-up support that is most meaningful.

In summary, the managers' learning activities have not been as well-attended as the employees' sessions, partly because managers have not been required to attend them. Employees, conversely, are filling their sessions. This phenomenon has created a bounce-back effect—that is, employees return from their one-and-a-half day sessions expecting to have a career development discussion with their managers. Feedback to the Career Partnership™ staff is that managers who have not taken the Supporting Career Development at AMD: The Manager's Role™ learning activities often have little understanding of the difference between career and performance development discussions or how to help them.

These management issues relate to the importance of the cultural shift cited earlier. The values of the organization must be in alignment with the shift. In this case, the implication is that managers must be held accountable for their part in the retention strategy. Thus, required attendance at the Supporting Career Development at AMD: The Manager's Role™ learning activities is gaining increased momentum. Another recommendation includes a review of rewards and recognition for managers who support their employees' career growth. This suggestion is gaining ground as employees are being viewed as valued intellectual capital—and consideration is being given to including managerial competencies in these areas as part of performance reviews. Again, the state of organization cultural readiness is critical. The issue of manager accountability was first brought up in the needs assessment stage, but it was not until some degree of pain was felt and data from employees was collected that serious movement began in earnest.

Another aspect of the AMD Career Partnership™ process includes a Career Partnership™ Center—a 1-stop shop for career development needs. It contains a career resource library, an online learning lab with individual workstations providing access to the AMD intranet, access to the Internet, and multimedia stations.

At AMD, it was felt that the culture required a substantial bricks-and-mortar statement in the beginning as a concrete demonstration of the organization's commitment to Career Partnership™. It was also deemed important to avoid any stigma associated with outplacement activities and to establish a place that was centrally located, easily accessible, welcoming, and that could also serve as a quiet area for employees. The COO agreed and granted a space of nearly 3,000 square feet that was located in the main corporate headquarters building.

Other services offered through the Center include registration for an on-site MBA program; a Career Partnership™ Web page with a description of learning activities and services offered, resources available, frequently asked questions, directions for registration, etc.; and a class on Work/Life Balance to help employees learn to minimize stress through the use of a variety of tools and processes to achieve a greater sense of balance in their work, family, and personal lives.

MULTIDIMENSIONAL EVALUATION

Evaluation and measurement occurred throughout the AMD Career Partnership™ process. The primary goal was to attain the highest level of evaluation possible to determine the impact of the initiative as a retention strategy. The intention from the beginning of the process was to move past the lowest level of evaluation up through various levels of measurement including:

- Did participants learn new skills during the training?
- Were participants able to apply the knowledge and skills when they returned to their jobs?
- Did the learnings—particularly as they related to career management as a retention strategy—make a difference to the individual?
- At the highest level of evaluation, did career management as a retention strategy make a difference to AMD in both quantitative (metrics) and qualitative (anecdotal) terms?

A second goal was to ensure that evaluation techniques were interwoven through all aspects of the design and development process. This was accomplished through application of 2 methodologies: formative and summative evaluation.

Formative evaluation occurred at every step of the process. It was a way to ensure that each step of the process was tested and reviewed with quantifiable feedback. This means examining what was done well in terms of content, materials, learning activities; systemic linkage attempts; what could have been improved, added, or deleted; and what changes should be made.

This methodology, based on the application of systematic instructional design processes, helped mitigate major obstacles in all aspects of the process.

By the time the Pilot phase occurred, the revisions had dropped significantly. Consequently, the ratings for the actual and ongoing Implementation phase were high while the revisions remained very low. That is not to imply that AMD Career Partnership™ is not adjusted over time as new needs emerge.

At the lower levels of evaluation, all learning activities were evaluated immediately following their conclusion. The coaches and instructors were provided with the summarized feedback, which was then analyzed for strengths and needed improvements.

In addition, quantitative data was provided on a regular basis, which demonstrated current usage of all services including participation in learning activities, usage of the Center, etc. (see Exhibit 2). Often, summaries of the data were presented at quarterly communications meetings and measured against previous quarters to determine if usage was increasing. At this point, the evaluation techniques shifted into higher levels in an attempt to measure the application of knowledge and skills to the individual and the impact on the organization over time.

Other recommended strategies not yet implemented include conducting one-on-one interviews with senior management and follow-up focus groups with managers and employees. The purpose would be to determine if each level of the organization that articulated the criteria for success for the initiative during the needs assessment had found that their needs were or were not being met. A second approach would be to examine exit interview data to determine the impact on retention. As one division vice president stated during the needs assessment, "Lack of career development discussion and follow-up should not be a reason for leaving AMD."

EVALUATION SURVEY SUMMARY

In the case of AMD Career Partnership™ 2 separate surveys (see Exhibit 3) were electronically distributed to employees and managers who had attended the Career Development courses. The entire program had been in full operation for approximately 18 months at the time of distribution.

The numbers indicate the company has impacted approximately 9% of the target population in Sunnyvale. Early review of the responses indicate no real surprises and appear to validate some initial assumptions. At the time of this writing, focus groups are underway and the survey data is being analyzed in depth to determine direct impact on retention.

General Findings

The number of attendees for the employee training was 233. A 33% response rate from this group and initial results from the employee survey indicate that:

- Career Partnership Services have had a moderately positive impact on factors such as employee development, individual contributions to AMD as a company, attitude towards AMD as a good place to work, and the decision to remain with the company.

- Services were rated "good" (based on a scale of 1–5 with 5 as "excellent").

- 55.9% of the respondents went on to explore educational opportunities.

- 52.9% of the respondents are seeking development opportunities in their current positions.

- The career coaching ratings had a positive slant from those who had used the service.

- The more supportive employees felt managers were of Career Partnership, the more positively it impacted their decisions to remain at AMD.

- The better the overall rating of the development discussion, the better the managers' abilities were rated and the more positive the impact.

The managers' survey was also distributed electronically to all 68 attendees and had a 24% response rate. Early findings indicate:

- The better the manager felt about the quality of the tools and information provided, the more likely they were to recommend the services to others.

- A higher number of development discussions took place when the manager felt the employee was well prepared.

- As more managers reported having development discussions with employees, the strength of the agreement that Career Partnership services were beneficial to the employee increased.

- As the agreement that Career Partnership services made a positive difference to the individual increased, employees were more likely to have development discussions.

As survey results are being analyzed, clear validation is emerging that when managers attend the classes and are prepared to conduct a development discussion with employees the reaction is positive. It is equally clear that when they do not attend it has a negative effect.

At this stage the assumption can be made that lack of management participation in the services offered could negatively impact retention. Conversely, managers' participation appears to have impact in helping the employees meet career goals.

A further measurement that has been used is a comparison of overall site voluntary turnover rates with the rates of those participating in the Career Partnership program. Results of this analysis show that the voluntary turnover rate for program participants is 12.3% less than that of the overall population. These results lend strong support to the Career Partnership business case. Turnover rates will continue to be a critical measurement for program success.

Additional external validation for career development as a retention strategy has surfaced from a number of sources (see Exhibit 4).

LESSONS LEARNED

AMD Career Partnership™ has made a definite impact on the recruitment and retention strategy. It is still a work in progress and continues to evolve as the initiative expands across sites. Yet career management as a retention strategy remains fairly new, unexplored territory for many organizations. During the development process of AMD Career Partnership™ numerous companies, from banks to pharmaceutical firms, utility companies to oil producers, hospitals to high-tech plants, visited AMD and benchmarked the process. This was primarily because designing and developing career management as a retention strategy is a challenging process to implement and manage upward, as well as to validate the value add. Yes, there have been successes, but the lessons learned have been numerous and invaluable.

AMD was invited to participate in several think tanks sponsored by leading-edge corporate researchers who brought together some of the organizations that had actually carried the strategy through to implementation and evaluation. The primary purpose was to examine the challenges faced and successes achieved, but most important, to discuss the lessons learned. Not surprisingly, these organizations had, for the most part, experienced very similar challenges and lessons. The synergy was truly amazing.

Here are some of the key lessons learned at AMD:

Lesson #1—A thorough needs assessment is critical to the success of any initiative. Time invested on the front end of a process greatly minimizes costly mistakes and delays later. A well-executed design plan, containing the results of the needs assessment and recommendations for all aspects of the process, serves as a valuable blueprint to guide development, implementation, and evaluation. The design plan should not be considered a static treatise—rather, it is a living document that is changed and adjusted as the process evolves to best meet the needs of the organization, management, and employees.

Lesson #2—Tie the initiative directly to a business case based on solid data. Credibility for an initiative is based on the direct impact to an organization's bottom line. Substantiating data to justify an investment in a program is essential to obtaining executive level support.

Lesson #3—Keep the "future perfect" in mind but start small. When presenting an executive summary, it is useful to have 2 or 3 back-up options for every strategy. It is easy to have an idealized view of what an initiative should look like in a "future perfect" world once one is armed with data from the needs assessment. Reality however, often intrudes in the form of budgetary concerns, time or resource constraints, cultural readiness, etc. A recommended approach would be to have 3 strategies: the ideal, a medium compromise, and a small but manageable aspect of the overall process. Frequently, an organization may start at a small level and, following successful validation, gradually move to the medium and ideal stages over time. There is no right or wrong approach. It is simply useful to constantly assess where the initiative is relative to the idealized version—and the milestones and objectives needed to achieve it.

It can be much easier to start small, thus the recommendation to begin with a pilot group of 6 to 8 people is preferred. Another approach would be to pilot in a small workgroup or division.

How to start small? Bring in guest speakers on hot topics for brown bag lunches. Introduce and integrate new concepts into existing initiatives such as management development training, new employee orientation, mentoring, job rotation programs, and so on.

Lesson #4—Dealing with the "I want it yesterday" syndrome. Once a demand for an initiative is made, the expectation is that a program will be delivered yesterday if not before with severe timelines and high expectations. An effective way to address this issue when needing to complete a needs assessment and design plan is to present a design, development, implementation, and evaluation strategy to senior executives. This strategy should be built on a solid business case, supported by external and internal data, with milestones identified for all phases such as needs assessment, conducting a pilot, and the benefits for using this approach. With this approach, it can be seen that a project is moving forward in an organized manner, and the results of each phase will be communicated on a regular basis. This buys time for the critical early steps of the initiative. This approach can falter if communications at all levels are not maintained on a regular basis.

Lesson #5—Accountability for managers is key to making a retention strategy work. AMD Career Partnership™ proved to be a tough culture shift and organizational readiness had a great deal to do with it. Early in the process, management accountability was identified as a high priority but it took approximately 4 years before significant movement occurred—not unusual according to several organizations dealing with career management as a retention strategy. A threshold of pain, such as increasing turnover in a specific division, can be a great motivator.

Neither is it enough to check the box by calling managers accountable for simply holding a career management conversation. Conducting follow-up evaluations is critical to determine if the manager took supportive action if the situation required it.

Lesson #6—Checking the box is easy; the cultural shift (values, beliefs, etc.) is the hard part. Learning activities and fancy Web pages can be implemented, mini-career centers can be in place, and resources made available. But the fundamentals required to catalyze the shift are necessary to create an infrastructure to sustain the process. Without them, an initiative can easily become flavor-of-the-month and disappear in time.

Lesson #7—It is easy to focus too much on the tools and online wizardry and lose sight of what is really important. While making performance development tools, processes and guidelines, as well as interactive exercises, available online is important, the fundamental change management occurs during the dialogue between the employee and the manager. That proved to be the critical game breaker for all involved.

Lesson #8—Never combine a career development with a performance development discussion. Doing so tends to force employees back into their current "job box," as performance management discussions tend to reflect on the past and skill expansion primarily within the immediate position. These required discussions also tend to be management-driven. Career development discussions on the other hand, should be initiated by employees, and they should focus on the future, either relative to expanding skills in the current position or out of the immediate job box altogether. These conversations should not be conducted in the manager's office but in neutral territory. Provisions should be made available for alternative resources if an employee does not feel comfortable having this type of discussion with a manager.

Lesson #9—More emphasis is needed on the changing role of HR representatives and management. The 3-way contractual agreement (the organization, management, and employees) leaves out a fourth and critical component. In the role of HR relative to career management as a retention strategy, HR must be viewed as proactive in helping resolve the turnover dilemma and, thus, emerging more as a business partner, or as the internal headhunter. It was not until after the launch of AMD Career Partnership™ that a tool was developed to help HR not only collect data to evaluate the reasons for turnover and the data behind it but to also translate that data into the dollar cost to the organization to justify front-end investment to mitigate loss of talent. In hindsight, this would have been useful much earlier in the process.

Lesson #10—Establish a "portfolio of consistencies." As the assessment and design phases are completed, it will be valuable to establish a foundation of philosophy, mission, learning activities, and resources so that practices may be replicated from site to site—and so that silo blockage, or the "not invented here" syndrome, can be avoided. Such an approach also minimizes time wasted in setting up the operations and logistics to support the initiative. In this manner, each site can celebrate and customize practices and materials to fit their local needs, yet the entire organization has a level of consistency relative to the overall initiative.

Exhibit 1 Career Partnership

CENTER DATA

WALK-INS*	PHONES	LAB #	LAB HRS	BOOKS

* INCLUDES: TUITION ASSISTANCE, SITN, ON SITE MBA, GENERAL QUESTIONS, TOURS ETC.

COURSE DATA

	EXEMPT	NON-EXEMPT	MANAGER	TTL #	TTL HRS	MALE	FEMALE	0-4.9 YRS	5-9.9 YRS	10 + YRS

COURSE DATA

TRAINING
TRAINING
WLB CLASS

	EXEMPT	NON-EXEMPT	MANAGER	TTL #	TTL HRS	MALE	FEMALE	0-4.9 YRS	5-9.9 YRS	10 + YRS

EVALUATION DATA
(SCALE OF 1 TO 4: WHERE 1 = STRONGLY DISAGREE AND 4 = STRONGLY AGGREE)

TRAINING
TRAINING
WLB CLASS

OCT	NOV	DEC	JAN	FEB	MAR	TOTAL

COUNSELING DATA
DOES NOT REFLECT REPEAT CLIENTS, ONLY NEW ONES. (40 APPTS. JAN-MAR.)

Exhibit 1. Career Partnership (Continued)

MALE

FEMALE

LENGTH OF EMPLOYMENT   <1 YR   1-5 YRS   5-10 YRS   10-15 YRS   15 + YRS

EDUCATIONAL LEVEL   HS   AA/AS   BA/BS   MASTERS

COUNSELING DATA - GENERAL REASONS FOR COMING

HIGH

MEDIUM

LOW

Exhibit 2. Employee Survey Questionnaire

How did you first hear about the?

___Fliers   ___Web site   ___Recommended by another employee

___Other:_____

Please rate the overall quality of the Career Partnership services that you have used by selecting from the rating scale below each item.

Career Self-Reliance Training (2 days)

1	2	3	4	5
Poor	Fair	No Experience	Good	Excellent

Career Partnership's Manager's Training

1	2	3	4	5
Poor	Fair	No Experience	Good	Excellent

Career Counseling

1	2	3	4	5
Poor	Fair	No Experience	Good	Excellent

Career Partnership Center Library

1	2	3	4	5
Poor	Fair	No Experience	Good	Excellent

Career Partnership Center's Multimedia lab

1	2	3	4	5
Poor	Fair	No Experience	Good	Excellent

If you have had a career development discussion with your manager please rate the following:

How well did the training provide you with the tools and information needed have a career development discussion with your manager?

1	2	3	4	5
Poor	Fair	No Opinion	Good	Excellent

Your level of preparedness

1	2	3	4	5
Poor	Fair	No Opinion	Good	Excellent

Rate your overall opinion of the Career Development discussion

1	2	3	4	5
Poor	Fair	No Opinion	Good	Excellent

Your Manager's ability to have a Career Development discussion as opposed to a performance review

1	2	3	4	5
Poor	Fair	No Opinion	Good	Excellent

Exhibit 2. Employee Survey Questionnaire (*Continued*)

Your Manager's supportiveness of your career development plan

1	2	3	4	5
Poor	Fair	No Opinion	Good	Excellent

Your Manager's ability to provide constructive suggestions

1	2	3	4	5
Poor	Fair	No Opinion	Good	Excellent

Your Manager's follow up

1	2	3	4	5
Poor	Fair	No Opinion	Good	Excellent

What actions have you taken due to your participation in the Career Self-Reliance course? Please check all that may apply.

___Create a Career Development Plan   ___Have a Career Development discussion with Manager

___Seek development opportunities in current position   ___Investigate additional training

___Explore educational opportunities   ___Update your resume

___Explore other positions at AMD   ___Conduct informational interviews and/or network

___Have taken no action since Career Self-Reliance Course

Other:_____

_____

If you have taken some action relative to your career development at AMD, has it resulted in any of the following? Please check all that apply.

___Expanded development in current position   ___Made a lateral move (changed jobs at same level)

___Received a promotion   ___Validated that you are currently in the best position

Exhibit 2. Employee Survey Questionnaire (*Continued*)

___It has not resulted in any changes

___Other:_____

Please rate Career Partnership services impact on the following

Your individual development (satisfaction and productivity)

1	2	3	4	5
Poor	Fair	No Impact	Good	Excellent

Your contributions to your group or department

1	2	3	4	5
Poor	Fair	No Impact	Good	Excellent

Your contributions to AMD as a company

1	2	3	4	5
Poor	Fair	No Impact	Good	Excellent

Your self confidence and self esteem

1	2	3	4	5
Poor	Fair	No Impact	Good	Excellent

Work-Life balance and dealing with stress

1	2	3	4	5
Poor	Fair	No Impact	Good	Excellent

Your attitude towards AMD as a good place to work

1	2	3	4	5
Poor	Fair	No Impact	Good	Excellent

Your decision to remain at AMD

1	2	3	4	5
Poor	Fair	No Impact	Good	Excellent

Your decision to come to AMD

1	2	3	4	5
Poor	Fair	No Impact	Good	Excellent

If you would be willing to participate in a focus group regarding Career Partnership services please include your name and extension. All responses to this survey and in the focus groups will be kept confidential.

Name: _____ ext:_____

Exhibit 3. Managers' Survey

Please rate the overall quality of the Career Partnership's Manager Training.

1	2	3	4	5
Poor	Fair	No Experience	Good	Excellent

Have you had any career development discussions with your employee? ___No ___Yes If yes, how many? ___

How well did the Manager's Training prepare you for a career development discussion with employees?

1	2	3	4	5
Poor	Fair	No Experience	Good	Excellent

How well did the Manager's Training provide you with the tools and information needed to assist employees in creating a career development plan.

1	2	3	4	5
Poor	Fair	No Experience	Good	Excellent

In the career discussion you have had with employees, the employee was well prepared to discuss their career and a career development plan.

1	2	3	4	5
Strongly Disagree	Disagree	No Opinion	Agree	Strongly Agree

In your opinion, Career Partnership services have made a positive difference to your employees at an individual level

1	2	3	4	5
Strongly Disagree	Disagree	No Opinion	Agree	Strongly Agree

Career Partnership services have made a positive difference to your group.

1	2	3	4	5
Strongly Disagree	Disagree	No Opinion	Agree	Strongly Agree

Career Partnership provides beneficial services to your employees for career development.

1	2	3	4	5
Strongly Disagree	Disagree	No Opinion	Agree	Strongly Agree

Career Partnership provides beneficial services to you as a manager.

1	2	3	4	5
Strongly Disagree	Disagree	No Opinion	Agree	Strongly Agree

I would recommend the Career Partnership Center's Services to AMD employees and managers

1	2	3	4	5
Strongly Disagree	Disagree	No Opinion	Agree	Strongly Agree

Exhibit 3. Managers' Survey (Continued)

Have employees taken action beyond the career discussion, to your knowledge.
___Yes ___No ___Unknown
If yes, what type(s) of action(s) and how many employees?

___Create a Career Development Plan   ___Have a Career Development discussion
                                                                   with Manager

___Seek development opportunities   ___Investigate additional training
in current position
___Explore educational opportunities   ___Update your resume
___Explore other positions at AMD   ___Conduct informational interviews
                                                                   and/or network

___Have taken no action since Career
Self-Reliance Course

Other:_____

How did you first hear about the Career Partnership Center?

___Fliers   ___Career Partnership Web site   ___Recommended by another
AMD employee
___Other:_____

Please rate the quality of any other Career Partnership services have you used
Career Self-Reliance course

1	2	3	4	5
Poor	Fair	No Experience	Good	Excellent

Career Counseling

1	2	3	4	5
Poor	Fair	No Experience	Good	Excellent

Career Partnership Center's Library

1	2	3	4	5
Poor	Fair	No Experience	Good	Excellent

Career Partnership Center's Multimedia Lab

1	2	3	4	5
Poor	Fair	No Experience	Good	Excellent

Comments _____
_____
_____
_____
_____

Exhibit 4. Recent External Data Validation

More recently, additional external data has surfaced to further validate career development as a recruiting and retention strategy. Here is a sample of the data:

"Is Your Company An Employer of Choice?"—In a Conference Board of New York survey, companies responded to the need for skilled employees in a tough labor pool by striving to become "employers of choice." Seventy-five percent of 102 companies are in the process of improving the way they are viewed by potential employees. What are the characteristics that define an employer of choice? According to HR executives, the top seven factors believed to have a "great deal" of impact are:

Career Development/Advancement	68%
Compensation Plan/Level	65%
Reputation in Community	61%
Management/Leadership Style	59%
Corporate Culture	56%
Profitability	51%

Also noted was that 68% of employees wanted to work at a company that offers both career development and advancement.

(Source: *Employee Relations Bulletin*, June 21, 1996)

54% of CEOs say *attracting* the right employees is much harder now than five years ago; 57% say *keeping* them is even tougher. The toughest to get and keep? IT professionals—you are competing with the world.

(Source: *Canadian Business Magazine*, 1999)

85% of employees leave due to reasons other than pay:
Poor supervisor skills/attitudes
No perceived career growth/opportunities
Job tasks not interesting or challenging
No opportunity to voice concerns

(Source: *Saratoga Institute Study*, 1997)

WetFeet.com (a career research site) says college students don't value pay as much as some other career-related items. In a survey of seniors and MBA candidates from more than 50 schools:

- 98% rated "working on a challenging and interesting assignment" as highly important
- More than 90% cited "good training for future work" and "great co-workers"
- Only 84% rated salary as important

(Source: WetFeet.com)

ABOUT THE CONTRIBUTORS

Beth Lama (blama@torchiana.com) is vice president, corporate career development at Torchiana, Mastrov, and Sapiro, Inc. Career Management Solutions, and former program manager of career partnership at Advanced Micro Devices. She is a pioneer in the development of proactive corporate career development programs, using a unique systems design model, which can directly impact recruitment, retention, and workforce planning. Lama has over 18 years experience working in Fortune 500 companies including Advanced Micro Devices, Inc., Apple Computer, Inc., and Hewlett-Packard, Inc. Her background includes career development, management development, succession planning, organizational change management, sales training, and leadership development. Most recently, Lama developed and managed one of the first company-wide corporate career development programs, entitled "Career Partnership." It is benchmarked as a "model of excellence" by numerous corporations throughout the United States and abroad. Lama has earned considerable recognition in the national media, including television and radio, and as a speaker at national and international conferences. She was selected to represent the views of several Fortune 500 companies on career development at a symposium, "Dialogue on Training and Employment Programs in America," sponsored by the Honorable Robert Reich, U.S. Department of Labor. Lama earned a bachelor of arts degree with honors in English from the University of the Pacific. She also received a teaching degree and conducted post-graduate work at San Jose State University. Professional affiliations include the National Career Development Association, the American Counseling Association, the Career Planning and Adult Development Network, the American Society for Training and Development, and the National Society for Performance and Instruction.

Lynda K. Munoz (lynda.munoz@amd.com) manages the Career Partnership Center at Advanced Micro Devices, Inc., in Sunnyvale, California. As a senior employee programs administrator, Munoz was instrumental in the design and implementation of the Career Partnership process at AMD. With over 25 years in Silicon Valley high-tech companies, Munoz's career includes career development, human resources, technical training, supervision, and manufacturing. Given her multidimensional experience, she has developed the reputation of approaching problems as opportunities and creating innovative solutions, resulting in continuous career growth and opportunity. A native of California, Munoz holds a certificate in Training and Human Resource Development from the University of Santa Cruz and has conducted undergraduate work in business from the University of Phoenix. She is certified in the use of the Career Architect suite of tools. Professional affiliations include the Career Planning and Adult Development Network, the American Society for Training and Development, the National Association for Female Executives, and the National Society for Performance and Instruction.

CHAPTER TWELVE

Allstate Insurance

A recruitment and selection process that leverages the Internet, internal database technology, and work analysis tools

INTRODUCTION

Background

Recruiting and selection is at the core of any organization's competitive advantage. The ability to attract, select, and retain highly skilled and motivated people is key to survival in today's constantly changing marketplace. Many companies are vying to attract the top echelon of the labor pool. Where these individuals seek employment cannot be left to chance. Corporations must aggressively market themselves and actively seek out the people who best match the organization's needs. Allstate is no exception.

Allstate is the second-largest personal lines insurance company in the United States, as well as a major life insurer. It insures 1 of every 8 homes and automobiles in the country, and provides insurance for more than 20 million consumers in the United States and Canada. Its parent company, the Allstate Corporation, is the nation's largest publicly held personal lines insurance company. Based in Northbrook, Illinois, Allstate has over 15,000 agents and 39,000 nonagent employees.

The recruitment and selection process at Allstate is one of the most critical of human resources processes. While other HR processes are important, a well-executed recruitment and selection process ensures that the right people are selected for the right jobs. Companies that fail to recruit and retain the best individuals for the job and the organization end up with only the "best of the rest." These organizations ultimately pay more for training, performance management, and additional recruitment to replace poor performers.

Allstate has always been committed to recruiting people who will best match the needs of the company. From hiring agents to claims adjusters to underwriters, to hiring home office, life, or sales personnel, the Allstate Insurance Company has consistently sought the most qualified individuals to fill its openings. However, simply matching Allstate's past recruiting successes will not be enough to maintain its rapid business growth requirements. To add the value the organization requires, recruiters must be competitive with professionals in other organizations looking for similar individuals. It is critical that Allstate's HR personnel have the training, processes, and leadership needed to meet the challenges of the twenty-first century. In order to ensure that the people selected will be the best match for the organization, HR professionals must work closely with their business partners as collaborators to fully understand the organization's needs.

The *Allstate Recruitment & Selection Process* is the company's process for attracting and hiring qualified employees and agents. This process enables HR selection professionals and line managers to consistently attract job applicants with the necessary skills, abilities, and other characteristics needed to fill openings identified during staffing planning and/or throughout the year. How?

- Ensuring that the approach is linked to strategic business plans
- Ensuring that the approach is proactive and responsive
- Providing a logical, systematic approach that integrates all critical recruitment activities
- Leveraging technology

The overall goals of the process are to help recruiters:

- Link department staffing plans more closely to business plans
- Conduct recruiting efforts more efficiently
- Leverage prospect and applicant pools to reduce recruiting cycle times
- Increase applicant and new hire quality

The phases of the Allstate Recruitment & Selection Process is depicted in Figure 1:

Note that "Measure" is not considered to be a distinct phase of the process. Because it is so critical to the success of the overall process, measurement has been highlighted, and a section of this case is dedicated to it specifically.

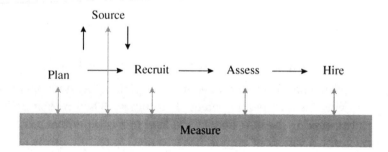

Figure 1 Recruitment & Selection Process

The purpose of each phase is listed below:

- *Plan*—To create strategies/plans to meet business staffing needs
- *Source*—To implement proactive sourcing plans to create a pool of prospects
- *Recruit*—To develop a strategy to fill an open position and to prescreen prospects

- *Assess*—To identify qualified applicants for an open position and to select the best qualified applicant
- *Hire*—To verify the best qualified applicant's background information and to hire a new employee or agent

To successfully execute the process in today's market, Allstate has embraced the use of technology. Technology can improve the company's selection processes as well as increase efficiencies.

The first section of this case reviews Allstate's approach to leveraging technology to recruit and select high-performing agents. This study will explain how technology was used to develop both a recruiting strategy and customized selection process for those agents. More general approaches for using technology at Allstate for recruitment and selection will be described later.

The design team for the agent selection effort consisted of:

- HR professionals within the Home Office Selection Team (including the HR director and two HR staff)
- One HR professional from the field who was assigned to this project full-time on a temporary basis
- Industrial/Organizational psychologists from the Allstate Research and Planning Center

Other people within Allstate also supported this effort at different times in the process (e.g., Sales and Legal professionals). Financial support and resources for the effort were provided by the Sales organization for whom this work was completed.

The Business Issues for Agent Selection

Why are recruiting and selection for agents so important? Allstate agents interact every day with customers and potential customers. Their role in delivering value is critical. Having the best people will lead to a competitive advantage.

For many years, a variety of approaches was used to recruit agents at Allstate such as job fairs, ads in local and national newspapers, and referrals from managers, employees, and agents. In the past 2 years, Allstate has also been using the Internet as a recruiting tool. That process will be described in more detail later in this chapter.

The selection process Allstate used in the past for selecting agents included a proprietary preemployment selection test. That test served the organization well and was utilized in the hiring process of agents for close to 10 years. It was designed to predict success in new business acquisition for employee agents. Because Allstate started hiring a different type of agent called exclusive agents (independent contractors) and job requirements changed, an updated selection process was needed. Also, with aggressive business growth goals for the organization, predicting performance for this new type of agent was critical to the organization's growth strategy as well as long-term strength and competitiveness.

A 2-phase approach was used to update the selection process being used for agent selection. In the first phase, in-depth analyses were conducted to update the scoring system of the current test. Specifically, relationships were examined between how agents answered the different questions on the test and performance on the job. Job performance in these analyses was measured by actual business results—new business acquired. Updates were made to the scoring system to ensure its maximum ability to predict performance on the job. The second phase of the process was to develop additional components for a new selection system that would predict other business outcomes (e.g., customer relationships/customer retention) as well as new business acquired.

Job Analysis

The process used to develop the new selection process was based on both a job analysis and other research of what defines a "star" performer. Data were collected from the following methods:

- Work/job analysis interviews with current agents at different performance levels
- Interviews with agency managers
- Benchmarking
- Analyses of longitudinal data files of test responses and business results
- Analyses of data from application forms

Based on these detailed analyses, the dimensions were identified that were critical for success and that distinguished "stars" from lower performers. There were a number of key features that distinguished star agents and low-performing agents. For example, star agents function more as managers and/or owners of their own businesses rather than as salespeople. Similarly, star agents focused on financial results and understood in detail how processes and policies would affect them financially.

It became evident that star agents use very innovative and creative processes to profitably build their businesses. For example, in several of the interviews conducted with this group, they indicated that certain markets were not being tapped. The star agent looked upon this as an opportunity to provide insurance products and services to these emerging markets. (See Exhibit 1 for the basic work analysis approach.)

The future selection of agents is based on the dimensions required for success as an agent. To ensure the best selection system, the design team determined how to improve the recruitment of star agents. The next steps related to the selection process included investigating selection tools already available that could help measure the dimensions identified as critical for success. Along with researching products, the design team interviewed various vendors and consultants to determine the fit between Allstate's needs and their products. After an extensive search it was determined that the best competitive advantage would be gained by custom building a selection process for future agent selection.

DESIGN AND STRUCTURE

After the job analysis work was completed, the team designed a technology-based selection system to increase chances of selecting high performers. There are several approaches to building such a system. The first is a common selection process for all positions in the company based on core competencies. Another is a customized process for each position. Finally, there can be a combination of the 2 approaches focusing on core skills but still allowing for customized tools for technical or other unique areas. There are advantages and disadvantages of each approach as shown in Table 1.

In addition to an overall strategy, there were other specific issues that needed to be considered:

- Technology capabilities to administer, score, and track a technology-based test
- Skill levels of those administering the test
- Ability to meet legal requirements and demonstrate validity
- Maintenance issues around a database, technical problem resolutions, upgrades
- Ensuring that all data would be uploaded into a centralized database so ongoing analyses could be conducted
- Consistency in how the selection tools are utilized for internal and external candidates

The early design of the selection process included these types of issues and many more. However, the design team made basic decisions early in the process to:

- Utilize a technology-driven system
- Consider cost-effectiveness of the final product
- Develop and communicate clearly the intent and business case for changing selection processes, and educate all users on the use of technology and how to use the newly created system to hire more high performers

Table 1. Advantages and Disadvantages of Selection System Approaches

Approach	Advantages	Disadvantages
Common Approach	• Relatively low cost • Relatively easy to administer • Assesses core skills required throughout organization • Reinforces the importance of core skills and values of the organization	• Does not assess unique skills of different positions
Customized Approach	• Can focus on full range of skills required including the unique requirements for a particular position • Can provide realistic job previews of individual positions	• Takes more time to develop than other approaches • Higher cost than other approaches • More difficult to administer than other approaches since each position has its own unique selection process
Blended Approach	• Assesses core skills required throughout the organization • Can consider the full range of skills required including the unique requirements for a particular position • Can provide realistic job previews of individual positions • Cost effective for the value obtained	• Takes more time to develop than common approach • Has higher cost than common approach

With these decisions as the basis for building the system, it was agreed that the customized process should be built for selecting agents. A customized system was chosen for several reasons. One primary reason was that the requirements for agents, especially agents who are not employees of the organization, are unique from other positions at Allstate. In addition, a customized approach was expected to provide the most competitive advantage.

Continuing with an effort to use technology to support the process, an online selection test for agent positions was built. To ensure that ongoing analyses could easily be conducted, a decision was made that any new system for selecting agents must include centralized electronic storage of data.

The agent position is one of the hardest positions to fill. Allstate looks for specific skills, abilities, and other characteristics in order to be certain to serve its customers expertly and efficiently. For example, agents must be able to bring in new business and retain customers (i.e., have both sales skills and customer relationship skills) and have the ability to manage an agency (e.g., financial management skills). Over this past year, the design team built a highly effective screening tool. The process has 3 main components: a scorable application form, a screening test, and a structured interview.

Agent Selection Process

The first component in the agent selection process is a scorable application form. It consists of many of the standard questions any company asks (e.g., name, work history, education, etc.). The design team added questions that have been shown in Allstate's research to be related to business acquisition skills. This application form is completed online and is scored as "proceed" or do not "proceed." This is the first step in the selection process for agents. To leverage technology further, the team will place the scorable application on Allstate's Internet site during the year 2000. (See Exhibit 2 for a sample view of Allstate's online application.)

The second component is the new screening test for Allstate's agent candidates. This test resides on agent hiring managers' laptops as well as those of HR professionals in the field. This is a fairly lengthy segment that consists of biodata (or biographical data) and situational questions. The biodata questions examine both past and current experiences and/or behaviors. For example, questions ask about prior experience selling insurance, prior experience dealing with customers, and a variety of other topics. The situational questions actually describe a situation, and the candidate is asked how he/she would handle this situation. Candidates will score as high, medium, low, or not qualified based on all their responses. Results to both the scorable application and screening test can be obtained in a matter of minutes.

The third component in the selection process is the structured interview. Based on the work analysis interviews of star agents and other research, structured, behavior-based interview guides were created. The questions focused on the skills and experiences of candidates on a number of dimensions related to success as an exclusive agent. The manager, trained in how to conduct interviews and evaluate candidates, then scores the answers to the questions based on the past behaviors and the relevant behavior being assessed.

Together, the scorable application form, screening test, and structured interview provide information to help the manager and/or HR professional determine which agent candidates are best matched to the opportunity.

Technology Support

Although not part of the formal process, reports are available that allow the field and Home Office to have immediate access to testing and hiring data on agent candidates company-wide through a database system.

The final design of the new system includes a total technology strategy for recruitment and selection. The master plan includes the ability to find candidates through the Internet, link candidates to a database management system for résumés, provide an online application through the Internet, and track candidates' flow as they move through the agent selection process. The strategy includes timelines for implementation and country-wide access.

In terms of sourcing candidates through the Internet, the design team analyzed the various search engines that are now available for the purpose of recruiting. They became experts in their use, both in posting a position as well as reviewing and categorizing résumés already provided by the site. Once they thoroughly understood this new process of finding candidates, they developed a training course to pass on their expertise to HR professionals in the field offices.

Internet sourcing strategies, the agent selection process, and the résumé tracking system have been implemented. The next phase includes having the online application on the Internet and linking that system to the résumé tracking system. One pilot test of the Internet-based, online application has been completed. That pilot test allowed centralized recruiters to screen candidates for a few individual regions. Although the technology was effective, the regions wanted more direct involvement in the recruiting and selection of candidates for their areas. Future pilot tests of the Internet, therefore, will be conducted with hiring managers and HR professionals within the regions.

IMPLEMENTATION

After the design of the technology processes, the next steps of agent selection implementation included:

- Testing the new tools and platform
- Reviewing current cutoff scores for the new tool

- Designing the rollout for the new online system country-wide
- Rolling out the online Internet system for the scorable application form

As the new agent selection process was implemented, a decision regarding the focus of scoring was needed. Specifically, a final determination needed to be made if the agent selection process was going to focus only on new business production (as in the prior test) or combine new business with a customer relationship element. A validation study provided evidence that both dimensions could be utilized with positive business results.

Some additional items that were considered included:

- If the focus for agents was exclusively on new business during the first 12 or 18 months, the new business option was the strongest.
- Using a combined key would help identify candidates who could both produce new business and develop strong customer relationships.
- The scoring system could be adjusted in the future as organizational needs and requirements change.

Implementation Issues

In implementing a new recruiting and selection system, there were a variety of other issues that needed to be considered. These issues were raised both in conjunction with agent recruiting and selection as well as recruiting and selection in general. These issues and questions are outlined below.

Knowledge/Skills of HR

- What are the challenges in placing staff into recruiting and selection positions?
- What training is in place to ensure consistent standards of excellence for recruiters and selection consultants?
- How is intellectual capital built in this area?
- Are there key resources to respond to specific topic areas? For what specific areas are those experts needed?
- How should technology or other tools be used to provide ongoing training and support?

Consistency

- What policies and guidelines are in place related to selection (e.g., retesting policies, handling of internal transfers)?
- How is adherence to internal policies and procedures assured?
- How will policies, guidelines, etc., be communicated?

Legal Requirements

- What current processes are in place to ensure that all legal requirements are met in the development and implementation of all selection policies and procedures?
- How are those processes communicated?

Involvement of Key Business Units

- Are partnerships in place with each client group to ensure involvement and buy-in in the development and implementation of new processes?

Communication Issues

- Are the processes in place to ensure that all the necessary groups understand selection strategies as well as policies and guidelines?

  Home Office
  Field Human Resources
  Client groups
  Organizational leaders

Transfer of Knowledge

- What processes are in place to ensure knowledge is transferred when people change positions (e.g., test administration, security, specific knowledge areas, etc.)?

Database Issues

- Who has (or will have) responsibility for maintaining the centralized database(s)?
- What processes have been established to define who will have access to information and what specific information each group will be able to access?
- How will privacy of information be protected?
- What security procedures will be developed to ensure that only those needing access to specific information for a legitimate business reason have access?

Ongoing Reviews

- Are processes in place to address compliance issues to ensure that policies and guidelines are being followed?
- Are processes in place to conduct ongoing reviews and analyses to monitor effectiveness, examine EEO-related issues, conduct analyses for different strategic purposes (e.g., HR planning), etc.?

Specific Implementation Plan

Specifically, the basic elements of the implementation plan for the agent selection process included:

- Developing the online selection system
- Conducting a usability test of the online selection system to determine aspects such as user-friendliness as well as image of the company
- Making revisions to the online system based on the usability test
- Making a decision on scoring options and scoring key
- Programming the selection test with the scoring key
- Testing and proofing the scoring system
- Designing training for test administrators
- Designing training for Field and Home Office users
- Writing job aids for future reference and training of new users
- Training in-house PC support to field questions and system problems
- Developing a process to monitor the system and continue to gather data

The new selection system was implemented in early 1999. The data are being tracked and monitored. A release of the system has just been rolled out that includes enhancements such as increased speed of the system. To date, the feedback has been very positive by system users. Early results are summarized in the next section.

EVALUATION

Since late 1998, data have been gathered on the performance of the new agent selection system. There is evidence to support that the new selection process is highly effective. Analyses have shown showed that those who perform better during the selection process produce better business results.

Data will continue to be collected, and ongoing analyses will be conducted. The following areas will continue to be:

- Passing rates
- Passing rates for protected EEO groups
- Score distributions
- Relationship of test scores to business results

Managers making hiring decisions base their decisions on the information gathered as part of the selection process. Communications to the regions and agency managers have clearly articulated the relationship between test results and agent business results. The new reporting system is expected to improve business results since the data on hiring quality can be reviewed instantly by agency managers, regional managers, and Home Office directors. Managers and directors are already using information from these reports to drive recruiting efforts to increase the number of people tested per hire to get the best candidates possible. A higher percentage of high-scoring candidates are, in fact, being hired than before the new system was implemented.

SUMMARY

Technology As a Strategy

Allstate's recruitment and selection process is heavily supported by technology (see Figure 2). The Human Resource team looks to the Internet for candidate leads, manages its candidate pool with a résumé software system, and screens for agents using an online test. The team will be using a scorable application for general employee selection by early 2000 and will have both the agent and employee applications available via the Internet early in the year 2000.

The résumé software system can manage the entire hiring process as it interfaces with other systems.

- A candidate can submit his or her résumé via the Internet, fax, or paper, which is then scanned into the résumé database by an Allstate recruiter. It is worth noting that a variety of methods are used to recruit employees and agents (e.g., Internet, newspapers, direct mailers, and other

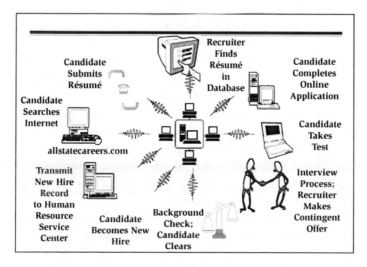

Figure 2 Recruitment and Technology-Based Selection

methods). Résumés obtained from each of these methods are entered into the database.

- A recruiter performing a match search for an opening will find those résumés in the database.
- The candidate will complete an application online (either via the Internet or Allstate laptop/desktops) which is automatically stored in the résumé database.
- Depending on the position for which the person applies, the candidate may take a screening test.
- If the candidate is qualified, the interview process will be initiated.
- If a contingent offer is made, the résumé system will send the information to the vendor who completes a background check which is required for many Allstate jobs.
- If the background check comes back clear, the candidate will officially become a hire, and the new hire's record will be transferred to Allstate's Human Resource Service Center.

With this system, the initial data remain intact eliminating much of the paperwork that was needed in the past. Once a candidate enters his or her information into the database via the application form, that information is transferred to all parts of the organization needing the information.

With the volume of résumés that come into Allstate, it is necessary to manage the data with a sophisticated system. A résumé system stores both résumés and job opening information and allows a user to search the database for résumés to match certain openings. The key piece in using this system is the description of openings. Skills are pulled off résumés and matched to openings that have a need for those skills. The opening must be written correctly in order for the system to find qualified matches.

Recruiters are dedicated to continually updating the résumé database with candidates. Currently it holds 140,000 résumés and is projected to store 300,000 by 2001. Allstate has filled over 6,000 openings using this system. The system goes beyond a matching system for candidates to openings. It allows the HR team to measure processes. For example, the system has the capability to identify which sources produce the best results. Specifically, it can determine how many résumés come from the Internet, which Internet sites result in the most candidates, the cost per hire, etc. In conjunction with other technology systems, the entire hiring process can be performed.

Technology provides a critical link that allows the organization to have both an efficient and effective recruiting and selection process.

What Happens Next?

Given the success of the new agent selection process, the new recruiting process, and the use of technology, these approaches are being expanded to other positions within the organization. Technology, for example, will be used extensively to support most recruiting and selection efforts in the future.

Although this case has focused on recruiting and selection, it is important to note that these processes are just two parts of the bigger picture and do not operate independently of other processes. Having a successful recruiting and selection strategy does not guarantee success. Success is also influenced by other factors such as orientation, training, management, work assignments, coworkers, rewards, recognition, development, and advancement.

Exhibit 1: Work Analysis Tool

Work Analysis
Document

Title:

Brand:

Department:

Work Group:

Reports to:

Person Interviewed:

Interviewer:

Date:

1a. PURPOSE OF WORK GROUP:

1b. PURPOSE OF JOB:

2. TASKS/MAJOR RESPONSIBILITIES

3. SKILLS FOR EACH TASK/MAJOR RESPONSIBILITY

4. INPUTS:

People:

Information:

Technology:

Facilities/Equipment:

Materials:

Exhibit 1. Work Analysis Tool (*Continued*)

---

5. COMPLIANCE/CONDITIONS:

External Factors:

Internal Factors:

Working Conditions:

6. CONSEQUENCES:

7. STANDARDS/MEASUREMENT

8. CRITICAL SUCCESS FACTORS:

Knowledge:

Skills:

Abilities:

Other Characteristics:

Computer Proficiency Required for this job:

Experience:
Length of time required: ☐ 1–2 years ☐ 3–5 years ☐ 6–8 years ☐ 9+ years

Formal Education:

Formal degrees, designations, licenses required to do the job:

Language proficiency required for the job:

Exhibit 2. Online Scorable Application Form

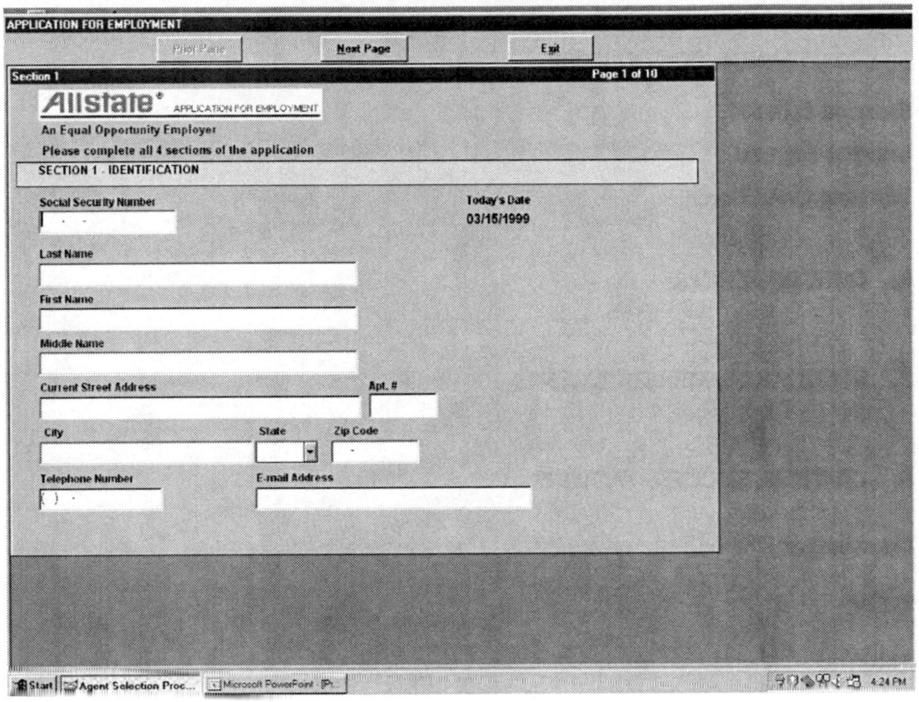
APPLICATION FOR EMPLOYMENT

Prior Page | Next Page | Exit

Section 1 — Page 1 of 10

Allstate® APPLICATION FOR EMPLOYMENT

An Equal Opportunity Employer

Please complete all 4 sections of the application

SECTION 1 - IDENTIFICATION

Social Security Number

Today's Date 03/15/1999

Last Name

First Name

Middle Name

Current Street Address — Apt. #

City — State — Zip Code

Telephone Number — E-mail Address

Start | Agent Selection Proc... | Microsoft PowerPoint — 4:24 PM

Above is the first page of the online scorable application form. It looks just like a regular application form. All the standard information is collected up front. The last section of the application contains a series of multiple choice questions.

ABOUT THE CONTRIBUTORS

Alice A. Cochrane (ACOCHRAN@allstate.com) is a senior manager in the Human Resource Shared Services of the Allstate Insurance Company corporate headquarters in Northbrook, Illinois. She has an MBA from the University of Maryland, College Park. She currently manages the Center of Excellence for recruitment and selection at Allstate, researching and implementing best practices throughout the Allstate Insurance Company. Other work has included designing and implementing Allstate's recruitment and selection process, designing sourcing strategies, and the Internet site for candidates found at allstatecareers.com. Cochrane received certification as a senior professional in human resources by the Society for Human Resource Management.

Ellen M. Papper, Ph.D. (EPAPP@allstate.com) is a senior research manager in Workforce Research at the Allstate Research and Planning Center, Allstate Insurance Company. She conducts research on a variety of topics including personnel selection, employee attitude and behavioral measurement, program effectiveness evaluation, employee communications, and external stakeholders' perceptions of the organization. Prior to joining Allstate, she worked as a research psychologist and consultant in the areas of selection, plant start-ups, surveys, teambuilding, and developmental feedback and as manager of Human Resource Planning with responsibility for selection, surveys, and performance management. She is a member of the Society for Industrial and Organizational Psychology, and received her Ph.D. in Industrial and Organizational Psychology from Bowling Green State University.

Acknowledgment

The authors would like to acknowledge all their colleagues within Allstate who were part of the design team. Their knowledge, time, and commitment to quality made the processes described in this chapter become a reality. In addition, they would like to thank all the agents, agency managers, HR professionals, and Allstate management who supported this work.

CHAPTER THIRTEEN

Cellular One

A focused employee retention initiative utilizing
career development, management training, team agreements,
and employee surveying as tools for creating a preferred
place of employment in the telecommunications industry

INTRODUCTION

The new knowledge economy now demands that people be considered *the* major corporate asset. Without great people, there is no great knowledge and there will be no great company.

Global competition, low unemployment, a shortened technology lifecycle, and changing demographics and employee work habits have created a lack of talent and a perceived skills gap between available talent and the talent required for companies to be productive at full capacity. Simply put, there are just not enough qualified workers to fulfill the business opportunities available in many industries. Employers today have found a dearth of workers "standing at the door." There are few people waiting to fill the positions vacated by unwanted turnover. The scramble is on to find new ways of keeping and gaining commitment from the best employees that employers already have.

Furthermore, companies without the best talent in their given market segment run the risk of providing mediocre customer service, demonstrating a lack of innovation, and producing poor business results—a definite formula for failure in today's fast changing world of multiple consumer choices.

In order to sustain the continuity of intellectual capital and service delivery, the best companies are now focusing on attracting and retaining top talent as a critical strategic business goal.

This case outlines a successful effort used by Cellular One to consciously increase employee retention and to become a preferred place to work amongst wireless communications employers.

The Business Issues

Cellular One is the leading wireless communications company in the San Francisco Bay Area. Cellular One's corporate vision is to enhance people's lives through wireless communications. In pursuing this vision, the company focuses on serving customer needs and uses the most advanced and progressive wireless communications technology to provide the products and services customers desire. As part of its "Customer Solutions" strategy, Cellular One is "dedicated to providing the best total solution to meet a customer's unique needs."

The wireless communications industry is currently growing at an explosive rate. There are now over 60 million subscribers and that number is expected to grow to more than 91 million by the year 2000. In addition, studies in the wireless industry demonstrate a growing pattern of higher employee turnover within the segment. Sensitivity to these trends catapulted the Cellular One management team to recognize that the ability to attract and retain scarce talent in the telecommunications industry would be a core driver of the business's ability to execute its strategic growth plan.

The Cellular One management team was also concerned about the cost of turnover. To this end, the company studied its direct costs related to:

- Recruiting
- Selection
- Training new personnel
- Losses in productivity due to new employee learning curves
- Lost opportunities while positions are vacant

As a result of this review, Cellular One's senior management team recognized that the costs associated with turnover and their impact on the corporation's profitability, coupled with the cost of lost opportunities to capture market share in a growth industry, created a compelling reason to launch an initiative focused on increasing employees' job satisfaction. Recognizing that next to the employee, the manager has the greatest impact on the employee's success or failure in the job, a major thrust of the initiative focused on leveraging and developing the strengths of Cellular One's managers and future leaders.

Cellular One designed a long-term strategic process to focus on employee retention and management development. While much progress has been made, Cellular One is now 3 years into a process that keeps revealing additional business challenges and areas for improvement. Cellular One remains committed to continued improvement in employee retention.

NEEDS ASSESSMENT

The first step in Cellular One's initiative was to determine the level of employee satisfaction and management capability. The Cellular One leadership team believed that a natural extension of increased employee satisfaction would mean longer employee lifecycles, increased motivation, stronger commitment to the organization, and better business performance overall.

Many organizations want to achieve this objective, yet there is uncertainty about what strategies will get them there. Surprisingly, companies often don't take the time to ask the target population what is important to them or how the company is doing on critical measures of employee satisfaction. Cellular One designed a process that would gather this information.

Cellular One used 2 employee surveys as the primary assessment methods.

The first assessment was conducting an annual Employee Satisfaction Survey (ESS), which is an annual practice at Cellular One that began in 1993. Employees at all levels in every location are asked to participate in a paper-and-pencil survey that is administered within a 2-week period. Seventy questions focus on 3 areas: the company, the work team, and the supervisor.

Internal marketing efforts lead to high levels of involvement in the ESS. The support of management and continually updated company-wide voice mails contribute to the consistently high levels of participation in the survey. Annually, posters (see Exhibit 1) are displayed in all conference and break rooms and are humorously, yet strategically, placed in all restrooms to remind employees of improvements that have been implemented in each department as a result of the previous survey. Cellular One also uses their intranet as a way to highlight and recognize prior year and ongoing improvements. Human Resources personnel travel to remote sites with popcorn and sodas to make participation easy and relaxed. For the past 3 years, Cellular One has had the following participation. One of Cellular One's goals was to make the survey more accessible to employees and easier for them to complete. In 1999, Cellular One migrated to an electronic version of ESS and still saw exceptional participation rates (Table 1).

Table 1. Survey Participation Rates

Year	Participation
1996	96%
1997	95%
1998	98%
1999	94% (Pilot of an electronic survey)

The Senior Management Team reviewed the 1996 results and opted to focus their efforts on improving management effectiveness. Survey scores and comments indicated that the following were the major areas in which employee satisfaction could be increased:

- Career Development
- Company Communication
- Development of Management Skills
- Perceived Fairness of Organizational Policies and Procedures

The second assessment method was conducting a pencil-and-paper survey called the Retention Assessment Profile. This survey measures the effectiveness of the retention management practices utilized by Cellular One managers. This 72-item survey, developed by a national management consulting firm, measures the importance and effectiveness of 6 management practices that are highly correlated with employee retention.

Supervisors received anonymous feedback on their retention practices from highly valued employees. This data was then compared to a national database comprised of technical companies. This data confirmed that the opportunities for increased employee job satisfaction were indeed consistent with the data obtained from the ESS effort.

The results of the survey became the launching pad for an ongoing effort to develop the managerial skills of Cellular One supervisors, managers, and directors. If successful, the Cellular One senior management team believed that the company would reap the benefits of extending the employee lifecycle, making recruiting easier, and improving the annual retention statistics.

A clear action plan addressing employee retention was then created by the president, vice presidents, and the organizational development director. This group then agreed to track progress at a monthly meeting dedicated to addressing the ESS results.

The president and CEO of Cellular One, who led the effort, stated:

"We have a lot of young supervisors and managers who want to do a good job. It's our responsibility to provide them with practical tools that will help them be more effective. The better the manager, the greater the likelihood that his or her employees will stay with the company."

DESIGN OF THE INTERVENTION

The goal of the employee retention action plan was to make Cellular One a preferred place to work by focusing its attention in 3 basic areas.

- Organizational Systems

- Management Practices
- Measurement and Management Accountability

ORGANIZATION SYSTEMS

A variety of organizational programs and systems were put into place to help increase management skills and improve employee retention. These programs and systems were based on the data discovered from the initial needs assessment. They included a career development program, an organizational policies and procedures audit, and a definition of systems that would define senior management's commitment to management competence and employee retention.

Here were some of the key actions that were taken in each area, as well as some employee reactions to the new commitments:

The Career Communications Program

As part of the early needs assessment process, entry-level employees in the Customer Operations department expressed an interest in advancing their careers. A "Career Communications" training program was piloted as a means of giving employees the tools to own their individual career development.

The program's philosophy, a model developed by Career Systems International, is that any career development system cannot be effective unless 3 key players—the employee, the manager, and the organization—do their part. At Cellular One, career development is viewed as an "ongoing process of self-discovery, learning, and planning that helps employees coordinate their professional goals with those of the company" (taken from *Career Communications: Takin' Charge,* developed by Career Systems International).

Pete Russell, manager of the Information Systems help desk, describes his experience:

> *"I took the training at a time when I found myself on an unfulfilling career path. Career Communications hit me like a bolt out of the blue. The ideas and the structure of the course provided me with concrete, methodical, yet personal guidance. The training also heightened my awareness of the partnership between myself, my career, and Cellular One."*

All Cellular One managers are trained to be facilitators of this career development process. The facilitator role includes "linking" employees to the right feedback, organizational information, access and visibility, assignments, and career options. Nancy Gortney, after 6 years in Engineering, applied for a lateral position in Marketing:

> *"My manager encouraged me to decide on my career development process. After some soul searching, I decided I wanted to broaden my career and that I needed a new challenge."*

The unrealistic expectation of reaching the vice president level in 2 years is addressed with the mantra "up is not the only way," also the title of Beverly Kaye's 1993 book, published by Davies Black. Employees are asked to open their minds to a new belief that "growing in place" or job enrichment is a viable option for their career development. Managers are responsible for constantly increasing the challenge or meaning of a particular job either by changing the job or crafting assignments that facilitate the development of skills critical to the business. This helps Cellular One do two things: (1) retain motivated employees in their current job, and (2) build the skills required to sustain the business. Employees stay motivated as they are given the opportunity to develop skills that can be transferred to a series of jobs within the organization. Cellular One has reaped the benefits by having talented employees to accept either lateral or vertical career moves. In some cases, employees have even taken "step down" positions for the sake of developing skills beneficial to their long-term career goals.

One of Cellular One's Training and Development specialists describes an opportunity she had to take on an additional assignment:

> "I was responsible for putting together a training program for managers on one of the company policies. As the project grew bigger, I was able to cross over and actually facilitate training on the company's progressive discipline process. In past jobs, I was only responsible for designing the training, and a subject matter expert was responsible for facilitating. As a result of facilitating this training, I was able to learn more about employee relations and human resource law. This kind of opportunity helped me develop valuable skills and it keeps my current job alive and interesting."

Measurements were initiated to track internal employee movement. Twenty-five percent of Cellular One's employees changed positions with a lateral move, a promotion, or a requested "demotion." Within a culture that values and encourages employee development, there is no stigma associated with applying for a job at a lower level to increase personal skills, learn another aspect of the business, or balance work and personal life. The stigma disappears when the culture truly values and encourages employee development.

Gina Rossi, a 4-year employee, applied for 2 lower-level positions.

> "Taking the voluntary 'down grade' from being a supervisor to a training coordinator opened many new doors for me. This move enabled me to develop project management skills, gain valuable training experience, and establish contacts within all the departments in the company. This was definitely the best career move I've ever made. The second 'down grade' enabled me to more effectively balance my personal and work life. Moving to the Livermore office allowed me to stay with the company. I have gained knowledge, experience, exposure, sanity (from a much reduced commute), and the ability to start a family and stay with Cellular One."

As a result of the success of this program in the customer operations group, the program was implemented company wide.

The Sales Career Development Program

The Cellular One Sales Leadership Team, made up of the sales vice president and direct reports, devoted resources to a "subsystem" of the Career Communications program called the *Sales Career Development Program*. This team believed that retaining top talent in sales would give Cellular One a competitive advantage in the wireless industry.

The goal of this program was to address the concerns of sales employees who could not identify career advancement opportunities within the sales organization. In addition, the goal was to clarify misperceptions that good people could only find advancement with other wireless companies. The Sales Leadership Team wanted to put "teeth" into true career development practices—that, in fact, skill development and actions are documented and taken seriously.

The program uses the following process:

Step 1: Complete a Skill Assessment Matrix (see Exhibit 2) to identify strengths and opportunities for improvement.

Step 2: Determine appropriate and realistic career goals, using the Career Path Options Matrix (see Exhibit 3).

Step 3: Identify assignments and training opportunities to help build skills and address improvement areas.

Step 4: Create a Career Development Plan (see Exhibit 4) for each employee.

Step 5: Review the plan on a quarterly basis and determine next steps.

Kari Gustafson, a Cellular One reseller account executive whose goal is to be promoted to reseller account manager, gave her reaction to the Sales Career Development Program.

> "It really lays out a path and gives direction. This was something that was lacking in the sales organization. Career 'discussions' always seemed to go well but most of the time they were documented on a dry erase board. At the end of the meeting, guess what, they got erased! It's nice to finally have some tools to get your strengths, options, and action plans down on paper. Following these steps has really brought some objectivity to a process that always seemed subjective in the sales department. The Career Path Options Matrix gives everyone the chance to see the big picture. Now I see what I have to do if I want to make a move."

Organization Policies and Procedures Audit Human Resources took the lead in coordinating the "owners" of 81 company policies. The owner's job is to systematically review and update each policy over a period of 18 months. Policies were reviewed and revised by the Senior Management team to ensure that each policy matched the goals and desired management practices of the organization. During the revision process all policies were moved from cumbersome binders to a Human Resources Intranet page. Now all employees can access any of the company policies anytime via the Cellular One Intranet.

Certain Cellular One departments took the policy review to a next step. For example, once the first policy review and revision cycle was completed, the Customer Operations management team determined that supervisors needed practical tools to assist them in uniformly applying and implementing the new policies. An intranet page for managers was created that provides information and resources about 1) how to apply certain policies in the call center and operations environment and 2) practical tools that could assist supervisors in bringing certain processes to life. Now, with "user friendly" policies and helpful hints, Cellular One supervisors and managers find it easier to create work environments that promote employee retention.

Tracy Gibson, director of Customer Care, describes the situation:

> "Our supervisors were asking for more information at their fingertips to educate their employees about compensation. We heard them, and put together a comprehensive section on the Web site that included frequently asked questions, common compensation, terms and definitions, how performance relates to compensation, and a general spreadsheet of salary and benefits. Our job is to translate for employees and the Web site helps us do that. Managers are now more educated and employees seem happier."

Policy Training

Quality Management Practices training was developed for all supervisors and managers. The training was designed to give policy information needed to make decisions and manage day to day. This training gives managers information to create work environments where everyone can contribute. For example, the training gives managers tips on dealing with workplace violence and harassment. It also provided managers with a matrix of all the leaves of absence available at Cellular One and how to determine what is best for an employee who needs to be out for an extended period of time. A variety of strategies were used including role-playing and case studies of real-life management and employee challenges. Executive sessions were created for vice presidents and directors to inform them of significant changes so that they were well-equipped to coach their managers and supervisors. As a result, the level of employee satisfaction at Cellular One remained stable during the new policy implementation period and had increased in some areas of the company.

Senior Management Commitment

The Organization Development group advised senior management to define the actions they would take to ensure that employees perceived the desired intent and integrity of the senior management's support to make positive company changes in response to the results of the ESS.

One important key senior management team action was the establishment of a regular and consistent data review meeting. On the first Wednesday of each month, the senior management team and director of Organization Development and Training can be found in an ESS meeting. The action plans created after the annual survey are tracked for completion, as are new action plans that are created and become defined throughout the year. The senior management team has defined these practices as "our Management Effectiveness focus." There is a senior management team belief that this focus requires a long-term commitment because the answers to employee retention and management competence are complex and multifaceted.

To ensure that the senior management team walks the talk, all employees rate the effectiveness of the Senior Management Team annually in the ESS survey (see Table 2). While the senior team anticipated a decrease in scores in 1997 due to significant changes in the business, the results from the management competence and employee retention initiatives were finally seen in the 1998 ratings.

The good news, however, is that in every year the effectiveness of the senior management team was measured, their scores compared to companies sampled in a national database were higher than the ratings given to leaders in the database companies.

Table 2. Senior Management Team Effectiveness As Rated by Cellular One Employees in the ESS (1996–1999)

Management Effectiveness Mean	1999	1998	1997	1996	Normative Data*
	77	75	68	70	
1. The Senior Management Team lets us know what the company is trying to accomplish.	79%	77%	72%	74%	71%
2. I have confidence in the fairness of the Senior Management Team.	N/A**	74%	68%	69%	55%
3. I believe that the Senior Management Team demonstrates our company values.	75%	76%	71%	73%	65%

*From Organizational Dynamics, Inc. database.

**Question eliminated from survey in 1999.

Another key action on the part of the Senior Management Team has been to make it a priority to participate in Cellular One management and employee training. On a rotating basis, each member of the Senior Management Team presents the opening of Cellular One's monthly New Hire and New Manager Orientation. This gives them the opportunity to stay connected to employees and demonstrate their commitment to the company values. In addition, there is always a vice president available to kick-off each of the required courses in the management training curriculum. JoAnn Penrith, vice president of Customer Operations, spends 20 minutes at the beginning of Quality Management Practices training program communicating her expectations of Cellular One leaders. Penrith says:

> *"Making myself visible and being willing to communicate my viewpoint helps accomplish 2 things: 1) it lets employees and managers know that the senior managers are real people and are interested in their day-to-day activities, and 2) as a senior person, anything you lend your name to takes on greater significance. Management training, and training in general, is one of those things."*

The Senior Management Team puts heavy emphasis on internal company communications. The Senior Management Team models the behavior they want by over-communicating about key company changes, initiatives, and results.

During an ESS action planning meeting, employees working in Santa Rosa, 60 miles north of Cellular One headquarters, requested more frequent and current information from the Senior Management Team. Coupling this request with the ESS data, the vice presidents and president created a communication action plan.

- An all-company meeting is held in January to celebrate business results.
- Town hall meetings are held midyear in 6 remote locations and corporate headquarters.
- Senior Management Team members rotate sending monthly voice mails to all employees highlighting the current business results and the employee bonus percentage based on those results.
- Detailed company results, critical business measures impacting the employee bonus, and ESS activities by department are updated monthly on the intranet.
- The president, vice president, and directors meet quarterly to discuss key business initiatives.
- Vice presidents cascade information throughout their organization using a combination of e-mail, voice mail, direct report meetings, and manager meetings.

Feedback from employees signaled to the Senior Management Team that the increase in communication allowed employees to understand the reasons for changes in the business. As a result, Cellular One no longer saw a decrease in productivity while employees had to dissect the latest rumor or search the Monster Board for more stable career opportunities. Instead, all the information is provided up front and Senior Management Team members are accessible to employees for questions and clarifications.

MANAGEMENT PRACTICES

To increase the effectiveness of company Management Practices as a method of retaining employees, Cellular One focused on the development of team agreements, instituted mandatory management training, and increased the level of accountability of the supervisor and management team. The following outlines the process Cellular One used and examples of key documents.

Team Agreement

In 1997, new members joined the Senior Management Team. They immediately began developing a Cellular One Team Agreement as a way to agree on behaviors that, if performed, would drive organizational success. The Team Agreement (see Exhibit 5) was refined until all members were comfortable with the commitments they created. After the senior leaders had time to internalize the behaviors, the Team Agreement was shared with the entire management team.

The Team Agreement is introduced to all employees in New Hire Orientation. They are asked to highlight the behaviors that would be essential to the job they were hired to do in the company. New Managers are introduced to the Team Agreement in New Manager Orientation and they are asked to create a plan for how they might coach their employees to live up to the team agreement everyday. As a result, Cellular One has established a set of behaviors that help create an open, honest, participative, and results-oriented environment. A section of the Cellular One Performance Management form titled "How You Do It" (see Exhibit 6) is used to give feedback to all employees on how they are doing with respect to the team agreement.

Mandatory Management Training

Levels of training were created by the Training Department to ensure that new supervisors and managers had a solid foundation in "What it Takes to be Successful at Cellular One" (see Exhibit 7) before moving to the second tier covering the "Essentials of Supervising and Managing" (see Exhibit 8). After a minimum of 6 months, supervisors and managers are required to begin the third level, "Managing Individuals and Teams" (see Exhibit 9). This curriculum focuses on the management practices identified by Integral Training Systems,

Inc., (ITS), which are highly correlated with low turnover and high employee satisfaction with the job, company, and manager. All managers were required to attend training to become familiar with the areas of the employee's job satisfaction that are within their control:

- The importance of hiring to cultural fit
- Giving realistic job previews to candidates during the hiring process
- How to set up clear goals and coaching to ensure success in the job
- Proving opportunity for learning new skills and developing professionally
- Being involved in career advancement
- Providing meaningful recognition
- Creating a supportive team environment

The Senior Management Team is committed to making sure all managers in their functional groups receive their required training. Quarterly training transcripts are provided to vice presidents who cascade the transcripts to directors, who hold career development discussions with managers or supervisors. Having seen the transcripts, vice presidents and even the president might casually encourage training in a hallway conversation.

The key to Cellular One's success in having such a high participation rate is the flexible approach taken in implementing the training. Eric Herkenrath, a trainer in Human Resources, says:

> "We've had to move away from the old paradigm of having 3-day or week-long training classes. We're just not in the kind of environment that can support managers being off the floors for that long of a stretch."

The delivery of training can be customized and is delivered in 4- or 8-hour modules to fit the scheduling needs of the target audience. Training is provided in field locations whenever possible so that the trainer commutes to a group rather than a group driving to the corporate offices.

MEASUREMENT AND MANAGEMENT ACCOUNTABILITY

Cellular One used 3 sources to evaluate and measure the success of their intervention. Exit interviews from 1997 and 1998 as well as key questions from the 1998 ESS were compared to data from 1999. Retention statistics were also gathered and reviewed.

Exit Interview Results

Cellular One has a process in place to obtain data from each employee who decides to leave the company (see Exhibit 10). The information collected from departing employees is used to identify trends and themes to help Cellular One identify areas and opportunities for improvement. In 1997 and 1998, the company collected data on the top 3 reasons employees left the company (Table 3):

It is notable that the top reasons employees leave the company are not factors in the control of management or related to the company culture. There was a 7% drop from 1997 to 1998 in those who left the company because of a perceived lack of opportunity. Cellular One attributes this to the "development" culture they set out to create and came to life in 1998.

The primary reasons employees now leave the company might be attributed to factors outside of the companies control (e.g., spousal relocation) or personal choice decisions (career change). Also, there may now be a natural time for all employees to leave a company. For example, the average tenure of employees that stay in a single company amongst all California corporations in 1999 is 3 years. If a company can extend this "natural lifecycle," then they are doing a good job in employee retention compared to the norm.

Here are quotes from exit interviews of employees who recently left Cellular One, 3 years after the initial management development initiative was put in place:

From Jason Walker, inside sales manager who worked at Cellular One for over 5 years:

> "There are a lot of reasons why I decided to leave Cellular One. First of all, I've been here since I graduated from college. For my development, I need to experience the outside. The commute was getting to me. I had the choice to telecommute but I would not be effective in this role. Changing jobs was a difficult decision to make. I would work here again in a second. This is a change and opportunity I have to make. I had a very positive experience here."

From Angie Petrella, Customer Operations employee who worked at Cellular One for over 5 years:

> "I want to spend more time with my baby. Even a part-time or job share would not have worked out because of the distance I commute. In each position I've held, I've always had opportunities to do a little more to help with my next position. All this seemed to be with thoughtful planning. It's been a great experience and I would probably still be here if not for my personal decision to spend more time with my son."

Table 3. Top 3 Reasons Employees Leave Cellular One (1997, 1998)

1997		1998	
Relocation & Personal	34%	Career Change	26%
Salary Increase	30%	Relocation	16%
Lack of Opportunity	21%	Lack of Opportunity	14%

Employee Satisfaction Survey (ESS) Data

Cellular One reviewed the results of key ESS questions and did comparisons to prior years to help evaluate the continued success of the retention intervention (Table 4).

Table 4. ESS Comparisons

QUESTION	1997	1998	1999	Percent Change '97 to '99
I have seen improvements as a result of ESS.	71%	71%	73%	+2.0%
The training I have attended has made me more effective in my job	70%	71%	77%	+7.0%
My supervisor discusses training and development goals with me.	72%	69%	78%	+6.0%
The senior management team communicates business issues on a regular basis.	72%	77%	80.4%	+8.0%

The ESS data indicated the following to Cellular One:

- Supervisor effectiveness increased during the 3-year period, especially in the area of training and developing employees.
- There is a high regard for senior management's commitment to sharing and communicating company information.
- Supervisors and the Senior Management Team remain committed to improving the company and culture.

Barrie Riddoch, a Cellular One store manager, comments on his perception of the results:

"Being a new manager as this initiative was underway, I was able to see the value from a growth standpoint. The training I received helped me be able to give better feedback to my employees and in the end it also helped me change careers within Cellular One."

Retention Data

Cellular One reviewed retention statistics for 1998 and 1999 in the job areas that are becoming harder to retain in the state of California. In all cases but one, Cellular One has been steadily seeing improvements (see Table 5). In the case

Table 5. Retention Statistics

Job Area	July 1998	July 1999	Percent Change
Finance	77.6%	81.7%	4.1%
Information Services	68.6%	83.6%	15.0%
Engineering	82.3%	78.5%	−3.8%

of engineering, the company is continuing to focus on more creative ways to retain this type of talent, knowing that these workers are in high demand all over the San Francisco Bay Area (due to proximity to Silicon Valley).

LESSONS LEARNED

Lesson #1—Management development and retention is a long-term strategic process. There were times when this effort looked too big to get underway. Then when it was, it seemed like it would never be done. Cellular One believes that it's critical to view this type of effort as a long-term strategic process that begins with a vision from the top and ends with measuring and continuous monitoring. It's important to be patient with the process and trust that incremental change and improvements will eventually get you to your goal. Even now, at the end of 3 years, there is still more work and the company realizes it will never really be "done." They continue to focus on what needs to happen next. Knowing that many large-scale change efforts often take 5–10 years, they are pleased with the results thus far.

Lesson #2—Senior Management must lead the management development and retention effort. At Cellular One, the program was lucky to have a CEO who was not only committed to this effort but was leading it almost daily. Her enthusiasm and charisma, coupled with her obsession about measurement, made it easy for her whole senior team to be on board. Meetings were dedicated to hearing about this initiative. Without active and visible support from senior leaders, the employee retention effort, or any effort requiring such commitment, would not have succeeded. The CEO strategically put members of her team in front of many employee groups to convey the message that they were in the business of employee satisfaction, employee retention, and building management capability. Fortunately for Cellular One, the leadership team takes on this role naturally. There was no confusion about the commitment from the Senior Management Team.

Lesson #3—Managers care about retention, but they don't "naturally" know how to do it. Attrition impacts a manager's department and his/her ability to achieve the objectives for which he/she is accountable. So, managers *do* care when a key person voluntarily leaves. However, in today's "do more with less" business world, managers feel pressed to get the work done and aren't always paying attention to the early warning signals employees demonstrate when they are beginning the road to dissatisfaction. These signals are always demonstrated long before the resignation occurs. Managers need education and training on their role. In addition, they need to know what *they* can do to increase employees' satisfaction and levels of commitment to the company, their jobs, and the quality of the relationships they have with their manager and peers. This is the "stuff" that keeps key people productive and in place.

Lesson #4—Linking initiatives enables managers to see the value of systematic retention approaches rather than a flavor-of-the-month program. In the case of Cellular One, linking the initiatives was a key part of brainstorming, designing, and implementing the intervention. Linking allowed managers to understand the importance of being asked to participate in required training and gave them insight into the value of using what they learned back on the job. Having 1 common goal (retaining top talent) that clearly linked to business success made the "events" of the design make sense.

Lesson #5—Employees must believe the assessment tool will lead to improvements. Your assessment tool must do a few things. First, it needs to give the organization a reading on the current situation. It's critical to demonstrate how a lack of attention to improvement areas will be detrimental to the business. In the case of Cellular One it was clear that if they did not address employee satisfaction and management capability, attrition would continue to drive up the cost of doing business. Based upon several years of results, employees at Cellular One are convinced that ESS will lead to improvements.

Lesson #6—Continual follow-up and reinforcement is crucial. This sends out the message that you are not going to ignore what you started. Cellular One knew that there were times when the initiative might slow down due to demands that are placed on the business during peak times. But as soon as things were under control, they were back on track, following up, checking deadlines, meeting commitments, or doing whatever it took. This practice communicates that they are serious about what they set out to do.

Lesson #7—Measure and share results widely. If you don't have a way of measuring, then you have no benchmarks. Cellular One used key measurements to determine progress and when to readjust their course. They were careful to determine what was needed to get measured so that they would not get caught in the trap of having meaningless measurement. The company continues to review exit interview, ESS, and retention data on a regular basis.

Exhibit 1. ESS Communication Posters

And the list of accomplishments...

Employee insights and suggestions often lead to better ways of doing business. Here are just a few of the 1998 success stories driven by *your* valuable ESS feedback:

Customer Ops

- Developed a secured Compensation Web Site for supervisors and managers in Customer Ops to be launched in July 1999.
- Began organizing Customer Ops Brown Bags in SSF, Santa Rosa, and Livermore locations to share best practices, develop relationships for support, and share tips for parents working in call centers.

Engineering

- Alternative work locations were established for Network Engineering and other departments where business operations would not be affected.

IS

- We need something here for IS. Did they continue computer upgrades??

Finance

- Formed the Finance Department Activities Committee to coordinate events and programs that promote teamwork, recognition and a healthy work environment.

Sales

- Developed a Sales Recognition program.

HR

- Increased benefits for part-time workers and added adoption reimbursement and the Commuter Check program.

Marketing

- Created a training library to provide information on internal and external training available in the Bay Area.

What's all this talk about electronic ESS?
More information will be coming soon to the ESS web site near you.
Stay tuned...

Goes on, and on, and on...

(*Continued*)

Exhibit 1. ESS Communication Posters (*Continued*)

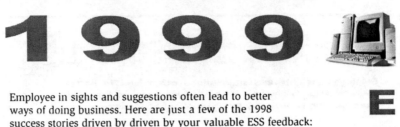

Employee in sights and suggestions often lead to better ways of doing business. Here are just a few of the 1998 success stories driven by driven by your valuable ESS feedback:

Customer Ops

• Weekly e-mails provide answers and explanations to compensation and benefits questions for all Customers Ops employees.
• Implemented scheduled "closedkey" time of the phones for Customer Care and Revenue Retention to follow-up on e-mail and customer issues.

Engineering

• Upgraded RF Engineering's test-drive equipment and personal computers.

IS

• Developed and implemented the change Control process for new hardware and software to test compatibility and performance.

Finance

• Quality-focused customer supplier meetings helped improve work processes and relationships among 8 inter-/intra departmental teams.

Sales

• Created a Career Development program implemented in June 1999.

HR

• Developed 4 new classes for Inside Sales and CORE employees and one new class for Customer Ops employees.

Marketing

• Created sub-team to address time management concerns.

What's all this talk about electronic ESS?
More information will be coming soon to the ESS Web site near you.
Stay tuned...

Exhibit 1. ESS Communication Posters (*Continued*)

We've all got a voice!

Employee in sights and suggestions often lead to better
ways of doing business. Here are just a few of the 1998
success stories driven by driven by your valuable ESS feedback:

Customer Ops

• Developed a secured Compensation Web site for supervisors and managers in
Customer Ops to be launched in July 1999.
• Began organizing Customer Ops Brown Bags in SSF, Santa Rosa, and Livermore
locations to share best practices, develop relationships for support, and share tips for
parents working in call centers.

Engineering

• Alternative work locations were established for Network Engineering and other
departments where business operations would not be affected.

IS

• Clarified roles and responsibilities for the Internet/Intranet sites and UNIX (within IS).
Also identified 29 shared responsibilities between IS and Engineering and clarified roles,
issues, priorities, and work teams.

Finance

• Formed the Finance Department Activities Committee to coordinate events and
programs that promote teamwork, recognition and a healthy work environment.

Sales

• Developed a Sales Recognition program that included the rollout of the "Spring Digital
Elite Contest", recognizing the efforts of 92 individuals who met aggressive digital targets.
• Developed sales-specific management training classes to be implemented in July 1999.

HR

• Increased benefits for part-time workers and added adoption reimbursement and the
Commuter Check program.

Marketing

• Created a training library to provide information on internal and external training
available in the Bay Area.

1999 *Electronic* ESS
Coming Soon...

Exhibit 2. Skills Assessment Matrix Sample

Basic Skills	Not Obsr'd	Devel Req'd	Meets Skills	Role Model
1. Communication Skills—ability to effectively communicate verbally and in writing • Engages in honest & open communication with everyone • Speaks and writes clearly, concisely, and persuasively • Uses appropriate grammar, enunciation, and tone • Actively listens and constructively acknowledges others opinions/concerns/feelings • Proactively solicits and communicates priorities and information • Demonstrates proper use of all communication tools (memos, letters, EM, one-on ones, meetings, VM, and telephone) • Directs communication to appropriate individuals/groups	❑	❑	❑	❑
Comments:				
2. Teamwork—Enhances work performance by establishing cooperative relationships • Constructively participates in team/group efforts • Willingness to prioritize team and company business interest over individual business interest • Includes all key customers and suppliers in decision-making and problem solving • Shares in the facilitation of team meetings/discussions to achieve objectives • Demonstrates flexibility and willingness to consider new/different ideas • Builds effective relationships with team/group based on respect & sensitivity to diversity	❑	❑	❑	❑

Basic Skills	Not Obsr'd	Devel Req'd	Meets Skills	Role Model
• Involves others and achieves results beyond individual capabilities				
• Takes a "we" approach to work and shares credit				
• Initiates help when other experience difficult				
• Volunteers for team projects or committee work				
• Values cultural diversity and works well with people from different backgrounds				
• Exercises tact and sensitivity in dealing with others, and compliments and praises their contributions				
Comments:				
3. Accountability, Judgment and Responsibility • Dependability: makes clear & complete commitments to internal & external customers • Exercises sound judgement • Demonstrates appropriate behaviors to safeguard Company assets/protect customer information • Takes ownership for projects and decisions, and avoids blaming others	❏	❏	❏	❏
Comments:				

Exhibit 3. Career Path Options Matrix—Sample

Positions/Job Descriptions	Skills/ Experience	Possible Primary Career Path	Possible Career Path Options
	Baseline Requirements: • Proficiency in Microsoft Office / Suite applications • College degree preferred but not required		
Director • Provides leadership and direction to sales teams and sales channel • Supervises and manages all aspects of sales including, hiring, training, motivating, coaching, problem-solving, and performance management • Ability to develop a vision, strategic plan and tactical actions to deliver business goals • Identifies and facilitates process improvements to improve sales effectiveness	• Successful sales management / marketing experience • Understands sales process • Intense desire to win/succeed • Ability to collaborate and to work cross-functionally • Strong program management experience • Strong leadership, analytical, financial, problem-solving, training, coaching, negotiating, presentation and selling skills	• VP Sales • Sales Director of other channel	• Marketing Director • Program Manager
Director, Sales Finance and Operations • Manage sales financial reporting and budget • Manage commission	• Financial management experience • Strong computer and analytical skills • Strong written and verbal	• VP Sales • Channel Director	• Marketing Director • Pricing Manager • Business Analysis

Exhibit 3. Career Path Options Matrix—Sample (*Continued*)

Positions/Job Descriptions	Skills/ Experience	Possible Primary Career Path	Possible Career Path Options
payment process for all channels • Manage the measurement and execution of sales contests • Co-develop channel strategy with directors and Marketing • Assess and develop new distribution opportunities • Responsible for broad-based internal sales recognition programs	communication skills • Negotiating experience • Strong team management experience		
Sales Operations Manager • Manages, develops and re-engineers operational processes • Recommends, prioritizes and leads changes to impact sales operational efficiencies • Responsible for the immediate operational response to competitive pressures • Partners with Product marketing to ensure timely and appropriate delivery of product / equipment / technology training	• Strong project and matrix management skills • Business strategy and analytical skills • Conflict Management skills • Presentation skills • Multi-tasking and fire-fighting ability • Strategic and tactical experience • Sales and management experience	• Director	• Sales Finance Manager • New Channel Manager • Indirect Channel Manager • CORE Regional Manager

Exhibit 4. Career Development Plan

I see the following skills as my current strengths:

-
-

I see the need to develop/improve my current skills in:

-
-

The following questions are designed to help you identify multiple career goals and options.

I would like to develop in the following areas of my current position (Enrichment option):

-
-

"Possible" jobs that I would like to have within the next 12–18 months:

-
-

I would like to develop in the following areas to assist me in attaining my short and long-term career objectives:

-
-

The following grid will help you identify your Career Development Plan:

Actions that I will take within the next 12 months to help build these skills in my current job and meet my career objectives:

Current position development:

Desired Skill	Development Assignment	Measure	Date

Exhibit 5. Cellular One Team Agreement

Build Partnerships

- Proactively seek out and enter into partnering opportunities with each other.
- Assure appropriate people are involved in critical issues.
- Celebrate and reward examples of teamwork.
- Be proactive in preventing and correcting dysfunctional alliances.

Share Information

- Talk and write candidly about issues—speak your point of view.
- All team members should facilitate meetings.
- Share knowledge and information in a timely manner.

Be Decisive

- Align quickly on key priorities.
- Have the discipline to reprioritize and communicate as appropriate.
- Ensure decisions are made at the appropriate level.
- Visibly support team decisions.

Build on Collective Thinking

- Openly encourage and be receptive to diversity of opinions.
- Proactively explore new concepts and ideas.
- Continuously build new skills, develop, and grow.
- Build on each other's ideas.
- Learn from our mistakes.

Meet Commitments

- Clearly define our commitments and keep them—both due dates and deliverables.
- Communicate to appropriate people when and why you can't keep a commitment.
- Don't commit if you think you can't do it—and learn to say no or not now.
- Follow company norms.

Be Accountable

- Take accountability for individual and team results.
- Deal directly with failure and develop action plans as well as contingency plans for improvement and resolution.

(Continued)

Exhibit 5. Cellular One Team Agreement (*Continued*)

Deliver Feedback Directly

- Provide constructive, direct, immediate, and specific feedback with the intent of resolving issues.
- Comments about a team member should be shared directly with that team member.

Develop and Delegate

- Seek out opportunities to develop and empower members of our team.
- Develop our teams' capability to manage the business effectively.

Create More Balance

- Acknowledge changing priorities and recognize when individuals have competing demands.
- Find ways to make the business fun.
- Use humor to help each other through our daily challenges.

Measure and Publish

- Always measure to test for success.
- Share results broadly.
- Use results to drive good business decisions.

Exhibit 6. Performance Management of Behaviors That Relate to the Team Agreement

Part II: "How You Do It"	Percent Weighting:	50%

Rate how employee performed on the overall category on a scale of 1–5 (quarterly increments). Use the comments section to highlight specific areas the employee excels in or needs improvement in.

EFFECTIVE COMMUNICATION SKILLS   Rating:_____

- Engages in honest and open communication with everyone
- Speaks and writes clearly, concisely and persuasively
- Actively listens and constructively acknowledges others' opinions/concerns/feelings
- Proactively solicits and communicates priorities and information

Comments:

TEAMWORK   Rating:_____

- Constructively participates in team/group efforts
- Willingness to prioritize team and company business interest over individual business interest
- Includes all key customers and suppliers in decision making and problem solving
- Shares in the facilitation of team meetings/discussions to achieve objectives
- Demonstrates flexibility and willingness to consider new/different ideas
- Builds effective relationships with team/group based on respect and sensitivity to diversity
- Demonstrates a basic understanding of Cellular One's Annual/Strategic Plan

Comments:

ACCOUNTABILITY, JUDGMENT, AND RESPONSIBILITY   Rating:_____

- Dependability: makes clear and complete commitments to internal and external customers
- Exercises sound judgement
- Demonstrates appropriate behaviors to safeguard company assets/protect customer information
- Takes ownership for projects and decisions, and avoids blaming others

Comments:

(Continued)

Exhibit 6. Performance Management of Behaviors That Relate to the Team Agreement (*Continued*)

INITIATIVE, RISK-TAKING, AND CREATIVITY   Rating:_____

- Takes initiative to develop cost-effective process improvements by using "kaizen"
- Seeks appropriate information about our business and industry developments
- Takes informed and thoughtful risks, when appropriate
- Anticipates problems and takes steps to resolve problems and minimize negative impact
- Responds quickly to company/management initiatives and executes with a sense of urgency

---

Comments:

MANAGEMENT EFFECTIVENESS (for management employees only)

                                                        Rating:_____

- Gains employee input and agreement on performance expectations and shares with employees
- Manages/coaches daily performance based on performance expectations
- Addresses ongoing nonperformance issues through progressive disciplinary process
- Tracks, reviews, and takes appropriate action based on Cellular One's attendance policy
- Conducts discussions with employee(s) on career goals/development and succession planning
- Provides thoughtful and timely recognition/rewards for employees
- Listens and responds to employee issue and problems in a considerate and timely manner
- Demonstrates support of company affirmative action program
- Consistently demonstrates behavior that support a harassment-free environment
- Seeks out information to audit the success of quality efforts

---

Comments:

"How You Do It" Rating: [   ]

Exhibit 7. Management Training Level I: What It Takes To Be Successful

WHAT	New Hire Orientation	New Manager Orientation
WHO	All newly hired supervisors, managers, directors	All newly hired or promoted supervisors, managers, directors
WHEN	Within one month of hire date (first Tuesday of each month)	Monthly sessions beginning September 1999
HOW	Classroom	Monthly sessions for all newly hired or ïpromoted managers
TOPICS	• Company overview • Benefits • Policies • The Employee Phone Program • Timesheets • Facilities and Data Security • Understanding Cellular One • Cellular One Products and Services • Intranet/Internet • Mitel Phone System	• Managing at Cellular One—What It Takes To Be Successful (guest speakers) • The Role of Human Resources • Our Quality Culture/Customer Obsession and Branding • Managing Performance • Staffing • Employee Satisfaction Survey • Finance • Payroll • Compensation • Company norms—E-mail, Voice Mail, Meetings • Management Training
Length	One day	One day

Exhibit 8. Management Training Level II: The Essentials of Supervising and Managing

WHAT	Quality Management Practice—1 Day	Performance Management Practices—1 Day	Behavioral Interviewing— 1 Day
WHO	Supervisors, Managers, Directors, VPs with at least one (1) direct report		Anyone responsible for the interview and selection process
WHEN	Within 1–6 months of employment		
HOW	Classroom		
CONTENT OBJECTIVE	**Managing the Work Environment** • Privacy and Confidentiality • Drug-Free Workplace • Violence in the Workplace • EEO/Affirmative Action • Harassment **Managing Leaves of Absence** • Medical • Pregnancy • Workers Comp • FMLA • Personal **How to Handle Injury in the Workplace** • Obligations Under IIPP • The Accident Investigation and Workers Compensation Processes **Compensation** • Terms • What Motivates/Retains/ Rewards • Pay Practices • How To Determine Salary • How To Do Salary Increases	**The Performance Management System at Cellular One** • Forms/The Formal Process • SMART Goals • Getting Input and Agreement • Developing a Training Plan **Facilitating Improved Performance** • Interaction Process • Communication Skills Needed to Give Good Feedback • Discussion Guidelines • Developing Plans—Monitoring Progress **Holding the Performance Discussion** • Preparing For the Review • Quarterly Employee Communication Sessions • The Annual Appraisal • The Appeal Procedure	**Interview and Selection Process at Cellular One** **Understanding Employment Laws** • EEOC/ADA • Asking Appropriate Questions **The Interviewing Process** • Preparing For the Interview • Determining Your Questions • Holding the Interview • Documenting the Interview • Closing the Interview • Assessing and Rating Your Candidate • Selecting Your Candidate • Making an Offer

Exhibit 8. Management Training Level II: The Essentials of Supervising and Managing

WHAT	Quality Management Practice—1 Day	Performance Management Practices—1 Day	Behavioral Interviewing— 1 Day
WHO	Supervisors, Managers, Directors, VPs with at least one (1) direct report		Anyone responsible for the interview and selection process
WHEN	Within 1–6 months of employment		
HOW	Classroom		
CONTENT OBJECTIVE	Rewards & Recognition	Policies relating to Managing Performance • Progressive Discipline Process • Attendance/ Occurrences • Punctuality, Documentation	
Length	One Day (Overview option for seasoned managers)	One Day (Overview option for seasoned managers)	One Day

Exhibit 9. Management Training Level III: Managing Individuals and Teams

WHAT	Quality Leadership Skills I	Quality Leadership Skills II	Career Communications	Retaining Top Talent	Conflict Management
WHO/ WHEN	Supervisors, Managers, Directors, VPs with at least one (1) direct report Within 6–18 months of hire (ideally)				
HOW	Classroom Training				
Content Objective	The Role of Leadership Feedback Assessment Personal Style (DiSC) The Role of the: • Pacesetter • Appraiser • Coach	Reconnection to QLS I Exploring the Team Concept Decision Making Styles in Teams Reaching Consensus Team Procedures for Giving Feedback Conducting Effective Team Meetings	Introduction to the Career Communications Model • PERSON • PERSPECTIVE • PLACE • POSSIBILITIES • PLAN Coaching Your Employees in the Career Development Process	Linking Retention Strategies to Business Goals The Cost of Attrition Awareness of the Ripple Effect The Retaining Top Talent Model Selective Retention Categories	Understanding Different Conflict Modes Conflict Self-Assessment Determine Your Usual Responses to Conflict Business Uses of the 5 Conflict Modes
Class Length	Two Days	Two Days	One Day	One Day	Half-Day

Exhibit 10. Exit Interview Form

Employee Name: _____ Job Title: _____

Department: _____ Supervisor: _____

Amount of time in present position: _____

Length of Employment at Cellular One: _____

Primary Termination Code: _____

HR Consultant/Generalist: _____ Date: _____

Termination codes: (please check all that apply)

CAR	Career Change	COM	Decreased Commute	MGT	Management Issues
OPP	Lack of Opportunity	PER	Personal Reasons	REC	Recruited by other Company
REL	Relocated	RET	Retirement	RNS	Transfer to Affiliate Organization
RTN	Return to School	SAL	Increased Salary	STR	Stress/Burnout
TRN	Training Issues	FIT	Poor Fit for Position		

1. What led you to the decision to leave the company?

2. What is your new position? Company?
   Position   _____
   Company   _____
   Salary % Increase   _____
   Special Benefits   _____
   Bonuses   _____

3. What could we have done to change your decision to leave?

4. What do you think are the driving factors for success at C-1?

5. Would you consider reemployment with Cellular One?

(Continued)

Exhibit 10. Exit Interview Form (*Continued*)

General Feedback

Have the employee rate each category. With each category ask why they rated it the way they did. If they rated a √ (Meets expectations) or a Δ (Below expectations) what could we do to improve? If it was a + (Above Expectations) what was good about it?

Category	+	√	Δ	N/A
Upper Management				
Immediate Supervisor				
Compensation				
Benefits				
Training				
Career Development				
Job Satisfaction				
Culture				
Work Environment (tools & equipment)				
Work Team				
Commute				
Reward/Recognition				
Company Communication				

6. What company policies helped or hindered you with your job?
7. What did you like best about working at Cellular One?
8. If you could change something at Cellular One, what would it be?
9. Is there anything else you would like to discuss?

ABOUT THE CONTRIBUTORS

Karen King (karen.king@cellone-sf.com) is director of Organization Development and Training at Cellular One—San Francisco. King has over 20 years of diversified business experience with a major emphasis in organization development, change management, training, total quality management, and managing assessment and survey processes. She has worked for organizations such as MCI Telecommunications and Litton Data Systems where she acted as a change agent for large-scale organizational change interventions. King has a proven record in OD implementations that result in increased client productivity and company revenue. King is currently responsible for all training and development at Cellular One, including sales, customer operations, and management training solutions. She oversees the company employee satisfaction process and works alongside senior management to design, facilitate, and measure improvement interventions. She was one of the key players in the design of the intervention described in this chapter. King has an MBA from the University of Colorado and has been active in the field of Organization Development for over 10 years. She has been working in the Bay Area since 1996.

Claire Meany (MeanyC@bactc.com) is manager of Organization Development and Training at Cellular One—San Francisco. Meany has a broad training and business background. She has worked in several Bay Area companies, doing internal organization development consulting and addressing a variety of leadership topics including change management, leadership development, facilitation, and coaching. She is currently responsible for designing and facilitating management development opportunities that reflect an understanding of business goals and strategies for all levels of leadership at Cellular One. Meany works closely with Senior Management to insure that future leadership development approaches support Cellular One's strategic initiatives. Meany received her bachelor's degree in psychology and Master's degree in human resource development from The George Washington University in Washington, D.C. She has been living and working in the Bay Area since 1990.

Dr. B. Lynn Ware, Ph.D (drware@itsinc.net) is the founder and president of Integral Training Systems, Inc. (ITS), an internationally known management and training consulting firm specializing in employee retention. ITS is on the forefront of finding proven solutions for solving other business challenges that arise from emerging workplace trends, such as managing Gen Xers and the effects of virtual management on productivity. ITS is dedicated to helping its clients create "employer of choice" environments, so that they can attract and keep the best talent in their respective industries. Ware is an industrial/ organizational psychologist. She has practiced for 20 years in the education and organization development field, focusing on increasing employee productivity and utilization. Some of her current clients include Bay Networks, Hewlett-Packard, Levi Strauss, Oracle Corporation, Prudential Securities, Sun Microsystems, and United Behavioral Health. Ware is frequently quoted on trends in employee retention strategies in numerous publications such as the Associated Press, *San Francisco Chronicle, Network World,* and *ComputerWorld* magazine. She has recently been featured on CNN as a national employee retention expert.

SECTION FOUR

PERFORMANCE MANAGEMENT

PERFORMANCE MANAGEMENT: AN INTRODUCTION
BY EDWARD E. LAWLER III

The performance management systems in most organizations are controversial, ineffective, and constantly under construction. They are so problematic that critics argue many organizations would be better off if they simply didn't have a performance management system, particularly one in which performance appraisals are tied to pay actions. But—and it is an important but—if individuals are not appraised, counseled, coached, and rewarded for performance, how can an organization produce the organized, coordinated, and motivated behavior that it takes to perform well? The answer most likely is that it can't.

Some performance management system clearly is needed in most large-complex organizations. The key questions thus become what should the system look like? How should it operate? And ultimately, how does an organization design and maintain an effective system? For years, researchers and practitioners have searched for the answers to these questions. Unfortunately, all too often, they have looked in the wrong places. They have focused too much attention on the technology of the appraisal process, focusing on such issues as what kind of rating scales to use and how to write better appraisals. Too little attention has

393

been focused on business strategy, organization design, and the performance management process.

The good news is that increasingly, organizations are looking in the right places for the keys to creating more effective performance appraisal systems and they are getting more positive results. Case Corporation and Sonoco Corporation are 2 organizations that seem to be on the right track with respect to creating effective performance appraisal systems. They appear to be on the way to avoiding the "damned if you do, damned if you don't" phenomena when it comes to performance appraisals. I am particularly impressed by how they have used their business strategy to focus their performance management system and their overall management approach. Getting the right fit with business strategy is an important key to creating an effective performance management system.

The performance management system needs to be driven by the business strategy and the senior management of an organization. Without leadership at the top, and a senior management group that models good performance appraisal behavior, it is impossible to have an effective performance management system. Senior management must see it as a critical tool in implementing their management style and the organization's business strategy. Only if it is positioned in this manner is it likely to be done well throughout the organization. Senior management must do more than simply articulate the need for effective performance appraisals; they must be role models of effective performance management behavior. This is the critical element in their providing leadership with respect to the performance management systems.

Once the issue of who supports and provides leadership for the performance appraisal system is satisfactorily dealt with, organizations need to answer the second most important question about performance management: What uses will be made of the data that are generated by it?

One of the longest running controversies in performance management involves whether a performance appraisal can simultaneously be used for development purposes and for compensation determination. The arguments are many and varied on both sides of this issue. It is clearly useful to have a performance management system that both helps people develop and rewards them in ways that motivate their performance. The reality, however, is that under some circumstances, it may not be possible or even advisable to tie performance to the rewards individuals receive. The reasons for this range all the way from the fact that rewards are not available and thus simply can't be distributed, to the fact that individuals are members of teams and are more appropriately rewarded as team members than as individuals.

Still, in many cases, individuals can and should be rewarded for their performance, and they should be counseled with respect to development and promotion opportunities. The challenge is to create a system that can clearly and effectively do both of these. There is no silver bullet here, but the evidence is clear that performance management is best done when discussions of development and pay are separated in time. Most individuals simply don't hear development feedback and do a good job of considering how they can improve their skills when they are also getting information about compensation. The pay information, particularly if it is negative, tends to overwhelm the information about development. This finding, however, doesn't rule out the fact that the same system can deal with reward issues and development issues. The key is separating the discussions and being explicit about the agenda of particular discussions. It is tied to the larger issue of organizations needing to make a clear, explicit statement about the role of the performance appraisal system and how the data from it will be used. Sonoco provides a good example of an organization that has done this.

It is obvious that performance appraisals should focus on performance, but what kind of performance should be measured? What to measure is a particularly difficult issue when the system is designed to deal with employee development as well as rewards. Clearly, for reward purposes, it is best to focus on comprehensive measures of tangible, operating results. If these cannot be obtained, it is probably best not to appraise and reward the job performance of individuals. When it is done in the absence of good, comprehensive measures, the performance of individuals is directed to what is measured and this creates problems because the unmeasured behaviors are no longer performed.

The situation with respect to measures is somewhat different when development is involved. Measures of operating performance usually are not sufficient. As you will see in the Case and Sonoco studies, it is often important to measure an individual's competencies and capabilities. Individuals often do not improve their performance unless they are given training and developmental coaching that helps them increase their knowledge, skills, and competencies. Indeed, companies are increasingly rewarding individuals for developing their competencies, knowledge, and skill, as well as for their performance. Thus, it is important that performance management systems do more than simply measure objective performance outcomes. They need to measure the underlying knowledge, skills, and competencies that lead to these results.

The challenge in measuring competencies and knowledge involves translating them into measures of observable behavior. Far too often, organizations focus on poorly defined and measured attributes of the individual, and as a result fail to give useful developmental feedback. For example, telling somebody they are unreliable and have poor skills rarely is useful feedback either for development purposes or for performance measurement purposes. Feedback needs to be much more specific; for example, X doesn't show up for work Y number of times or X does not know how to set up a machine so that it operates at a 6-sigma quality level. Overall, a good rule is that measures that are gathered for different uses need to focus on different things.

The final key issue in performance management concerns who actually does the performance management activities. Traditionally the answer to this was obvious: the boss. In knowledge work and high-technology situations, this answer is often either completely or partially wrong. Depending on the measures that are being collected and the purpose of the appraisal, the best judge of an individual's skills and performance may be subordinates, customers, peers, or bosses. In short, whomever has a clear line of sight to observe that individual's behavior and performance.

The challenge in performance management systems is to collect valid data from individuals who have the chance to see the relevant performance and behavior of the individual. One approach that is used by both Case and Sonoco is the 360-degree appraisal. It is an increasingly popular approach and can be particularly useful in providing feedback for development purposes. Using 360-degree appraisals when rewards are involved is more problematic because of the competitiveness and political issues that may come into play. Thus, it is not surprising that Sonoco uses them only for developmental reviews.

Overall, I believe a number of forces are converging to improve the quality of the performance appraisals that are conducted in most corporations. More and more CEOs are realizing that performance management systems are a powerful way for them to influence the strategic direction of the business. This recognition is the most important building block for an effective system. Information technology is helping by providing online aids and educational opportunities for individuals who are appraisers and appraisees. Finally, more and more organizations are attending to the right issues in the design of their appraisal process and making informed decisions about how it should be carried out. Thus, there is good reason to believe that we will see an increasing number of organizations that have effective performance management systems.

Edward E. Lawler III (elawler@ceo.usc.edu) is a professor of management and director of the Center for Effective Organizations in the Marshall School of Business at the University of Southern California. He has been honored as a top contributor to the fields of organizational development, organizational behavior, and compensation. He is the author of more than 200 articles and 30 books. His most recent books include *Strategies for High Performance Organizations— The CEO Report* (Jossey-Bass, 1998), *The Leadership Change Handbook* (Jossey-Bass, 1999), and Rewarding Excellence (Jossey-Bass, 2000).

CHAPTER FOURTEEN

Case Corporation

A performance management and development process designed for managers and individual contributors that includes setting expectations, driving continuous communication about performance, and assessing employees against performance results, development results, and competencies

INTRODUCTION

Background

Case Corporation is a leading worldwide designer, manufacturer, and distributor of agricultural and construction equipment, and it offers a broad array of financial products and services. Headquartered in Racine, Wisconsin, Case had revenues of $6.1 billion in 1998 and sells its products in over 150 countries through a network of approximately 4,900 independent dealers. Case employs approximately 17,700 employees around the world.

In February 1998, Case Chairman and Chief Executive Officer Jean-Pierre Rosso shared his perspective with leaders from around the globe. His view was of an organization at a crossroads. In the period from 1994 to 1997, Case executed a financial turnaround, the need for which had been building since the early 1990s. Recent history of this manufacturer of agricultural and construction equipment included financial turmoil in the early 1990s. After an initial public offering in 1994, Case developed and executed a restructuring plan in accordance with the mission of the organization. Industry analysts considered this financial turnaround to be a true success story, but it also provided new challenges for leaders throughout Case. Although management of financial assets improved dramatically in a short period of time, Case demonstrated that more effective management of human assets offered a new challenge for the organization. With senior leaders increasing their focus on the people practices, human resource leaders launched a number of initiatives aimed at developing leaders' skills in driving individual and team performance, and then providing systems to support these efforts. Among these initiatives were the development of leader and individual contributor competency models and integrated HR applications based on these models.

Development of Competency Models

When he joined the organization in 1994, Rosso put in place a strategic framework to guide the future of the organization. This framework, still used today, includes Case's mission, strategic imperatives, and operating principles. As a visual reminder for Case employees, the framework is posted in offices, hallways, and manufacturing plants.

Developing competency models for leaders and individual contributors involved understanding current competencies and, based on the strategic framework, desired behaviors for the future. To capture and describe the current state, Case conducted an intensive study of what key performers do on the job. The project team collected data from over 70 interviews with leaders around the world and through focus groups and subject matter expert panels. The competencies identified for leaders and individual contributors were charted against the operating principles. The result was 2 competency models, *Leadership* and *Individual Contributor,* that were vertically integrated and directly linked to the operating principles, strategic imperatives, and company's mission. As shown in Exhibits 1 and 2, each competency was aligned with Case's business goals and strategy. For the first time, employees could see how their behaviors directly supported the company's mission.

Competency models can be useful tools for communicating leaders' expectations of employees, but these models alone will not impact performance. To align performance with business goals, competencies must be integrated into business tools and processes for managing people. Case recognized the need to build integrated HR systems based on the competency models. Identification of Leadership and Individual Contributor competencies became a common framework with which managers and leaders could select, develop, and evaluate employees. With competencies as the unifying element for driving human performance, a variety of applications were developed (see Exhibit 3). These applications included selection, development, performance management, career planning, and succession planning.

The following HR applications are now integrated at Case:

- Performance Management and Development
- Targeted Interviewing
- 360-degree Feedback and Development Planning
- Human Resource Planning

Performance Management and Development (PM&D) is designed to support yearly objective setting, development planning, and appraisal. Targeted Interviewing helps managers identify candidates who embody the behaviors required to meet business unit and organizational goals. 360-degree Feedback and Development Planning specify the behaviors that employees must focus on to achieve desired results. Human Resource Planning (HRP) allows employees to express career aspirations and managers to create succession plans based on competencies needed to fulfill organizational roles. All of these applications were designed to promote a comprehensive approach to managing people.

Each of these applications includes tools, a process, and skill-building elements to provide managers with the training and support required for managing their people. Using competencies to integrate these applications allows managers to easily reinforce behaviors that Case needs to compete in the global marketplace.

FROM THE "WHAT" TO THE "WHAT AND HOW" OF PERFORMANCE MANAGEMENT

The Context for Performance Management at Case

As a global organization, Case and its leaders at all levels must have the tools to create and execute strategy around the world. With global commerce increasing, the complexities of managing across country boundaries and in multiple cultural settings present greater challenges for employees at all levels. Case's system for managing people must to be flexible enough to be adapted by different business units, divisions, and cultural settings. Yet, the system must also ensure that corporate-wide strategy is aligned and executed consistently throughout the world.

Blueprinting the Process for Managing Performance While the impetus created by a successful financial turnaround created a sense of urgency for managing human assets more effectively, specific input from employees and managers was required to determine the process and tools that would best support performance management. As an initial step, a project team was established. They utilized a blueprinting approach to identify all stakeholders, assess the current state of performance management and appraisal, define the intended future state, and outline a process for filling gaps. The team conducted end-user focus groups to explore satisfaction and effectiveness levels for the current performance management process.

Focus group data clearly indicated a need to develop a simple, easy-to-use system that would decrease the emphasis on formal performance management discussions and ratings (formal appraisal). Instead, it would drive ongoing feedback and open discussion between employees and their managers. Employees expressed a need to increase dialogue with their managers regarding expectations and actual performance in terms of competencies and results. Focus group data indicated the following gaps:

- Existing performance definitions were used inconsistently throughout the company
- It was difficult to link top-down objectives and business goals with individual performance

- There was a lack of understanding regarding how this process related to other HR processes
- The focus was exclusively on the "what" of performance, e.g., results

The project team, in conjunction with senior leaders and business unit leaders, developed a plan and a set of goals. These goals included:

- Raising the bar for employee performance to drive better operational and financial performance
- Emphasizing the ongoing nature of performance communication and management
- Developing user-friendly tools and a solid process for setting expectations and reviewing performance
- Defining the leadership and employee behaviors necessary for competitive advantage
- Linking all HR processes

With these goals in mind, Case leadership leveraged components of the existing process and enhanced and improved upon those aspects of the process that would create value in the eyes of the customer. The "customers" here were managers and employees.

Design and Development of Performance Management Process and Tools

Business unit leaders and managers were anxious to obtain the tools and support that would help them to better manage individuals' contributions to the company. Although Case's performance management process took approximately 4 months to develop, the sense of urgency created by key stakeholders provided a source of momentum for the project team. The key success factor in gaining key stakeholders' "buy-in" was their participation in the design and development of the performance management process and tools.

The team used the following overall process:

1. Conducted a project planning meeting to identify required resources and determine project timeframe
2. Met with key stakeholders and senior leaders to gain support and gather input
3. Collected data from focus groups to understand the effectiveness of the existing system, perceptions about that system, and manager skill gaps; focus group participants included managers, individual contributors, business unit leaders, and human resource professionals
4. Analyzed data and reviewed best practice tools and processes
5. Designed prototype tools and outlined the process

6. Collected data from focus groups with key stakeholders regarding the prototype tools and process; stakeholders included senior leaders, business unit leaders, managers, individual contributors, and human resource professionals

7. Refined the tools and process with ongoing feedback first from human resource professionals and then from business leaders and line managers (the primary source of input)

8. Developed training for managers to acquire competencies for ongoing feedback and communication, expectation setting, and performance evaluation

9. Piloted the training program with business leaders and line managers

10. Rolled out training for all competency-based HR processes

DRIVING CONTINUOUS COMMUNICATION ABOUT PERFORMANCE AND DEVELOPMENT

Communication about performance and development must, of course, occur more than a few times a year. Although informal communications are often the most effective, formal systems must support these efforts. Case leadership emphasized the importance of both the achievement of results and how the work would be done. Three major shifts in the performance management and development process enable Case leaders to truly drive continuous communication. These shifts include integrating HR processes, focusing on development as a priority, and defining "how" the work would be done through behavioral competency definitions.

Integrating Human Resource Processes

In order to maximize the contribution that each individual and team makes to the organization on an ongoing basis, Case developed a number of human resource processes around a single framework: the competencies. By integrating applications such as selection, performance management, and 360-degree assessment and development planning, Case management created a standard set of criteria for the management of human assets. This represented the first shift in how the new Performance Management and Development process became an integral part of managing the business.

As the Targeted Interviewing process was introduced, managers learned to select employees based on data about competencies. Competency information on candidates is now a tool for the hiring manager to use in working with the new employee to plan initial development steps.

Case's 360-degree feedback and development planning process provided additional reinforcement in the process of competency acquisition. With an eye on diagnosing development needs and identifying learning opportunities, Case introduced a 360-degree feedback system where employees nominate their own raters and receive feedback on each of the competencies. The development planning tools were designed to enable individuals to understand their strengths and their development needs. Customized planning tools assist in determining the best developmental activities and in planning and discussing ongoing development. This process provides a structure to ensure that competencies are a focal point and key aspect of communication between employees and their managers.

Making Development a Priority

The inclusion of development objectives in the performance agreement was a second major shift in performance management at Case. In the past, organizations could expect employees to stay with 1 company for many years, perhaps for an entire career. Today, few organizations would consider this a realistic expectation. Developing employees means helping individuals to understand their strengths and development needs, providing them with opportunities to gain new skills and knowledge, and ensuring continual feedback and support to enhance their learning. By incorporating development objectives into expectation setting and performance reviews, Case is demonstrating a commitment to support employee learning and growth.

Defining Behaviors Required for Achieving Individual and Organizational Results

The focus of performance management also shifted from simply appraising performance to viewing employee performance in terms of "what" results are achieved and "how" employees achieve these results. The "how" of performance is based on the competency models. The models provide behavioral criteria against which employees can be assessed. Competency performance standards were developed to support managers' understanding of what each competency "looks like" in action and to provide employees with detailed descriptions of behavioral expectations (see Exhibit 4). These performance standards describe the observable behaviors at 4 levels: no evidence, somewhat effective, effective, and exceptional. The introduction of measurable components enables managers to more effectively measure employee contributions.

PERFORMANCE MANAGEMENT AND DEVELOPMENT PROCESS

Case's Performance Management and Development process was designed to enable employees and managers to work in partnership to create and manage individual objectives and demonstrate appropriate behaviors. Ultimately, the organizational goal is to achieve increasingly strong levels of performance. For employees, this is achieved through 3 yearly formal discussions and ongoing informal coaching and feedback.

Employees are assessed against what they do and how they do it. Performance results, or "what" an employee accomplishes, are based on the key results expected during the year. These Performance Objectives reflect the overall strategy of the company and the business unit or division as they are cascaded down based on business goals. In addition, 1 or 2 development goals are set for the individual. These can be derived from the 360-degree feedback. "How" an employee accomplishes these results refers to the competencies appropriate to their position, whether leader or individual contributor. Managers are assessed against the Leadership competency model, which includes specific behaviors required of good performance coaches. These behaviors include Foster Open Communication, Team Leadership, and Develop Others. As a result, managers are accountable for "how" they manage and coach.

Each component of PM&D comprises a conversation between the employee and the manager, documentation of ratings, and a summary of progress. While the tools designed to support the process offer an opportunity to record formal discussions, the process emphasizes continual coaching by reinforcing the need for communication about performance. The PM&D process comprises the following components.

- *Performance Agreement*—Setting performance and development objectives and measures at the beginning of the year and revising as necessary throughout the year. For development objectives, key actions required to achieve those objectives must be defined.

- *Performance Results*—Determining progress against measures at mid-year and year-end.

- *Competency Assessment*—Formally evaluating at year-end the level at which employees demonstrate each competency. Levels correspond to specific definitions of the competency: no evidence, somewhat effective, effective, and exceptional.

- *Performance Summary*—Summarizing the employee's performance throughout the year in terms of competencies, performance results, and development compared to objectives. This section includes an overall rating against performance expectations and manager and employee comments and is completed at year-end.

- *Career Development*—Planning career progression based on 3 primary career paths: functional specialist, cross-functional generalist, and general management. At mid-year, employees have the opportunity to reflect on their long-term career goals and plan the steps necessary to achieve them.

- *Human Resource Planning/Career Planning*—Assessing, from an organizational standpoint, each employee's potential future growth in the organization. At mid-year, managers assess employees' potential for organizational planning purposes. Competencies are a key to this planning process. The HRP process strengthens Case leadership by ensuring that every position is filled appropriately according to both organizational and employee needs. When considered in conjunction with career development, the HRP process provides guidance to the individual for personal, long-term development.

ENHANCING MANAGERS' SKILLS IN MANAGING PERFORMANCE

Case recognized the need to develop a training program to provide managers with an opportunity to learn about the new PM&D process and to gain some additional skills that would assist in increasing the effectiveness of the process. In addition, the PM&D process was designed to be self-reinforcing. The competencies identified for leaders targeted the behaviors required of coaches and managers who set performance expectations, assess the "what" and "how" of performance, and provide ongoing feedback to help employees continually develop (see Exhibit 5 for a list of the competencies and definitions).

As a part of the PM&D introduction and on an ongoing basis for new managers, business unit and corporate Human Resources and Organization Development professionals conduct training sessions. The goals of the training are to:

- Expose managers to new thinking about performance management
- Demonstrate integration with other HR processes
- Emphasize manager's roles and responsibilities
- Build skills in:

  Writing effective performance agreements

  Communicating about development

  Delivering continual constructive feedback

  Appraising performance

See Exhibit 6 for the training agenda.

At the end of 1998, training sessions were delivered to managers and supervisors. The focus of these sessions was to enable managers to work with employees to set performance expectations in the form of performance and development objectives and measures and to provide ongoing feedback against these objectives. Learning objectives for this session included:

- Understanding the importance of Performance Management and Development for achieving Case's mission
- Explaining the Case competency models and their use in Performance Management and Development
- Creating Performance Agreements that are challenging and aligned with Case's mission
- Communicating effectively about performance and development
- Conducting formal mid-year check-in discussions with employees to assess progress to date against objectives and consider development planning needs

Managers were provided with an opportunity to develop basic skills enabling them to build upon existing capability and to utilize the PM&D process in a way which enhanced employee performance. In some business units a second training session was planned for year-end as a refresher and skill practice in constructively reviewing and appraising performance.

GLOBAL APPLICATION

As with any global organization, flexibility is key to the success of the PM&D initiative at Case. The roles of Corporate Organization Development, Human Resources, and business unit leaders who developed the PM&D process were:

1. To create a system that business units could adapt, if necessary
2. To provide standard tools that are flexible enough to work with the standard process or with modifications

Similarly, the design and development of the training program provided for adaptation as necessary by specific business units or divisions.

To facilitate global acceptance of the process, business unit leaders and HR professionals from around the globe were included in focus groups and design discussions throughout the project. Leaders from across the globe participated in the development of the competency models.

Case, as a global organization, is not immune to the notion that within the organization, there are units or divisions utilizing different management tools and processes. One example is the Asia Pacific unit (APAC).

Prior to the development of the new Performance Management and Development process, the HR group in APAC took the lead in adapting existing tools and processes to better meet their needs. Their successes and lessons learned provided a learning opportunity for the PM&D project team as well. APAC utilized existing Case HR processes such as Human Resource Planning and Performance Alignment and built a set of resources to help managers implement the tools and processes. While remaining true to the spirit of the tools and process utilized throughout Case, APAC took it to the next step. The value of this work for the project team (and as a result, for employees throughout Case) was twofold. First, some of the work that was done was able to be integrated into the new process and tools, and second, it provided a solid example of how a somewhat standardized process could be easily adapted for use in particular groups.

After the new worldwide PM&D process was developed, local adaptations were made. In the European unit, the Business Unit head delivered numerous written communications about the process. In addition, the Performance Management and Development training was done in a "phased" or just-in-time approach. Of course, materials were translated into appropriate languages as needed in different areas of the world.

IMPLEMENTATION

With the need for both consistency and flexibility in mind, the project team developed an implementation plan. First, each business unit had the responsibility to manage their own rollout. Master trainers were selected to work with each business unit to ensure consistency in the concepts and skill-building elements delivered to managers. As described earlier, a training session for managers was delivered as soon as possible to leverage the momentum created by the rollout of this process at the end of 1998. Trainers from all business units were required to attend train-the-trainer sessions to ensure consistency of the message.

In addition, trainers and Organization Development representatives conducted several large group-orientation sessions for employees to familiarize them with the tools and process and with the training their managers would receive. The components of this session included:

- A videotape of senior managers discussing the importance of PM&D
- A discussion of results and competencies as criteria for measurement
- An exercise demonstrating the importance of identifying key competencies
- An overview of Case's integrated competency-based applications
- An introduction of the PM&D process and tools

- A discussion of roles and responsibilities of both managers and employees

EVALUATION

Feedback from managers and business leaders throughout Case has been overwhelmingly positive, particularly in terms of the addition of competencies to the process. In addition, managers reacted positively to the simplicity and practicality of the process and tools, particularly to the definitions of competencies at specific levels of performance. These performance standards for the competencies provide for a more detailed understanding of the behaviors required; this is beneficial on a worldwide basis due to cultural differences and "distance" between employees and managers working in different locations.

Perhaps one of the strongest testimonies for the new process occurred when Case dealers who had seen the new tools inquired about using them for their dealerships. At this point, the development team knew they had created tools that truly added value to the business.

There are still some issues surrounding the elements that remained from the previous Performance Management process (Performance Alignment). In particular, the summary rating that managers are asked to complete at the year-end performance review still presents a challenge in that some managers may attempt to use year-end ratings to justify merit increases. Clearly defined measurable components such as the competencies and performance objectives aim to reduce this problem. The overall process is designed to achieve a level of rigor in assessing individual performance. The process itself, combined with reinforcing behaviors for managers to act as performance coaches as outlined in the Leadership Competency Model, minimizes this effect.

Case is currently in the process of evaluating this overall effort. Members of the Organization Development group will conduct focus groups with managers and employees and will distribute surveys to a random sample of both managers and employees. The project team will use the data collected to determine how managers are applying what they have learned in facilitating ongoing dialogue with employees about performance. This data from end users provides opportunities to further refine and enhance Performance Management and Development at Case. (See Exhibit 7 for a sample of the survey questions.)

KEY CHALLENGES AND LESSONS LEARNED

Throughout the course of this work, members of the project team have gained support, acceptance, feedback, and participation from people at all levels, from locations around the globe and from all units and divisions. No project comes without its challenges. This project team met numerous challenges successfully:

Lesson # 1—Gain common understanding of the importance of competencies. Many of Case's business leaders, managers, and employees were involved in the development of the competency models either through interviews, focus groups, or validation surveys. Common understanding and endorsement of the importance of competencies as criteria for the behaviors of leaders and individual contributors was critical to the success of this work.

Lesson # 2—Engage senior leaders. Project champions worked closely with senior leaders to truly drive buy-in and support for this initiative throughout the course of the project. Since performance management is a leadership responsibility, this level of involvement was crucial to the initiative's success.

Lesson # 3—Overcome the compensation hurdle. If compensation is tied to performance reviews, address the compensation issues as well. The process redesign explained here did not change the compensation element, as it appeared that the organization was not ready for such large-scale change. But the power of compensation for employees should be a critical consideration in redesigning performance appraisal processes.

Lesson # 4—Link to other management processes. When designing and implementing a new performance management system, the links to other systems must be explicit. As managers and employees began to utilize the performance management tools and process, selection and 360-degree tools and processes were delivered to the organization in tandem.

Lesson # 5—Focus on the technological needs of the organization. Focus on the technological needs of the organization and develop online capability simultaneously. While the PM&D tools are available online, Case is currently working to develop a database to collect, store, and retrieve all performance management data and written feedback both from managers and employees.

Lesson # 6—The plan is only as good as the implementation. Creating a decentralized rollout plan encourages involvement and ownership at the business unit level. While this approach lessens the "corporate HR program" impact, it depends entirely on the skill, commitment, and motivation of those empowered to deliver. The results vary accordingly.

Lesson # 7—Solicit input. Creating something that enables the business to move forward is extremely rewarding. There are decisions made along the way in any project that will affect the outcome either for better or for worse. Involving others to collect input and to gain their commitment is critical. The project team valued the incredible depth and detail of feedback from business leaders across the organization on prototype materials and pilot sessions. A true "customer orientation" served the team well.

SUMMARY

Case built upon an existing foundation of performance management expertise by developing a process that reflected best practices. By taking the time to define what the best managers do to enhance individual performance, Case was able to capture and share a tremendous depth of experience, knowledge, and skill. The result is an ongoing community of learning in which employees at all levels continually assess how they are adding value to the organization and what they can do to improve.

There are 2 critical aspects of this work that enable managers to more effectively manage people. First, people are hired, assessed against, evaluated on, and provided with feedback regarding a constant set of criteria. Competencies provide a common language with which work can be discussed. Second, development is a priority for everyone. Individuals are held accountable for learning and improving themselves as contributors. This new partnership enables both the employee and the organization to benefit immediately and into the future.

Responses from managers have shown that Case has overcome some of the hurdles that impacted managers' ability to drive improved individual performance. Clearly, the performance bar has been raised and employees understand how their contribution helps the organization to achieve its objectives. Competencies are becoming a way of life. Human Resource systems are clearly linked to each other, and more important, to the business.

The future of Performance Management and Development at Case is continuously evolving in response to business needs. As external forces affect the work of the organization, business strategies change accordingly. As the business and the workforce continue to evolve, so will the Performance Management and Development process. With this new foundation, Case can manage both the "what" and the "how" of success into the future.

Exhibit 1. Leadership Competency Model

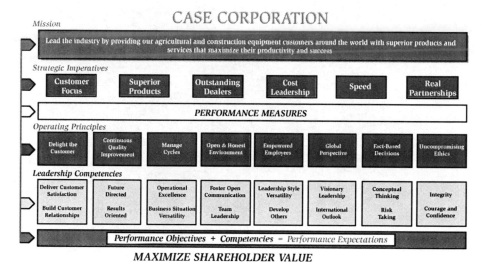

CASE CORPORATION

Mission

Lead the industry by providing our agricultural and construction equipment customers around the world with superior products and services that maximize their productivity and success

Strategic Imperatives

| Customer Focus | Superior Products | Outstanding Dealers | Cost Leadership | Speed | Real Partnerships |

PERFORMANCE MEASURES

Operating Principles

| Delight the Customer | Continuous Quality Improvement | Manage Cycles | Open & Honest Environment | Empowered Employees | Global Perspective | Fact-Based Decisions | Uncompromising Ethics |

Leadership Competencies

| Deliver Customer Satisfaction | Future Directed | Operational Excellence | Foster Open Communication | Leadership Style Versatility | Visionary Leadership | Conceptual Thinking | Integrity |
| Build Customer Relationships | Results Oriented | Business Situation Versatility | Team Leadership | Develop Others | International Outlook | Risk Taking | Courage and Confidence |

Performance Objectives + Competencies = Performance Expectations

MAXIMIZE SHAREHOLDER VALUE

Exhibit 2. Individual Contributor Competency Model

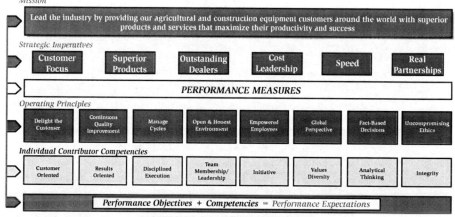

CASE CORPORATION

Mission

Lead the industry by providing our agricultural and construction equipment customers around the world with superior products and services that maximize their productivity and success

Strategic Imperatives

| Customer Focus | Superior Products | Outstanding Dealers | Cost Leadership | Speed | Real Partnerships |

PERFORMANCE MEASURES

Operating Principles

| Delight the Customer | Continuous Quality Improvement | Manage Cycles | Open & Honest Environment | Empowered Employees | Global Perspective | Fact-Based Decisions | Uncompromising Ethics |

Individual Contributor Competencies

| Customer Oriented | Results Oriented | Disciplined Execution | Team Membership/ Leadership | Initiative | Values Diversity | Analytical Thinking | Integrity |

Performance Objectives + Competencies = Performance Expectations

MAXIMIZE SHAREHOLDER VALUE

Exhibit 3. Case's Integrated Competency-Based Applications

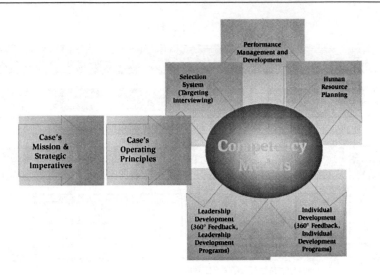

Exhibit 4. Performance Standards

Components of a Competency Model - Example

Continuous Quality Improvement Cluster

Results Oriented

Personally strives for excellence in performance by surpassing established standards. Establishes a high standard of performance that extends into the organization.

Performance Standards:

	Somewhat Effective:	Effective:	Exceptional:
N O E V I D E N C E	Meets all required standards; is viewed within own function as a pace setter; is sometimes satisfied with meeting standards when with a bit more effort or care those same standards could have been exceeded.	Continually exceeds required standards; is seen throughout the organization as a bellwether; drives self to achieve outstanding results but may not inspire others to do so.	Is driven to exceed established standards; drives self and the organization to continuously set new standards of excellence; establishes a standard that is considered an industry benchmark.

Exhibit 5.   Leadership Competencies

International Outlook—Maintains international competitive advantage by recognizing and valuing cultural differences. Integrates cultural differences into personal and business actions.

Conceptual Thinking—Ability to identify and recognize business trends, patterns, or connections that are not obviously related and/or go beyond the confines of one's own function or business. Uses this information to deal with business problems or create opportunities.

Risk Taking—Pursues a course of action without necessarily having all questions answered. Takes independent action to meet critical business objectives, while balancing the uncertainty of a situation with common sense.

Operational Excellence—Recognizes the importance of the tactical component of leadership. Ensures that the expectations, e.g., strategic initiatives, of key stakeholders are met or exceeded.

Business Situation Versatility—Develops distinctive strategies and action plans to meet the challenges of different business situations (e.g., start-up, fast growth, steady state, turnaround, close-down, merger/acquisition).

Foster Open Communication—Promotes a free flow of timely and accurate information and communication throughout the organization. Creates an environment where everyone is able to communicate with candor.

Team Leadership—Creates an environment that encourages teamwork. Enables team performance by meeting its needs and tending to its challenges.

Integrity—Shows commitment around issues of ethics, principles, and Case's values. Models and reinforces ethical behavior in self and others. Acts consistently with his/her shared values and beliefs.

Courage and Confidence—Confronts problems early on, drives hard on the right issues, and takes a firm stand in the face of controversy. This is the ability to realistically appraise one's own strengths and weaknesses and a belief in one's own capacity to accomplish tasks and solve problems. This confidence allows the person to express themselves in increasingly challenging circumstances.

Future Directed—Identifies problems and/or opportunities that impact achieving Case's business objectives. Develops a plan of action to address these issues in a way that will favorably impact business performance.

Results Oriented—Personally strives for excellence in performance by surpassing established standards. Establishes a high standard of performance that extends into the organization.

(Continued)

Exhibit 5. Leadership Competencies (*Continued*)

Leadership Style Versatility—Plays a variety of leadership roles (e.g., Pacesetting, Democratic, Affiliative, Coaching) as appropriate. Adapts style and approach to match the needs of different individuals and teams and to differentiate situations.

Develop Others—Promotes long-term development of Case employees by assessing an individual's fit and aspirations with job requirements. Creates a climate where everyone stretches beyond how they currently perform.

Deliver Customer Satisfaction—Creates satisfaction by meeting and exceeding internal and external customer needs accurately and quickly. Takes any reasonable action to ensure obligations and promises are fulfilled.

Build Customer Relationships—Serves internal and external customers by understanding their needs. Implements ways to exceed their expectations.

Exhibit 6. Performance Management and Development Training Agenda

Part One (Full Day)

Session Opening

Section One: Introduction to Performance Management and Development

Section Two: Introduction to Competencies at Case

Section Three: The Performance Agreement—Setting Objectives

Section Four: Communicating About Performance and Development

Part Two (Half Day)

Review of Part One

Section Five: Reviewing Performance

Section Six: Planning Individual Development

Section Seven: Summary and Common Questions and Answers

Exhibit 7. Sample Evaluation Questions

1. Which of the following have you completed for your direct reports this year? (Check all that apply.)

   ___ Year-end performance review regarding your performance last year

   ___ Objectives (performance and development)

   ___ Mid-year review of performance results

   ___ HRP form

2. To what extent do the following statements describe you?

   Scale:

   5 = To a very great extent

   4 = To a great extent

   3 = To some extent

   2 = To a little extent

   1 = Not at all

   A. I serve as a model of good performance.

   B. I discuss with my direct reports the relationship between their objectives and those of the organization.

   C. I hold my direct reports accountable to achieve their development objectives.

   D. I hold my direct reports accountable to achieve their performance objectives.

   E. I encourage my direct reports to discuss their development needs with me.

   F. I provide my direct reports with balanced and timely feedback.

   G. I coach my direct reports in specific areas.

   H. I provide support and resources (time, $, etc.) to my direct reports for their development.

   I. I have regular discussions with my direct reports about their objectives and progress toward them.

   J. I stress the importance of development to career progress.

   K. I show an interest in my employees' development.

3. To what extent does each of the following statements describe Case Corporation?

   Scale:

   5 = To a very great extent

   4 = To a great extent

   3 = To some extent

   2 = To a little extent

   1 = Not at all

Exhibit 7. Sample Evaluation Questions (*Continued*)

At Case Corporation:

    A. Managers and supervisors are rewarded for developing others.
    B. Managers deal effectively with poor performance issues.
    C. People are rewarded based on how well they meet their objectives.
    D. Development is irrelevant to getting ahead.
    E. Development is an annual requirement for everyone.
    F. Development is only for people whose performance is below par.
    G. Developing new competencies is valued.
    H. Development is only for a select few in the organization.
    I. We dedicate enough resources to provide development opportunities for employees.
    J. It is difficult to get information about career opportunities within the company.
    K. Outstanding performance is rewarded at Case.

4. To what extent does each of the following statements describe the current Performance Management and Development Process?

    Scale:
    5 = To a very great extent
    4 = To a great extent
    3 = To some extent
    2 = To a little extent
    1 = Not at all

    A. The Performance Management and Development Process is an improvement over the old process.
    B. The roles of management and employees are clear in the Performance Management and Development Process.
    C. I understand the competency model I will be evaluated against this year.
    D. I understand the competency model I will be evaluating my direct reports against this year.
    E. I feel comfortable evaluating my direct reports on their competencies.
    F. The performance standards (rating scale for competencies, 0–3) are useful for clarifying and evaluating the competencies.

ABOUT THE CONTRIBUTORS

Karen Garoukian Ferraro (karenferraro@casecorp.com) is director of worldwide organization development at Case Corporation and principal of KGF Consulting, L.L.C. She has worked for over 16 years in organization development, executive coaching, and human resource management for 3 Fortune 500 companies. Ferraro's recent work in the area of leadership competencies has been featured in publications such as *Training* magazine. She is a frequent speaker on topics including leadership 360-degree feedback, performance management, and competency development.

Kristine Rainge (krainge@linkage-inc.com) has worked in the organizational development arena for over 6 years, designing, developing, and implementing systems to enhance human performance in organizations. Her expertise lies in the areas of assessment and development, selection, and performance management. As a consultant at Linkage, Inc., Rainge has worked with clients across industries to assess and build tools, training, and processes enabling individuals and organizations to achieve peak performance.

Scott Nelson (snelson@linkage-inc.com) is the Midwest regional director for Linkage, Inc. He is responsible for overall operations in the Midwest, including client management, service delivery, and regional marketing initiatives. Nelson has over 15 years of experience working in both the public and private sectors of Human Resource Planning and Development. In his previous roles, Nelson's work has focused on a variety of competency-based applications such as assessment centers, selection systems, individualized executive coaching, multirater feedback and development processes, and customized training programs.

Jim Kane (jkane@linkage-inc.com) has over 20 years of experience in such areas as operations management, quality system management, process development, and human resource system development. As a principal consultant at Linkage, Inc., Kane's expertise focuses on improving the efficiency and effectiveness of work groups via a systematic approach to managing data collection, problem solving, and decision making. Kane's most recent work includes enabling leaders at all levels to engage in "Powerful Conversations," interactions that progress from shared feelings, beliefs, and ideas to an exchange of wants and needs to clear action steps and mutual commitments.

CHAPTER FIFTEEN

Sonoco

A performance management system designed to develop employees' knowledge of their roles and responsibilities while aligning their performance in support of the company's strategic business goals through such tools as 360-degree feedback and a focused competency model

INTRODUCTION

Sonoco is a 100-year-old packaging company. With sales that top $2.6 billion, Sonoco has more than 16,500 employees in 250 different locations, on 5 continents and in 31 countries.

Sonoco is not a household name, but its wide range of packaging solutions makes it possible for customers to make and distribute a broad array of products for consumers around the world. From the composite canisters used for snacks, cookies, or nuts to the plastic bags used in the grocery stores, to the protective packaging used for large appliances, more and more products in more and more places are either wound on or contained in a Sonoco package during their life cycle. See the company Web site at www.sonoco.com for more information.

BACKGROUND

Organizational Structure

Sonoco has 9 manufacturing divisions, the largest of which are Industrial Paper (IPD), Consumer Products (CPD), Flexible Packaging, and High Density Film. A vice president who reports to 1 of 2 executive vice presidents heads each division. These 2 executive vice presidents in turn report to the president and CEO of Sonoco, P. C. Browning.

Sonoco is only 25% unionized and prefers to keep the majority of the organization nonunion.

SYSTEM SPECIFICS

Key Objectives

The goal of Sonoco's Performance Management System (SPMS) is to help employees understand their roles within the organization and align their performance in support of business goals. A secondary goal of the system is employee development.

The old performance management system, in place for 15 years, needed replacing because it was:

- An event and not a process
- Not a serious business initiative
- Characterized by infrequent training
- Manager-driven
- Plagued with meaningless numerical scores for evaluating employees' past performance
- Not connected to future employee development

In contrast, SPMS was designed to:

- Act as a process and not an event
- Increase employee involvement and communication at every step of the cycle
- Examine how performance results were achieved and how to successfully achieve results in the future
- Make employees accountable for the success of the performance management process

The need for change occurred in 1995 because Sonoco was experiencing a changing business environment. Specifically, Sonoco acquired several companies, resulting in division reengineering. Each division of Sonoco was engaged in its own performance management system with little coordination among the divisions. Additionally, senior management was concerned with the quality of its work force and they recognized the lack of employee development in the old system.

System Basics

SPMS and leadership development systems were developed simultaneously, though not by design. There is overlap between the 2 systems because they are both focused on development and based on competencies. A multirater 360-degree feedback tool was developed for the leadership development program, something that was foreign to Sonoco's culture until recently. All parts of the leadership development system are now linked back to the performance management system.

The performance management system is based on competencies identified as key to Sonoco's success. Sonoco uses 4 core competencies for all employees and adds additional competencies for those in leadership positions. All employees are assessed on:

- Business and Technical Knowledge
- Communications
- Customer Satisfaction Through Excellence (both internal and external)
- Teamwork and Collaboration

Leaders in Sonoco are evaluated against 3 additional competencies:

- Visionary Leadership, Accountability, and Commitment
- Coaching and Developing Others
- Innovation and Risk-Taking

Executive leaders have 1 additional competency: diversity.

Available to employees are complete explanations of why these competencies are important, behavioral examples of desirable behavior, and examples of poor behavior.

A cascading process links organizational objectives to the division objectives, to department objectives, and down to the individual objectives.

Unique to Sonoco's system is that employee 360-degree ratings are confidential and intended only for employee development. Though the information resides on a company server, management has promised employees not to access the information—choosing not to retrieve the information even when it would have been helpful for evaluative decision making (i.e., deciding to promote, demote, or fire an employee). The approach is intended to make employees feel confident about using the online tools and evaluate themselves accurately.

The succession planning process uses the development information supplied by the performance management and leadership development programs. Leaders of each division present information about their high-potential employees to the corporate review group. For three-and-a-half days, the corporate review group, consisting of the top 6 executives, the CEO, the CFO, and the vice president of Human Resources, discusses successful employees within each division of the company. The vice president of HR generates a summary of the discussions and the high-potential employees.

Later, when positions become available, the list is reviewed to see who would be appropriate to fill the vacant position. Inclusion on the list does not guarantee promotion. Rather, those on the list are examined closely to see that they have the necessary skills for advancement or that they are receiving the development opportunities needed for advancement. The process creates equity within the succession planning system because candidates across all divisions are considered for advancement.

The Process

January to March The performance management process starts with a formal performance planning meeting based on the key initiatives laid out in Sonoco's business plan. Individual performance objectives are established based on the objectives of the organization. Employees and supervisors discuss employee competencies and outline a development plan for the year. Developmental feedback based on last year's performance is incorporated into the conversation.

April to June Employees meet with supervisors to discuss compensation changes.

June to August Business objectives and employee performance are reviewed in the middle of the year. This is a formal process and employees are responsible for initiating the conversation with their supervisors. Throughout the entire performance period, however, managers and employees should be talking informally about performance plans, objectives, competencies, and developmental plans.

Also in the middle of the year is a formal meeting between managers and subordinates to discuss career plans. This process needs improvement. Right now, career-planning meeting does not receive a lot of attention, nor does it occur as often as it should. The HR Council is working to provide timelines and guidelines to employees and managers. The guidelines suggest that participants use data gathered during the goal-setting period to frame the career-planning discussion and to set a time for the career meeting during the midyear discussion.

December At year's end, the employees complete a self-assessment and initiate a formal meeting with their supervisors. Together they discuss employee accomplishment of individual objectives, and the manager signs the form. Areas for development are identified and noted for further discussion at next year's performance planning meeting. There should be no surprises at this year-end meeting if open manager-employee communication took place throughout the performance cycle. No numerical rating is given. All feedback is narrative to indicate employee strengths, weaknesses, individual objectives, and the development plan for the next year.

Who Is Involved in Conducting Performance Appraisals?

The responsibility falls on the employee for initiating the required discussions for performance management. The conversations with managers are to clarify business objectives and how they translate to individual objectives and for the managers to provide feedback on performance.

In November and December of 1995, Sonoco worked with DDI to implement the multirater 360-degree performance appraisal with 250 employees in the leadership development program. The 360s were not software-based at that time. Employees were told that it would be 18 to 24 months before anybody would be evaluated on the 360s again. The delay is based on research suggesting that it takes close to a year for the feedback to be digested and for employees to react by creating development plans. Then, another year must pass before raters have the opportunity to observe the employee's new job behaviors. The HR Council prolonged the period further when it decided to push the 360-degree system downward into the organization, assessing 1,000 to 1,200 employees and to switch to a software-based 360-degree system. Sonoco is rolling out the 360-degree system to the employees now.

Supervisors rate the remaining employees who are not in the 360-degree system. SPMS requires supervisors to provide narrative feedback on performance and not simply meaningless numerical ratings.

Providing Thorough and Meaningful Feedback

A quantitative, 15-item survey questions employees and managers on the value and effectiveness of Sonoco's performance management system. Qualitative, open-ended questions gather information on SPMS from employees and managers through interviews. Some of the questions in these instruments evaluate the effectiveness of supervisor feedback.

The HR Council, consisting of the VP of Human Resources and other senior human resource professionals, does not check up on individual managers to see that they are providing the necessary feedback. Supervisory training incorporates specific training on coaching. Individual feedback on coaching is provided to managers in the leadership group through the 360-degree feedback system. Eventually this system will be pushed further down into the organization so that all supervisors can monitor their feedback and coaching skills.

Differences in the System Between Levels of Employees

Sonoco's Performance Management System is used for only the salaried employees (approximately 4,000 individuals). Sonoco is implementing the performance management system in a top-down format and is piloting a system for the hourly employees (approximately 12,500). The new system is designed to replace an older performance management system for the hourly workers.

All covered employees are evaluated on the same core competencies. Additional competencies exist for those who are more senior in the organization and covered under the leadership development program.

Identifying and Dealing with High and Poor Performers

The present system is designed primarily as a developmental tool and not for administrative decision making. High-potential employees who are ready for the advancement into the leadership development program are identified in the succession planning process.

The Most Effective Components of Sonoco's Performance Management System

- The system is no longer a backroom event and is now a forward-looking process. SPMS is becoming part of the regular employee-manager conversation at Sonoco that is fundamental to the job. The system focuses on development as the employees look to the future, rather than simply rating employees on past performance.

- The competency-based system helps employees understand Sonoco's values and direction, thus guiding individual performance toward organizational goals.

- SPMS puts the responsibility on the employees to complete their assessments instead of making it a manager responsibility. The system enhances buy-in because employees are active participants in their own performance management. Many employees like that they choose for themselves which areas they need to develop.

- The training method employed by Sonoco across its geographically dispersed workforce communicates system specifics and fosters commitment to SPMS.

- The 360-degree feedback system is integrated with the performance management system, as both are based on the same competencies. This arrangement permits employees to develop themselves on areas that need improvement. Development materials supporting the competencies are readily available. In addition, by tracking the aggregate results of the

360-degree feedback system Sonoco can monitor organizational effectiveness on the core competencies, using the information to drive organization-wide performance.

The Least Effective Components of Sonoco's Performance Management Process

- The formal midyear meeting for career planning needs improvement in the future. Sonoco needs to ensure that the meeting occurs and that it accomplishes its purpose.

- Sonoco still has work to do to get all system users to acknowledge that performance management is a routine part of their jobs.

SYSTEM DESIGN

How Was the Current System Designed?

The HR Council is a group at Sonoco that started meeting three-and-a-half years ago to provide strategic direction for human resources in Sonoco. The Council consists of 7 people, including the director of organizational development and is led by the vice president of Human Resources. Other members on the HR Council include the vice president of Employee Relations and the vice presidents from each of the 4 largest manufacturing divisions at Sonoco. The HR Council designed SPMS. Meanwhile, the 9 vice presidents who decided on the core and leadership competencies for Sonoco developed the leadership development program.

The competencies were the most time consuming and difficult part of the system to develop. The HR Council worked with the leadership development team and senior management to develop the competencies. The Council began by benchmarking what other organizations were doing with competencies. After a year of brainstorming, discussion, writing and rewriting, getting feedback, and tweaking, the competencies were completed. The group carefully examined the vision of Sonoco and how it needed to direct its efforts toward the vision.

The HR Council agrees that the best approach is to do your best with choosing the competencies and then agree to reexamine them a year later to see if they need changing. The HR Council did just that, changing the competencies later by adding the diversity competency for the executive leaders.

Much of the design and implementation process used cross-functional teams to build commitment to the performance management system. These teams worked on various components of the SPMS system with the HR Council. The council benchmarked the practices in other organizations, designed the performance management process, and then sought feedback from future system users and made changes before implementing SPMS throughout Sonoco.

The Role of Key Stakeholders The HR Council is responsible for overseeing the system's success. With the HR Council, Sonoco wants employees to understand that someone is looking at the system but it does not want them to feel policed.

Occasionally, some policing is necessary. A date is applied to electronic forms and to the review. If an HR manager finds that a supervisor's employee performance plan for the year was not finalized until October then the supervisor is questioned. This enforcement tactic has generally been effective.

The continued use of the system is a joint responsibility. Employees have the primary responsibility of scheduling the meetings with their managers and initiating all processes. If employees do not take the initiative, then managers are to remind the employees that action is expected.

Taking Team and Individual Performance into Account

One of the 4 core factors is *Teamwork and Collaboration*. SPMS recognizes that collaborating with others is critical to improving work efficiency and quality. The factor evaluates the degree to which an employee 1) empowers and/or involves others in decision making, 2) supports and contributes to team success, 3) establishes strong, positive working relationships, and 4) handles conflict constructively.

Ensuring That Effective Coaching Takes Place

All managers receive special training on coaching and counseling employees on performance. The training consists of a 1- to 2-day course with videotaped role play and feedback from peers. Reactions to the training are positive and, though participation in training is voluntary, the number of people signing up demonstrates the program's success. Further, the SPMS evaluations indicate that the training is favorable.

The training effectiveness can also be monitored through the results of the 360-degree feedback system used for leaders, since coaching is one of the competencies evaluated.

Much of the guidance in SPMS occurs between the employees and the online tools. The employees rate themselves on performance using these online tools.

Setting Realistic But Challenging Goals

SPMS is developmental in nature. The responsibility is on the employees to set challenging goals for themselves. They have considerable freedom to decide how challenging the goals should be. Employees are encouraged to develop themselves and obtain coaching from their supervisors.

Exceptional Tools in SPMS

- The software aids employees with defining their developmental needs and linking those needs with the appropriate resources for improvement.

- The 360-degree feedback system is online, easy to use, and provides valuable developmental feedback to covered employees.

SYSTEM INTEGRATION WITH COMPENSATION

The Relationship Between Performance Management and Compensation

The compensation system is deliberately not linked to SPMS. Compensation decisions are based on many factors, including judgments of individual performance and the performance of the organization as a whole. Meetings on performance occur early in the year, and meetings on pay occur toward the middle of the year. The separation of these meetings is intentional. This way the developmental focus of SPMS is not lost, and ratings are less likely to be inflated by managers trying to increase the pay of employees.

Sonoco has recently switched to a broadband compensation system that pays employees based on their value to the organization (even if it is above market value), as opposed to the old system that paid employees in relation to the midpoint for their position.

SYSTEM DEPLOYMENT

How the System Was Deployed

Training was key to deploying SPMS and represented a significant investment for Sonoco. A train-the-trainer program had the master trainer (who has since become the director of Organizational Development) travel to Sonoco sites throughout the world to train the trainers local to those sites.

In 1995, high-potential onsite trainers were asked to volunteer to learn about SPMS and then present it to employees at their locations. This method created buy-in at the sites because the trainers were recognized onsite as members of the local employee community, as opposed to having offsite trainers come in present the material to employees and leave. All trainers were heavily involved in wording and presenting the material.

Each training session involved a maximum of 6 trainers at a time. The first day of training talked about basic presentation skills and discussed SPMS basics. Trainers left for the day with the homework of studying the performance management system. Each trainer presented the system to the group the next day. Following each training session was a round of developmental feedback for the presenter to point out areas of strength, successful ways to make the training real to participants, and suggestions for improvement. The sessions were feedback intensive. Typically, there were 2 or 3 presentations a day Tuesday through Friday or until training was complete.

The newly trained trainers presented SPMS to the senior management of their region or division on the following Monday and Tuesday. At the end of each day, the veteran trainers gave more feedback to the novice SPMS trainers. Finally, senior managers receiving the training would provide feedback to the whole training team on how to improve training as they pushed the SPMS system down through the organization.

The HR Council asked trainers to be local experts—champions of the performance management process. As the local experts on SPMS, their role was to answer questions for employees and managers covered in the system. The veteran SPMS trainers left the site after senior management was trained. Now, the newly developed trainers presented SPMS to supervisory-level exempt employees, and then to nonexempt employees. Sonoco is still working on how to train hourly employees.

Managers trained in the system participate both days, whereas employees need only attend the first day. It is during the second day that managers engage in the role playing on coaching and feedback sessions. Supervisors are also trained on how to set objectives, observe performance, and record behavioral examples. Options for future training on coaching are presented.

After the training, managers working with employees have the role of telling employees that SPMS is the new standard for performance management and then asking subordinates what they need to cope better with the change.

Ensuring That Appraisers and Appraisees Fulfill Their Roles

The SPMS assessment and interview indicate at the organizational level the overall success at getting employees and managers to fulfill their roles in the system.

Appraisees SPMS places the burden of managing the performance management system on employees. There is no enforcement of the system because the HR Council does not want to police the employees. Evaluative data on the use of SPMS indicates that the HR Council needs to continue to communicate the importance of SPMS and to create further buy-in for SPMS. In terms of tracking employee use of the online software, the SPMS software does track the number of hits to the site but cannot distinguish whether it is 1 person logging on numerous times or many different people each logging on once.

Appraisers As stated previously, online performance plan forms are electronically dated, and managers who are late to put together performance plans for their employees at the beginning of the cycle are identified and questioned.

Ongoing Resources Provided to Help Maintain Commitment

The HR Council ensured that each division had a plan to keep SPMS a high-profile initiative. The Council sponsored an intranet site for sharing ideas on how to promote the system across the organization. Division leaders were given the flexibility to choose their own methods for building and maintaining commitment.

For example, the manager of Organizational Development for the Industrial Products and Paper Division takes responsibility for keeping SPMS in the spotlight in his division. He continually communicates the importance of SPMS. Periodically, he releases a newsletter on SPMS to covered employees describing what the HR Council is doing with performance management and what users of the system need to be doing with it.

The director of Corporate Reporting and Accounting chose another method to build commitment to SPMS. She chose to set up a team to discuss how the performance management process is progressing. Members of the team, who are all trained in SPMS, provide coaching to one another during these meetings.

After the system was rolled out, the director of Organizational Development and the vice president of Human Resources went to Sonoco's executives and explained to them what their role would be in the system. Going into those meetings, they knew that they would have executive-level support, but they wanted to be sure that the executives demonstrated their support for SPMS. In turn, Peter Browning (president and CEO) and other executives addressed their direct reports. The executives explained to the managers their new supervisory role in the system: to explain business objectives, prepare developmental plans, and provide coaching and feedback to employees on an ongoing basis.

Resistance Encountered

Employees Some employees prefer not to take responsibility for their performance. Heavy coaching with these employees was important (emphasizing that SPMS is the new system and the manager would help the employee to adapt to the change). "SPMS is too time consuming," was a common complaint. Upper management's visible support within each division helped minimize resistance. At the same time, many employees embraced the new system because they realized that they had the control to influence their own development; their managers were not telling them what to improve.

Managers Training was designed to prevent resistance by giving managers the coaching skills they need to operate under the new system. A few managers do not take the system seriously because they see it as an employee responsibility only. Some managers express that they do not like the forms and consider SPMS to be time consuming. The HR Council is addressing all of these issues. To counter the time-consuming complaint, they suggest that in the long term managers will save time because the Council suggests not to revisit the same performance issues repeatedly.

Senior Management Senior management supports the SPMS initiative.

Continuous Improvement Efforts

Working with DDI, the HR Council developed an assessment measure to evaluate SPMS. Consisting of a quantitative questionnaire and a qualitative interview, data from these instruments are leading to changes in SPMS, including changes to the forms, competencies, and training.

The HR Council is pushing the 360-degree feedback system further down into the organization because it is so useful.

Unlike with the previous performance management system, the HR Council agreed that SPMS needs to remain high profile, be subject to continuous improvement, and require refresher training. The HR Council has been successful at all 3 endeavors during the past 2 years.

INFORMATION TECHNOLOGY SYSTEMS

Successfully Leveraging Technology

As described previously, the following processes are automated with SPMS:

- Software helps employees develop their skills. The software developed by DDI enables employees to identify the developmental activities and resources available to them so that they can improve their work performance. Further, the OPAL (Online Performance and Learning) allows the information to be exported into the performance planning forms.

- New software from Mindsolve enables the 360-degree ratings to be done online. Raters are selected by the individual, the software e-mails the raters requesting feedback, and the assessment is completed online. The software compiles the results so that the employees requesting feedback can see them.

The 360-degree feedback system and OPAL are both intranet-based and located on the company server. Remote sites can access the system through the Internet. However, security is not an issue.

OPAL and Performance Planning Forms The flexible software developed by DDI is known as OPAL, which requires a name and password for secure entry. Users can build development plans to guide them during the next year. Nobody other than the individual has access to user information, so it makes sense to be honest and use the system to one's advantage. There are 3 sections to the software: Developer, Assessor, and Advisor.

Users can customize the Developer component to their part of the organization. The software helps users find resources and learning opportunities to develop themselves on the core competencies. Some of the learning resources are in the library, but many are described as things the person can do on the job to develop him or herself. The on-the-job development piece is in keeping with the philosophy that 70–75% of development occurs on the job. Later, users can enter information into the OPAL database to indicate which resources and pieces of advice they found helpful to their development. The software even warns users about behaviors they can overdo and how to avoid this. OPAL is available to all employees who can link in through a desktop, whether they are covered by the 360-degree feedback system or not.

Assessor and Advisor are the other parts of system. Assessor allows employees to complete self-assessments on the competencies. Advisor allows supervisors to volunteer feedback to the employees. Sonoco uses neither of these components now because it is still in the early stages of its system development and is developing the system in steps.

Sonoco's performance management form is divided into 4 sections. The software allows users to work offline and then go online when they are ready. The performance management system tracks which employees are using the forms. The system also tracks the progress of the employees.

In Section 1, users start with creating objectives. Employees can write in the objectives; emphasize certain text with bold, italics, and underline; and expand the text box to accommodate their typed objectives.

Section 2 presents users with the 4 core competencies and the 3 leadership competencies. Employees rate themselves on how well they perform on each relevant competency. The numerical ratings were added to the system to further connect the 360-degree feedback system with OPAL in mind; otherwise, ratings probably would not be have been included in OPAL. The system does not allow users to create new competencies for themselves.

Section 3 has a career and development planning form. The software displays activities and timing of the development plan. Sonoco wants to take the next step and further integrate this section with its succession planning process to identify for employees the possible career paths.

Section 4 allows for written comments by employees and supervisors on how they feel about the performance management process. They both sign off electronically and indicate with whom the information can be shared (e.g., compensation manager).

Lastly, OPAL allows users to look at ideas for developing their competencies and then export the information to Sections 2 or 3 of their performance management plan.

The 360-degree Feedback System Mindsolve, based in Florida, put together the 360-degree feedback online software and customized it to Sonoco's competency-based system. Mindsolve set up the software, and Sonoco's people administrate the system. Sonoco is currently rolling out the new procedure.

The database containing 360-degree assessments and development information resides on a company server with a megabyte of RAM and 400 megabytes of hard-drive space. Employees have been assured that management will not view individual information. Employee trust existed from the beginning. It continues to develop as management stands by its commitment not to access individual data from the server.

The software operates as follows for an individual software user:

1. Employees receive e-mail on Lotus Notes when somebody else has selected them as participants for 360-degree feedback.

2. They download software to their machine.

3. Next, the employees log on to the software as users and select who they want to rate their performance. The software users type the names and e-mail addresses of those who should rate them. The raters' job titles are displayed. Supervisors are automatically identified. Users select others who are their direct reports, who work upstream/downstream, as well as team members who have had the opportunity to observe their performance. The software displays the names and titles of those who the users have picked. E-mail is sent to all raters saying that they have been selected to rate the users. Then the raters download the software, engage in steps 1 through 3 of the sign-up process, and provide feedback.

4. With steps 1 through 3 completed, the users move to the rater screen (now the users becomes the raters). This screen displays the competency in the upper right corner with a behavioral statement. The definition of the competency is available by clicking on the competency word on the screen. The raters select the person they want to rate. Next, they select a box indicating the level of performance they think the person demonstrates on the particular competency.

The choices are:

- Top 5% of company
- Usually exceeds expectations
- Usually meets and sometimes exceeds expectations
- Usually meets expectations
- Usually below expectations

There is a text box available for the raters to enter comments.

5. Next, another person's name comes up on the same competency and the raters repeat the process until they have rated all people requesting ratings. This method allows them to rate each person against the descriptors for the competency and to see how they compare with one

another on the same competency. This allows raters to make adjustments when they are done and provides a chance to review all rated employees in comparison with one another. Thus, it is important to rate groups of like individuals together in 1 session. Raters can decline to rate someone if they do not match well with the rest of the people being rated at the time. Rating continues until all competencies and people are covered. Note that the system will not allow more than 20 people to select any 1 rater.

Users are not trained in this system since it is very intuitive. The software provides online instructions that answer why it is important to use the system, what the data are used for, and who receives the data. The software also contains an online tutorial that visually demonstrates the rating process to the rater.

The HR Council suggests several advantages of the software-based system. Computer software takes the boredom out of the paper-and-pencil rating system. The process is quicker online and more enjoyable. Employees choose who they want to have rate them (with their supervisor a mandatory rater), and managers review employee decisions. Managers cannot make changes to the raters selected. Managers can encourage changes through conversation, but the employee must decide whether to make the changes.

The software compiles all ratings so that group data can be analyzed.

Challenges and Obstacles to Using Technology

The greatest challenge is to decide what to automate and how to do it. Cost is the only obstacle. The technology exists to link all HR and performance management systems together.

SYSTEM RESULTS

Performance Management Process Effectiveness

Sonoco has enlisted the assistance of DDI to develop an organizational audit/assessment of SPMS. Using the quantitative survey discussed earlier, data were collected in October 1998 from 1,000 employees (a 70% response rate). One hundred percent of surveyed employees completed the qualitative interview. Some changes for the system have already been identified and are being communicated to employees now. For example, the forms are now using Lotus Notes and are simpler to follow, the performance management process is streamlined for those who do not supervise others, and the second day of training is continually being improved. The audit has the added benefit of demonstrating to employees that SPMS is a high priority for the organization.

The aggregate results of executive group performance on the 360-degree feedback system demonstrated that some competency areas need strong performance improvement (indicating that the respondents, including the group members themselves, provided candid feedback on the instrument). The leadership group did not dispute the data. Instead, they discussed the data openly and decided on methods for improving in the future. This demonstrates that the data produced by SPMS can drive change and improvement.

Evaluation of the return on investment (ROI) of the performance management system does not occur at this time because of the difficulty in isolating the factors influencing the success criteria. This is an area that Sonoco would like to learn about from other organizations that have such an evaluation system.

Distribution of Employee Performance Results

Numerical scores are only used for developmental purposes in SPMS and the 360-degree feedback system; they are not used to make promotional or pay decisions. That is, the 360-degree feedback results are used to identify competency areas that need improvement organization-wide.

Balancing the Flexible Distribution of Performance with a Finite Compensation Budget

Many other factors besides performance affect pay, so there is no conflict between the distribution of pay and performance. Linking pay too strongly to organizational performance could potentially result in a situation where the company performs poorly one year, lowers pay for high-performing employees, and loses them because the market is paying more money.

NEXT STEPS/OVERALL

How Sonoco Would Improve the System If It Were to Redesign

SPMS is a flexible system that is still under development. Further assessment data are needed before the HR Council can understand the success of the system and evaluate which components should have been designed differently. Recommendations for minor adjustments are identified in the Continuous Improvement section, as well as in this section.

Lessons Learned

- Deriving the core competencies for the organization is a very difficult and time-consuming step, but it is well worth the effort. One must continue to work to refine the competencies that drive the system.

- Communication is very important to the process. One must strive continually to communicate the system throughout the organization.
- Benchmarking is a valuable practice in itself, but those doing the benchmarking must examine whether the practice they are thinking of adapting will fit with their own organizational culture. The practice may need to be modified to fit with one's own organizational culture.
- Using team-based processes with input from as many people as is practical is a great technique for encouraging buy-in. Use the opportunity to tell team members what you are doing and why you are doing it.
- Implementation must be consistent. Training materials cannot be presented in slightly different ways. Doing so can affect how the information is perceived (e.g., some managers have missed the point that SPMS is a joint responsibility because they perceive the role to be an employee-only responsibility).
- A powerful commitment-building technique is to have local trainers work with senior management to push the system downward into the organization. This process creates instant buy-in from senior managers, gives an opportunity for them to ask questions and provide suggestions for how to roll out the system, and creates champions for performance management.

Next Steps

- Continuing to develop and redefine the competencies to be sure that they align with Sonoco's business strategy as the company expands globally and as leadership changes.
- Expanding the use of the 360-degree feedback system. The HR Council wants to use the data for evaluative purposes, too, but it does not want to lose the developmental focus.
- Moving to collect the 360-degree feedback data on a Sonoco intranet as opposed to using an outside source to collect the data. The system will assist with selecting raters and gathering data.
- Rolling out new online tools that will take the 360-degree feedback ratings and generate a list of resources and developmental opportunities for users based on their scores.
- Piloting and rolling out a performance management system for the nonexempt and hourly employees.
- Improving the formal midyear career plan meeting between supervisors and employees.
- Integrating competencies into the selection process.

- Plotting performance versus potential on a grid as part of a succession planning process that is in development.

- Working to get performance management to be part of the regular conversation at Sonoco and building user acceptance.

- Keeping an open mind and constantly scanning the horizon for other ideas to help evolve the performance management and other human resource systems at Sonoco.

ABOUT THE CONTRIBUTORS

Rick Maloney (Rick.Maloney@sonoco.com) joined Sonoco Products Company in the spring of 1991 and was assigned to work on the development of its company-wide performance management and development systems. Over the past 5 years, Maloney has developed and implemented Sonoco's organizational development systems. During this time, Sonoco has become recognized as a leader in fully integrated performance management and development systems. Within the past 3 years, Maloney has been asked to make numerous presentations across the United States and abroad on the development and implementation of competency-based, developmentally focused performance management. Born in Winchester, Virginia, Maloney attended Bridgewater College. Majoring in psychology, he worked his way through school as a behavior modification trainer working primarily with autistic children at DeJarnette Center for Human Development. This center was a leader in the use of behavior modification programs to deal with autism rather than the use of drugs to suppress autistic behaviors. Maloney has also served as a senior human resource generalist for the James River Corporation and the Interstate Paper Company.

Derek A. Smith (Dsmith@linkage-inc.com) is a research consultant at Linkage, Inc., where he has led numerous projects in research and organizational development. Most recently, he led a study with Dr. Edward Lawler III on performance management and worked with Dr. Noel Tichy on the application of action learning to leadership development and change management. His previous work assignments included developing and validating personnel selection tests and procedures; designing, implementing, and evaluating training programs; designing systems for employee evaluation and development; and employing data-based decision tools using statistical analysis. Prior to joining Linkage, Inc., Smith developed training programs and survey instruments for Square D, Pillsbury, and the City of Murfreesboro Fire Department. Smith earned a bachelor's degree at Castleton State College and a master's degree in industrial/organizational psychology at Middle Tennessee State University.

COACHING AND MENTORING

COACHING AND MENTORING: NEW TWISTS, OLD THEME—AN INTRODUCTION
BY BEVERLY KAYE

In the world of organization and human resource development, the concepts of mentoring and coaching are nothing new. Both have always "been there," usually happening informally, but occasionally "designed" as interventions to solve particular business issues.

The last 5 years have seen a groundswell in both arenas. And it's not just been more of the same; organizations have begun to use mentoring and coaching more purposefully. HR and OD practitioners have worked to utilize both interventions to meet pressing business problems having to do with the development and retention of talent, as well as the growth of future leaders. These interventions have been more systemic, more thoughtful, and more innovative than ever before.

The case studies that follow illustrate this trend. Both were motivated by specific business drivers, both were preceded by intensive research, both were implemented over time, and both were evaluated seriously. Readers will find them instructive, detailed, and engaging.

Usually a section introduction calls for a definition of terms. In this case, this is easier said than done. The literature has defined coach, mentor, and manager in a great variety of ways. Some say that the coach, the mentor, and the manager are 3 distinct people—different in position, role, and responsibility. Others say they are one and the same. They are intertwined. If you forced me to choose, I'd side with the group that suggests they are, in fact, very different. Although I also suggest that any manager worth his or her "salt" *should* do both. The best of managers do some coaching and some mentoring as part of their management or leadership responsibilities. Those who subscribe to the latter definition invest heavily in training their managers in both of these roles.

The following table distinguishes some of the characteristics between a mentor, a coach, and a manager who is "just" managing.

Coach	Mentor	Manager
Has an individual perspective: provides insight and perspective aligning an individual's developmental goals with those of the organization.	Has a horizontal/systemic perspective: provides insight and perspective that matches the flow of business across several different functions.	Has a vertical perspective: provides key insights and perspectives about the function or department they manage.
Provides an external mirroring: models effective two-way communication and feedback in order to improve the performance of the learner.	Provides indirect authority: not responsible for managing the performance of the learner.	Provides direct authority: responsible for the learner's performance and success on the job.
Advice to further development: shares confidential and personal feedback but encourages learner to share development plans with others.	Advice to broaden viewpoint: allowed to share information to which the learner is seldom privy.	Advice on Performance Improvement: able to provide feedback on an on-going basis so the learner knows how he or she is performing in relation to goals and objectives.
Foster self-insight: concerned with helping the learner grow through introspection and feedback from others.	Foster self-responsibility: concerned with helping the learner take charge of his or her own growth.	Foster accountability: responsible for monitoring performance and progress through appraisals and other formal systems.
Concerns about personal growth: concerned that the learner is successful at learning and becoming a more effective leader.	Concerns about thinking: ultimately concerned that the learner gains perspective and is successful at learning.	Concerns with productivity: concerned with the learner's success on the job.

So, what's your reward for carefully reading these 2 case studies? For one, you will find that they were both sparked by similar issues. You might think about which of these is also represented in your own organization.

Dow Corning's process began with a warning signal from their attitude survey, which indicated only a 33% satisfaction level with career opportunities. The warning light flashed because Dow recognized there could be severe performance implications from individuals not satisfied with their jobs. They also knew that it was vital to develop a particular set of competencies if the organization was to remain competitive into the twenty-first century. Similarly, the senior team at MediaOne recognized that they too needed to develop particular skill sets as they moved into a new industry. Their concerns about their own leadership bench strength and talent shortage led them to realize that they would have retention risk problems if they didn't take this seriously.

Each employed several models of coaching and mentoring throughout their process. As you review their methodologies, consider which might fit into your own culture, if tailored properly.

MediaOne used external coaches at very senior levels, and internal (HR) coaches at the leader level. All offered their coachees one-on-one sessions where their 360-degree feedback was reviewed. Peer coaching was also introduced as individuals met in trios to work on development plans. Managerial coaching was also expected as managers continued the work begun with the coaches with their own direct reports. Dow Corning's program emphasized the manager as the major coach and mentor. Instituted as a global educational effort, all Dow managers learned the skills and art of development coaching. The responsibility was directly on their plates. Coaches were utilized as secondary resources through their career resource center. They also used members of their Operating Committee to participate in brown bag lunches designed to raise a variety of career topics. In this way, even more leaders were able to coach and mentor.

Serious, long-term coaching and mentoring interventions like the following case studies described are indeed "bigger than a breadbox." They all took great commitment and great resources to implement. If you are looking at these cases as ideas to mirror, don't feel you need to do it this big. You *can* start small. Here are some "musts" to use as a check sheet.

1. Define your target group.

2. Decide on your Mentoring or Coaching philosophy.

3. Train or "buy" your coaches, or do both.

4. Educate your learners on what to ask for and how to manage the coaching relationship.

5. Evaluate the intervention, learn from mistakes, and continue.

My own recent research on retention suggests loud and clear that stars don't leave organizations for dollars. They leave because no one in the organization seemed to care about their learning and their growth. They leave if they feel they are not being developed. Whether you train your own managers to be effective coaches and mentors, whether you institute a formal mentoring program using your senior execs, or whether you employ external or internal coaches, it is important that this message gets out loud and clear. Author and career consultant Donald Miller said something that I have never forgotten:

> *"Behind every successful person, there is one elementary truth. Somewhere, someway, someone cared about their growth and development."*

Dr. Beverly Kaye (Beverly.Kaye@csibka.com), president of Career Systems International, has delivered organizational career development programs for the past 20 years. Kaye is the author of *Up is Not the Only Way* (Davies-Black, 1997) and co-author of *Designing Career Development Systems* (Jossey Bass, 1986), and *Love 'Em or Lose 'Em: Getting Good People to Stay* (Berrett-Koehler, 1999). Kaye consults to major Fortune 500 companies across the country and is the recipient of several prestigious career development awards for her contribution to the field.

CHAPTER SIXTEEN

Dow Corning

A Global Career Development Process (Career Fitness) for all employees designed to create a culture for continuous learning and personal responsibility for career growth through career management, coaching, and advising

INTRODUCTION

Dow Corning Corporation is the global leader in the manufacture of silicone and silicon-based products with approximately $2.7 billion in sales and 9,000 employees. It is a 56-year-old joint venture between Dow Chemical and Corning Inc., with its stock solely held by the 2 partners in the joint venture. While corporate headquarters are located in Midland, Michigan, there are facilities in 33 countries outside the United States. The company had long held the philosophy of "promote from within." In general, long-term employment was an expectation held by most employees. In terms of employee development, this meant a somewhat patriarchal approach to career development and a sense of entitlement among employees.

In mid-1994, an employee expectation survey of 75% of the global employee population showed only a 33% level of satisfaction with opportunities for career growth. Naturally, this raised concerns on the part of executive management. Although turnover had been steady at about 5% per year for sometime, there was a concern about losing high performers in the workforce. In addition, management was concerned about the level of performance if employees were not satisfied with opportunities for career growth. Executive management requested that Human Resources initiate a project to determine the possible causes for this low level of satisfaction and recommend changes to improve employees' satisfaction in this area.

The request was significant in 2 ways. First, it was not a specific request for a class or event—rather, it was a request for understanding the causes of the dissatisfaction. Second, it gave human resources the opportunity to operate as a business partner and take a strategic role—rather than the traditional transactional role.

The project began in 1994. The first report to executive management was made in October of the same year.

The Business Issues

In 1995, Dow Corning was beginning a process of change that would impact everything and everyone in the organization over the next 5 years. Known as Project PRIDE, it was the implementation of an enterprise-wide software suite to drive the business processes of the entire company. Implementation of the software was in itself a huge step toward globalization. In May of 1995, Dow Corning entered Chapter 11. This resulted in new concerns about employee retention, as "headhunters" descended en masse on employees at all levels in the organization and changed the timeline for implementation of the process. It was clear that new ways of thinking about employee development must be created. The issues were articulated as:

1. How do we attract and retain high-performing employees?
2. How do we prepare employees for the change in our organization?
3. How do we empower our employees to take personal responsibility for their careers during this period of significant change in the organization?
4. How do we create a culture that demands continuous learning at all levels?
5. How do we improve employee satisfaction with opportunities for career growth when the organization is flattening?
6. How do we do this in a way that meets the needs of a diverse global audience?

NEEDS ASSESSMENT

The employee expectation survey of 1994 had included the Americas and Europe, but not Asia. The needs assessment for this current project would draw information from all areas. However, due to the structure of the organization and the mass of momentum and literature about employee development, the assessment would focus largely on the United States.

Corporate Education, Training and Development undertook the first 2 phases of the Needs Analysis:

1. Understanding executive management's view of Dow Corning's knowledge needs for the future
2. Understanding the best practices in the field for developing employees to meet organizational needs

In phase 1 of the needs analysis, the top 16 executives in the company were interviewed. Each interview was conducted by 2 people. One individual was from Corporate Education, Training and Development. One individual was from the Education, Training and Development staff of the major functions in the organization (Manufacturing and Engineering, Marketing and Sales, and Science and Technology). The interviews were essentially free form in nature, focusing on the skills for the future.

The outcome of these interviews was a list of competencies needed for all employees for the future. The competencies fell into 3 major categories:

1. Managing Change For the Future
2. Maximizing People's Effectiveness
3. Maximizing Business Effectiveness

Phase 2 of the needs assessment involved benchmarking with external organizations to determine the best practices in the field. To a certain extent, it was fortunate that a large body of literature on the subject was being produced during this time—resulting in excellent source material about the leaders in the field. The bibliography at the end of this case includes a list of references from the initial research. During July and August of 1994, 9 organizations were interviewed. The primary focus of the interviews was employee development. The following diagram (Table 1) shows a list of the practices that were seen as exemplary in the organizations interviewed. The table is a summary of key concepts and practices from Dow's Benchmarking and Needs Analysis Project, in October 1994.

In late 1994, a report was made to the Global Operating Committee (the top 16 executives in the company) with the following 3 recommendations:

1. Create a team of Global Operating Committee members, called the Board of Governors, to direct the efforts of a Learning and Development organization (replacing Corporate Education, Training and Development)
2. Develop, at a very high level, the competencies that are necessary to move the organization into the twenty-first century
3. Create teams to address Leadership Development and Career Development

These recommendations were unanimously accepted—with the first priority given to creating the Board of Governors and establishing competencies for the twenty-first century. The Board of Governors consisted of the 5 members of the Operating Committee (representing all functions and areas) and the director of Learning and Development. It was led by the CEO. In addition, Dave Ulrich, from the University of Michigan, served as a consultant to the group. In 1995, the Board of Governors approved a list of competency clusters for leadership in

Table 1. Benchmarking Employee Development Chart

Concept or Practice	Definition	Where seen
Corporate University	Typically defined as the "home base" for training activities. May be an actual place or a "virtual" university. Frequently offered as a catalog of training programs. Usually includes alliances with outside trainers.	Motorola*** Boeing* Raychem* Corning** Kodak** Intel**
Career Center	A resource for individual employees to use in assessing and enhancing their employability, either internally or externally. There is a very strong difference of opinion whether the center should do outplacement.	Career Action Center* Raychem* Corning** Intel** Boeing*
Collaborative Learning/Theory Practice Interplay	An approach to education based on the theory that effective learning is multidirectional—not just 1 way from teacher to student. This also involves "theory practice interplay" which centers on the student's exploration or application and constant reinforcement of learning how to learn.	Evergreen State*
Employability and Career Self-Reliance	". . . the ability to actively manage your work life in a rapidly changing environment, and the attitude of being self-employed whether you are inside or outside of an organization." (Quoted from "Career Self-Reliance: Your Path to the Future" by Betsy Collard) In this practice it is common for all employees to be required to have an up-to-date résumé.	Career Action Center* Raychem* Intel** Corning**
Job Posting	Defined by most as a listing of open positions inside the company, although senior management positions are typically excluded. In some areas, companies may include external positions as well.	Raychem* Corning**

Table 1. Benchmarking Employee Development Chart (*Continued*)

Concept or Practice	Definition	Where seen
360-degree Performance Assessment	A performance evaluation that includes self-appraisal, peer/internal customer/suppliers appraisal, and management appraisal.	Boeing* Evergreen State* Corning**
Distance Learning & Non-Classroom Learning	Both the ability to get instruction at distant sites (may include video/CD tools and video conference) and the use of on-the-job and other learning experiences outside the traditional classroom setting.	Corning** Raychem* Evergreen*

*Personal Interview
**Telephone Interview
***Referenced in Literature

Dow Corning. The competencies, when implemented and executed with excellence, address the following 5 trends:

1. A dramatically changing organization—moving from a functional focus to a process-driven focus

2. Increasing global competition resulting in new pricing and quality pressures

3. Expansion into new global markets, resulting in a shift in sales and technology away from the United States

4. Increased emphasis on eliminating barriers to productivity—between individuals, geographies, cultures, genders, teams, and internal organizations

5. Increasing focus on business processes requiring continuous growth of information technology—related to the implementation of an enterprise resource planning software

These competency clusters became known as Dimensions and formed the foundation for both Leadership Development and Career Development. The 6 Dimensions are:

1. *Valuing Learning*—the creation of a culture that advocates continuous learning at all levels

2. *Creating a Facilitative Environment*—leadership that empowers employees through emphasis on collaboration, participation, and assurance of decision making at the lowest possible level

3. *Energizing Performance*—a focus on setting and achieving high performance goals with visible alignment to challenging business strategies

4. *Leading Change*—helping all employees adapt to the ever increasing speed of change

5. *Sans Frontières (Operating without Borders)*—embracing diversity, in all its forms, and using that diversity to meet the challenges of the future

6. *Customer Driven*—a focus on customer service that enables Dow Corning to attain levels of customer satisfaction that are higher than competition

In early 1995, 2 teams were formed:

1. The Global Leadership Team—5 members of the Learning and Development Organization, representing Europe, Asia, and the Americas

2. The Global Career Development Team—3 members of the newly formed Learning and Development Organization representing Europe, Asia, and the Americas

The Global Leadership Team was given the responsibility of translating the Dimensions into skills and behaviors and creating an appropriate curriculum to develop these skills in leaders and in all employees.

The Global Career Development Team was given the responsibility to determine the best process for career development and the resources required to support it.

The newly formed Learning and Development Organization was asked to provide resources for the Leadership Development and Career Development teams.

The focus of the remainder of the case will be on the Career Development segment of the project. Since it is not possible to entirely separate the 2 segments, you will see some outcomes of the Leadership Development segment as they were incorporated into the Career Development process.

DESIGN AND STRUCTURE OF THE CAREER DEVELOPMENT PROCESS

Models

In 1995, a Learning and Career Center pilot was proposed—to be established in the largest population center of Dow Corning, yet to perform at a global level. This center would both test the concepts of career development and offer a tangible resource for employees interested in continuous learning.

It was widely agreed that learning programs would be the most effective way to introduce the concepts of career development to employees. The basic

Table 2. Career Fitness Model

Individual	Manager	Organization
Person—understand who I am, articulate my values, interests and style.	**Listen**—facilitate discussion of employee's values, interests and style.	**Embrace** diversity—insist upon an appreciation for the diversity of all people in the organization.
Perspective—understand my personal skill level, how my personal skill level is perceived by others and what my reputation in the organization is.	**Level**—assess employees candidly, with empathy, on skills and potential. Help employees understand how reputations are formed and changed.	**Establish** competencies—create and communicate the competencies needed for the organization and individuals to be successful.
Place—understand the world of work, both internal and external to Dow Corning .	**Leverage**—advise employees how their skills fit into organizational needs.	**Explain**—articulate the culture of the organization in clear terms and make it available for all to see.
Possibilities—recognize the choices I have for career growth.	**Look Ahead**—forecast opportunities that may exist in the future.	**Expand**—design HR systems to help employees see development opportunities and build skills for future growth.
Plan—create a personal development plan to make your career goals a reality.	**Link**—connect employees to people and resources for development.	**Empower**—allow employees to take personal responsibility for their career goals.

The 5 goals established for the process are:

1. To give employees visibility into the opportunities for career growth
2. To create a culture in which the employee takes personal responsibility for his or her own career growth and forms a partnership with his or her manager to establish and attain goals
3. To focus employees on the development needs that will give them and the organization competitive advantage in any market

concepts of the program were designed by Human R⌐
1995. The model from this early concept was a simple
3 questions (Who am I?, What can I do?, and What are
sent key elements of career development and are inten
the model was expanded to show that the junction of the
sents the contribution the individual can make to the organiza⌐
the model was expanded into the Career Fitness Model (Figu.
below:

The Career Fitness concepts carry through the model below (deve
Beverly Kaye) which explains roles and responsibilities in the partι.
between individuals, managers, and the organization (Table 2).

Goals

The original purposes of the career development process were aligned with the
Dimension of Valuing Learning. This is best articulated in the Mission Statement
for Learning and Development created by the Board of Governors:

"We will provide the resources to assure that our employees have the skills and
knowledge to execute our business strategies successfully. These skills make our
employees readily employable outside of our company—but they choose to stay
here because their expectations for satisfying work and opportunities for growth
are met."

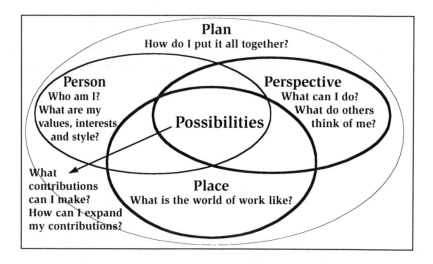

Figure 1 Dow Corning's Career Fitness Model

This model used courtesy of Beverly Kaye Associates and Career Systems International.
Copyrights apply.

4. To help employees prepare for and adapt to the changes brought on by business process reengineering initiatives and the implementation of enterprise resource planning software

5. To communicate all of the Dimensions and Skills developed by the Global Leadership Team

Benefits

The organization benefits from a strong career development process in several ways:

A solid process for career development helps to retain high-performing employees. Internal research indicates the cost to replace an employee ranges from 1.5 to 2 times the employee's annual salary—so a high turnover rate can be quite expensive to an organization. Dow Corning historically had a turnover rate of less than 5% annually. A combination of dissatisfaction with opportunities for career growth, Chapter 11, and competitors aggressively recruiting employees could increase turnover.

A study from Sears (written by Anthony Rucci, published in the *Harvard Business Review* in April 1998) demonstrated that employee satisfaction was linked to both customer satisfaction and profitability. There is significant opportunity to improve overall employee satisfaction by increasing the satisfaction with opportunities for career growth.

In *The Fifth Discipline Fieldbook* (1994), Peter Senge states, ". . . the only sustainable source of competitive advantage is your organization's ability to learn faster than its competition." This is done through providing employees the resources to create developmental plans that are both meaningful to the individual and aligned to the needs of the business.

The benefits to the organization are directly aligned with the original goals of the practice, and the Learning and Development Organization is held accountable by senior management for demonstrating the benefits. In addition, managers and employees benefit in several ways.

The benefits to the manager are:

- Open communication with the employee about career goals and needs
- More opportunities to link career development coaching and overall performance improvement
- A more satisfied and more productive employee

The benefits to the individual are:

- A broad understanding of the personal and organizational factors influencing career development, giving the individual a strong basis for career decision making

- A comprehensive set of tools and resources for developing a career plan
- New insights into the opportunities for growth in the organization
- Methods for managing the personal development necessary to meet future requirements resulting from ongoing organizational change

Prior Work Referenced

This process has its foundation in work started in the 1970s and continuing throughout the 1990s by career development leaders including Thomas Gutteridge, Zandy Liebowitz, Beverly Kaye, Caela Farren, and Beverly Bernstein. Their work was visionary and presented a formula that in practice still appears to be state of the art. In their book *Organizational Career Development,* the best practices in organizations in the 1990s were described in detail. Drawing upon this work, the Dow Corning design was expanded to offer a complete set of the recommended practices to employees:

- A tangible representation of the company's interest in individual career development (the Learning and Career Center)
- A globally communicated and consistent process for career development
- Options for all learning styles—classroom training, library resources, and computer-based career planning
- One-on-one career advising

Beverly Kaye's book *Up Is Not the Only Way* (1993) provided the premise that enrichment and not promotion is the career development way of the future. This premise was a key selling point for managers who were concerned that employee expectations would focus on promotion or leaving the company.

External guidance came from benchmarked companies, including Raychem, Boeing, Motorola, Chrysler, and the Career Action Center. Consultant partners were a rich source of experiences and ideas. Networking in career development sessions at professional society meetings and conferences resulted in additional ideas for improvements in the process.

Additional research was done prior to implementation of the Career Development process to determine employee needs using focus panels representing all levels and functions. Many ideas from these panels were incorporated into the design of the physical facilities and the design of the offerings. Exhibit 1 summarizes this research.

IMPLEMENTATION

Phase I—The primary development of the concepts and process occurred between July 1994 and November 1996.

Phase II—The development of a tangible resource for career development and ongoing learning (the Learning and Career Center) occurred between January 1995 and November 1996.

Phase III—The transition from a U.S.-based process to a globally acceptable process occurred between March 1997 and May 1998. There is currently the capability to deliver workshops in all locations, globally, using local facilitators. Translations in French, German, and Japanese will be completed in 1999.

Phase IV—Expansion of learning solutions to meet career needs of new employees and "near retirement" employees was initiated in the United States in 1998. Global adoption of these programs is under review.

Phase V—The development of real or virtual Learning and Career Centers in Europe and Asia began in 1999 and will continue through 2000.

The concepts of the process are expected to remain intact, but the application of the concepts will continue to evolve as organizational and individual needs change.

Location/Target Audience

This process was initiated in the United States (Midland, Michigan, in August 1996), with approximately 2,500 people having been exposed to the process at various levels through December 1998. Approximately 200 people in Europe and approximately 300 people in Asia have been exposed to the process.

It is projected that learning solutions will be delivered to approximately 500 people per year over the next 5 years.

All full-time and part-time employees, approximately 9,300 people worldwide, are eligible to participate in the career development process. Contract workers, student workers, and retirees are not eligible to participate. Family members are being considered for future participation, but are not eligible today.

Resources

The following (Table 3) describes the resources allocated for the various stages of the Career Development Process.

Content

This process integrates a number of learning and development approaches and practices to achieve aligned outcomes. Alignment is accomplished using globally consistent models and competencies. The competencies form the "backbone" of all Learning and Development initiatives—including the Human Resources Systems module of the enterprise resource planning software.

Learning and Development is challenging and changing the paradigm that classes are the only learning solution for employees. The Career Development programs—workshops, workbooks, computer-based learning, and career

Table 3. Career Development Process Resources Chart

Component	Resources	Effort/Capital/Budget
Needs Analysis	2 Senior Learning and Development (L&D) Specialists	3 months
Learning and Career Center Design	1 Senior L&D Specialist, 2 L&D Coordinators, 1 Facility Planner, 1 Facility Engineer, 1 telephone specialist, and 1 computer specialist	4 months; $500K for center remodeling and furnishings
Learning and Career Center Implementation	1 Career Center Manager, 1 Career Center Operations Administrator, 3 receptionists/training administrators	$500K annual budget for facility, SW&B, library resources and career advising
Global Career Development Team	1 Americas representative (Global Manager of Career Development), 1 European representative (Area L&D Manager) and 1 Asian Representative (Area L&D Manager)	Approximately 3 months per person per year—ongoing effort
External Consultants	External facilitators: 5 facilitators for Americas 2 facilitators for Europe 6 facilitators for Asia	Approximately 800 hours per year 1997–1998
Learning Solution Delivery	Software Self-paced Workbooks 2-day workshop	$50 per person $200 per person $600 per person (includes facilitator cost)
	Library Resources	$20K per year budget for resources

advising—all follow the same model but accommodate various learning styles and needs and decrease the need for traditional classroom learning.

Career Fitness workshops reinforce individual responsibility for career development using action learning principles. Extensive personal preparation is required to complete the program effectively. Classroom activities are designed to be highly interactive. Lecturing is minimized. Group or paired activities make up the majority of the sessions. The 2-day program can be delivered in a 1 + 1 (one day of classroom activities followed by a second day 2 weeks later). I can also be delivered in a 4 × 4 (four 4-hour modules scheduled weekly) format to allow action items to be accomplished. Action items include feedback discussions with managers or associates, informational interviewing, and values discussions with spouses or significant others.

Career Fitness for New Employees is designed for employees with less than 1 year of service. It focuses on self-awareness, relating to your manager, understanding the organization, and the need for continuous learning.

Career Fitness and Coaching workshops are offered to managers to enable them to help employees with career issues. These workshops take managers through the entire Career Fitness program—so they learn how to manage their own careers, then an additional day is spent on coaching. Managers practice the skills of Listening, Leveling, Leveraging, Looking Ahead, and Linking, as described in the model earlier in the case.

Retire Fit is a program designed for employees who are over 35 years old. This program helps employees plan for their post-work future—spouses and life partners are invited to participate with the employee.

CareerPoint® Software is a self-paced network-based program that allows employees to go through the career development process. It was customized to include the Career Fitness Model and terminology.

Career Advising provides employees the opportunity to work one-on-one with an external career advisor in a totally confidential setting. The career advisor uses the Career Fitness model for career development and expands on the Person (Who am I?) segment through the use of style, interest, and values instruments. The advisor typically takes a more in-depth approach to helping the employee articulate skills, network, and interview internally.

Library Resources on career development are extensive and include books, videos, and audiotapes. They are accessible online and are available for checkout to all employees—globally.

Peripheral programs that facilitate open discussion between managers and individuals have been created to reinforce and enhance classroom learning. Two concepts have been implemented:

1. *Brown Bag Lunches*—Informal sessions led by a senior manager. The manager discusses the competencies needed to accomplish the goals of his or her organization, the behaviors that are expected of individuals in these positions, and his or her personal career path. The managers use the Dow Corning Competency Model (shown in Exhibits 2–6) to describe the skills they seek in employees. They emphasize the employee's responsibility for his or her own career development and continuous learning through stories of their own careers. These lunches are designed to give employees new insights

into organizations with which they may be unfamiliar—focusing on the internal World of Work.

2. *Hot Career Topics*—Panel discussions of topics suggested by employees. These discussions focus on the world of work in a broader context. Topics such as Novel Work Arrangements and International Assignments have been covered. The panelists are directly involved in the topic. For example, the panelists for International Assignments were the Manager of Relocation and 3 couples who had been or are currently on international assignments. Sharing candid real-life stories about the challenges and rewards of their assignments provided attendees with new perspectives.

The Learning and Career Center Newsletter provides employees with articles on the career development process and other learning information. Recently, this newsletter was introduced online to the full global audience.

Partnerships

Evidence of partnerships within and outside the organization has been seen in several ways.

The senior management support for this initiative has been unprecedented. In a time of unparalleled change and turbulence in the organization, significant resources were allocated to implement this practice. Throughout the imple mentation process, these managers demanded new levels of excellence from Learning and Development and from themselves. They have willingly partici- pated in programs and communications, continually emphasizing the need for ongoing development.

All members of the Operating Committee and many other senior managers (about 30 total) have participated in Brown Bag Lunches and Hot Career Top- ics. At first, participation was by invitation. Now managers volunteer and even insist on participating. Managers frequently ask to bring their entire staff to the Learning and Career Center (LCC) for a tour and discussion of the options avail- able to them. The outcome has always been that the manager encourages the use of the facility and the programs.

Managers frequently ask for a representative of the LCC to come to their site to give an overview of the process and options, or to bring a full program to a specific group of people.

The partnership with Japan has been one of the strongest. The approach was designed to enable Japanese managers to use the style of decision making most comfortable to them. The approach was top-down, phased in gradually to allow discussion and make appropriate cultural adaptations. It was clear that con- sensus decision making would be used to determine when and how to proceed from one step to another.

External partnerships include strong relationships with consultant partners. The process of developing new programs and options for employees is continuing with these partners. These include Creating Meaningful Development Assignments (Beverly Kaye and Associates) and annotations for all library resources (Career Development Services). Learning & Development personnel have been very active in the ASTD and IQPC, sharing information about Dow Corning's activities with other organizations. In conjunction with consulting partners, benchmarking opportunities for organizations are provided on a regular basis.

EVALUATION

The Global Career Development Process is evaluated in several ways:

- *Level 1 evaluations* (taken from Donald Kirkpatrick's model, outlined in his book *Evaluating Training Programs: The Four Levels* [Barrett-Koehler, 1998])—Each program is evaluated for general satisfaction. Results are tabulated and tracked to assure ongoing quality of delivery and tools. The level of satisfaction exceeds 80% on average. Exhibit 7 shows the format used for this evaluation.

- *Level 2–4 evaluations* were initiated in 1997. In conjunction with an outside firm, focus panels were held to determine the extent of application of learning and to develop anecdotal information about return on investment. The outcomes of these panels were very positive, indicating strong application of learning. There were several examples of return on investment. In one example, an employee decided, as a result of Career Fitness, that he could take on additional responsibilities from a vacant position. As a result of follow-up discussions with his manager, the old position was eliminated with cost savings of approximately $70,000 per year. See Exhibit 8 for a summary of results from this evaluation.

- A survey of all Career Fitness participants is planned for late 1999. This survey will focus on employee satisfaction and application of learning.

- Additional measures include:

    Demographic studies to determine the usage patterns of Center offerings
    Cost tracking—overall Center expenses are tracked, allocated to programs or services, and used to calculate charges for offerings
    Phone inquiry trends
    Library check-outs
    Career Advising issue trends (see Exhibit 9)
    Company-wide employee satisfaction surveys (planned for fourth quarter, 1999)

Results

Specific Behaviors Significant *voluntary usage* of the process has occurred. Since the emphasis is on employee ownership and responsibility for his or her career, all programs in the United States were voluntary. Approximately 35% of the Midland audience has participated in some form of career development activity during the past 3 years. This is higher than had been projected.

Career Fitness is the first learning solution to be *implemented globally*. This represents a major behavioral change for the organization. The acceptance of the program at all sites has been very high.

Business support of the Career Fitness process has been high. One commercial unit included a variable compensation goal to have 90% of their employees have an agreed-upon development plan by year-end. This not only encouraged participation, but linked compensation to career planning and ongoing development. Key managers reinforced the learning by participating in the full session with their employees. In addition, the entire management team participated in a Career Coaching session to prepare themselves for the newly educated workforce. Approximately 120 employees participated in Career Fitness Workshops for this Commercial Unit.

Managers participating in the Career Fitness and Coaching Workshops frequently recommended that all their employees use one or more of the Center's options for career development.

It is difficult to determine if these behaviors are long term in nature. It is evident, however, that the concept is being internalized on a broad scale in the short term. The ongoing demand for expanded services indicates a high level of interest in the process.

These behaviors contribute to the achievement of the original purpose and aims of the practice in the following ways:

- The behaviors exhibited by managers in supporting the process have encouraged individuals to participate and have emphasized the need for the individual to take the lead in their own development. The feedback discussions between managers who participate in the Career Fitness and Coaching program and individuals who participate in the Career Fitness Workshop are richer and more meaningful than previous career development discussions.

- Individuals are demonstrating a desire for continuous learning in their development planning.

- Development plans include action items based on the competencies that are derived from business strategies.

Success Stories A number of "success" stories were sent to the attention of the center staff indicating that learning was being applied. Many told of finding positions that were linked with short-term and long-term career goals. Others discussed improvements in interviewing and résumé writing skills.

Key Impacts Integration of the global competencies into all Human Resources practices is occurring. This is facilitated by the Global Leadership Team's efforts at defining competencies and learning solutions (see Exhibits 2–6). In addition, the implementation of the enterprise resource planning software requires reengineering of the work flow processes in the organization. Ultimately, this means each position must be redesigned to meet the needs of the new workflow. Employees need to understand the skill sets of future positions in order to begin to determine areas where development is needed. The human resources module of the enterprise resource planning software incorporates the global competencies into a database. This module will allow employees to "see" all positions in the company along with the skills that are required to do the work. Employees can then compare their qualifications with the requirements to determine skill gaps for development.

In addition, efforts regarding the center and the process have increased significantly. A newsletter featuring various career topics is published 5–6 times per year. In these days of information overload, it has been surprising to see a huge response to this publication. Calls increase by more than 20% the week following a newsletter release. Programs mentioned in the newsletter are filled rapidly. Individuals say they both use and save articles that were of particular interest to them. In July 1999, this newsletter was introduced to the total Dow Corning population via the intranet. Within 48 hours of publication, there were more than 2,000 hits to the Web site. The ongoing interest in this publication reemphasizes the need employees have for information and learning around career development and demonstrates a growing mindset for continuous learning (see Exhibit 10).

LESSONS LEARNED

Lesson #1—Get help early. There is a wealth of information and guidance in this field. The individuals who participate are very open and willing to help the novice. It is also very easy to get on the wrong track, so you can avoid mistakes by seeking help in the early phases of your project.

Lesson #2—Career planning should neither be linked to outplacement nor to correcting poor performance. Career planning must focus employees on development for the future. A number of people in the original research and benchmarking gave this advice. Interviewing people who had tried to combine career development and outplacement made it even clearer that a career development process commingled with outplacement was doomed to failure.

Lesson #3—Good facilitators are critical. Many programs appear deceptively simple, but require skilled facilitators to deliver. Having an external facilitator work with an internal facilitator was been very beneficial in the Career Fitness series.

Lesson #4—Competencies that support business strategies must *be the basis for development.* Programs without this underpinning have very limited success. This can make the implementation of the process more complicated, but the effort will pay dividends in the long run.

Lesson #5—Senior management must visibly support this effort. It is not enough to simply provide funding—employees want to see senior managers demonstrate their commitment to career planning. Dow Corning managers participating in the Brown Bag Lunch series told stories of their own career planning. This made them more "human" to employees and demonstrated the struggles that even top performers have with career issues.

Lesson #6—Communicate, Communicate, Communicate! One-time communications efforts simply will not work. An ongoing communication effort that reinforces the career development process is an absolute necessity. Keeping in mind that the intent of communication is for the receiver to understand the message will make the process much more successful.

SUMMARY

Dow Corning's Career Development process is a globally implemented intervention designed for and used by all levels of employees. It has been successful because:

- There was a clearly defined need.
- The business case was developed and articulated to show the link of career development to competitive advantage.
- A competency model was developed to give employees a sense of the skills required for the future.
- Senior management commitment and participation in the process were highly visible.
- There was global participation in the development of the tools and programs.
- There was extensive communication to all levels of the organizations, with messages developed to target specific needs.

- Multiple learning solutions allowed employees with different learning styles to find a way to use the process.

Evaluations have indicated a significant level of awareness for personal responsibility for career development and continuous learning among employees participating in the programs. Anecdotal evidence of success has come from success stories within the organization.

It is expected that the concepts of the process will remain intact over the short-term horizon, but the method of delivery is expected to evolve using more "virtual" delivery methods.

Exhibit 1. Qualitative Evaluation of Employees and Managers' Attitudes Toward the Concept
of a Career Management Center, Executive Summary

BACKGROUND AND OBJECTIVES

Dow Corning employees have indicated through employee expectation surveys
that they were not totally satisfied with career development issues within
the company. As a result, human resources explored a number of other major
companies in terms of how they managed the career development process.
The common element was the presence of a CAREER MANAGEMENT CENTER,
which was a separately managed facility. As a result, Dow Corning developed
plans for such a center to be potentially implemented in the Midland area. Prior
to this implementation, management was interested in testing the concept with
employees to determine the most appropriate implementation program. More
specifically, the objectives of this effort were to determine:

- The most critical issues and concerns in terms of career management issues
  at Dow Corning (with the goal to understand unaided issues)

- How well Dow Corning did in terms of meeting employee needs (using a
  TEN-POINT scale), including:

  Areas of improvement (unaided comments that could be related to the
  new Center concept)

  The role of supervision and management in the career development
  process

- An overall evaluation of the new CAREER MANAGEMENT CENTER concept, following a brief presentation of the concept:

  Using a rating on a TEN-POINT scale describing the pros and cons of the
  concept on an overall basis

  A rating of the "free-standing" (or separate facility) concept, with the
  goal to understand perceptions about having a separate physical center

  Perceptions of the potential "ambiance" of the facility (e.g., "feel,"
  "tone," "design," etc.)

  Reactions to specific elements of the center (e.g., library, counselors,
  etc.) Reactions to a combination training facility

  An evaluation of the preferred location, including several Midland
  options (both onsite and offsite)

  Preferred hours of operation

  Perceptions of family services through the center

  Communication issues, including ways to introduce the concept and
  potential messages that would get the attention of employees

Exhibit 1. Qualitative Evaluation of Employees and Managers' Attitudes Toward the Concept of a Career Management Center, Executive Summary (*Continued*)

METHODOLOGY

FIVE in-depth focus groups were conducted in Midland in late February and early March 1996 among a diverse group of Dow Corning employees and managers. A total of 46 employees and managers participated in the focus groups. The respondents were internally recruited on a random basis, with the goal to generate a broad mix of gender, functions, locations, and years with Dow Corning. The groups were conducted as follows:

		Number of Respondents		
Group	Date	Female	Male	Total
EXEMPT/NON-SUPV	February 28	3	3	6
	March 1	3	6	9
NON-EXEMPT	March 1	7	1	8
	March 6	8	1	9
MANAGERS	March 6	3	11	14
Total		24	22	46

The respondents averaged 16.5 years of experience, with the managers representing the most experience at 24.3 years. The years of Dow Corning experience were as follows:

	Year of Experience			
Group	1–10	11–20	21+	Average
EXEMPT/NON-SUPV	7	6	2	12.9
NON-EXEMPT	8	6	3	13.3
MANAGERS	1	4	9	24.3
Total	16	16	14	16.5

Based on an interpretive opinion (moderator's judgment), we suggest that the following breakdown will shed some light on the stage in life represented by the respondents:

- "Early career" respondents were primarily younger and on a strong promotional track.
- "Mid-career" employees were still upwardly mobile with 20 years or so of Dow Corning experience.
- The "late-career" employees were waiting to retire, or very satisfied with their role, with a lot of Dow Corning years behind them.

(Continued)

Exhibit 1. Qualitative Evaluation of Employees and Managers' Attitudes Toward the Concept of a Career Management Center, Executive Summary (*Continued*)

| Group | Number of Respondents | | | |
	Early Career	Mid-Career	Late-Career	Total
EXEMPT/NON-SUPV	6	7	2	15
NON-EXEMPT	6	8	3	17
MANAGERS	2	3	9	14
Total	14	18	14	46

It must be noted that qualitative focus group research cannot be statistically projected to the entire employee population.

- The results are directional in nature, and should be supplemented with management judgment and experience.

- Several TEN-POINT scale sequences were utilized during the discussions. The numerical values and mean ratings should not be viewed in a statistical sense. Rather, the analysis was designed to generate a basis for discussion.

IMPLICATIONS

The following discussion is based both on the results of this research and the knowledge and experience of the Mar-Quest Research professional staff. The implications should be viewed along with Dow Corning philosophies and internal requirements.

- Of critical importance was the fact that many of the INITIAL CONCERNS (prior to presenting the concept) of the employees in all groups, regardless of being exempt, non-exempt, or managerial, could potentially be solved with the Career Development Center concept. The result of these concerns showed some significant frustration among many of the employees (e.g., younger, fewer years at Dow Corning, nonexempt, etc.), which would impact the ratings in the Employee Expectations studies. We suggest that any process or program that will reduce the following concerns will be very well received, if managed properly.

  Many of the respondents mentioned "networking" within Dow Corning. This was especially true with new employees and the nonexempt employees. Many employees did not know where to go for help, both within their departments and functions, and within other functions. This created frustration, particularly among the nonexempt employees.

  Understanding their own "skill sets" and then "matching" those skills with potential job opportunities were important to them.

Exhibit 1. Qualitative Evaluation of Employees and Managers' Attitudes Toward the Concept of a Career Management Center, Executive Summary (*Continued*)

Although most employees realized that they were primarily responsible for managing and taking the initiative to develop their careers, many did not know how to do that.

"Time" was a concern in all of the groups, as most employees were so busy with their jobs, that they did not have time to think about or take any steps to further their career development.

One of the biggest concerns about career development was the role of supervisors and managers in the process. The concerns related to inconsistencies in the way managers handled career management between managers and between departments.

- Of concern was the "feeling" that some managers either did not want to spend the time on career management or that they were uncomfortable with it (e.g., did not know how to deal with it, etc.).

- Providing a manager "buy-in" will be critical in any new career management program, including sensitization, training, and managing the process.

Several employees were frustrated with the See Jobs network. Most liked the fact that the jobs were posted, but felt that the postings were in some cases only a formality (e.g., departments already had people in mind). They also did not get any feedback on why they were not selected if they had applied for a position.

On an overall basis, the CAREER MANAGEMENT CENTER concept was very well received, with a rating of 8.4 (on a TEN-POINT scale, where 1 = do not like at all to 10 = like very much). The ratings were very positive in all of the employee groups, with many of the initial concerns addressed by the new concept. Thus, we suggest that Dow Corning management should move ahead with the implementation of the Center, using both this research and other internal and external input as guidelines.

- The research suggested that positioning will be very important in generating employee comfort levels. That is, it should NOT (in any way) be associated with out-placement and/or downsizing. Otherwise, there will be a tremendous stigma and barrier to use. It should be positioned as being a positive, and forward-looking program that will assist the employees with their Dow Corning experience (and beyond).

- The "library" concept and "software" were liked by most of the respondents. Several even wondered of the software would be available for use in their offices (e.g., through the LAN). Human resources must deal with this issue in terms of communicating the need to have centralized control over the process, rather than having it be available at individual work stations.

(*Continued*)

Exhibit 1. Qualitative Evaluation of Employees and Managers' Attitudes Toward the Concept of a Career Management Center, Executive Summary (*Continued*)

- The idea of an "independent counselor" being available was very well-received, but the management of that process must be carefully done and communicated to all employees.

  The counselor must understand the structure and culture of Dow Corning, as well as know how the networking process takes place. Many of the panelists were not sure this would happen, which suggests a need to ensure that this does happen and then communicate to employees (otherwise the employees will not use the Center).

  The manager group was concerned that the counselors would give feedback to the employees that was inconsistent with what management wanted them to hear. This must be understood.

  Although there was some suggestion that Dow Corning middle managers and/or retirees should serve as counselors, we suggest that this might not generate the level of confidentiality that must exist.

- A major key to making the center a success will be in creating "buy in-on the parts of the middle managers and supervisors.

  The employees said that they did not want to feel as if they were "sneaking off" to go to the center.

  Having strong support from upper management will help in this process.

  Training supervisors and managers in managing career development using the center MUST happen in order to make the center an effective tool. The training should concentrate on consistency of response and support to those employees that want to use the center.

- In terms of their likelihood to use the center, nonexempt employees were the most likely to use it, while the managers were the least likely.

  This was a function of many nonexempt employees wanting to improve their status (e.g., move to exempt), but being early in their careers at Dow Corning. Most of the managers were in mid- to late-careers and did not personally feel a need to use it.

  Those who were satisfied in their current positions also were less likely to offer high ratings, but did say that if they were interested in a move, they would be very likely to use the center.

- We suggest that management should move ahead with the FREE-STANDING (or separate entity) concept for the center.

  The concept of having all of the resources housed in one "self-contained" place was well-received.

Exhibit 1. Qualitative Evaluation of Employees and Managers' Attitudes Toward the Concept of a Career Management Center, Executive Summary (*Continued*)

Of critical importance, however, was the need to have a "real person" (that was very knowledgeable) available for immediate assistance in finding what they wanted at the center.

- In terms of the "feel" or AMBIANCE of the center, the respondents offered thoughts that it should be very functional, yet not be ostentatious (expensive was the wrong impression in today's environment).

  The feel should be more like a library, with furnishings and colors being soft, comfortable, and "nonthreatening."

  We suggest that internal space design consultants review the results of this effort to understand the overall needs of the employees.

- We suggest that developing a "multipurpose" positioning for the center, with TRAINING also being a key element, will be a very effective drawing power for the concept.

- In terms of LOCATION, we suggest that an "off-site" option will be the most effective in generating use in a "nonthreatening" way.

  Most employees wanted the convenience of the center being located at their site. However, many also thought that a "neutral" site would be less threatening and more convenient for ALL Midland-based employees.

  They wanted to have a facility that was convenient to them (e.g., on the way home, close to expressway, easy to find, etc.). Thus, of the sites evaluated, the Waldo/U.S. 10 area was the most acceptable possibility. A site on Rodd Street by the Post Office was not desirable because of traffic congestion and a lack of perceived accessibility. Thus, we suggest that management move ahead with the Waldo/U.S. 10 options.

- The general tone of the groups indicated that the services of the center should not be initially offered to FAMILY members, at least until it was established and the "capacity" of the center was fully utilized by employees. Further, charging for services at "this time" would create some problems with those paying the charge.

- Providing retirement planning services should be considered as an additional benefit to that employee so inclined.

- Most employees wanted the option to access to the center during working hours AND after hours. We suggest that it be open a couple of days a week from 7:00 a.m. to 9:00 p.m. and on some Saturday mornings. These hours would give employees more options, as well as offer them a way to "escape" the scrutiny of their peers and supervisors (if deemed necessary).

(*Continued*)

Exhibit 1. Qualitative Evaluation of Employees and Managers' Attitudes Toward the Concept of a Career Management Center, Executive Summary (*Continued*)

- In terms of COMMUNICATIONS, the panelists indicated the following issues for consideration:

    They wanted to know about the specific services offered and feel comfortable that their discussions were kept confidential.

    In addition, the role of the counselors must be structured so that employees feel comfortable that the counselors understand the Dow Corning culture and structures.

    They also wanted to be sure that management was behind the effort, with supervisors and managers trained in administering the process to employees (e.g., supported employee use of the center).

    We further suggest that the benchmarking of the center concept against other major programs added considerable value the credibility of the idea. This should be communicated to employees.

- In terms of introducing the new Center concept, we suggest that the following be considered:

    A series of introductory announcements be made, using internal news sheets and bulletin boards to reach employees.

    Utilize management forums to further introduce the concept so that top management will show endorsement.

    PROFS did not appear to be a good vehicle since not all employees had access.

    The potentially most effective way to merchandise the concept will be to have open houses to "show off" the facility, along with some presentations and demonstrations.

Exhibit 2. Dow Corning's Competency Model

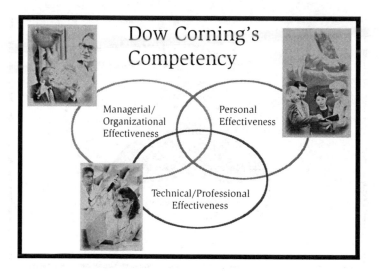

Three Circle Profile

Learning and Development uses a 3-Circle Profile (see Exhibit 3) to categorize the skills that are needed for Dow Corning to be successful. These skills were developed by a global Learning and Development team and senior management several years ago. The Managerial and Organizational Effectiveness circle houses dimensions and skills that are needed by leaders in Dow Corning. Note the use of the word LEADERS, not MANAGERS. The emphasis here is: "You can be a leader without having the title of manager." Dow Corning expects all of us to have some level of proficiency in these skills. The skills in this circle are considered transferable skills; that is, they are useful in many jobs and are strategic in nature. The Personnel Effectiveness circle houses dimensions and skills that are needed by everyone (i.e., communication and interacting with others). These skills are also considered transferable skills and are foundational in nature. The first 2 circles combined house fewer than 50 skills. The third circle houses more than 1,000 Technical and Professional Effectiveness skills—skills that are job or position-specific. It includes scientific skills and a wide range of skills that define specific needs both technical and professional.

Exhibit 3. 3-Circle Profile

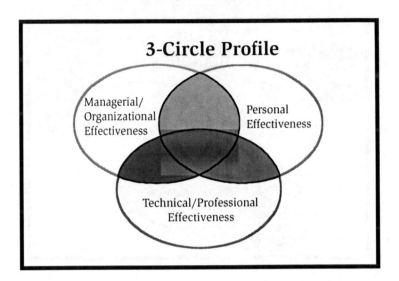

Description

Some skills seem to fall between 2 circles (for example, problem solving is considered a personal effectiveness skill and is used by everyone at a basic level). Yet, problem-solving skills may also be used at a highly technical level by engineering groups within the organization. Some skills may seem to fit into all circles. We consider project management a Managerial and Organizational Effectiveness skill. To a project leader, it is a tool for managing the process. To a facilities engineer, it is a tool for laying out specific tasks in his or her work and is viewed as technical effectiveness. To a communications person, it could be viewed as a tool for communicating activities—personal effectiveness. The circles overlap deliberately. Jobs, positions, and individuals must have skills from all 3 circles in order to be successful at Dow Corning.

Dimensions and Skills

Dimensions serve to group knowledge and skills into logical categories within the 3 circles. The word *dimension* is defined as an area of knowledge and/or skill that is causally related to performance outcomes.

Moving down a level, a skill is the ability to perform a certain physical or mental task, while knowledge refers to the information a person has in a specific content area. Skills and knowledge are further defined by sample behaviors. Sample behaviors are the observable actions that indicate whether a person possesses a particular skill or knowledge.

Exhibit 4. Managerial and Organizational Effectiveness Competencies

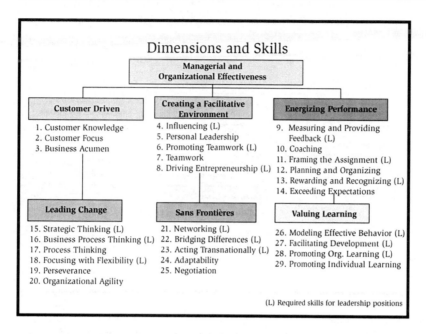

The 6 dimensions on this slide all fit within the Managerial and Organizational Effectiveness circle. You might think about them as strategic skill groupings representing our keys to competitive advantage in the future. They are defined as:

1. *Valuing Learning*—the creation of a culture that advocates continuous learning at all levels

2. *Creating a Facilitative Environment*—leadership that empowers employees through emphasis on collaboration, participation, and assurance of decision making at the lowest possible level

3. *Energizing Performance*—a focus on setting and achieving high performance goals with visible alignment to challenging business strategies

4. *Leading Change*—helping all employees adapt to the ever increasing speed of change

5. *Sans Frontières (Operating without Borders)*—embracing diversity, in all its forms, and using that diversity to meet the challenges of the future

6. *Customer Driven*—a focus on customer service that enables Dow Corning to attain levels of customer satisfaction that are higher than competition

Exhibit 5. Personal Effectiveness Skills

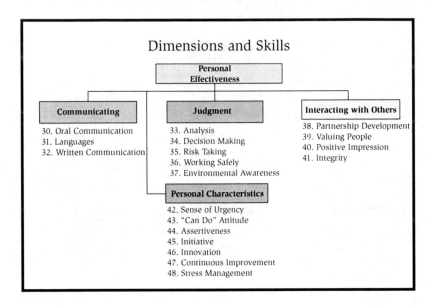

The 4 dimensions on this figure represent the Personal Effectiveness circle. Personal Effectiveness skills can be thought of as the basic building blocks for success in Dow Corning (or any other organization, for that matter). They are "transferable" to any position.

Definitions of the Dimensions in this circle are:

1. *Communication*—the ability to deliver a message orally or in writing in such a way that the receiver understands the message in the way intended

2. *Personal Characteristics*—attributes or attitudes that contribute to the way in which an individual accomplishes his or her work

3. *Judgment*—the ability to use rational processes to make timely, sound decisions

4. *Interacting with Others*—the ability to collaborate and work effectively with others within the organization or external to the organization

Exhibit 6. Technical and Professional Effectiveness Skills

Dimensions and Skills

> **Technical /Professional Effectiveness**

- Technical/Professional Effectiveness skills are job specific.
- Dow Corning has identified over 1000 skills in this grouping.

Technical Effectiveness skills are related to the core competencies of the organization and are proprietary in nature. These skills are position specific and often are not transferable to another position.

For example, writing a product market plan is a technical or professional skill for a marketer, and design of experiments is a technical skill for a research chemist or chemical engineer. If a marketing professional moved into a technical position, it is unlikely that he or she would be able to use the skill of writing a product market plan. By the same token, design of experiment skills would not be useful in a marketing position.

Exhibit 7. Career Fitness Evaluation Form, Level 1

DOW CORNING LEARNING AND DEVELOPMENT PROGRAM FEEDBACK FORM

Learning and Development is continually looking to improve the quality and relevance of the courses being offered to you, our clients. Please spend a few minutes evaluating the program you have just attended.

CAREER FITNESS WORKSHOP

Please circle the appropriate answer.

Q1. How relevant to your needs were the following topics in this training course?

Introducing ways to self-manage career	Not relevant	Fairly relevant	Relevant	Very relevant
Giving a clearer picture of self	Not relevant	Fairly relevant	Relevant	Very relevant
Compare your manager's assessment of your skills to your own assessment	Not relevant	Fairly relevant	Relevant	Very relevant
Giving a clearer picture of the factors that impact careers today	Not relevant	Fairly relevant	Relevant	Very relevant
Developing a personal action plan	Not relevant	Fairly relevant	Relevant	Very relevant

Q2. How did the following topics meet your expectations?

Introducing ways to self-manage career	Not at all	Fairly well	Well	Very well
Giving a clearer picture of self	Not at all	Fairly well	Well	Very well
Compare your manager's assessment of your skills to your own assessment	Not at all	Fairly well	Well	Very well
Giving a clearer picture of the factors that impact careers today	Not at all	Fairly well	Well	Very well
Developing a personal action plan	Not at all	Fairly well	Well	Very well

Exhibit 7. Career Fitness Evaluation Form, Level 1 (*Continued*)

Q3. What do you think about the time allocated to the following topics?

Introducing ways to self-manage career	Too little	Just right	A little too long	Far too long
Giving a clearer picture of self	Too little	Just right	A little too long	Far too long
Compare your manager's assessment of your skills to your own assessment	Too little	Just right	A little too long	Far too long
Giving a clearer picture of the factors that impact careers today	Too little	Just right	A little too long	Far too long
Developing a personal action plan	Too little	Just right	A little too long	Far too long

Q4. The balance of lectures, discussions, and activities held my interest.

   Not at all   Fairly well   Well   Very well

Q5. How was the trainer's overall knowledge of the subject?

   Bad   Satisfactory   Good   Excellent

Q6. How were the ideas and concepts communicated clearly?

   Not clearly   Fairly clearly   Clearly   Very clearly

Q7. How did the trainer(s) interact with the participants? (i.e. answer questions, encourage participation, etc.)

   Badly   Fairly well   Well   Very well

Q8. How well did this training meet your expectations regarding each of the following?

* **Quality of the material** (workbook, overhead, etc.)	Not Met	Met	Exceeded
* **Facilities** (training room, overhead projector, etc.)	Not Met	Met	Exceeded
* **Location**	Not Met	Met	Exceeded
* **Pre-course arrangements, info & agenda**	Not Met	Met	Exceeded
* **Pre-course lecture and/or work (if applicable)**	Not Met	Met	Exceeded

(*Continued*)

Exhibit 7. Career Fitness Evaluation Form, Level 1 (*Continued*)

Q9. For any areas where expectations were not met, please briefly explain reasons.

....

....

....

Q10. Would you recommend this course to others?

No   Yes

Q11. If yes, to whom?

....

Q12. Did you have a pre-course discussion with your manager?

No   Yes

Q13. What improvements, if any, would you suggest?

....

....

....

Q14. Please rate how valuable you felt these tools were:

	Not at All Valuable			Very Valuable	
a. Career Action Inventory	1	2	3	4	5
b. Invest in Your Values	1	2	3	4	5
c. Interest Cards	1	2	3	4	5
d. WorkStyle Patterns™	1	2	3	4	5
e. Myers-Briggs Type Inventory	1	2	3	4	5
f. Learning Zones	1	2	3	4	5
g. Career Leverage Inventory	1	2	3	4	5
h. Connections: A Networking Map	1	2	3	4	5

Exhibit 8. Career Fitness Evaluations, Level 2–4

Purpose of Analysis

Management has perceived training's effect on productivity and profits to be mainly a question of faith rather than a question of evidence. In fact, training is often seen as having no effect at all, and is only tolerated as part of the "cost of doing business." To change this perception and quantify training's effect, the training department at Dow Corning initiated the analysis of frequently offered training program. The program analysis followed one predetermined objective: Quantify the impact of Dow Corning Career Fitness Training.

To determine this impact, the investigation analyzed the relationship between company goals, management goals, training department goals, trainers, participants, and job performance. In short, the analysis determined what employees learned, how this learning changed job performance, and the added value of those changes. In addition, the analysis established the evaluation process as an ongoing alignment of training to changing Dow Corning needs, strategies, and initiatives.

The analysis unfolded during 3 distinct stages:

- The evaluation of training program modules.
- The determination of training's effect on the job.
- The assessment of value added changes due to the training.

Evaluation of Training Program Modules

Pre- and post-training work sessions, with training managers and training instructors, coupled with workshop observation determined the following:

- Identified specific Competency Goals for the Career Fitness class
- Recommended testing procedures to assess the degree of competency for each goal
- Determined the participants' degree of success in achieving classroom goals

Determining Effects of Training on the Job

This part of the evaluation occurred approximately 8 weeks after the completion of the Dow Corning training program. At 8 weeks, changes had the opportunity to develop, but were still new enough to observe. Of course, the goal was to discover the effects of the training program back on the job.

What changes in thinking and in behavior did we see after the training? What areas of productivity improvement were identified and measured? To identify these changes, the analysts:

- Interviewed participants
- Collected and analyzed impact data such as career goal creation, action plan creation, technical skill improvement, managerial skill improvement, mentoring incidence rates, and process improvements

(Continued)

Exhibit 8. Career Fitness Evaluations, Level 2-4 (*Continued*)

Assessing the Value-Added of Dow Corning Career Fitness Training

What was the value-added of the changes caused by the Dow Corning Career Fitness Training. When possible, the changes were estimated in terms of dollars. When not possible, the description was concrete, specific, and detailed so that it could be evaluated against the stated goals of training. In addition, the analysis:

- Identified the Dow Corning Career Fitness Training costs
- Identified the participants to assign value to any changes
- Assigned value to the training benefits
- Compiled a cost-benefit analysis of the results

Results and/or Objective of the Analysis

Ultimately, this analysis determined whether the established training curriculum aligned employee learning and development with the main business goal of driving market leadership. Furthermore, this template established the evaluation process as an ongoing alignment of training to changing business needs, strategies, and initiatives.

Establishing Training's Impact on the Job

To determine training's impact back on the job, we generally conduct follow-up interviews 8 weeks after the completion of the training. At 8 weeks, changes have had the opportunity to develop but are still new enough to observe. (Analyst's note: Due to scheduling concerns and the lack of an available target audience, the Career Fitness participants were interviewed 3 to 6 months after the program. We believe this lag did not influence our ability to determine impact.)

What changes in thinking and in behavior did we see after the training? What areas of productivity improvement were identified and measured? To identify these changes, we analyzed each Career Fitness module separately through interviews with participants.

Questions and Answers

- *During the Career Fitness workshop, you identified your personal values with a yellow, red, or green sticker. Identify 1 value change from a red or yellow sticker to green.*

  Percentage of participants who improved the rating of a personal value: 60% (9/15)

  Mentioned Responses—Actions Taken

- Transferred
- Assumed new work responsibilities
- Created résumé
- Networked

Exhibit 8. Career Fitness Evaluations, Level 2–4 (*Continued*)

- Became a mentor
- Participated in additional training

During the career fitness workshop, each participant identified a personal value he or she thought was lacking. During the several months after the training, a significant percentage took an action step to realize this value more in their lives. This question identified those individuals who had changed or began to change one of their identified personal values. Briefly, this question answers which individuals acted.

While many individuals mentioned improving their relationship with family or friends, 4 individuals dramatically changed their work behavior. One person, concerned with career advancement, transferred from her current position to a new position. This move aligned more closely with her goal to "advance career issues." Another Dow Corning employee, who was near retirement-age, initiated a mentoring relationship with a younger colleague. This new relationship coincided with the participant's need to "influence others." The third Career Fitness participant assumed more work-related responsibilities to better align his position to his personal work style. Finally, the last individual, who made a significant work-related change, networked more aggressively with colleagues. His ability to "influence others" has improved.

To recap, a significant majority acted on their personal values. Each found that their behavioral change helped them more fully realize their personal values. Surprisingly, a significant percentage of these changes helped Dow Corning. Enhanced networking or mentoring either improve communication among colleagues or transfer skills from one work generation to the next. Career transfers and assuming new responsibilities strengthen the link between work and personal satisfaction.

- *Previously, you identified an area in which you had a high interest but low ability. What steps did you take to improve your ability in this area?*

  Percentage of participants who raised their skill levels in an interest area: 67% (10/15)

Many participants acted to improve one or more of their skill areas or performance gaps after the Career Fitness workshop. We consider this an indication of real change. Not only did these individuals identify their personal performance gaps, many closed their gaps and skill deficiencies.

Most notably, one participant's improved business awareness skills resulted in substantial savings for Dow Corning. Wishing to understand business concepts better, this individual began a mentoring relationship with a more experienced colleague. During the countless hours together and, specifically, a long car trip to a client location, the participant attained substantial benefit from the relationship.

(Continued)

Exhibit 8. Career Fitness Evaluations, Level 2–4 (*Continued*)

According to the participant, Dow Corning considered developing a new product. After proceeding with the development of this new product, the individual discussed the merits of the product with his mentor. The mentor relayed several personal experiences and suggestions for effective product development. Following his mentor's suggestion, the individual realized that the product would most likely not succeed in the market place. The new product would not capture significant market share or provide any new manufacturing insight for Dow Corning. Subsequently, the Career Fitness participant scrapped the project and dismantled the development team, saving substantial costs in the process.

In another instance, an individual realized significant productivity improvements and cost-savings after acting on his skill deficit. For example, after focusing on his questioning techniques, this participant eliminated several unnecessary procedures and documents in his department. Because of his improved questioning techniques, he identified new methods and procedures to document injury reports at the Midland manufacturing facility. As a result, he saved time and his department went injury-free last year.

Obviously, the benefits to Dow Corning are substantial when employees take an active interest in improving their skill levels. Generally, employees that make concerted personal efforts to improve skills result in significant benefits to both the individual and the company. Even though the percentage of participants who realized a personal improvement that directly benefited Dow Corning's improvement was small, those who did substantially impacted Dow Corning's bottom-line.

- *Did you have a conversation with anyone about your reputation and/or skills?*

  Percentage of participants who had a conversation about their reputation and/or skills: 86% (13/15)

A near-perfect percentage of focus panel participants held a skill and reputation conversation with either a colleague or manager. Sixty percent spoke with their manager while the remainder discussed their reputation with colleagues and/or their network.

Once again, several of these conversations positively impacted Dow Corning. One individual attended a training program on the use of a new electron microscope. Another began to shadow her manager so that she could improve her negotiating skills. Others realized their influence and place within Dow Corning.

Most significantly, one participant recognized that he did not have enough work to do in his current position. After outlining his capabilities and skills, he and his manager both agreed that the participant had the time and skills to

Exhibit 8. Career Fitness Evaluations, Level 2–4 *(Continued)*

assume a second position. Consequently, this conversation eliminated the need for a second employee in their department. When the Career Fitness participant assumed the new responsibilities, the department saved substantial dollars in salaries and benefits that would have been paid to a second employee.

- *Did you have a discussion with your manager about your development goals and/or actions?*

  Percentage of participants who discussed with their managers their development goals and/or actions: 60% (9/15)

Immediately following the Career Fitness workshop, many participants discussed their development goals with their managers. Although several mentioned that they held this conversation during their annual or PIP review, we do not consider that an acceptable answer. Why? According to the stated Career Fitness workshop goals, the participants were to discuss their goals and create action plans immediately after the awareness-building exercises. Otherwise, the workshop information would not be of benefit. Because they lack both immediacy and alignment to the Career Fitness workshop, annual reviews do not fulfill the above requirements.

Nonetheless, most participants outlined their career interests and goals with their managers. On one occasion, an individual discussed the difference between his current position and his work style patterns, improving the balance between his job and personality preferences.

- *Did your manager assist you with your development goal(s) or career action plan(s)?*

  Percentage of managers who assisted the participants with their development goals and/or career action goals: 33% (5/15)

As mentioned earlier, detailed development plans allow the participant to have a meaningful career discussion with their manager. Without a meaningful development plan in place, any conversations will be broad and generally vague. If you remember, the Career Fitness participants were to complete their development plans after the workshop. Only one-third of the Career Fitness participants held substantial discussions with their manager. Subsequently, they were the only participants to receive career development direction and guidance from their managers.

Nonetheless, those participants who did have a substantial conversation with their manager made significant progress. To achieve their career goals and objectives, several added or deleted unsatisfactory job responsibilities while others received helpful advice and/or recommendations from their managers.

As examples, one manager modified a participant's schedule so that she could attend graduate school and proceed toward her career goal. Another manager helped draft the participant's detailed career plan with many different options and

(Continued)

Exhibit 8. Career Fitness Evaluations, Level 2–4 (*Continued*)

development possibilities. Additionally, this same manager and the participant created a skill improvement plan to close the individual's skill performance gaps. As a result, the participant rejected, on 2 different occasions, job offers that failed to fit into his career action plan.

- *Has your overall Career Fitness improved since the workshop?*

  Percentage who believe that their career fitness has improved since the workshop: 67% (12/15)

A slightly higher percentage considered their career development improved, yet they had not taken the necessary steps to warrant that satisfaction. Like some typical Level 1 response sheets, we expect they were only providing us the anticipated answer.

However, many individuals did experience significant career development improvement. Two-thirds of the interviewed participants took an active role in their career development. Some of the more significant actions or insights were:

- Leadership development
- Performance gap analysis
- Career plan development
- Job transfers
- Work style acceptance
- Reestablished personal/professional relationships
- Improved networking
- Mentoring

In 2 cases, the Career Fitness program provided substantial benefit either to the participant or to Dow Corning. In the first instance, one individual found less confusion in his department about individual responsibilities. The department coordinated their job responsibilities around those individual capabilities. As a result, the department eliminated an unnecessary position. This move saved a considerable sum in salary and benefits.

Another participant considerably improved her motivational and leadership effectiveness. With her enhanced effectiveness, she improved her working relationship with a particular building. To recognize this improvement, Dow Corning gave her a cash award.

Although we can question the degree to which all participants improved their Career Fitness, career development provided substantial benefits to both the individual and Dow-Corning. To Dow Corning's benefit, improved efficiencies eliminated 2 unnecessary positions; a mentoring relationship provided a scrapped project; and improved career development saved time. For the participants, one rejected poorly aligned job offers, others established mentoring and networking relationships, and many showed technical and interpersonal skill improvement.

Exhibit 9. Career Advising Demographics and Issues

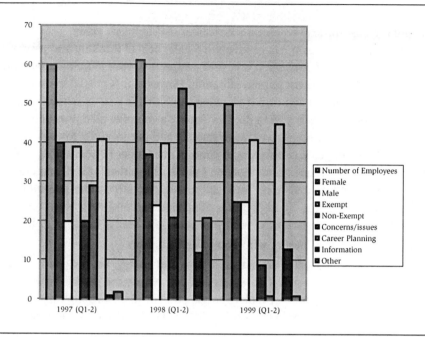

Career Advising Demographics and Issues

Exhibit 10. An Excerpt From the December 1998 Learning and Career Center Newsletter

Plan . . .

Charting the best route to reaching your career development goals

Successfully managing your career involves a great deal of thinking and assessment about the kind of *person* you are, your *perspective*, your *place* of employment and the *possibilities* inherent in your situation. However, it is crucial to quickly put all this thinking together and turn it to action—and that is exactly what a career development plan can help you to do. Developing a cohesive plan puts you "in the driver's seat" and helps you to move steadily and purposefully toward your career development goals. In this final section of our Career Fitness series, we'll help you to answer the question, "How do I put it all together?" We'll acquaint you with the Force Field Analysis tool, walk you through a 6-step career development planning process, explain the importance of networking, and even help you prepare for a development discussion with your manager. Ready? Let's get rolling . . .

Spotting shortcuts and detours with Force Field Analysis

Achieving a career goal takes considerable time and energy. So, it's good to know what you are up against—what shortcuts and detours are out there—before you start. Force Field Analysis is a problem-solving tool available through the Learning and Career Center that may help. Force Field Analysis worksheets are used to identify "forces for" and "forces against" achieving each of your goals. A "force for" is something that can contribute to your success, while a "force against" may hinder your progress. These forces may be related to:

- **Skills,** both those you possess and those you need to develop.
- **The environment,** including organizational needs, budget, and time.
- **Relationships,** existing connections with contacts and those that need to be nurtured.
- **Internal forces,** including courage, drive, persistence, and interest, as well as fear, low self-confidence, and lack of motivation.

It is helpful to do 3 Force Field Analyses, 1 for each of your three primary career goals, with a friend or colleague. Your Career Fitness Development Plan will be based on those forces that are in your power to control and are related to at least two of your goals.

Your development plan: 6 simple steps to getting there

It's time to create your plan! There are 6 basic steps to a Career Fitness Development Plan:

1. **Designate development areas.** Development areas capture the key skills and strategies you need to develop to move toward your goals, as indicated by your Force Field Analyses. If a "force for" or "force against" appears with 2 or more of your goals and is within your power to control (not an environmental factor) then you should consider it a vital development area. Skill development in vital areas can translate to progress toward more than 1 goal and prepare you for several possibilities simultaneously.

Exhibit 10. An Excerpt From the December 1998 Learning and Career Center Newsletter (*Continued*)

2. **Establish success indicators.** For each development area, establish your vision of success. Define deliverables, expected outcomes, and measures that will help you complete this sentence: "I'll know I've succeeded when . . ." And remember, the clearer you can make your success vision, the more energy and commitment you'll have to make it a reality.

3. **Assign learning activities.** This is perhaps the most critical and thought-provoking stage of the planning process . . . the point at which you identify assignments, projects, courses, and tasks you can take on to address each development area. When generating potential learning activities, gather ideas and input from others, and try to be as specific as possible. "Build in" opportunities to practice new skills, so that you can learn by doing.

4. **Investigate resources.** Discover the books, courses, online information, associations, or people that can help you develop your skills and achieve your goals.

5. **Identify feedback providers.** Name the people who can provide feedback on your performance as you learn and develop. Those who are already experts at what you are trying to learn can accelerate your learning process.

6. **Set deadlines.** Give yourself concrete timing milestones. Include a "first step" that can be taken in the next 24 or 48 hours, such as buying a book, watching a training video, scheduling a meeting, or asking a friend to review your development plan. Also, be sure to set a completion date by which you want to achieve each development assignment and related activities.

Making connections for your journey

When you are establishing a career path, the art of networking is an important development skill. People connections can be wonderful resources (step 4 above) and feedback providers (step 5). It is important to consider what you want, who can help you, how they can help, the odds of getting what you want from them, and what you can offer in exchange for their assistance. The primary responsibility for your career development rests with you. *You* must initiate the career development process and work to ensure its success. Your manager can be a key connection along the way. Begin sharing your ideas about direction, goals and development strategies with your manager; maintain open and honest communication. Then work together to build and revise your development plan. Your manager should be able to help you further your career development by: arranging useful contacts, communicating your plan to those who could provide you with future opportunities, and connecting you with learning re-sources for implementing your plans.

This article is adapted from Career Fitness, *produced by Beverly Kaye Associates and Career Systems International for Dow Corning. Copyrights apply.*

Bibliography

Brinkergoff, Robert and Stephan Gill, *The Learning Alliance*, San Francisco: Jossey-Bass, 1994.

Filipczak, Bob, "The Training Manager in the 90's," *Training*, June 1994, p. 31.

Ford, Don, "Benchmarking HRD," *Training and Development*, June 1993, p. 36.

Geber, Beverly, "Re-Engineering the Training Department," *Training*, May 1994, p. 27.

Gutteridge, Thomas, et al, *Organizational Career Development*, San Francisco: Jossey-Bass, 1993.

Heskett, James, et al, "Putting the Service-Profit Chain to Work," *Harvard Business Review*, March/April 1994, pp. 164–174.

Kaye, Beverly, *Up Is Not the Only Way*, Washington, D.C.: Career Systems, Inc., 1993.

Kimmerling, George, "Gathering Best Practices," *Training and Development*, Sept. 1993, p. 28.

Mirlaglia, Joseph, "An Evolutionary Approach to Revolutionary Change and the Implications For Human Resources Practice," unpublished, 1994.

O'Reilly, Brian, "The New Deal—What Companies and Employees Owe One Another," *Fortune*, June 13, 1994, p. 44.

Redding, John and Ralph Catellanello, *Strategic Readiness: The Making of the Learning Organization*, San Francisco: Jossey-Bass, 1994.

Rucci, Anthony, et al, "The Employee Customer-Profit Chain at Sears," *Harvard Business Review*, January/February 1998, pp. 82–97.

Richman, Louis, "The New Worker Elite," *Fortune*, Aug. 22, 1994, p. 56.

Robinson, Dana and James Robinson, *Training For Impact*, San Francisco: Jossey-Bass, 1989.

Senge, Peter, *The Fifth Discipline Fieldbook*, New York: Currency Doubleday, 1994.

Ulrich, Dave, *Learning Organization, Culture Change and Competitiveness: How Managers Can Build Learning Capability*, Lexington, MA: ICEDR, 1993.

Ulrich Dave, et al, "Employee and Customer Attachment: Synergies for Competitive Advantage," *Human Resource Planning*, vol. 14, no. 2, pp. 89–102.

Wick, Calhoun and Lu Leon, *The Learning Edge*, New York: McGraw-Hill, 1993.

ABOUT THE CONTRIBUTOR

Judy Milam Mason (judy.mason@dowcorning.com) joined Dow Corning in 1989 and is currently the global manager of Career Development for Dow Corning. Prior to joining Dow Corning, Mason was employed by Baxter Healthcare and held positions in product development, manufacturing, marketing, and sales. She was also employed by Parke, Davis Company and held positions in quality assurance, manufacturing, and research and development. She has presented at training and OD conferences on career development for the past 2 years. In May 1999, she was recognized by the American Society of Training and Development with an Excellence in Practice Award for Dow Corning's Career Development Process. She received a bachelor of arts degree in biology from Shorter College in Rome, Georgia.

CHAPTER SEVENTEEN

MediaOne Group (AT&T)

A coaching and mentoring program leveraging 360-degree assessment, individual coaching, follow-up surveys, and customized coaching workshops that is designed for the follow-on support and development stages of the leadership development system at MediaOne

BACKGROUND

MediaOne Group is an international broadband technology company offering cable television, high-speed Internet access, telephone, and interactive digital TV options via its broadband network, as well as international wireless services. MediaOne Group serves over 13 million customers in 16 countries, with its 16,000 employees generating $7.4 billion in revenues in 1998. A spin-off of US West in 1997, MediaOne Group is now undergoing a merger with AT&T, expected to close in the first quarter of 2000.

Leadership and employee development have always been critical business priorities at MediaOne Group (M1G) for several reasons. The first and most important is that M1G is paving the way for a new industry—the broadband industry. This calls for a whole new skill set for all levels of employees. Related to this is the need for first-rate customer service—thousands of M1G employees interact with customers everyday, and each of those interactions calls for exceptional customer service skills and business knowledge. Finally, the intense competition for talent in the industry requires that M1G invest heavily in skills development, not only to increase competency levels but as an employee satisfaction lever to promote retention.

BUSINESS DIAGNOSIS

The M1G Executive Team identified leadership development as one of their top 5 business priorities in early 1996, shortly after they were identified as a separate business within US West and received a targeted stock on the NYSE. The business drivers were quite clear to them:

- They were forging a new industry—the broadband industry—requiring a whole new skill set.
- Through the succession planning process, they identified that there was a shortage of "ready now" candidates for future leadership positions.
- Succession planning data also identified a shortage of high-quality general management, marketing, and technical leadership talent for domestic and international positions.
- There was a shortage of diversity candidates.
- The external environment was very competitive regarding talent, raising retention risks.
- Recruiting statistics indicated that there were fewer internal and external recruiting sources with expected shortages through 2002.

Based on the above business drivers, the CEO and his team decided to invest in the creation of a leadership development system that would accomplish 3 major objectives:

1. Develop the needed skill sets to compete in the newly formed broadband industry.
2. Develop leadership talent for the future, ensuring that shortage areas and diversity issues were considered.
3. Implement a system that would increase employee satisfaction levels through leadership development in order to positively impact retention.

With this preliminary business diagnosis, a more in-depth assessment was conducted. To begin, a team of learning and development experts was formed to oversee the system implementation. To complete the business diagnosis phase, the following steps were implemented: 1) *Focus groups* were conducted with employees throughout the company to identify needed competencies; 2) *Interviews* were conducted with the top 40 executives to analyze gaps and identify preferred development options; 3) *Best practice research* was conducted utilizing a literature review and visits to best practice companies. From these steps, the final business diagnosis was completed and competency assessments were developed. The primary development methodology selected was coaching and mentoring. The following paragraphs describe these three steps in more detail.

Focus Groups for Competency Model Development

In order to identify needed leadership competencies, M1G hired Keilty, Goldsmith & Company to run focus groups with leaders and conduct interviews. Beginning with the CEO and his team, the executives sketched out the competency profile of the ideal MediaOne Group leader of the future. After a series of revision sessions, the draft competency model was then tested with focus groups of leaders throughout the company. At the end of the 3-month process, the model was validated, but it was determined that there were some differences between *senior* leadership competencies (directors, VPs, and officers) and leadership competencies (managers and supervisors). Because of this, 2 similar but aligned competency models were created (see Table 1).

Both leadership competency models were organized into the 4 clusters of Business Knowledge, Strategic, People/Relationships, and Personal, but there are some minor variations. The Senior Leadership Competency Model has 17 competencies, whereas the Leadership Competency Model has 19. The major difference is illustrated in the Strategic cluster, wherein the Senior Leadership model focuses on *visionary thinking, shaping strategy,* and *global perspective,* and the Leadership model focuses more on strategic alignment with the 4 competencies of *acquiring strategic knowledge, influencing strategy, enterprise perspective,* and *leading change.* In the Senior Leadership Model the *leading change* competency falls under Industry/Business Knowledge. Another minor change is with the People/Relationships dimension, the Senior Leadership Model calls for *developing and motivating others,* whereas the Leadership Model uses the competency of *managing performance,* which is more the daily domain of frontline supervisors and managers.

Though MediaOne Group's original intent was to have only 1 leadership competency model, the focus groups composed of supervisors and managers clearly pointed out the need for 2, stating that the competencies required for frontline managers and supervisors were different than those required of senior management. Therefore, the 2 leadership competencies models were created, but they still illustrate the alignment of competencies between both groups.

Top 40 Interviews

In addition to the development of the competency models, 1-hour interviews were conducted with the top 40 executives in the company, including the CEO. The purpose of these interviews was to verify common understanding of vision, values, and strategy; to recognize current and future threats and opportunities to the business; to identify the company's current strengths and skill gaps; and to discuss preferred leadership development methodologies.

An interviewing template was developed and approved, and 1 person was selected to conduct all the interviews over a period of 1.5 months. The majority

Table 1. M1G Leadership Competency Models

SENIOR LEADERSHIP MODEL (Directors, VPs and Officers)	LEADERSHIP MODEL (Managers and Supervisors)
STRATEGIC DIMENSIONS • *Visionary Thinking* • *Shaping Strategy* • *Global Perspective*	STRATEGIC ALIGNMENT • *Acquiring Strategic Knowledge* • *Influencing Strategy* • *Enterprise Perspective* • *Leading Change*
BUSINESS DIMENSIONS • Functional Depth & Breadth • Operational Excellence • Customer Driven • Decision Making • *Leading Change*	BUSINESS MANAGER • Functional Depth & Breadth • Operational Excellence • Customer Driven • Decision Making
PEOPLE/RELATIONSHIP DIMENSIONS • Communication & Interpersonal Effectiveness • Teamwork • *Develops and Motivates Others* • Creates and Maintains People Networks	PEOPLE/RELATIONSHIP DIMENSIONS • Communication & Interpersonal Effectiveness • Teamwork • *Managing Performance* • Creates and Maintains People Networks
PERSONAL DIMENSIONS • Integrity • Self Esteem and Confidence • Self Discipline and Motivation • Adaptability • Passion and Optimism	PERSONAL DIMENSIONS • Integrity • Self Esteem and Confidence • Self Discipline and Motivation • Adaptability • Passion and Optimism

Italics font designates differences in competency models.

of the interviews were face-to-face, with the exception of interviews with international executives, which were conducted via telephone. A qualitative research methodology was employed to analyze the interview results. Paraphrased comments and quotes were coded by theme, then sorted by code, and a frequency count was used to determine strength of the theme (thematic analysis).

Skill Gaps The results of the assessment validated the competency model further, and also highlighted preliminary skill gaps which required more immediate focus. These were the need to enhance *operational skills* to succeed in this new industry of broadband, as well as *general leadership development,* with an emphasis on *developing and motivating employees.*

Development Methodology—Preference for Coaching The needs assessment also clearly described the preferred leadership development methodology which was a desire for *individual coaching* (see Exhibit 1). When probed on the rationale for selecting this method, executives responded that since the company was in a start-up mode and less than 2 years old, that it did not make sense to implement a more traditional classroom method. Since most senior managers were on the move with very busy schedules, the most effective development would be one that could come to them in a variety of locations, and be focused on their specific development needs. Executive coaching seemed ideal for this because it offered offer flexible on-the-job development activities.

Best Practice Research

The last piece of the business diagnosis was to conduct a literature review on best practices in leadership development and visit some of the identified best practice companies. Several firms were identified to conduct the literature review on best practices in leadership development. All of the articles were sorted by program type and analyzed to see which options might fit within the M1G culture and assist in our specific competency development. Companies utilizing coaching and action learning were specifically targeted for analysis.

Then visits were arranged to GE, Motorola, and American Express to learn more about their best practice leadership development systems. In addition, interviews were arranged with experts who had established leadership development systems at Amoco, AlliedSignal, Sun Microsystems, PepsiCo, Texas Instruments, and Weyerhauser. Assistance in completing the best practice research was provided by Executive Development Associates and Global Consulting Alliance.

Final Analysis

At the conclusion of the business analysis phase, a synthesis of all the business drivers, leadership competencies, gaps, preferred learning formats, and best practice research was conducted. This resulted in the development of a Leadership Development Strategy (see Exhibit 2) and Process Model (see Exhibit 3) with a 360-degree assessment and coaching at the heart of the system.

The Process Model provides an overview of the leadership development process, but the specifics are outlined in the next sections of the case which describe the 360 assessment, the design and development of the 3 types of coaching utilized, as well as the supporting curriculum and on-the-job activities. In general, the model illustrates that each individual leader must complete a 360 assessment based on their specific leadership competency model. Next, they attend a 1-day workshop where they meet their private coach—an external coach for senior leaders and an internal coach (certified HR or Learning and Development representative) for leaders. A second option for participants who cannot attend the workshop is to meet in a private one-on-one "tutorial" with their coach where they review what is covered in the workshop and then move into the analysis of the 360 results.

The third phase is to create a Development Plan, which is limited to 3 development items and is endorsed by the participant's manager. The coach assists in the creation of the plan and recommendation of development activities. Depending on their situation, participants can select options from the Executive Development Portfolio or the Management and Supervisory Training curriculum offered through the corporate university, Broadband U. The coach also continues to meet with the participant 3 more times over a period of 6 months to provide additional development tips. At 5 months, a 1-page follow-up survey with the 3 development items is distributed to original 360 raters. The coach and leader then meet to discuss results. The Development Plan is integrated into the succession planning process and the performance appraisal system as a public document—however the 360-feedback report is confidential to the leader and coach and is used only for developmental purposes.

ASSESSMENT

Since one of MediaOne Group's key values is "Data Driven Decisions," use of assessments to gather leadership competency data was readily accepted and endorsed by the top executive team. Several different assessment processes are used.

360 Assessment

The two leadership competency models were translated into two 360 assessment instruments. They were entitled the Senior Leadership Effectiveness Inventory (SLEI), which is composed of 76 items, and the Leadership Effectiveness Inventory (LEI), composed of 79 items. Both are designed around satisfaction scales. Focus groups and interviews were conducted to validate the assessment items. In addition, 3 pilot workshops using the 360 assessment were held. After several months and some revisions, the 360 instruments were validated. Examples of the items under the Customer Driven competency are listed in Exhibit 4.

Assessment Plus, an external assessment center located in Atlanta, was identified to process the results and maintain a confidential database. The company can request group reports on top 10 strengths and bottom 10 development areas, but individual data is confidential. The bottom 10 development area data and critical business issues were used to identify top priority training modules and Executive Development Portfolio options.

Coaching Debrief

It is M1G's policy never to give a participant his or her 360-degree feedback report without a coach present to debrief the results. If the participant attends the workshop, they receive their report there, learn how to interpret it, and then meet privately with their coach for one hour to analyze the results. If they do not attend the workshop, they receive their report when they meet one-on-one with their coach in a 4- to 6-hour private tutorial.

The 360 assessment includes 4 major sections:

1. Overall competency rating bar chart
2. Top 10/Bottom 10
3. Rater Comments on what participant does well/areas for improvement
4. Detailed item analysis for all 76 items

The 360 report also shows the average composite of direct report, peers/others, and customer ratings, with a minimum of 3 responses required to maintain rater confidentiality. The ratings of the participant's manager are not confidential and are illustrated separately.

After helping the participant interpret the report, the coach assists him or her in identifying major themes and messages, and then identifying 1 strength and 2 to 3 development areas to document on the Development Plan (see Exhibit 5). Participants are encouraged to select 1 strength to share with others in some way, as well as areas for improvement. Participants are limited to 3 improvement areas, because with the hectic schedules of a start-up company such as MediaOne Group, attempting to work on more often results in failure to achieve any of them. If a participant elects to only work on 1 development area, that is also fine.

After meeting with the coach to analyze the 360 results and begin drafting the Development Plan, the participant schedules a 1-hour meeting with his or her manager, to be completed within the next 30 days. The purpose of the meeting is to share the draft Development Plan and receive input and endorsement from the manager on the items selected, as well as potential development activities. The participant also follows-up with all raters to thank them for the feedback and to announce publicly what he or she is planning to work on. This not only role models the leader's commitment to professional development, but enlists the help of others in improving development areas. The leader also asks others for ideas and input into his or her Development Plan within the first 30 days.

The philosophy at M1G is that everyone has strengths and development needs; and therefore everyone needs a Development Plan. This is a public document to be shared with others, so that others can assist in the development and provide ongoing feedback.

Mini-Metrics (Follow-up Survey)

A second assessment piece is the follow-up survey, or mini-metrics, which is distributed 5 months after the initial 360 assessment (see Exhibit 6). Again,

Assessment Plus distributes and compiles the results of the follow-up surveys which are customized for each participant based on his or her top 3 development needs. In addition, the survey includes 2 other questions: 1) Did this leader follow-up with you regarding his or her development areas? And 2) On a scale of 0% to 100%, what percentage rating would you give this leader regarding improvement in his or her leadership skills over the last 6 months?

Quarterly/Annual Company Assessment Report

The follow-up surveys provide very useful statistics concerning how much improvement leaders have made across the company as a whole using the coaching and 360-assessment process. It is always run on an annual basis at year-end, and occasionally on a quarterly basis if requested by management for mid-term reporting purposes.

Second Assessment Cycle

Leadership development is considered to be an ongoing process that never ends. Every leader will always have something to learn and work on. Therefore, the 360-assessment process is ongoing. All leaders are encouraged to complete it every 12 to 18 months—depending on their specific job situation.

DESIGN & DEVELOPMENT

Design and development of the M1G Leadership Development System was based on the components of the Process Model. The first step was to complete the design of the 360-degree assessment, then the work on the other components followed. Other design and development components included: 1) 360 Workshop (1 day); 2) Coaching Options; and 3) Leadership Development Curriculum, which is composed of the Executive Development Portfolio and Managerial/Supervisory Curriculum. All components were designed with the total performance management system in mind, meaning that they were linked by the Competency Models to staff/recruiting, performance appraisal, career planning, and succession planning.

360 Workshop (1 day)

The design of the 1-day 360 debrief workshop was the first step of the process. The workshop was designed around a meeting with individual coaches, so all participants meet together in the morning, and then during the afternoon there are rotational sessions. The windowpane for the workshop is illustrated in Table 2.

The morning session is facilitated by a consultant and a M1G trainer presenting the review of the M1G Leadership Development System. Also, a M1G executive welcomes participants and reiterates how important the 360-coaching process is for development. Participants enjoy the 1-hour of reflection time,

Table 2. 360 Workshop

Morning—8 a.m. to 12 noon	Afternoon—1 p.m. to 6 p.m.
• Welcome & Introductions (30 min)	• Lunch (60 min)
• Review of M1G Leadership Dev. System (30 min)	• Rotational Sessions (1 to 5 p.m.)—each person attends each of the following at different times:
• Feedback Perceptions (30 min)	—One Hour with Private Coaching
• Break (15 min)	—One Hour of Reflection Time
• Company Feedback Data (60 min)	—One Hour of Peer Coaching
• How to Interpret a Feedback Report (30 min)	
• Private Time to Review Your Report Data (30 min)	—One Hour of Mini-Tutorial
• Preparing for Coaching/ Afternoon Sessions (30 min)	• Preparing for Re-Entry/ Conclusion (60 min)

during which they are encouraged to go to a quiet spot—often outdoors—and reflect on the feedback, as well as review development activities in the 360 Executive Development Resource Guide. The book lists on-the-job developmental activities for each of the competency items.

Participants also rate the peer coaching section highly. Here they meet in a trio with peers and each shares one development area they are thinking of working on. They ask peers for ideas on development options. The 1-hour minitutorial is a brief overview on a specific competency item. It is customized for each session and based on the class "group" feedback. In most cases it is a mini-session on Change Management or Coaching/Developing Others. The Reentry portion at the conclusion of the class prepares participants to go back and thank raters for feedback, as well as to meet with their manager. The coaching process is described in the Performance Coaching section below.

The 360 Workshop was also designed to be offered in 3 formats: 1) 1-Day Open Enrollment Format for mixed groups of executives; 2) 1-Day Team Format for an intact executive teach who also wanted to spend time looking at their intact team data—i.e., as an executive team, what are their strengths and what are their development areas?; and 3) Private Coaching Format—for leaders who miss the workshop due to vacation, schedule conflict, or some other reason. In this case, they meet with their private coach for 4 to 6 hours and receive a minitutorial on the workshop in additional to debriefing their 360 report.

Coaching Options

M1G offers its leaders 3 major coaching options: performance coaching, in-depth developmental coaching, and OJT coaching. The most common one is performance coaching using the 360 data. This type of coaching is offered during the afternoon session of the 360 workshop as well as in the private coaching session. Here the leader meets with an external coach (for executives) or internal coach (for managers/supervisors) and discusses the 360 feedback implications. Together the coach and leader identify 1 strength and 1–3 development items on which to focus. The coach provides some development activity suggestions, and all of these are documented on the Development Plan (see Exhibit 5). Then the coach prepares the leader to discuss the draft plan with the manager and direct reports upon return to work. The coach then meets with the leader 3 more times over a period of 6 months to assess progress, provide encouragement, and assist with any obstacles to development. This performance coaching process is outlined in Exhibit 7.

In-depth Developmental Coaching is used with high-level executives as both a reward and a chance to improve in certain areas. This type of coaching is usually reserved for the top 60 executives, and it involves the selection of the appropriate external coach who will work with the executive closely for up to 1 year. The first 2 months usually involve intensive data collection, using a multitude of assessment instruments and 360 interviews with the majority of the executive's direct reports, peers, customers, manager—and even external raters, such as family or community members. The coach will often "shadow" the executive on the job, observing him or her in interactions and other business situations. After data collection, the coach debriefs the executive in a 2- to 3-day session where they mutually "make sense of the data" and select specific themes on which to focus. From here a customized development plan is prepared and the coach continues to work with the executive—usually meeting with him or her at least once a month for the reminder of the year until the plan has been implemented.

The third coaching option is OJT Coaching, and this is basically an expectation that M1G managers will begin coaching their direct reports on the job in an ongoing formal and informal basis. The formal coaching is tied to the M1G performance appraisal system, wherein a manager meets with each employee 4 times a year to set performance objectives, provide feedback on progress, and coach on ways to improve development areas or excel in a strength area. As leaders complete the 360 process, they also meet with their manager to discuss their Development Plan, providing another formal coaching opportunity for managers. Informal coaching is an expectation that managers will look for the "1-minute" coaching opportunities to encourage or improve performance—depending on the situation.

Leadership Development Curriculum

The heart of M1G's leadership development strategy is based on the 360-assessment feedback and a personal relationship with a coach. However, a supporting leadership development curriculum was needed to provide development activities that could not be achieved only through coaching. With this in mind, the Executive Development Portfolio was created for executives (directors, VPs, and officers), and a Managerial/Supervisory Training Curriculum was put together for frontline supervisors and managers. Both rest on a foundation of core leadership training classes and on-the-job development activities (see Exhibit 8).

Highlights of the Executive Development Portfolio include the Strategic Forums, the Leadership Institute, and Targeted External Education. Descriptions of the offerings are provided in an excerpt (see Exhibit 9) from the actual brochure, which is distributed to every executive each year describing the portfolio.

Highlights of the Managerial/Supervisory Curriculum include the one week Leading the Way course (see Table 3) which welcomes new leaders into the M1G culture and leadership system. It is offered once a month on a traveling basis through all the M1G regions. Other courses in the curriculum are offered through M1G's Broadband University, which comprises 6 learning centers throughout the United States. Based on their specific development needs, leaders sign up for courses that will help them close developmental gaps.

Table 3. Windowpane for "Leading the Way" Course

Day 1	Day 2	Day 3	Day 4	Day 5
• Welcome & Intro. by Executive Sponsor	• Region 1 Business Update	• Region 3 Business Update	• Region 5 Business Update	• Region 7 Business Update
• M1 Past, Present, Future	• Coaching for Excellence	• Objective Setting	• Working Within the Law	• Development Planning
				• Close at Noon
• Merger Transition	• Region 2 Business Update	• Region 4 Business Update	• Region 6 Business Update	
• Managing Performance	• Coaching for Excellence — continued	• Managing Business Improvement	• Working Within the Law (cont.) • Graduation Dinner	

(For front-line supervisors.)

IMPLEMENTATION

The implementation of the M1G system was based on a cascade approach. The CEO and his team attended the first 360-Assessment Workshops, were matched with an external executive coach, and began the development process. A few of the top executives opted for the In-depth Developmental Coaching option as an add on to the regular Performance Coaching. The top executives role-modeled the process well, and each took turns introducing the 360 session to other executive teams.

In addition, the CEO and other key executives sponsored the Strategic Forums by helping to design them, select speakers, introduce the sessions, and participate in the complete day. Obviously, the CEOs were also intimately involved in the implementation of the Exchange and Shadow Board sessions. Finally, top executives stayed close to the process through the annual succession planning and approved all the recommendations for high potentials to attend Targeted External Education Programs (see Exhibit 9).

After the CEO and his top team completed the 360 process, all the other executive teams scheduled and completed the process over the next year. Then the system cascaded to the next level, which consisted primarily of the director population. A goal was set to have all 500 executives (directors, VPs, and officers) through the process at least 1 time within a 2-year period. New executives who were promoted or hired externally waited until they were on the job at least 4 months before completing the process—and many used the Private Coaching option. Several top executives began a second and even third round of their 360 assessment during the first 2 years.

During the fourth quarter of each year, a mini-needs assessment is conducted via e-mail and telephone conversations with top executives in order to identify the strategic business issues of the next year. This data is used to determine what topics should be used for the Strategic Executive Forums. The 360 database, which stored all the company data on leadership strengths and development areas, is also a source of information in considering new training classes for Broadband University and other leadership sessions.

After the second year, when the majority of all executives had completed the 360 process at least once, had been assigned a coach, and had been participating in the Executive Development Portfolio options, the 360 process was started with managers and supervisors. The rationale for waiting was to ensure that all executives were familiar with the system and could be good "managerial coaches" to the frontline supervisors and managers. Even though the 360 was delayed for this population, they still were being developed by attending the 1-week "Leading the Way" course and other Broadband University offerings.

Another reason for the delay with the population was that internal coaches had to be identified and certified to administer the managerial/supervisory LEI 360. To meet this need, an LEI Coaching Certification class was developed (see Table 4), and specific acceptance criteria were identified. These criteria are as follows:

- At least 5 years experience in HR, HRD, or L&D
- Previous experience coaching employees in training or employee relations contexts
- Familiarity with the 360-assessment process
- Must have participated in a 360-assessment process in the past
- Ability to suggest practical development suggestions, e.g., on the job changes, etc.
- Willingness to be assertive and "tough" as needed
- Excellent interpersonal skills, especially listening

Currently, the 360 process is being implemented with the supervisory/ managerial population. It follows the same process as the executive population.

Table 4. Windowpane for the LEI Coaching Certification

Day 1 (6 hours)	Day 2 (5–6 hours)
Welcome & Introduction (15 min)	Review of Report Interpretation Homework (30 min)
Overview of the Leadership Development Process (30 min)	The Coaching Session (90 min)
The Role of the Coach (30 min)	Process Steps
Process Logistics (30 min)	Handling the Emotional Aspects of Coaching
Break (15 min)	Demo
360 Report Interpretation (120 min)	Coaching Lab (up to 110 min)
Homework—Interpreting 2 Reports (2 hours)	Preparing for the Lab/Break (30 min)
	Individual Role Plays w/ Group Feedback (20 min EACH)
	Certification Exam (15 min)
	Individual Certification Discussions (15 min EACH)

Class is limited to 8 participants; requires 2 instructors.

The only difference is the use of an internal coach and different developmental activities, primarily the Managerial/Supervisory Training Curriculum.

ON-THE-JOB SUPPORT

As anyone who works in corporate America today knows the frantic business schedules which control our lives leave little time for personal development, even with the best of intentions. Therefore, on-the-job support has been critical to the success of this system. This type of support comes from a variety of mechanisms, with the main focus being the *executive coach*. A primary part of the coach's role is to play the part of "goad master"—reminding the leader to take his or her Development Plan off the back burner and pay some attention to it. The coach also tries to weave developmental activities into regular job responsibilities. In most cases, more than 75% of development activities are what the company refers to as "Current Job Adjustments," or making minor changes to the way employees interact with others on a daily basis, as well as enlisting their help and advice on others' development areas. Therefore, as the coach continues to "check-in" with the leader over a period of 6 months, in most cases, the Development Plan is implemented.

The *leader's manager* is also expected to assist in this process, beginning with the follow-up conversation and endorsement of the Development Plan. Progress checks and feedback should occur during regularly scheduled interim performance management discussions. The leader is also reminded by the coach and 2 letters, which are automatically sent by Assessment Plus at 2 and 4 months, to follow-up with the manager and direct reports to ask for feedback and suggestions on progress.

The *HR and Learning & Development Community* are also available to provide on the job support through advertisement of learning opportunities in Broadband U, as well as providing nominations or recommendations to certain Executive Development Portfolio programs.

Finally a list of formal *Individual Development Activities* is provided as part of the Leadership Development Curriculum. An excerpt of 4 of the most common on-the-job development activities is provided in Exhibit 10.

EVALUATION AND RESULTS

The M1G Leadership Development System is evaluated in a variety of ways, using the first 3 levels of Kirkpatrick's Evaluation. Level 1 includes post workshop evaluation forms for the 360 workshop, as well as all the offerings in the Executive Development Portfolio and Supervisory/Managerial Training Curriculum.

Level 1 results (reaction) for the first 210 participants through the 360 Workshops are as follows:

Satisfaction Level = 4.7 on a 5.0 point scale

General Feedback on benefits includes:

- Simple and easy to do.
- The feedback is extremely helpful. I liked having the day set aside to focus on the feedback and creating the development plan.
- Getting direct input from those individuals that are nearest to a manager's performance. Offering a systematic approach to using the evaluations to develop personal management skills.

Level 2 (learning transfer) and 3 (application to job) results are calculated via three sources for the 360 Coaching Process: 1) 7-month Email Follow-Up Survey to Participants; 2) 5-month Mini-Metrics Survey; and 3) Success Stories Provided by Coaches. Results of each of these are described below:

7-month Follow-up Survey to Participants

With this survey, participants are asked 3 primary questions. The results for the previous year are listed after the question. 1) How many times did you meet with your coach? *Ave.: 3.25;* 2) Did you complete your Development Plan? *All answered YES;* 3) Self-reported % increased effectiveness as a leader? *36.25%.* These results indicate that the process is working very well. Participants should have at least 3 follow-up conversations with their coach after the initial meeting. In most cases this is happening, and in some cases, the participants elect to continue the relationships with the coach—budgeting continued coaching through their own department. (Currently the 6-month coaching process is funded through the corporate Executive Development budget.) The fact that all participants responding had completed their Development Plan is positive, and a self-reported increased effectiveness of 36% after 6 months is also positive.

5-month Mini-Metrics Survey

This survey is a mini-360 which is distributed at 5 months to direct reports and peers/others who rated the leader the first time around. Most current results of this survey (though it is optional and not all participants elect to complete it), indicate 79% of Direct Reports reported that their managers are perceived to be more effective as a result of the 360-Coaching Process, and 86% of peers reported that the manager was perceived to be more effective (see Exhibit 11). This is exceptionally positive Level 3 data, though the responding numbers of leaders was rather low.

In general, the evaluation results for the M1G Leadership Development System have been very positive to date. The company has increased its succession planning benchstrength and has made great inroads in increasing diversity in top executive positions. They have also increased the number of leaders with high-quality general management skills and broadband technology knowledge. However, for marketing and technical leadership talent, the company had to recruit externally as the need was too immediate to expect a leadership development program to produce it overnight.

Feedback from the leaders indicates that they are especially appreciative of the flexibility of the system in that it provides them with development opportunities and follow-up conversations with coaches—wherever and whenever they need it. They are also pleased with the simplicity of the process and the rigorous use of assessment data. Though M1G is not successful in helping every leader improve, the company has made great inroads in increasing the leadership skills of many in its employment. And the journey is a continuous one. The philosophy at MediaOne Group is: Leaders will always have development needs (due to changing markets, job positions, technology, etc.), so everyone has a Development Plan.

Key Learnings

Key learnings from the implementation of this coaching-based executive development system can be separated into 2 categories—success factors and areas for improvement, described below:

Success Factors

- *Top-Level Endorsement:* Getting the support of the CEO and top executive team went along way towards making the system successful. Their positive comments, encouragement, and involvement made it a success.

- *CEO Sponsorship:* Having the 3 CEOs sponsor the Forums and Exchange sessions created a huge customer pull. Other executives and high potentials wanted to be nominated and invited to attend.

- *Role-Modeling:* By having the top executive teams go through the process first and then role-model it to others, it created a large "customer-pull" and helped make implementation move more smoothly.

- *Outsourcing Scoring:* By outsourcing the scoring and report generation components of the 360, it created much more confidence in the confidentiality and "development focus" of the system.

- *Database:* Setting up a database to analyze 360 data for the whole company provided very useful information and raised the level of credibility of the process.

- *Evaluation Results:* Calculating results to Level 3 (and in some cases to Level 4) went a long way in proving the success of the system.

- *Strategic Linkage:* Linking the topics of the Forums to strategic business issues—identified by an advisory board—created a lot of interest in the events and raised the level of credibility.

- *Top Name Speakers:* By bringing in "world class speakers" who had a lot of credibility and excellent speaking skills, many executives were excited about attending the programs. In addition, we designed these sessions to promote application to the workplace.

- *System Linkage:* Linking the executive development system to the succession planning, staffing, and performance appraisal system through the competency models added a simplicity and seamlessness that was appreciated by all.

Areas for Improvement

- *New Topics for Second Cycle:* As executives began to repeat the 360 for their second time through the cycle, it became obvious that new material was needed for the 1-day workshop. However, since the workshops have first-time people in them as well, it is not clear yet how to revise this issue.

- *Top Priority Development Areas:* The database clearly points out 2 major development areas for the company, but we have not yet determined the best methodology to address these. Some of it is occurring through coaching, but other methods are probably needed as well.

- *Accountability Via Succession Planning:* Executives have been asking to go through the process, but no accountability system is in place to "require" that they do. Closer scrutiny of this should occur during succession planning, e.g., "Have they gone through the 360 executive coaching process yet?" or "What forums, exchanges, etc. have they participated in?"

- *Executive Teaming:* The need to provide more services around the area of executive "teambuilding" has increased. As new executives are added to a team, business needs shift, natural conflicts arise—all of these issues increase the need for more focus in this area.

- *Executive Orientation:* Focus is needed to assist new executives to "hit the ground running." There is an orientation process for executives, at MediaOne, but it is optional and rarely used.

- *Retention:* Despite all of the company's efforts to retain employees, it still loses some that they would prefer not to. The executive development system is just one component of retention, but it is an important one. There is still more work to do in this area.

- *Merger Uncertainty:* With the company's impending merger with AT&T, it is unclear what will happen with this system. In many cases, it has already slowed down. However, we have added workshops and discussion sessions on "The Role of the Leader During a Merger."

Exhibit 1. Preferred Learning Formats

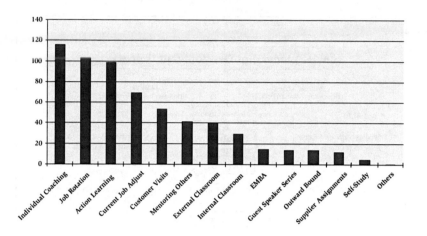

Exhibit 2. Leadership Development Strategy

MediaOne Group Leadership Development Strategy

Development of highly competent and experienced leadership,
including sufficient benchstrength for the future
via a 360-competency assessment model, individual coaching,
and flexible focused development activities
that positively impact the execution of business strategy
and the personal growth and job satisfaction of our leaders.

Exhibit 3. Leadership Development Process Model

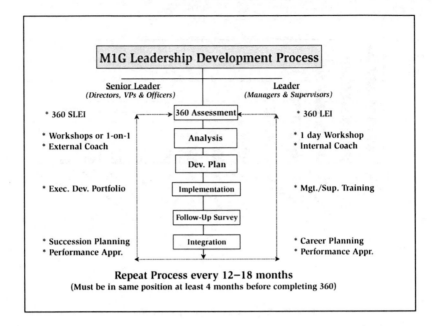

Exhibit 4. 360 Assessment Items for Customer-Driven Competency

Customer Driven is demonstrating appropriate attention to the customer, providing superior service, growing the customer base, and promoting customer loyalty.

HOW SATISFIED ARE YOU WITH THE WAY THIS LEADER:	Very Dissatisfied	Dissatisfied	Neither S or D	Satisfied	Very Satisfied	Not Applicable
▫ Listens to what customers want/need, creates tailored approaches, and even challenges and leads customers to stretch beyond perceived needs.	1	2	3	4	5	na
▫ Delivers high-quality services to customers, delivers on commitments made to customers, and exceeds expectations of customers.	1	2	3	4	5	na
▫ Interacts personally with customers.	1	2	3	4	5	na
▫ Increases size and loyalty of the customer base.	1	2	3	4	5	na

Exhibit 5. Development Plan Form

Media●ne Group

DEVELOPMENT PLAN

NAME: _____ DATE: _____

Strength: Your Plan to Capitalize on a Strength (share it with others and utilize it in some way to link to company goals. Hint: Use your Model of Excellence to identify required competencies)

Strength   *Action Plan, including Deadline*

Development Areas: Your Plan to Improve 2 to 3 Development Areas (Hint: Use your Model of Excellence to identify required competencies)

Development Areas   *Action Plan, including Deadline*

Career Goals

Exhibit 6. Mini-Metrics Survey

MINI-METRICS SURVEY REGISTRATION FORM

Name: _____

Address: _____

_____

_____

_____

Work Phone: _____ Work Fax: _____

E-Mail Address: _____

Number of raters you plan to survey (up to 16 total) _____ Direct Reports
_____ Peers

Your raters will be asked to rate the extent to which you have increased or decreased in effectiveness, and the scale they will use to respond to is as follows:

-3	-2	-1	0	1	2	3
Less Effective			No Change			More Effective

Items you want to include on your mini-survey:

1. _____

2. _____

3. _____

PLEASE SEND SURVEYS TO ME TO DISTRIBUTE NO LATER THAN

Insert Date _____

Please mail or fax to:

Assessment Plus
1217 Rockbridge Road, #7
Stone Mountain, GA 30087
Fax: (770) 465-9007

Exhibit 7. Performance Coaching Process

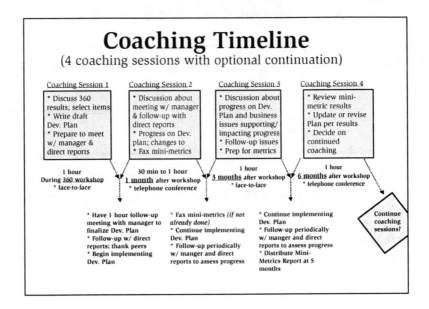

Exhibit 8. Leadership Development Curriculum

Executive Development Portfolio
(Directors, VP's & Officers)

Management Development Series
(Mangers & Supervisors)

Targeted External Education
(by nomination) * CTAM * CCL * EMBA
* USC-Telcom * Betsy Magnus * 14 Seats

Targeted Internal Education
(based on individual development needs)
* Project Management * Finance
* Change Management * Product Know.
* Business Process Improvement * Other

Strategic Forums *(by invitation)*
* 1 day Forums * Shadow Board
* Leadership Conferences * The Exchange

LEI 360 Workshop

SLEI 360 Workshop

Leading The Way (1 week)
Introductory Leadership Course for managers
& supervisors. Covers business issues, HR
policies, and key leadership skills

Leadership Institute (3 days)

Individual Development Options *(based on individual development needs)*
* Current Job Adjustments * Work Assignments * Job Rotation * Coaching
* Self-Study * Project Team Work * Mentoring * Intranet * Community Work

Core Leadership Courses
* Performance Management (LINC) Series * Facilitative Leadership * Coaching for Performance

Exhibit 9. 1999 MIG Executive Development Portfolio Excerpt

Executive Development Forums: One-day forums on strategic business topics and needed capabilities. Featuring expert speakers in the morning and application discussions in the afternoon. Two sessions offered in 1999:

1. *Customer Focus:* What are the new best practices in customer focus and satisfaction? Hear from a world-class expert on customer satisfaction and loyalty issues, as well as feedback from our own customers. Then participate in group discussions to identify actions to enhance our customer focus. By invitation.

2. *Product Leadership*: Learn more about our products and the future direction of new products from product development experts in our company. In the afternoon, listen to an external expert describe the competitive direction of the industry, and then participate in group discussions regarding product issues and new directions. By invitation.

The Exchange: Small interactive group discussions of 2 hours in length with one of our CEOs and a group of 15 to 20 directors and new VPs. Discussion topics would be "hot issues and topics" within the organization. The format would be informal, beginning with introductions, and then the CEO would speak for 15–20 minutes on issues that "keep him/her awake at night. Participants would be encouraged to respond, as well as to bring up issues from their region, function, and/or business unit. Offered once a quarter; by invitation.

Shadow Board: Bi-annual meetings of 1 day in length for 10–15 high potential leaders to serve on a "shadow board." Scheduled one day before the MediaOne Executive Team meets for their meeting. The purpose would be to let the high potentials work the Executive Team agenda 1 day in advance, thus experiencing the issues and decisions which the Exec. Team must handle. Two members of the Shadow Board then attend the Exec. Team meeting the next day to observe and share the Shadow Boards' observations on the agenda items. Offered twice in 1999; by invitation.

External Executive Development Programs: Senior leaders are encouraged to attend external executive education programs, (e.g. Harvard, CCL, Stanford, Insead, AMA, CTAM, Betsy Magnus, etc.) to address specific development needs that are documented on their Development Plan. The Leadership Development Program provides advice and assistance in identifying and registering for these programs, though they must be funded by the individual department.

Executive Teaming: Take the 1-on-1 executive coaching process to the next level by bringing in an executive coach to work with your team over a period of 3 to

(*Continued*)

Exhibit 9. 1999 M1G Executive Development Portfolio Excerpt (*Continued*)

6 months. The coach will attend your regular staff meetings; and offer tips on accelerated decision-making, group dynamics; business process improvement issues, etc. Or schedule a customized team-building session around a specific topic, such as creativity, collaboration, cross-functional teams, strategic change process for teams, and other. Currently all executive teaming must be funded by the individual department.

MediaOne Group Leadership Institute: Targeted at directors and new VPs, the institute covers strategic business information regarding products, competitors, customers, and markets, as well as reviewing mission, values, strategy, and critical business priorities. In addition, specific leadership skills are covered such as change management, conflict resolution, and coaching. Participants will complete the 360 SLEI Coaching Process, the Myers-Briggs Type Indicator, and work in cross-functional teams. An action learning project will continue back on the job. To be offered on a quarterly basis in different regions across the company during 2000.

Exhibit 10. Excerpt from Portfolio of Individual Development Activities

_____**Current Job Adjustments**: Leaders develop in current job position by adjusting behavior to address a specific development issue, e.g. spend more time giving direct reports feedback, dealing with conflict, using active listening skills, holding more staff meetings, etc. May also include introducing new challenges to the current assignment, and/or increasing the complexity or scale of the job, e.g. adding more direct reports.

_____**Work Assignments**: Leaders develop new skills/knowledge by participating in new work assignments, such as a special work project or taskforce. This could also include making visits to customers or suppliers. In some cases, it could be a short-term work assignment at the supplier's company. It could also be a community involvement project (see www.volunteermatch.com for development ideas; or being a member on a Board of Directors.)

_____**Job Rotation**: Leaders develop new skills by working in different departments and job locations—often international offices. World-class companies insure that there is an overlap between the incoming and outgoing executive and that lessons learned are documented in a corporate database. The overlap insures continuity for employees, customers, and suppliers, and the database prevents repeating mistakes and accelerates individual and organizational learning.

Exhibit 11. Success Stories Provided by Coaches

The executive coaches are requested to share special success stories as they occur, making sure to maintain the confidentiality of the leader. Following are excerpts from 3 of these success stories.

"I just received this week a 3-page, single-spaced e-mail from one of the leaders in your organization. It documented the changes that had actually happened (i.e., the office did get ORGANIZED! It took 2 1/2 days! But now they can find things and won't be breaking their promises!) This person also gave a major speech that was very much a success. Making presentations needed a lot of attention. This time they practiced it . . . in front of real live people . . . 3 times . . . instead of winging it which was the usual style . . . and not too successful."

"I wanted to share with you a success story about one of your VPs I am coach-ing. I just completed our 3 month face-to-face coaching session with him recently. Since our first meeting in June, he has made a dramatic change in his personal leadership style based on his 360 feedback, and has received extremely positive responses from his team. He had worked hard to foster open communi-cation, and to be a better listener. As a result, his team members are more relaxed around him, they modeled his behavior, and become more open toward each other. He was very pleased with the outcome and is encouraged to continue his efforts. It was great to see the progress he had made in such a short time."

"Sam (not the participant's name) was lukewarm at the onset. 'What do you think? (about the 6 month coaching process we were embarking on),' I asked at the end of the 360-feedback session. 'Well, I'm not sure. We'll just wait and see, won't we?' Sam has strong integrity, great job knowledge, and he holds people accountable. He is clear and direct. But sometimes he's very INTENSE, perceived as a little gruff. It was clear from the feedback that he was far from good at pos-itively recognizing others. . . . In the first phone conversation, I learned Sam was not programmed to positively recognize others. He wasn't raised with it, so he never saw it. But after some discussion, he agreed to think about it. He thought for 2 weeks. I mailed a couple information pieces. He came back said he really wanted to do it. So the plan . . . he announced it to his group (so they wouldn't faint when they saw this new behavior), chose 30 minutes every Friday to review what he had discussed that week with each direct report. Had he recog-nized them in some way? How did it feel? If he had not recognized a person, why not? This a.m. I receive a voice mail from Sam who wants me to know that he is working the plan. And IT'S WORKING! And two of his people came by this week AND TOLD HIM THEY WERE SEEING A CHANGE AND HOW MUCH THEY APPRECIATED IT."

ABOUT THE CONTRIBUTOR

Elizabeth "Liz" Thach, Ph.D. (lthach@mediaone.com) is director of leadership and organization development for MediaOne Group, based in Denver, Colorado. She currently has over 16 years experience in the field of human resource development, specializing in international leadership development and the application of communication technology to workplace performance. Prior to coming to MediaOne, Thach worked at Compaq Computer, Amoco Corporation, and Texas Instruments. In these positions, she was deeply involved in a variety of large-scale organizational change projects, and also had the opportunity to work in over 15 countries around the world. Thach is an avid writer, having published more than 20 articles in the field of human resource development. She has presented at numerous conferences, both in the United States and abroad. Thach holds a doctorate in HRD from Texas A&M University; a master's degree in organizational communication and management from Texas Tech University, and a bachelor's degree in English from College of Notre Dame in Belmont, California.

PART THREE

CONCLUSION

by Louis Carter

RESEARCH: OD/HRD TRENDS AND FINDINGS

To provide additional context for the case studies presented in this book, we asked our contributors to reflect on 6 critical areas of their OD/HRD initiatives in an online survey. Areas covered by this survey include: 1) company and initiative background, 2) business diagnosis, 3) resistance to change, 4) design and implementation, 5) evaluating the initiative, and 6) summary.

Although the initiatives in this book cover a broad range of organization and human resource development topic areas, they are all bound by 1 key characteristic: change. As Linda Ackerman says in the book *Organization Development Classics,* "Change is one of those words that serves as a melting pot for scores of concepts and methods. . . . For example, it can mean planning, training, problem solving, innovation, leadership . . . and the list goes on!"[1] Within this section, you will see that we have researched the most pressing organization and human resource development issues that have arisen from managing change in this handbook.

1. Company and Initiative Background

The organizations in this book represent a range of employee sizes, revenues, and industries. The following Figure 1 represents the different industries represented in this survey and the handbook.

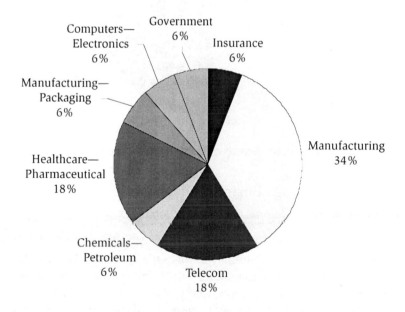

Figure 1 Allocation of Organizations Studied, by Industry

Average revenue for the 17 companies represented in the book is $13.4 billion. On average, the initiatives discussed in this book have been in place for 3.7 years. Thus, the initiatives are new enough to contain novel, innovative practices, and old enough to have undergone scrutiny through careful evaluation. The average number of employees for the organizations represented in this handbook is 39,432 (Figure 2).

For some organizations, there was a positive correlation between the amount of money budgeted for the initiative and the amount of employees dedicated to the initiative (Table 2). The organizations that did not have a positive correlation between the number of employees dedicated full-time to the initiative and the amount of money budgeted, spent more of their money outsourcing work to external consulting firms.

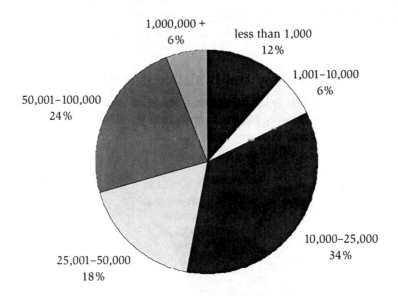

Figure 2 Number of Employees Represented by Organizations

2. Business Diagnosis

"It is thrifty to prepare today for the wants of tomorrow"

Aesop, *The Ant and the Grasshopper*

Before engaging in any change initiative, it is sage advice to diagnose the business. One hundred percent of the organizations followed this advice by engaging in a needs assessment to determine the best course of action for their initiatives. This high percentage may be indicative of the kind of care that best-practice companies take to ensure that they are successful with their initiatives.

Table 1. Amounts Budgeted to Initiative (By Type of Initiative, n = 12)

Initiative	Annual Average Amount Budgeted
Organization Development & Change(OD&C)	$15,625,000 (n = 4)
Leadership Development (LD)	$2,000,000 (n = 3)
Coaching & Mentoring (C&M)	$1,200,000 (n = 2)
Recruitment & Retention (R&R)	$500,000 (n = 2)
Performance Management (PM)	$250,000 (n = 1)

Table 2. Annual Investment of Employee Time and Dollars on Initiatives, n = 12

U.S. Dollars Budgeted	Employees Dedicated on a Full-Time Basis	Type of Initiative
$36,000,000	35	OD&C
$8,000,000	55	LD
$2,500,000	3+	OD&C
$2,000,000	4	LD
$2,000,000	4	LD
$1,500,000	3	C&M
$1,000,000	10	OD&C
$900,000	2	C&M
$750,000	8	R&R
$500,000	1	OD&C
$250,000	1.5	PM
$250,000	2	R&R

Organizations today operate in an increasingly challenging environment. They must not only face the demands of their end-users and competitors, but they have to listen carefully and respond to the needs of one of their most important customers—their employees. It is not surprising then, that rapid growth, response to employee surveys, improving productivity, and improving customer focus were among the top 4 reasons organizations implemented their OD/HRD initiatives (Table 3).

3. Resistance to Change

"A body at rest remains at rest and a body in motion continues to move at a constant velocity unless acted upon by an external force."

Sir Isaac Newton's first law of physics

The most difficult obstacles to implementing change are usually cultural, organizational, or psychological, rather than technical factors. (See Table 4.) Most

Table 3. Top Four Reasons Organizations Engaged in Initiatives,
in Order of Frequency

Engagement Reason
1 Rapid growth
2 Response to employee surveys
3 Improve productivity
4 Improve customer focus

Table 4. Types of Resistance That Were Encountered, in Order of Frequency

Types of Resistance
1 Fear of change, the unknown and loss of control
2 Time constraints
3 Lack of skills to deal with people or understand the tools of the initiative
4 Averse to "touchy-feely" people issues
5 Negative expectations that initiative is a "flavor of the month"

technical factors are masking a deeper issue. All organizations in this book encountered resistance of some sort—be it cultural, organizational, psychological, or technical. Many of the organizations indicated that fear of change was a predominate factor that influenced resistance to the initiative. Several organizations emphasized that employees resisted because their work schedules did not allow them to commit the time necessary to engage in the initiative. Other resistance factors included a disgust with "touchy-feely" people issues and a distrust of the genuine nature of the initiative (flavor-of-the-month). Lastly, several organizations indicated that employees did not feel qualified to engage in the initiative, due to a lack of skills. Our lesson here is that, when engaging in a change project, it is imperative that you be aware and sensitive to the underlying issues that affect an employee's willingness or readiness for change. As we have learned from Nortel's change capability evaluation, a client's readiness for change is more a function of the organizational system, timing, and situation than a personal attack on the efficacy of the initiative.

Reducing Resistance

"Companies cannot legislate their employees' feelings, but companies do rent their behavior."

Harvard Business Review, November/December 1993

Surely, these organizations don't need to gain the commitment of everyone in the organization to be successful, but a critical mass is necessary. The time of the consultant or change agent is best spent identifying the key stakeholders who compose the critical mass and dealing with the issues and concerns that they are grappling with. For most organizations, change was facilitated, by and large, by communication to the organization that senior management was committed to change (Table 5). Focus groups, stakeholder assessments, clear action plans, and teams comprising different levels of the organizations follow.

The survey probed deeper to how senior leaders supported the initiative. Results indicated that in more than half the organizations, the senior leaders frequently modeled the desired behavior in accordance with the initiative. Additionally, they allocated the necessary funds to sustain the project's success. Half of the contributors indicated that a moderate portion of the senior leader's compensation is tied to the success of the initiative.

Table 5. Reducing/Overcoming Resistance and Gaining Commitment to the System, in Order of Frequency

	Steps Taken
1	Senior management communicated their support for the new system
2	Use organization-wide communication on the need for change
3	Senior management were strong models/champions for the system
4	Design team consisting of persons from different levels/departments of the organization
5	Implementation team consisting of persons from different levels/departments of the organization
6	Communicated a vision for how the organization would operate after the change
7	Conduct employee focus groups
8	Conduct manager focus groups
9	Survey users of system for input into the new system change
10	Other

4. Design and Implementation

Design There appears to be a trend in designing change initiatives that are integrated with other human resource systems. (See Table 6 below.) This trend follows the theory that change initiatives need to fit within the structure of the whole system. As Thomas Cummings and Ann Feyerherm point out in *Practicing Organization Development*, "The key concept in open-systems theory is congruency or fit among the components. They must fit with one another to attain the most effective results."[2] All of the contributors indicated that their OD/HRD initiative was designed to integrate with other human resource systems within the organization.

Implementation To shed more light on the implementation process, we studied the different categories of change agents, the techniques they used to ensure accountability on the part of senior executives, and the activities performed by senior executives that demonstrate visible commitment to the initiative.

As Rothwell, Sullivan, and McLean (1995) point out, the change agent or "champion of change" usually takes on 3 critical roles. The first role is that of the envisioner who articulates a clear and credible vision of the new organization and its strategy and generates pride and enthusiasm. The energizer, the second role, is someone who demonstrates excitement for changes and models the behaviors linked to them. Lastly, the enabler allocates resources for implementing change, uses rewards to reinforce new behaviors, and builds effective top-management teams and management practices.[3] For all of the organizations, there was either a group of change "champions" or a single change "champion" who exercised these roles.

Table 6. Internal Systems That Support Initiatives, in Order of Frequency

	Internal Systems
1	Training & Education
2	Coaching & Mentoring
3	Leadership Development
4	Employee Opinion Surveys
5	Tie Compensation to Performance
6	Succession Planning
7	Work/Life Balance Policies
8	Performance Management/Appraisal
9	Recruitment: Obtaining Applicants
10	Selection: Selecting Hires from Applicants
11	Benefits Administration

Categories of Change Agents or Change "Champions" We have identified 7 different groups of change agents or "champions" of change within this short study of organization initiatives (Table 7). These categories need further explanation.

- First, we have found that the majority of organization initiatives are driven jointly by 2–3 officers, usually chief executive, chief operating or chief information officers, and a host of senior executive titles such as OD director, senior vice president, or senior VP of human resources.
- The second category of "champions" falls under the category of the president or chief executive officer.
- The third category, senior executive can take the form of any of the senior executive titles mentioned above.
- The fourth category, manager, falls under such titles as general manager or plant manager.
- The fifth category, driven jointly by managers ranges from business group leaders to a team of managers.
- The sixth category, OD task force or council, comprises a host of managers, executives, officers, and employees from all levels of the organization.

Techniques Used to Enlist Support To accomplish the tasks necessary to implement change projects, consultants and change agents, in general, must be able to enlist the support of others, within their department or division and from their network in the larger organization. Techniques used to ensure accountability include tying the initiative success to changes in base or bonus pay, and using the performance review to evaluate activities or results. The most popular of these options (64% of the contributors) is using the performance management system to guide and evaluate the behavior of the senior management team toward supporting the initiative. Similar results emerged for managers (59% of the contributors). Tying performance ratings to the initiative was common for only 35% of the contributors.

Table 7. Champions of Change, in Order of Frequency

Champion	
1	Driven jointly by officers and senior executives
2	President or officer
3	Senior executive
4	Manager
5	Driven jointly by managers
6	OD task force or council

Activities Performed by Senior Executives That Demonstrate Visible Comitment Lastly, we identified 5 activities performed by senior executives that demonstrated visible commitment to the initiative. (See Table 8.) These activities illustrate the leadership group's (comprising senior-most leaders and direct reports) visible commitment to the initiative.

Table 8. Activities Extensively Performed By Senior Executives, in Order of Frequency

	Activity
1	Allocates funds for the initiative
2	Models the behaviors consistent with the initiative
3	Integrates the initiative into overall strategic plan
4	Participates in initiative education/training
5	Frequently articulates the business case for the initiative
6	Has a portion of compensation tied to the initiative

5. Evaluating the OD/HRD Initiative

Evaluation is often not given the attention it deserves. However, it is quite possibly the most important component of the OD/HRD process. Evaluation, as defined by Beckhard and Harris, "is a set of planned, information-gathering and analytical activities undertaken to provide those responsible for the management of change with a satisfactory assessment of the effects and/or progress of the change effort."[4] Nearly all of the organizations have systems in place to evaluate the effectiveness of the initiative. Methods vary on the different ways in which evaluation can be implemented (Table 9).

Four different methods of implementing evaluations were leveraged by organizations in this handbook. The first type of evaluation was organization assessments/surveys/tracking that occurred on a formative and summative basis. Formative evaluations are conducted during the intervention while summative evaluations are conducted immediately after the completion of the intervention. These evaluations were most prevalent within organization development and change initiatives as well as performance management initiatives. Another point at which an evaluation can be conducted is longitudinal. Longitudinal evaluations are conducted at a specified time after the completion of the intervention.[5]

Table 9. Evaluation Method Usage, in Order of Frequency

	Evaluation Method Usage
1	Organization Assessments/Surveys/Tracking
2	Level 1–4 Evaluations
3	Feedback sessions that evaluate the program's success against its original objectives
4	Continuous Improvement Efforts

Some Level 1–4 evaluations were performed on a longitudinal basis.

Level 1–4 evaluations were used predominately in leadership development and coaching and mentoring case studies, due to the fact that these case studies delivered formalized training programs. Level 1–4 refer to Donald Kirkpatrick's methods of evaluation that can be divided into 4 categories, and include data drawn largely from interviews or questionnaires. Level 1–4 evaluations were conducted on a formative, summative, and longitudinal basis.

1. *Reaction Evaluations* measure the participant's initial response or feeling from the training.

2. *Learning Evaluations* are administered in the form of tests or questionnaires and measure how well participants have learned facts, ideas, concepts, or theories.

3. *Behavior Evaluations* measure the effect of training on job performance.

4. *Results Evaluations* measure the effect of training on the achievement of organizational goals.

The third evaluation delivery method was feedback sessions. Feedback sessions were leveraged mostly by organization development and change initiatives. The fourth delivery method, continuous improvement efforts, pays homage to the action research model of organization development. The action research model incorporates continuous feedback mechanisms so that the organization development system continuously evolves.

6. Summary

Book contributors indicated the impact of the initiative on a range of outcomes. (See Table 10.) There was widespread agreement among the contributors on the outcomes reported. They disagreed more frequently on the impact that the initiative had on other measures of organization effectiveness such as increased market share, and employee recruitment.

When asked to indicate the top 3 critical success factors for their initiatives, contributors indicated behavioral, strategic, and cultural factors (Table 11). The

Table 10. Positive Results of Organization Effectiveness, in Order of Frequency

	Impact of Initiative
1	Employee retention
2	Employee job satisfaction
3	Organizational effectiveness (e.g., coordination and communication)
4	Financial results
5	Customer satisfaction
6	Strategic effectiveness
7	Team performance
8	Employee productivity
9	External image/reputation

Table 11. Top 3 Critical Success Factors for Initiatives, in Order of Frequency

Ranking	Critical Success Factor
1	Linking OD/HRD to critical business issues
2	Support and involvement of senior management
3	Those affected by the initiative believed in the need for change

results underscore the importance of making a strong business case for the change initiative. By linking the initiative to critical business issues, contributors were able to obtain buy-in from senior management and those affected by the change, thus increasing the likelihood for success. "Change readiness" also arose as a strong theme for success. The contributors strongly agreed that when employees believe that change needs to happen, they were more likely to participate in activities and become more supportive of the initiative.

Key Learnings When asked in an open-ended question for the 3 most effective components of the initiative, contributors presented a range of answers from issues around communication, to the alignment of business issues (Table 12). Some of the most powerful key learnings centered around the challenges inherent in creating an organizational culture that supports and nurtures learning and continuous improvement.

These best practice organizations overcame obstacles in their struggle for success (Table 13). Some of the greatest challenges occurred around global, technological, managerial, and cultural aspects of the change initiative.

Table 12. Top Ten Effective Components of Initiatives, in Order of Frequency

Ranking	Most Effective Components of Initiative
1	A common vision to guide efforts
2	An effective champion to continually drive for change
3	Thorough needs assessment
4	Strong, consistent communication efforts
5	"No exception" training
6	Creating a knowledge-sharing and learning environment
7	Consistent implementation in a global environment
8	Demonstration of senior management commitment (e.g., through brown bag lunch days, CEO kick-off of initiative)
9	Alignment of culture change with business strategy
10	Infrastructure support: environment + resources = commitment

Table 13. Challenges or Obstacles to Change

1	Helping employees understand new technology applications
2	Achieving change with a geographically dispersed population of employees
3	Managing costs, time, and resource allocation
4	Gaining project sponsorship across the organization
5	Planning for the future when change is so fast
6	Maintaining the change momentum
7	Continuing to improve the company while fighting the perception that "We are the best. How could we get any better?"
8	Creating realistic accountability to ensure that managers follow through in support of the initiative

The Future: Continuous Organizational Development

Contributors were asked to indicate where they envision their organization is heading with its initiative within the next 5 to 10 years. Responses indicate that the contributors want to keep the organization on a track to continuously learn and develop its capabilities. Comments from some contributors indicate that they want to leverage lessons learned from this experience. Some contributors commented that they want to firmly ingrain the initiative into the organization to the point that it is almost invisible to the user, making it an accepted part of life at the company. Other contributors will continue to refine the present initiative in place, while others will expand their efforts into other business lines. Survey results clearly indicate that the present state of the initiatives represented in this book represent snapshots of moving targets. Further growth and innovation is inevitable for these best practice organizations, as they work to stay ahead of their competitors by embracing change and continuously learning and improving.

ENDNOTES

1. Van Eynde, Hoy, and Van Eynde. *Organization Development Classics*, San Francisco: Jossey-Bass, 1997.

2. Rothwell, Sullivan, and McLean. *Practicing Organization Development*, San Francisco: Jossey-Bass, 1995. p. 205.

3. Tushman, M., M. Newman, and D. Nadler. "Executive Leadership and Organizational Evolution: Managing Incremental and Discontinuous Change." In R. Kilmann and J. Covin (eds.), *Corporate Transformation*, San Francisco: Jossey-Bass, 1988. pp. 102–130.

4. Beckhard and Harris. *Organizational Transitions*, Reading, MA: Addison-Wesley, 1977. p. 86.

5. Rothwell, Sullivan, and McLean. *Practicing Organization Development*, San Francisco: Jossey-Bass, 1995. p. 313.

ABOUT LINKAGE, INC.

Linkage, Inc. (www.linkageinc.com) is a global leader in creating organizational development, leadership, coaching and mentoring, and corporate education programs, research, and resources that achieve measurable business impact. Combining the world's most renowned thought leaders, "best-in-class" educational resources, and a highly experienced team of consultants, Linkage has delivered programs to more than 9,000 individuals, including employees of 80 of the Fortune 100 companies. Clients include Lucent Technologies, Merck, Harvard University, Brigham & Women's Hospital, Skudder Kemper Investments, McDonald's, Toyota, Xerox, and a host of other organizations in the major vertical industries.

Linkage's Suite of Leadership and Organizational Development Products & Services

Linkage, Inc. prides itself in providing practical, cost-effective, and results-oriented leadership and organization development programs and systems. Linkage provides one-stop-shopping for its clients' leadership and organizational development needs.

World-class consulting, training, research, distance-learning programming, videos, and books.

Leadership/Organizational Development Consulting and System Development— Through a multimode systemic model for building an organizational or human resource development program, Linkage provides "best-in-class" OD/HRD consulting. Linkage leverage's its multimode model for designing, implementing, and providing ongoing support for OD/HRD systems such as performance management, leadership development coaching and mentoring and change management. Clients include Brown University, Case Corporation, Toyota, American Home Products, Ralston Purina, and ITOCHU International.

Global Institute for Leadership Development (GILD)—Co-chaired by Warren Bennis (leadership author and expert) and Phil Harkins (Linkage's president and CEO), GILD provides high-level programs and services targeted at the long-term leadership development of individuals and teams from the world's foremost organizations.

The Executive Leadership Development Program—This program, Linkage's core leadership workshop, is an experiential, interactive session that provides proven models, tools, and processes to help participants become more impactful leaders. The program is designed to provide an intensive 3-day session that helps leaders to continuously improve skills, increase knowledge, and develop their leadership competencies.

The Best of Organizational Development Conference (ODC)—The event brings together Organizational Development, Organizational Effectiveness, HR professionals, academics, and practitioners to address the compelling issues and challenges facing Organizational Development professionals today. ODC is designed to provide the most comprehensive learning forum and a compilation of the best thinking and applications of OD tools, skills, and methodologies.

The Essential Coach—Enables managers and leaders to shape and direct their behavior to increase their personal effectiveness by measuring the critical capabilities required for powerful coaching. The Essential Coach is available as both a self-managed assessment and a 360-degree assessment.

Leadership Assessment Instrument (LAI)—Developed by Linkage, in partnership with Warren Bennis, the LAI measures the critical capabilities required for high-performance leadership across all industries and functions. The LAI is available as both a self-managed assessment and as a 360-degree assessment.

Complete Consultant—Categorizes the broad range of roles that HR/OD consultants perform by measuring the competencies within each role that drive superior results and work outputs. The Compleat Consultant is available as both a self-managed assessment and a 360-degree assessment.

Center for Organizational Research—Linkage's Research Group provides benchmarking and best practice research to help guide decision making on key leadership and organizational development issues, bringing the industries' key leaders and best practitioners to work directly with the client.

The Linkage Toolkit for Developing Leaders—Linkage's products group has brought together its most valuable tools from its conferences, workshops, consulting, and research into one volume that coaches leaders at all levels of the organization to become more effective and successful. This particular coach represents what Linkage has been learning about leadership for quite some time. And it is a multi-faceted coach. It not only provides tools but assessments. It not only helps you think about yourself but your impact on others. Its is also a very pragmatic coach who wants you out on the playing field applying what you have learned. Best of all, it is a remarkably comprehensive coach—Linkage's toolkit is packed with all sorts of helpful instruments, cases, diagnostics, and advice. In many ways, this volume is like a filled-to-the-gills tool box.

Linkage's Best Practice Guidebooks—Linkage's products group has also created self-directed, self-paced, practical guidebooks that provide best practice tools, processes and models needed to be an effective manager or change leader, improve processes and enable teams. All processes, models, and tools have been integrated and implemented with positive measurable change at such organizations as **Raytheon, Morton, Beatrice Foods, Ellerbe Beckett, GE Capital,**

Barclays Bank, and Volvo. The guidebooks have been effectively used by vice presidents, managers, supervisors, work team leaders, project managers, and other industry leaders across all major vertical industries. For more information on these books, visit: http://www.linkageinc.com/products.

ABOUT THE EDITORS

Louis Carter

Managing Editor/Consultant, Linkage, Inc.

Louis Carter is Director of Products and leadership consultant at Linkage, Inc., where he implements and manages best practice training and development programs as well as publishes best practice resources. Lou leads Linkage Press, Linkage's Publishing division, that produces best practice resources in organization and leadership development. Prior to joining Linkage, Lou was a research consultant for Gemini Consulting, as well as Director of Strategy and Development for an insurance and investment services firm. He has also worked as an analyst for two Wall Street Investment Banking firms, as well as a writer for a Boston-based news station. His work has been featured in the *Supervisors Guide to Quality and Excellence, Investors Business Daily,* and *Bankers and Tradesman.* His best practice work has also been featured at the International ASTD conferences, and Linkage workshops and events. Carter's book, Linkage Inc.'s *Best Practices in Leadership Development Handbook,* which he co-edited with Marshall Goldsmith and Warren Bennis was published in 2000 by Jossey Bass, and his new books, *The Linkage Toolkit for Developing Leaders* and *Best Practices in Knowledge Management & Organizational Learning Handbook* were published in 2001 by Linkage Press.

David Giber, Ph.D.

Vice President of Consulting Services, Linkage, Inc.

David Giber (DGiber@linkage-inc.com) is a leading expert in designing and implementing integrated leadership development programs that achieve organizational effectiveness and measurable change. He has served in director-level HR positions for major organizations in various vertical industries for over 15 years, and has consulted with a wide variety of domestic and global organizations on such issues as succession planning, management development, workforce assessment, competency modeling, and developing performance and compensation systems. He has designed and managed training and development programs worldwide for such firms as SIAC, Digital Equipment Corporation, Keane, Inc., New York Airlines, and Goldman Sachs. He has also developed competency models and competency-based human resource systems for such organizations as the Principal Financial Group, Levi Strauss, LEGO Systems, Harvard Community Health Plan, Unum Insurance, and others. Giber received his bachelor's degree from Stanford in 1976 and his Ph.D. in industrial/organizational psychology from Duke University in 1980.

Marshall Goldsmith, Ph.D.
Keilty, Goldsmith & Company

Marshall Goldsmith (marshall@kgcnet.com) is one of the world's foremost authorities in helping leaders achieve positive, measurable change in behavior: for themselves, their people, and their teams. Goldsmith has been ranked in the *Wall Street Journal* as one of the "Top 10" consultants in the field of executive development. His work has received national recognition from the Institute for Management Studies, the American Management Association, the American Society for Training and Development, and the Human Resource Planning Society. His coaching process has been positively described in both the *New York Times* and the *Financial Times*. Goldsmith has co-edited (with Frances Hesselbein and Dick Beckhard) the books *The Leader of the Future, The Organization of the Future,* and *The Community of the Future,* which have sold over 400,000 copies in 14 different languages. Goldsmith has an MBA from Indiana University and a Ph.D. from UCLA. Before forming KGC, he was an associate dean at Loyola Marymount University and a director at the Center for Leadership Studies.

INDEX

HOW TO USE THE CD-ROM

SYSTEM REQUIREMENTS

Windows PC

* 486 or Pentium processor-based personal computer
* Microsoft Windows 95 or Windows NT 3.51 or later
* Minimum RAM: 8 MB for Windows 95 and NT
* Available space on hard disk: 8 MB Windows 95 and NT
* 2X speed CD-ROM drive or faster

Netscape 3.0 or higher browser or MS Internet Explorer 3.0 or higher

Macintosh

* Macintosh with a 68020 or higher processor or Power Macintosh
* Apple OS version 7.0 or later
* Minimum RAM: 12 MB for Macintosh
* Available space on hard disk: 6MB Macintosh
* 2X speed CD-ROM drive or faster

Netscape 3.0 or higher browser or MS Internet Explorer 3.0 or higher

NOTE: This CD requires Netscape 3.0 or MS Internet Explorer 3.0 or higher. You can download these products using the links on the CD-ROM Help Page.

GETTING STARTED

Insert the CD-ROM into your drive. The CD-ROM will usually launch automatically. If it does not, click on the CD-ROM drive on your computer to launch. You will see an opening page. You can click on this page or wait for it to fade to the Copyright Page. After you click to agree to the terms of the Copyright Page, the Home Page will appear.

MOVING AROUND

Use the buttons at the left of each screen or the underlined text at the bottom of each screen to move among the menu pages. To view a document listed on one of the menu pages, simply click on the name of the document. To quit a document at any time, click the box at the upper right-hand corner of the screen.

Use the scrollbar at the right of the screen to scroll up and down each page.

To quit the CD-ROM, you can click the Quit option at the bottom of each menu page, hit Control-Q, or click the box at the upper right-hand corner of the screen.

TO DOWNLOAD DOCUMENTS

Open the document you wish to download. Under the File pulldown menu, choose Save As. Save the document onto your hard drive with a different name. It is important to use a different name, otherwise the document may remain a read-only file.

You can also click on your CD drive in Windows Explorer and select a document to copy it to your hard drive and rename it.

IN CASE OF TROUBLE

If you experience difficulty using the *Best Practices in Organization Development and Change* CD-ROM, please follow these steps:

1. Make sure your hardware and systems configurations conform to the systems requirements noted under "Systems Requirements" above.

2. Review the installation procedure for your type of hardware and operating system. It is possible to reinstall the software if necessary.

3. You may call Jossey-Bass/Pfeiffer Customer Service at (415) 433-1740 between the hours of 8 A.M. and 5 P.M. Pacific Time, and ask for Jossey-Bass CD-ROM Technical Support.

Please have the following information available:

* Type of computer and operating system
* Version of Windows or Mac OS being used
* Any error messages displayed

Complete description of the problem.

(It is best if you are sitting at your computer when making the call.)